Hadoop in Action

Hadoop in
Action

CHUCK LAM

MANNING
Greenwich
(74° w. long.)

For online information and ordering of this and other Manning books, please visit
www.manning.com. The publisher offers discounts on this book when ordered in quantity.
For more information, please contact

Special Sales Department
Manning Publications Co.
180 Broad St.
Suite 1323
Stamford, CT 06901
Email: orders@manning.com

Manning Publications Co.   Development editor: Cynthia Kane
180 Broad St.   Copyeditor: Composure Graphics
Suite 1323   Proofreader: Katie Tennant
Stamford, CT 06901   Composition: Composure Graphics
                            Cover designer: Marija Tudor

ISBN: 9781935182191
Printed in the United States of America
1 2 3 4 5 6 7 8 9 10 – MAL – 15 14 13 12 11 10

brief contents

PART I   HADOOP–A DISTRIBUTED PROGRAMMING
          FRAMEWORK.. 1

  1 ■ Introducing Hadoop   3
  2 ■ Starting Hadoop   21
  3 ■ Components of Hadoop   37

PART II   HADOOP IN ACTION 61

  4 ■ Writing basic MapReduce programs   63
  5 ■ Advanced MapReduce   102
  6 ■ Programming Practices   134
  7 ■ Cookbook   160
  8 ■ Managing Hadoop   173

PART III HADOOP GONE WILD............................191

  9 ■ Running Hadoop in the cloud   193
  10 ■ Programming with Pig   212
  11 ■ Hive and the Hadoop herd   246
  12 ■ Case studies   266

v

contents

preface   xiii
acknowledgments   xv
about this book   xvii
Author Online   xix
about the author   xx
about the cover illustration   xxi

PART I   HADOOP—A DISTRIBUTED PROGRAMMING
FRAMEWORK.. 1

1 **Introducing Hadoop   3**

1.1 Why "Hadoop in Action"?   4

1.2 What is Hadoop?   4

1.3 Understanding distributed systems and Hadoop   6

1.4 Comparing SQL databases and Hadoop   7

1.5 Understanding MapReduce   8
Scaling a simple program manually 9 ▪ Scaling the same program in MapReduce 12

1.6 Counting words with Hadoop—running your first program   14

1.7 History of Hadoop   19

1.8   Summary   20

1.9   Resources   20

2   Starting Hadoop   21

2.1   The building blocks of Hadoop   21
NameNode 22 ▪ DataNode 22▪ Secondary NameNode 23
JobTracker 24 ▪ TaskTracker 24

2.2   Setting up SSH for a Hadoop cluster   25
Define a common account 26 ▪ Verify SSH installation 26 ▪ Generate SSH key
pair 26 ▪ Distribute public key and validate logins 27

2.3   Running Hadoop   27
Local (standalone) mode 28 ▪ Pseudo-distributed mode 29 ▪ Fully distributed
mode 31

2.4   Web-based cluster UI   34

2.5   Summary   36

3   Components of Hadoop   37

3.1   Working with files in HDFS   38
Basic file commands 38 ▪ Reading and writing to HDFS programmatically   42

3.2   Anatomy of a MapReduce program   44
Hadoop data types 46 ▪ Mapper 47 ▪ Reducer 48 ▪ Partitioner—redirecting
output from Mapper 49 ▪ Combiner—local reduce 50 ▪ Word counting with
predefined mapper and reducer classes 51

3.3   Reading and writing   51
InputFormat 52 ▪ OutputFormat   57

3.4   Summary   58

PART II   HADOOP IN ACTION..61

4   Writing basic MapReduce programs   63

4.1   Getting the patent data set   64
The patent citation data 64 ▪ The patent description data   65

4.2   Constructing the basic template of a MapReduce program   67

4.3   Counting things   72

4.4   Adapting for Hadoop's API changes   77

4.5   Streaming in Hadoop   80
Streaming with Unix commands 81 ▪ Streaming with scripts 82
Streaming with key/value pairs 86 ▪ Streaming with the Aggregate package 90

4.6   Improving performance with combiners   *95*

4.7   Exercising what you've learned   *98*

4.8   Summary   *100*

4.9   Further resources   *101*

5 *Advanced MapReduce*   **102**

5.1   Chaining MapReduce jobs   *103*
      *Chaining MapReduce jobs in a sequence 103 ▪ Chaining MapReduce jobs with
      complex dependency 103 ▪ Chaining preprocessing and postprocessing steps   104*

5.2   Joining data from different sources   *107*
      *Reduce-side joining 108 ▪ Replicated joins using DistributedCache 117
      Semijoin: reduce-side join with map-side filtering 121*

5.3   Creating a Bloom filter   *122*
      *What does a Bloom filter do? 122 ▪ Implementing a Bloom filter 124
      Bloom filter in Hadoop version 0.20+ 131*

5.4   Exercising what you've learned   *131*

5.5   Summary   *132*

5.6   Further resources   *133*

6 *Programming Practices*   **134**

6.1   Developing MapReduce programs   *135*
      Local mode 135 ▪ Pseudo-distributed mode 140

6.2   Monitoring and debugging on a production cluster   *145*
      *Counters 146 ▪ Skipping bad records 148 ▪ Rerunning failed tasks
      with IsolationRunner 151*

6.3   Tuning for performance   *152*
      *Reducing network traffic with combiner 152 ▪ Reducing the amount of input
      data 152 ▪ Using compression 153 ▪ Reusing the JVM 155 ▪ Running with
      speculative execution 156 ▪ Refactoring code and rewriting algorithms 157*

6.4   Summary   *158*

7 *Cookbook*   **160**

7.1   Passing job-specific parameters to your tasks   *160*

7.2   Probing for task-specific information   *163*

7.3   Partitioning into multiple output files   *164*

7.4   Inputting from and outputting to a database   *169*

7.5   Keeping all output in sorted order   *171*

7.6   Summary   *172*

8   *Managing Hadoop   173*

    8.1   Setting up parameter values for practical use   *174*

    8.2   Checking system's health   *176*

    8.3   Setting permissions   *178*

    8.4   Managing quotas   *179*

    8.5   Enabling trash   *179*

    8.6   Removing DataNodes   *180*

    8.7   Adding DataNodes   *180*

    8.8   Managing NameNode and Secondary NameNode   *181*

    8.9   Recovering from a failed NameNode   *183*

    8.10   Designing network layout and rack awareness   *184*

    8.11   Scheduling jobs from multiple users   *186*
        Multiple JobTrackers 186 ▪ *Fair Scheduler 187*

    8.12   Summary   *189*

PART III   HADOOP GONE WILD..191

9   *Running Hadoop in the cloud   193*

    9.1   Introducing Amazon Web Services   194

    9.2   Setting up AWS   *194*
        Getting your AWS authentication credentials 195 ▪ *Getting command line tools 198* ▪ *Preparing an SSH key pair 200*

    9.3   Setting up Hadoop on EC2   201
        Configuring security parameters 201 ▪ *Configuring cluster type 202*

    9.4   Running MapReduce programs on EC2   *203*
        Moving your code to the Hadoop cluster 204 ▪ *Accessing your data from the Hadoop cluster 204*

    9.5   Cleaning up and shutting down your EC2 instances   *209*

    9.6   Amazon Elastic MapReduce and other AWS services   *209*
        Amazon Elastic MapReduce 209 ▪ *AWS Import/Export 210*

    9.7   Summary   *211*

10   *Programming with Pig   212*

    10.1   Thinking like a Pig   *213*
        Data flow language 213 ▪ *Data types 213* ▪ *User-defined functions 214*

10.2 Installing Pig 214

10.3 Running Pig 215
Managing the Grunt shell 216

10.4 Learning Pig Latin through Grunt 217

10.5 Speaking Pig Latin 221
Data types and schemas 222 ▪ Expressions and functions 223
Relational operators 225 ▪ Execution optimization 233

10.6 Working with user-defined functions 233
Using UDFs 234 ▪ Writing UDFs 234

10.7 Working with scripts 237
Comments 237 ▪ Parameter substitution 238 ▪ Multiquery execution 239

10.8 Seeing Pig in action—example of computing similar patents 240

10.9 Summary 245

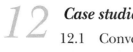

Hive and the Hadoop herd 246

11.1 Hive 247
Installing and configuring Hive 248 ▪ Example queries 250 ▪ HiveQL in
details 254 ▪ Hive Sum-up 260

11.2 Other Hadoop-related stuff 262
HBase 262 ▪ ZooKeeper 262 ▪ Cascading 263 ▪ Cloudera 263
Katta 263 ▪ CloudBase 264 ▪ Aster Data and Greenplum 264
Hama and Mahout 264 ▪ search-hadoop.com 264

11.3 Summary 265

Case studies 266

12.1 Converting 11 million image documents from the
New York Times archive 267

12.2 Mining data at China Mobile 267

12.3 Recommending the best websites at StumbleUpon 272
Distributed beginnings at StumbleUpon 273 ▪ HBase and
StumbleUpon 274 ▪ More Hadoop at StumbleUpon 281

12.4 Building analytics for enterprise search—IBM's Project ES2 282
ES2 architecture 285 ▪ ES2 crawler 287 ▪ ES2 analytics 288
Conclusions 296 ▪ References 297

appendix HDFS file commands 298

index 302

preface

I've been fascinated by data for a long time. When I was an undergrad in electrical engineering, I discovered digital signal processing and gravitated toward it. I found out that music, video, photos, and lots of other stuff could be viewed as data. Computation was creating and enhancing those emotional experiences. I thought that was the coolest thing ever.

Over time, I continued to get excited by new aspects of data. The last few years had exposed me to social and big data. Big data was especially intellectually challenging for me. Previously I had learned to look at data from a statistician's point of view, and new types of data had "only" asked for new mathematical methods. It wasn't simple, but at least I had been trained for that, and there was also a wealth of resources to tap into. Big data, on the other hand, was about system-level innovations and new ways of programming. I wasn't trained for it, and more importantly, I wasn't alone. Knowledge about handling big data in practice was somewhat of a black art. This was true of many tools and techniques for scaling data processing, including caching (for example, memcached), replication, sharding, and, of course, MapReduce/Hadoop. I had spent the last few years getting up to speed on many of these skills.

Personally I have found the biggest hurdle to learning these techniques is in the middle of the learning curve. In the beginning it's pretty easy to find introductory blogs and presentations teaching you how to do a "Hello World" example. And when you're sufficiently well-versed, you'll know how to ask additional questions to the mailing lists, meet experts at meetups or conferences, and even read the source code yourself. But there's a huge knowledge gap in the middle, when your appetite is whetted but you don't quite know what questions to ask next. This problem is especially acute for the newest technologies, like Hadoop. An organized exposition that starts with "Hello World" and takes you to the point where you can comfortably apply Hadoop in practice is needed. That's what I intend this book to be. Fortunately I've found Manning's *In Action* series to be consistent with this objective, and they have excellent editors that helped me along the way.

I had a fun time writing this book, and I hope this is the beginning of your wonderful journey with Hadoop.

acknowledgments

Many people have inspired and made contributions to this book. First and foremost I want to thank James Warren. He led analytics at RockYou, and together we evangelized the use of Hadoop throughout the organization. I learned a lot from him, and he even lent a hand in some of the initial writings.

I've been lucky to have many people contribute interesting case studies from outside the Web 2.0 industry. For this I need to thank Zhiguo Luo, Meng Xu, Shaoling Sun, Ken MacInnis, Ryan Rawson, Vuk Ercegovac, Rajasekar Krishnamurthy, Sriram Raghavan, Frederick Reiss, Eugene Shekita, Sandeep Tata, Shivakumar Vaithyanathan, and Huaiyu Zhu.

I also want to thank the many reviewers of this book. They provided valuable feedback to my early drafts. In particular, Paul O'Rorke was the technical reviewer that went beyond his call of duty and made some wonderful suggestions on how to make the manuscript better. I look forward to seeing him author his own book at some point. I also enjoyed many long chats with Jonathan Cao. His expertise in databases and large-scale systems provided a broad perspective to understanding the capabilities of Hadoop.

The other reviewers who read the manuscript numerous times during development and whom I'd like to thank for their invaluable feedback include the following: Paul Stusiak, Philipp K. Janert, Amin Mohammed-Coleman, John S. Griffin, Marco Ughetti, Rick Wagner, Kenneth DeLong, Josh Patterson, Srini Penchikala, Costantino Cerbo, Steve Loughran, Ara Abrahamian, Ben Hall, Andrew Siemer, Robert Hanson, Keith Kim , Sopan Shewale, Marion Sturtevant, Chris Chandler, Eric Raymond, and Jeroen Benckhuijsen.

I've been blessed to work with a wonderful group of people at Manning. Special thanks go out to Troy Mott, who got me started on this writing project and has been patient enough to see me finish it. Thanks also to Tara Walsh, Karen Tegtmeyer, Marjan Bace, Mary Piergies, Cynthia Kane, Steven Hong, Rachel Schroeder, Katie Tennant, and Maureen Spencer. Their support is simply phenomenal. I couldn't imagine a better group of people to work with.

Needless to say, all the people who contribute to Hadoop and help grow its ecosystem deserve praise. Doug Cutting got it all started, and Yahoo had the foresight to support it early on. Cloudera is now bringing Hadoop to a broader enterprise audience. It's an exciting time to be part of this growing Hadoop community.

Last, but not least, I want to thank all my friends, family, and colleagues for supporting me throughout the writing of this book.

about this book

Hadoop is an open source framework implementing the MapReduce algorithm behind Google's approach to querying the distributed data sets that constitute the internet. This definition naturally leads to an obvious question: What are *maps* and why do they need to be *reduced*? Massive data sets can be extremely difficult to analyze and query using traditional mechanisms, especially when the queries themselves are quite complicated. In effect, the MapReduce algorithm breaks up both the query and the data set into constituent parts—that's the *mapping*. The mapped components of the query can be processed simultaneously—or *reduced*—to rapidly return results.

This book teaches readers how to use Hadoop and write MapReduce programs. The intended readers are programmers, architects, and project managers who have to process large amounts of data offline. This book guides the reader from obtaining a copy of Hadoop to setting it up in a cluster and writing data analytic programs.

The book begins by making the basic idea of Hadoop and MapReduce easier to grasp by applying the default Hadoop installation to a few easy-to-follow tasks, such as analyzing changes in word frequency across a body of documents. The book continues through the basic concepts of MapReduce applications developed using Hadoop, including a close look at framework components, use of Hadoop for a variety of data analysis tasks, and numerous examples of Hadoop in action.

MapReduce is a complex idea both conceptually and in its implementation, and Hadoop users are challenged to learn all the knobs and levers for running Hadoop. This book takes you beyond the mechanics of running Hadoop, teaching you to write meaningful programs in a MapReduce framework.

This book assumes the reader will have a basic familiarity with Java, as most code examples will be written in Java. Familiarity with basic statistical concepts (e.g., histogram, correlation) will help the reader appreciate the more advanced data processing examples.

Roadmap

The book has 12 chapters divided into three parts.

Part 1 consists of three chapters which introduce the Hadoop framework, covering the basics you'll need to understand and use Hadoop. The chapters describe the hardware components that make up a Hadoop cluster, as well as the installation and configuration to create a working system. Part 1 also covers the MapReduce framework at a high level and gets your first MapReduce program up and running.

Part 2, "Hadoop in action," consists of five chapters that teach the practical skills required to write and run data processing programs in Hadoop. In these chapters we explore various examples of using Hadoop to analyze a patent data set, including advanced algorithms such as the Bloom filter. We also cover programming and administration techniques that are uniquely useful to working with Hadoop in production.

Part 3 is called "Hadoop gone wild" and the final four chapters of the book explore the larger ecosystem around Hadoop. Cloud services provide an alternative to buying and hosting your own hardware to create a Hadoop cluster and any add-on packages provide higher-level programming abstractions over MapReduce. Finally, we look at several case studies where Hadoop solves real business problems in practice.

An appendix contains a listing of HDFS commands along with their descriptions and usage.

Code conventions and downloads

All source code in listings or in text is in a `fixed-width font like this` to separate it from ordinary text. Code annotations accompany many of the listings, highlighting important concepts. In some cases, numbered bullets link to explanations that follow the listing.

The code for the examples in this book is available for download from the publisher's website at www.manning.com/HadoopinAction.

Author Online

The purchase of *Hadoop in Action* includes free access to a private forum run by Manning Publications where you can make comments about the book, ask technical questions, and receive help from the author and other users. You can access and subscribe to the forum at www.manning.com/HadoopinAction. This page provides information on how to get on the forum once you're registered, what kind of help is available, and the rules of conduct in the forum.

Manning's commitment to our readers is to provide a venue where a meaningful dialogue between individual readers and between readers and the author can take place. It isn't a commitment to any specific amount of participation on the part of the author, whose contribution to the book's forum remains voluntary (and unpaid). We suggest you try asking the author some challenging questions, lest his interest stray!

The Author Online forum and the archives of previous discussions will be accessible from the publisher's website as long as the book is in print.

about the author

Chuck Lam is currently founding a mobile social networking startup called *RollCall*. It's building the social secretary for active individuals.

Previously Chuck was a Senior Tech Lead at RockYou. There he developed social applications and data processing infrastructure handling hundreds of millions of users. He applied A/B testing and statistical analysis to tune the virality of social apps. He also optimized RockYou's ad network with the use of real-time and social data. He was able to improve response rates dramatically, sometimes by an order of magnitude.

Chuck first got interested in big data when he began his PhD study at Stanford. He learned of the significant effect big data has on machine learning and began to explore its consequences. His thesis, "Computational Data Acquisition," was the first to investigate creative approaches to data acquisition for machine learning, adopting ideas from areas such as open source software and online games.

about the cover illustration

The figure on the cover of *Hadoop in Action* is captioned "A young man from Kistanja, Dalmatia." The illustration is taken from a reproduction of an album of Croatian traditional costumes from the mid-nineteenth century by Nikola Arsenovic, published by the Ethnographic Museum in Split, Croatia, in 2003. The illustrations were obtained from a helpful librarian at the Ethnographic Museum in Split, itself situated in the Roman core of the medieval center of the town: the ruins of Emperor Diocletian's retirement palace from around AD 304. The book includes finely colored illustrations of figures from different regions of Croatia, accompanied by descriptions of the costumes and of everyday life.

Kistanja is a small town located in Bukovica, a geographical region in Croatia. It is situated in northern Dalmatia, an area rich in Roman and Venetian history. The word "mamok" in Croatian means a bachelor, beau, or suitor—a single young man who is of courting age—and the young man on the cover, looking dapper in a crisp white linen shirt and a colorful, embroidered vest, is clearly dressed in his finest clothes, which would be worn to church and for festive occasions—or to go calling on a young lady.

Dress codes and lifestyles have changed over the last 200 years, and the diversity by region, so rich at the time, has faded away. It is now hard to tell apart the inhabitants of different continents, let alone of different hamlets or towns separated by only a few miles. Perhaps we have traded cultural diversity for a more varied personal life—certainly for a more varied and fast-paced technological life.

Manning celebrates the inventiveness and initiative of the computer business with book covers based on the rich diversity of regional life of two centuries ago, brought back to life by illustrations from old books and collections like this one.

Hadoop–A Distributed Programming Framework

Part 1 of this book introduces the basics for understanding and using Hadoop. We describe the hardware components that make up a Hadoop cluster, as well as the installation and configuration to create a working system. We cover the MapReduce framework at a high level and get your first MapReduce program up and running.

Introducing Hadoop

This chapter covers

- The basics of writing a scalable, distributed data-intensive program
- Understanding Hadoop and MapReduce
- Writing and running a basic MapReduce program

Today, we're surrounded by data. People upload videos, take pictures on their cell phones, text friends, update their Facebook status, leave comments around the web, click on ads, and so forth. Machines, too, are generating and keeping more and more data. You may even be reading this book as digital data on your computer screen, and certainly your purchase of this book is recorded as data with some retailer.[1]

The exponential growth of data first presented challenges to cutting-edge businesses such as Google, Yahoo, Amazon, and Microsoft. They needed to go through terabytes and petabytes of data to figure out which websites were popular, what books were in demand, and what kinds of ads appealed to people. Existing tools were becoming inadequate to process such large data sets. Google was the first to publicize *MapReduce*—a system they had used to scale their data processing needs.

---

[1] Of course, you're reading a legitimate copy of this, right?

This system aroused a lot of interest because many other businesses were facing similar scaling challenges, and it wasn't feasible for everyone to reinvent their own proprietary tool. Doug Cutting saw an opportunity and led the charge to develop an open source version of this MapReduce system called Hadoop. Soon after, Yahoo and others rallied around to support this effort. Today, Hadoop is a core part of the computing infrastructure for many web companies, such as Yahoo, Facebook, LinkedIn, and Twitter. Many more traditional businesses, such as media and telecom, are beginning to adopt this system too. Our case studies in chapter 12 will describe how companies including New York Times, China Mobile, and IBM are using Hadoop.

Hadoop, and large-scale distributed data processing in general, is rapidly becoming an important skill set for many programmers. An effective programmer, today, must have knowledge of relational databases, networking, and security, all of which were considered optional skills a couple decades ago. Similarly, basic understanding of distributed data processing will soon become an essential part of every programmer's toolbox. Leading universities, such as Stanford and CMU, have already started introducing Hadoop into their computer science curriculum. This book will help you, the practicing programmer, get up to speed on Hadoop quickly and start using it to process your data sets.

This chapter introduces Hadoop more formally, positioning it in terms of distributed systems and data processing systems. It gives an overview of the MapReduce programming model. A simple word counting example with existing tools highlights the challenges around processing data at large scale. You'll implement that example using Hadoop to gain a deeper appreciation of Hadoop's simplicity. We'll also discuss the history of Hadoop and some perspectives on the MapReduce paradigm. But let me first briefly explain why I wrote this book and why it's useful to you.

1.1 Why "Hadoop in Action"?

Speaking from experience, I first found Hadoop to be tantalizing in its possibilities, yet frustrating to progress beyond coding the basic examples. The documentation at the official Hadoop site is fairly comprehensive, but it isn't always easy to find straightforward answers to straightforward questions.

The purpose of writing the book is to address this problem. I won't focus on the nitty-gritty details. Instead I will provide the information that will allow you to quickly create useful code, along with more advanced topics most often encountered in practice.

1.2 What is Hadoop?

Formally speaking, Hadoop is an open source framework for writing and running distributed applications that process large amounts of data. Distributed computing is a wide and varied field, but the key distinctions of Hadoop are that it is

- *Accessible*—Hadoop runs on large clusters of commodity machines or on cloud computing services such as Amazon's Elastic Compute Cloud (EC2).

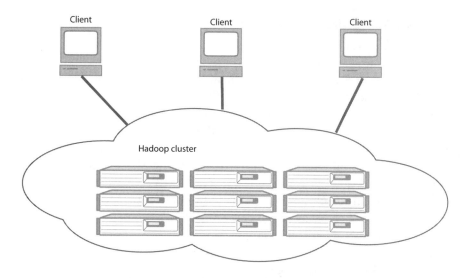

Figure 1.1 A Hadoop cluster has many parallel machines that store and process large data sets. Client computers send jobs into this computer cloud and obtain results.

- *Robust*—Because it is intended to run on commodity hardware, Hadoop is architected with the assumption of frequent hardware malfunctions. It can gracefully handle most such failures.
- *Scalable*—Hadoop scales linearly to handle larger data by adding more nodes to the cluster.
- *Simple*—Hadoop allows users to quickly write efficient parallel code.

Hadoop's accessibility and simplicity give it an edge over writing and running large distributed programs. Even college students can quickly and cheaply create their own Hadoop cluster. On the other hand, its robustness and scalability make it suitable for even the most demanding jobs at Yahoo and Facebook. These features make Hadoop popular in both academia and industry.

Figure 1.1 illustrates how one interacts with a Hadoop cluster. As you can see, a Hadoop cluster is a set of commodity machines networked together in one location.[2] Data storage and processing all occur within this "cloud" of machines. Different users can submit computing "jobs" to Hadoop from individual clients, which can be their own desktop machines in remote locations from the Hadoop cluster.

Not all distributed systems are set up as shown in figure 1.1. A brief introduction to other distributed systems will better showcase the design philosophy behind Hadoop.

---

[2] While not strictly necessary, machines in a Hadoop cluster are usually relatively homogeneous x86 Linux boxes. And they're almost always located in the same data center, often in the same set of racks.

1.3   *Understanding distributed systems and Hadoop*

Moore's law suited us well for the past decades, but building bigger and bigger servers is no longer necessarily the best solution to large-scale problems. An alternative that has gained popularity is to tie together many low-end/commodity machines together as a single functional *distributed system*.

To understand the popularity of distributed systems (scale-out) vis-à-vis huge monolithic servers (scale-up), consider the price performance of current I/O technology. A high-end machine with four I/O channels each having a throughput of 100 MB/sec will require three hours to *read* a 4 TB data set! With Hadoop, this same data set will be divided into smaller (typically 64 MB) blocks that are spread among many machines in the cluster via the Hadoop Distributed File System (HDFS). With a modest degree of replication, the cluster machines can read the data set in parallel and provide a much higher throughput. And such a cluster of commodity machines turns out to be cheaper than one high-end server!

The preceding explanation showcases the efficacy of Hadoop relative to monolithic systems. Now let's compare Hadoop to other architectures for distributed systems. SETI@home, where screensavers around the globe assist in the search for extraterrestrial life, represents one well-known approach. In SETI@home, a central server stores radio signals from space and serves them out over the internet to client desktop machines to look for anomalous signs. This approach moves the data to where computation will take place (the desktop screensavers). After the computation, the resulting data is moved back for storage.

Hadoop differs from schemes such as SETI@home in its philosophy toward data. SETI@home requires repeat transmissions of data between clients and servers. This works fine for computationally intensive work, but for data-intensive processing, the size of data becomes too large to be moved around easily. Hadoop focuses on moving code to data instead of vice versa. Referring to figure 1.1 again, we see both the data and the computation exist within the Hadoop cluster. The clients send only the MapReduce programs to be executed, and these programs are usually small (often in kilobytes). More importantly, the move-code-to-data philosophy applies within the Hadoop cluster itself. Data is broken up and distributed across the cluster, and as much as possible, computation on a piece of data takes place on the same machine where that piece of data resides.

This move-code-to-data philosophy makes sense for the type of data-intensive processing Hadoop is designed for. The programs to run ("code") are orders of magnitude smaller than the data and are easier to move around. Also, it takes more time to move data across a network than to apply the computation to it. Let the data remain where it is and move the executable code to its hosting machine.

Now that you know how Hadoop fits into the design of distributed systems, let's see how it compares to data processing systems, which usually means SQL databases.

1.4 Comparing SQL databases and Hadoop

Given that Hadoop is a framework for processing data, what makes it better than standard relational databases, the workhorse of data processing in most of today's applications? One reason is that SQL (*structured* query language) is by design targeted at structured data. Many of Hadoop's initial applications deal with unstructured data such as text. From this perspective Hadoop provides a more general paradigm than SQL.

For working only with structured data, the comparison is more nuanced. In principle, SQL and Hadoop can be complementary, as SQL is a query language which can be implemented on top of Hadoop as the execution engine.[3] But in practice, SQL databases tend to refer to a whole set of legacy technologies, with several dominant vendors, optimized for a historical set of applications. Many of these existing commercial databases are a mismatch to the requirements that Hadoop targets.

With that in mind, let's make a more detailed comparison of Hadoop with typical SQL databases on specific dimensions.

SCALE-OUT INSTEAD OF SCALE-UP

Scaling commercial relational databases is expensive. Their design is more friendly to scaling up. To run a bigger database you need to buy a bigger machine. In fact, it's not unusual to see server vendors market their expensive high-end machines as "database-class servers." Unfortunately, at some point there won't be a big enough machine available for the larger data sets. More importantly, the high-end machines are not cost effective for many applications. For example, a machine with four times the power of a standard PC costs a lot more than putting four such PCs in a cluster. Hadoop is designed to be a scale-out architecture operating on a cluster of commodity PC machines. Adding more resources means adding more machines to the Hadoop cluster. Hadoop clusters with ten to hundreds of machines is standard. In fact, other than for development purposes, there's no reason to run Hadoop on a single server.

KEY/VALUE PAIRS INSTEAD OF RELATIONAL TABLES

A fundamental tenet of relational databases is that data resides in tables having relational structure defined by a schema. Although the relational model has great formal properties, many modern applications deal with data types that don't fit well into this model. Text documents, images, and XML files are popular examples. Also, large data sets are often unstructured or semistructured. Hadoop uses key/value pairs as its basic data unit, which is flexible enough to work with the less-structured data types. In Hadoop, data can originate in any form, but it eventually transforms into (key/value) pairs for the processing functions to work on.

FUNCTIONAL PROGRAMMING (MAPREDUCE) INSTEAD OF DECLARATIVE QUERIES (SQL)

SQL is fundamentally a high-level declarative language. You query data by stating the result you want and let the database engine figure out how to derive it. Under MapReduce you

---

[3] This is in fact a hot area within the Hadoop community, and we'll cover some of the leading projects in chapter 11.

specify the actual steps in processing the data, which is more analogous to an execution plan for a SQL engine. Under SQL you have query statements; under MapReduce you have scripts and codes. MapReduce allows you to process data in a more general fashion than SQL queries. For example, you can build complex statistical models from your data or reformat your image data. SQL is not well designed for such tasks.

On the other hand, when working with data that do fit well into relational structures, some people may find MapReduce less natural to use. Those who are accustomed to the SQL paradigm may find it challenging to think in the MapReduce way. I hope the exercises and the examples in this book will help make MapReduce programming more intuitive. But note that many extensions are available to allow one to take advantage of the scalability of Hadoop while programming in more familiar paradigms. In fact, some enable you to write queries in a SQL-like language, and your query is automatically compiled into MapReduce code for execution. We'll cover some of these tools in chapters 10 and 11.

OFFLINE BATCH PROCESSING INSTEAD OF ONLINE TRANSACTIONS
Hadoop is designed for offline processing and analysis of large-scale data. It doesn't work for random reading and writing of a few records, which is the type of load for online transaction processing. In fact, as of this writing (and in the foreseeable future), Hadoop is best used as a write-once, read-many-times type of data store. In this aspect it's similar to data warehouses in the SQL world.

You have seen how Hadoop relates to distributed systems and SQL databases at a high level. Let's learn how to program in it. For that, we need to understand Hadoop's MapReduce paradigm.

1.5   *Understanding MapReduce*

You're probably aware of data processing models such as pipelines and message queues. These models provide specific capabilities in developing different aspects of data processing applications. The most familiar pipelines are the Unix pipes. Pipelines can help the *reuse* of processing primitives; simple chaining of existing modules creates new ones. Message queues can help the *synchronization* of processing primitives. The programmer writes her data processing task as processing primitives in the form of either a producer or a consumer. The timing of their execution is managed by the system.

Similarly, MapReduce is also a data processing model. Its greatest advantage is the easy scaling of data processing over multiple computing nodes. Under the MapReduce model, the data processing primitives are called *mappers* and *reducers*. Decomposing a data processing application into mappers and reducers is sometimes nontrivial. But, once you write an application in the MapReduce form, scaling the application to run over hundreds, thousands, or even tens of thousands of machines in a cluster is merely a configuration change. This simple scalability is what has attracted many programmers to the MapReduce model.

> **Many ways to say MapReduce**
>
> Even though much has been written about MapReduce, one does not find the name itself written the same everywhere. The original Google paper and the Wikipedia entry use the CamelCase version *MapReduce*. However, Google itself has used *Map Reduce* in some pages on its website (for example, http://research.google.com/ roundtable/MR.html). At the official Hadoop documentation site, one can find links pointing to a *Map-Reduce Tutorial*. Clicking on the link brings one to a *Hadoop Map/Reduce Tutorial* (http://hadoop.apache.org/core/docs/current/mapred_ tutorial.html) explaining the *Map/Reduce* framework. Writing variations also exist for the different Hadoop components such as *NameNode* (*name node*, *name-node*, and *namenode*), *DataNode*, *JobTracker*, and *TaskTracker*. For the sake of consistency, we'll go with CamelCase for all those terms in this book. (That is, we will use *MapReduce*, *NameNode*, *DataNode*, *JobTracker*, and *TaskTracker*.)

1.5.1 *Scaling a simple program manually*

Before going through a formal treatment of MapReduce, let's go through an exercise of scaling a simple program to process a large data set. You'll see the challenges of scaling a data processing program and will better appreciate the benefits of using a framework such as MapReduce to handle the tedious chores for you.

Our exercise is to count the number of times each word occurs in a set of documents. In this example, we have a set of documents having only one document with only one sentence:

Word	Count
as	2
do	2
i	2
not	1
say	1

> *Do as I say, not as I do.*

We derive the word counts shown to the right.

We'll call this particular exercise *word counting*. When the set of documents is small, a straightforward program will do the job. Let's write one here in pseudo-code:

```
define wordCount as Multiset;
for each document in documentSet {
    T = tokenize(document);
    for each token in T {
        wordCount[token]++;
    }
}
display(wordCount);
```

The program loops through all the documents. For each document, the words are extracted one by one using a tokenization process. For each word, its corresponding entry in a multiset called `wordCount` is incremented by one. At the end, a `display()` function prints out all the entries in `wordCount`.

> **NOTE**   A multiset is a set where each element also has a count. The word count we're trying to generate is a canonical example of a multiset. In practice, it's usually implemented as a hash table.

This program works fine until the set of documents you want to process becomes large. For example, you want to build a spam filter to know the words frequently used in the millions of spam emails you've received. Looping through all the documents using a single computer will be extremely time consuming. You speed it up by rewriting the program so that it distributes the work over several machines. Each machine will process a distinct fraction of the documents. When all the machines have completed this, a second phase of processing will combine the result of all the machines. The pseudo-code for the first phase, to be distributed over many machines, is

```
define wordCount as Multiset;
for each document in documentSubset {
    T = tokenize(document);
    for each token in T {
        wordCount[token]++;
    }
}
sendToSecondPhase(wordCount);
```

And the pseudo-code for the second phase is

```
define totalWordCount as Multiset;
for each wordCount received from firstPhase {
    multisetAdd (totalWordCount, wordCount);
}
```

That wasn't too hard, right? But a few details may prevent it from working as expected. First of all, we ignore the performance requirement of reading in the documents. If the documents are all stored in one central storage server, then the bottleneck is in the bandwidth of that server. Having more machines for processing only helps up to a certain point—until the storage server can't keep up. You'll also need to split up the documents among the set of processing machines such that each machine will process only those documents that are stored in it. This will remove the bottleneck of a central storage server. This reiterates the point made earlier about storage and processing having to be tightly coupled in data-intensive distributed applications.

Another flaw with the program is that `wordCount` (and `totalWordCount`) are stored in memory. When processing large document sets, the number of unique words can exceed the RAM storage of a machine. The English language has about one million words, a size that fits comfortably into an iPod, but our word counting program will deal with many unique words not found in any standard English dictionary. For example, we must deal with unique names such as *Hadoop*. We have to count misspellings even if they are not real words (for example, *exampel*), and we count all different forms of a word separately (for example, *eat, ate, eaten,* and *eating*). Even if the number of unique words in the document set is manageable in memory, a slight change in the problem definition can explode the space complexity. For example, instead of words in documents, we may want to count IP addresses in a log file, or the frequency of bigrams. In the case of the latter, we'll work with a multiset with billions of entries, which exceeds the RAM storage of most commodity computers.

> **NOTE**　A bigram is a pair of consecutive words. The sentence "Do as I say, not as I do" can be broken into the following bigrams: *Do as, as I, I say, say not, not as, as I, I do*. Analogously, trigrams are groups of three consecutive words. Both bigrams and trigrams are important in natural language processing.

`wordCount` may not fit in memory; we'll have to rewrite our program to store this hash table on disk. This means we'll implement a disk-based hash table, which involves a substantial amount of coding.

Furthermore, remember that phase two has only one machine, which will process `wordCount` sent from *all* the machines in phase one. Processing one `wordCount` is itself quite unwieldy. After we have added enough machines to phase one processing, the single machine in phase two will become the bottleneck. The obvious question is, can we rewrite phase two in a distributed fashion so that it can scale by adding more machines?

The answer is, yes. To make phase two work in a distributed fashion, you must somehow divide its work among multiple machines such that they can run independently. You need to *partition* `wordCount` after phase one such that each machine in phase two only has to handle one partition. In one example, let's say we have 26 machines for phase two. We assign each machine to only handle `wordCount` for words beginning with a particular letter in the alphabet. For example, machine A in phase two will only handle word counting for words beginning with the letter *a*. To enable this partitioning in phase two, we need a slight modification in phase one. Instead of a single disk-based hash table for `wordCount`, we will need 26 of them: `wordCount-a`, `wordCount-b`, and so on. Each one counts words starting with a particular letter. After phase one, `wordCount-a` from each of the phase one machines will be sent to machine A of phase two, all the `wordCount-b`'s will be sent to machine B, and so on. Each machine in phase one will *shuffle* its results among the machines in phase two.

Looking back, this word counting program is getting complicated. To make it work across a cluster of distributed machines, we find that we need to add a number of functionalities:

- Store files over many processing machines (of phase one).
- Write a disk-based hash table permitting processing without being limited by RAM capacity.
- Partition the intermediate data (that is, `wordCount`) from phase one.
- Shuffle the partitions to the appropriate machines in phase two.

This is a lot of work for something as simple as word counting, and we haven't even touched upon issues like fault tolerance. (What if a machine fails in the middle of its task?) This is the reason why you would want a framework like Hadoop. When you write your application in the MapReduce model, Hadoop will take care of all that scalability "plumbing" for you.

1.5.2   *Scaling the same program in MapReduce*

MapReduce programs are executed in two main phases, called *mapping* and *reducing*. Each phase is defined by a data processing function, and these functions are called *mapper* and *reducer*, respectively. In the mapping phase, MapReduce takes the input data and feeds each data element to the mapper. In the reducing phase, the reducer processes all the outputs from the mapper and arrives at a final result.

In simple terms, the mapper is meant to *filter and transform* the input into something that the reducer can *aggregate* over. You may see a striking similarity here with the two phases we had to develop in scaling up word counting. The similarity is not accidental. The MapReduce framework was designed after a lot of experience in writing scalable, distributed programs. This two-phase design pattern was seen in scaling many programs, and became the basis of the framework.

In scaling our distributed word counting program in the last section, we also had to write the partitioning and shuffling functions. Partitioning and shuffling are common design patterns that go along with mapping and reducing. Unlike mapping and reducing, though, partitioning and shuffling are generic functionalities that are not too dependent on the particular data processing application. The MapReduce framework provides a default implementation that works in most situations.

In order for mapping, reducing, partitioning, and shuffling (and a few others we haven't mentioned) to seamlessly work together, we need to agree on a common structure for the data being processed. It should be flexible and powerful enough to handle most of the targeted data processing applications. MapReduce uses *lists* and *(key/value) pairs* as its main data primitives. The keys and values are often integers or strings but can also be dummy values to be ignored or complex object types. The map and reduce functions must obey the following constraint on the types of keys and values.

In the MapReduce framework you write applications by specifying the mapper and reducer. Let's look at the complete data flow:

	Input	Output
map	<k1, v1>	list(<k2, v2>)
reduce	<k2, list(v2)>	list(<k3, v3>)

1 The input to your application must be structured as a list of (key/value) pairs, `list(<k1, v1>)`. This input format may seem open-ended but is often quite simple in practice. The input format for processing multiple files is usually `list(<String filename, String file_content>)`. The input format for processing one large file, such as a log file, is `list(<Integer line_number, String log_event>)`.

2　The list of (key/value) pairs is broken up and each individual (key/value) pair, <k1, v1>, is processed by calling the map function of the mapper. In practice, the key k1 is often ignored by the mapper. The mapper transforms each <k1, v1> pair into a list of <k2, v2> pairs. The details of this transformation largely determine what the MapReduce program does. Note that the (key/value) pairs are processed in arbitrary order. The transformation must be self-contained in that its output is dependent only on one single (key/value) pair.

　　For word counting, our mapper takes <String filename, String file_content> and promptly ignores filename. It can output a list of <String word, Integer count> but can be even simpler. As we know the counts will be aggregated in a later stage, we can output a list of <String word, Integer 1> with repeated entries and let the complete aggregation be done later. That is, in the output list we can have the (key/value) pair <"foo", 3> once or we can have the pair <"foo", 1> three times. As we'll see, the latter approach is much easier to program. The former approach may have some performance benefits, but let's leave such optimization alone until we have fully grasped the MapReduce framework.

3　The output of all the mappers are (conceptually) aggregated into one giant list of <k2, v2> pairs. All pairs sharing the same k2 are grouped together into a new (key/value) pair, <k2, list(v2)>. The framework asks the reducer to process each one of these aggregated (key/value) pairs individually. Following our word counting example, the map output for one document may be a list with pair <"foo", 1> three times, and the map output for another document may be a list with pair <"foo", 1> twice. The aggregated pair the reducer will see is <"foo", list(1,1,1,1,1)>. In word counting, the output of our reducer is <"foo", 5>, which is the total number of times "foo" has occurred in our document set. Each reducer works on a different word. The MapReduce framework automatically collects all the <k3, v3> pairs and writes them to file(s). Note that for the word counting example, the data types k2 and k3 are the same and v2 and v3 are also the same. This will not always be the case for other data processing applications.

Let's rewrite the word counting program in MapReduce to see how all this fits together Listing 1.1 shows the pseudo-code.

Listing 1.1　Pseudo-code for map and reduce functions for word counting

```
map(String filename, String document) {
    List<String> T = tokenize(document);
    for each token in T {
        emit ((String)token, (Integer) 1);
    }
}
reduce(String token, List<Integer> values) {
    Integer sum = 0;
```

```
    for each value in values {
        sum = sum + value;
    }
    emit ((String)token, (Integer) sum);
}
```

We've said before that the output of both map and reduce function are lists. As you can see from the pseudo-code, in practice we use a special function in the framework called `emit()` to generate the elements in the list one at a time. This `emit()` function further relieves the programmer from managing a large list.

The code looks similar to what we have in section 1.5.1, except this time it will actually work at scale. Hadoop makes building scalable distributed programs easy, doesn't it? Now let's turn this pseudo-code into a Hadoop program.

1.6   Counting words with Hadoop—running your first program

Now that you know what the Hadoop and MapReduce framework is about, let's get it running. In this chapter, we'll run Hadoop only on a single machine, which can be your desktop or laptop computer. The next chapter will show you how to run Hadoop over a cluster of machines, which is what you'd want for practical deployment. Running Hadoop on a single machine is mainly useful for development work.

Linux is the official development and production platform for Hadoop, although Windows is a supported development platform as well. For a Windows box, you'll need to install cygwin (http://www.cygwin.com/) to enable shell and Unix scripts.

> **NOTE**   Many people have reported success in running Hadoop in development mode on other variants of Unix, such as Solaris and Mac OS X. In fact, MacBook Pro seems to be the laptop of choice among Hadoop developers, as they're ubiquitous in Hadoop conferences and user group meetings.

Running Hadoop requires Java (version 1.6 or higher). Mac users should get it from Apple. You can download the latest JDK for other operating systems from Sun at http://java.sun.com/javase/downloads/index.jsp. Install it and remember the root of the Java installation, which we'll need later.

To install Hadoop, first get the latest stable release at http://hadoop.apache.org/core/releases.html. After you unpack the distribution, edit the script conf/hadoop-env.sh to set JAVA_HOME to the root of the Java installation you have remembered from earlier. For example, in Mac OS X, you'll replace this line

```
# export JAVA_HOME=/usr/lib/j2sdk1.5-sun
```

with this line

```
export JAVA_HOME=/Library/Java/Home
```

You'll be using the Hadoop script quite often. Let's run it without any arguments to see its usage documentation:

```
bin/hadoop
```

We get

```
Usage: hadoop [--config confdir] COMMAND
where COMMAND is one of:
  namenode -format      format the DFS filesystem
  secondarynamenode     run the DFS secondary namenode
  namenode              run the DFS namenode
  datanode              run a DFS datanode
  dfsadmin              run a DFS admin client
  fsck                  run a DFS filesystem checking utility
  fs                    run a generic filesystem user client
  balancer              run a cluster balancing utility
  jobtracker            run the MapReduce job Tracker node
  pipes                 run a Pipes job
  tasktracker           run a MapReduce task Tracker node
  job                   manipulate MapReduce jobs
  version               print the version
  jar <jar>             run a jar file
  distcp <srcurl> <desturl> copy file or directories recursively
  archive -archiveName NAME <src>* <dest> create a hadoop archive
  daemonlog             get/set the log level for each daemon
 or
  CLASSNAME             run the class named CLASSNAME
Most commands print help when invoked w/o parameters.
```

We'll cover the various Hadoop commands in the course of this book. For our current purpose, we only need to know that the command to run a (Java) Hadoop program is `bin/hadoop jar <jar>`. As the command implies, Hadoop programs written in Java are packaged in jar files for execution.

Fortunately for us, we don't need to write a Hadoop program first; the default installation already has several sample programs we can use. The following command shows what is available in the examples jar file:

```
bin/hadoop jar hadoop-*-examples.jar
```

You'll see about a dozen example programs prepackaged with Hadoop, and one of them is a word counting program called... `wordcount`! The important (inner) classes of that program are shown in listing 1.2. We'll see how this Java program implements the word counting map and reduce functions we had in pseudo-code in listing 1.1. We'll modify this program to understand how to vary its behavior. For now we'll assume it works as expected and only follow the mechanics of executing a Hadoop program.

Without specifying any arguments, executing `wordcount` will show its usage information:

```
bin/hadoop jar hadoop-*-examples.jar wordcount
```

which shows the arguments list:

```
wordcount [-m <maps>] [-r <reduces>] <input> <output>
```

The only parameters are an input directory (`<input>`) of text documents you want to analyze and an output directory (`<output>`) where the program will dump its output. To execute `wordcount`, we need to first create an input directory:

```
mkdir input
```

and put some documents in it. You can add any text document to the directory. For illustration, let's put the text version of the 2002 State of the Union address, obtained from http://www.gpoaccess.gov/sou/. We now analyze its word counts and see the results:

```
bin/hadoop jar hadoop-*-examples.jar wordcount input output
more output/*
```

You'll see a word count of every word used in the document, listed in alphabetical order. This is not bad considering you have not written a single line of code yet! But, also note a number of shortcomings in the included `wordcount` program. Tokenization is based purely on whitespace characters and not punctuation marks, making *States,* *States.,* and *States:* separate words. The same is true for capitalization, where *States* and *states* appear as separate words. Furthermore, we would like to leave out words that show up in the document only once or twice.

Fortunately, the source code for `wordcount` is available and included in the installation at src/examples/org/apache/hadoop/examples/WordCount.java. We can modify it as per our requirements. Let's first set up a directory structure for our playground and make a copy of the program.

```
mkdir playground
mkdir playground/src
mkdir playground/classes
cp src/examples/org/apache/hadoop/examples/WordCount.java
➥ playground/src/WordCount.java
```

Before we make changes to the program, let's go through compiling and executing this new copy in the Hadoop framework.

```
javac -classpath hadoop-*-core.jar -d playground/classes
➥ playground/src/WordCount.java
jar -cvf playground/wordcount.jar -C playground/classes/ .
```

You'll have to remove the output directory each time you run this Hadoop command, because it is created automatically.

```
bin/hadoop jar playground/wordcount.jar
➥ org.apache.hadoop.examples.WordCount input output
```

Look at the files in your output directory again. As we haven't changed any program code, the result should be the same as before. We've only compiled our own copy rather than running the precompiled version.

Now we are ready to modify `WordCount` to add some extra features. Listing 1.2 is a partial view of the WordCount.java program. Comments and supporting code are stripped out.

Listing 1.2   WordCount.java

```
public class WordCount extends Configured implements Tool {

  public static class MapClass extends MapReduceBase
    implements Mapper<LongWritable, Text, Text, IntWritable> {

    private final static IntWritable one = new IntWritable(1);
    private Text word = new Text();

    public void map(LongWritable key, Text value,
                    OutputCollector<Text, IntWritable> output,
                    Reporter reporter) throws IOException {
      String line = value.toString();
      StringTokenizer itr = new StringTokenizer(line);
      while (itr.hasMoreTokens()) {
        word.set(itr.nextToken());
        output.collect(word, one);
      }
    }
  }

  public static class Reduce extends MapReduceBase
    implements Reducer<Text, IntWritable, Text, IntWritable> {

    public void reduce(Text key, Iterator<IntWritable> values,
                       OutputCollector<Text, IntWritable> output,
                       Reporter reporter) throws IOException {
      int sum = 0;
      while (values.hasNext()) {
        sum += values.next().get();
      }
      output.collect(key, new IntWritable(sum));
    }
  }

  ...
}
```

① **Tokenize using white spaces**

② **Cast token into Text object**

③ **Output count of each token**

The main functional distinction between WordCount.java and our MapReduce pseudo-code is that in WordCount.java, map() processes one line of text at a time whereas our pseudo-code processes a document at a time. This distinction may not even be apparent from looking at WordCount.java as it's Hadoop's default configuration.

The code in listing 1.2 is virtually identical to our pseudo-code in listing 1.1 though the Java syntax makes it more verbose. The map and reduce functions are inside inner classes of WordCount. You may notice we use special classes such as LongWritable, IntWritable, and Text instead of the more familiar Long, Integer, and String classes of Java. Consider these implementation details for now. The new classes have additional serialization capabilities needed by Hadoop's internal.

The changes we want to make to the program are easy to spot. We see ① that WordCount uses Java's StringTokenizer in its default setting, which tokenizes based only on whitespaces. To ignore standard punctuation marks, we add them to the StringTokenizer's list of delimiter characters:

```
StringTokenizer itr = new StringTokenizer(line, " \t\n\r\f,.:;?![]'");
```

When looping through the set of tokens, each token is extracted and cast into a `Text` object ❷. (Again, in Hadoop, the special class `Text` is used in place of `String`.) We want the word count to ignore capitalization, so we lowercase all the words before turning them into `Text` objects.

```
word.set(itr.nextToken().toLowerCase());
```

Finally, we want only words that appear more than four times. We modify ❸ to collect the word count into the output only if that condition is met. (This is Hadoop's equivalent of the `emit()` function in our pseudo-code.)

```
if (sum > 4) output.collect(key, new IntWritable(sum));
```

After making changes to those three lines, you can recompile the program and execute it again. The results are shown in table 1.1.

Table 1.1 Words with a count higher than 4 in the 2002 State of the Union Address

11th (5)	citizens (9)	its (6)	over (6)	to (123)
a (69)	congress (10)	jobs (11)	own (5)	together (5)
about (5)	corps (6)	join (7)	page (7)	tonight (5)
act (7)	country (10)	know (6)	people (12)	training (5)
afghanistan (10)	destruction (5)	last (6)	protect (5)	united (6)
all (10)	do (6)	lives (6)	regime (5)	us (6)
allies (8)	every (8)	long (5)	regimes (6)	want (5)
also (5)	evil (5)	make (7)	security (19)	war (12)
America (33)	for (27)	many (5)	september (5)	was (11)
American (15)	free (6)	more (11)	so (12)	we (76)
americans (8)	freedom (10)	most (5)	some (6)	we've (5)
an (7)	from (15)	must (18)	states (9)	weapons (12)
and (210)	good (13)	my (13)	tax (7)	were (7)
are (17)	great (8)	nation (11)	terror (13)	while (5)
as (18)	has (12)	need (7)	terrorist (12)	who (18)
ask (5)	have (32)	never (7)	terrorists (10)	will (49)
at (16)	health (5)	new (13)	than (6)	with (22)
be (23)	help (7)	no (7)	that (29)	women (5)
been (8)	home (5)	not (15)	the (184)	work (7)
best (6)	homeland (7)	now (10)	their (17)	workers (5)
budget (7)	hope (5)	of (130)	them (8)	world (17)
but (7)	i (29)	on (32)	these (18)	would (5)
by (13)	if (8)	one (5)	they (12)	yet (8)

Table 1.1 Words with a count higher than 4 in the 2002 State of the Union Address (*continued*)

camps (8)	in (79)	opportunity (5)	this (28)	you (12)
can (7)	is (44)	or (8)	thousands (5)	
children (6)	it (21)	our (78)	time (7)	

We see that 128 words have a frequency count greater than 4. Many of these words appear frequently in almost any English text. For example, there is *a* (69), *and* (210), *i* (29), *in* (79), *the* (184) and many others. We also see words that summarize the issues facing the United States at that time: *terror* (13), *terrorist* (12), *terrorists* (10), *security* (19), *weapons* (12), *destruction* (5), *afghanistan* (10), *freedom* (10), *jobs* (11), *budget* (7), and many others.

1.7 *History of Hadoop*

Hadoop started out as a subproject of Nutch, which in turn was a subproject of Apache Lucene. Doug Cutting founded all three projects, and each project was a logical progression of the previous one.

Lucene is a full-featured text indexing and searching library. Given a text collection, a developer can easily add search capability to the documents using the Lucene engine. Desktop search, enterprise search, and many domain-specific search engines have been built using Lucene. Nutch is the most ambitious extension of Lucene. It tries to build a complete web search engine using Lucene as its core component. Nutch has parsers for HTML, a web crawler, a link-graph database, and other extra components necessary for a web search engine. Doug Cutting envisions Nutch to be an open democratic alternative to the proprietary technologies in commercial offerings such as Google.

Besides having added components like a crawler and a parser, a web search engine differs from a basic document search engine in terms of scale. Whereas Lucene is targeted at indexing millions of documents, Nutch should be able to handle billions of web pages without becoming exorbitantly expensive to operate. Nutch will have to run on a distributed cluster of commodity hardware. The challenge for the Nutch team is to address scalability issues in software. Nutch needs a layer to handle distributed processing, redundancy, automatic failover, and load balancing. These challenges are by no means trivial.

Around 2004, Google published two papers describing the Google File System (GFS) and the MapReduce framework. Google claimed to use these two technologies for scaling its own search system. Doug Cutting immediately saw the applicability of these technologies to Nutch, and his team implemented the new framework and ported Nutch to it. The new implementation immediately boosted Nutch's scalability. It started to handle several hundred million web pages and could run on clusters of dozens of nodes. Doug realized that a dedicated project to flesh out the two technologies was needed to get to web scale, and Hadoop was born. Yahoo! hired Doug in January

2006 to work with a dedicated team on improving Hadoop as an open source project. Two years later, Hadoop achieved the status of an Apache Top Level Project. Later, on February 19, 2008, Yahoo! announced that Hadoop running on a 10,000+ core Linux cluster was its production system for indexing the Web (http://developer.yahoo.net/blogs/hadoop/2008/02/yahoo-worlds-largest-production-hadoop.html). Hadoop had truly hit web scale!

What's up with the names?

When naming software projects, Doug Cutting seems to have been inspired by his family. *Lucene* is his wife's middle name, and her maternal grandmother's first name. His son, as a toddler, used *Nutch* as the all-purpose word for *meal* and later named a yellow stuffed elephant *Hadoop*. Doug said he "was looking for a name that wasn't already a web domain and wasn't trademarked, so I tried various words that were in my life but not used by anybody else. Kids are pretty good at making up words."

1.8   Summary

Hadoop is a versatile tool that allows new users to access the power of distributed computing. By using distributed storage and transferring code instead of data, Hadoop avoids the costly transmission step when working with large data sets. Moreover, the redundancy of data allows Hadoop to recover should a single node fail. You have seen the ease of creating programs with Hadoop using the MapReduce framework. What is equally important is what you didn't have to do—worry about partitioning the data, determining which nodes will perform which tasks, or handling communication between nodes. Hadoop handles this for you, leaving you free to focus on what's most important to you—your data and what you want to do with it.

In the next chapter we'll go into further details about the internals of Hadoop and setting up a working Hadoop cluster.

1.9   Resources

The official Hadoop website is at http://hadoop.apache.org/.

The original papers on the Google File System and MapReduce are well worth reading. Appreciate their underlying design and architecture:

- *The Google File System*—http://labs.google.com/papers/gfs.html
- *MapReduce: Simplified Data Processing on Large Clusters*—http://labs.google.com/papers/mapreduce.html

Starting Hadoop

This chapter covers
- The architectural components of Hadoop
- Setting up Hadoop and its three operating modes: standalone, pseudo-distributed, and fully distributed
- Web-based tools to monitor your Hadoop setup

This chapter will serve as a roadmap to guide you through setting up Hadoop. If you work in an environment where someone else sets up the Hadoop cluster for you, you may want to skim through this chapter. You'll want to understand enough to set up your personal development machine, but you can skip through the details of configuring the communication and coordination of various nodes.

After discussing the physical components of Hadoop in section 2.1, we'll progress to setting up your cluster in sections 2.2. and 2.3. Section 2.3 will focus on the three operational modes of Hadoop and how to set them up. You'll read about web-based tools that assist monitoring your cluster in section 2.4.

2.1 The building blocks of Hadoop

We've discussed the concepts of distributed storage and distributed computation in the previous chapter. Now let's see how Hadoop implements those ideas. On a fully configured cluster, "running Hadoop" means running a set of daemons, or resident programs, on the different servers in your network. These daemons have specific roles; some exist only on one server, some exist across multiple servers. The daemons include

- NameNode
- DataNode
- Secondary NameNode
- JobTracker
- TaskTracker

We'll discuss each one and its role within Hadoop.

2.1.1   NameNode

Let's begin with arguably the most vital of the Hadoop daemons—the NameNode. Hadoop employs a master/slave architecture for both distributed storage and distributed computation. The distributed storage system is called the *Hadoop File System*, or HDFS. The NameNode is the master of HDFS that directs the slave DataNode daemons to perform the low-level I/O tasks. The NameNode is the bookkeeper of HDFS; it keeps track of how your files are broken down into file blocks, which nodes store those blocks, and the overall health of the distributed filesystem.

The function of the NameNode is memory and I/O intensive. As such, the server hosting the NameNode typically doesn't store any user data or perform any computations for a MapReduce program to lower the workload on the machine. This means that the NameNode server doesn't double as a DataNode or a TaskTracker.

There is unfortunately a negative aspect to the importance of the NameNode—it's a single point of failure of your Hadoop cluster. For any of the other daemons, if their host nodes fail for software or hardware reasons, the Hadoop cluster will likely continue to function smoothly or you can quickly restart it. Not so for the NameNode.

2.1.2   DataNode

Each slave machine in your cluster will host a DataNode daemon to perform the grunt work of the distributed filesystem—reading and writing HDFS blocks to actual files on the local filesystem. When you want to read or write a HDFS file, the file is broken into blocks and the NameNode will tell your client which DataNode each block resides in. Your client communicates directly with the DataNode daemons to process the local files corresponding to the blocks. Furthermore, a DataNode may communicate with other DataNodes to replicate its data blocks for redundancy.

Figure 2.1 illustrates the roles of the NameNode and DataNodes. In this figure, we show two data files, one at /user/chuck/data1 and another at /user/james/data2. The data1 file takes up three blocks, which we denote 1, 2, and 3, and the data2 file consists of blocks 4 and 5. The content of the files are distributed among the DataNodes. In

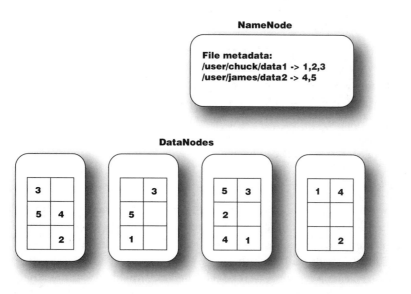

Figure 2.1   NameNode/DataNode interaction in HDFS. The NameNode keeps track of the file metadata—which files are in the system and how each file is broken down into blocks. The DataNodes provide backup store of the blocks and constantly report to the NameNode to keep the metadata current.

this illustration, each block has three replicas. For example, block 1 (used for data1) is replicated over the three rightmost DataNodes. This ensures that if any one DataNode crashes or becomes inaccessible over the network, you'll still be able to read the files.

DataNodes are constantly reporting to the NameNode. Upon initialization, each of the DataNodes informs the NameNode of the blocks it's currently storing. After this mapping is complete, the DataNodes continually poll the NameNode to provide information regarding local changes as well as receive instructions to create, move, or delete blocks from the local disk.

2.1.3   Secondary NameNode

The Secondary NameNode (SNN) is an assistant daemon for monitoring the state of the cluster HDFS. Like the NameNode, each cluster has one SNN, and it typically resides on its own machine as well. No other DataNode or TaskTracker daemons run on the same server. The SNN differs from the NameNode in that this process doesn't receive or record any real-time changes to HDFS. Instead, it communicates with the NameNode to take snapshots of the HDFS metadata at intervals defined by the cluster configuration.

As mentioned earlier, the NameNode is a single point of failure for a Hadoop cluster, and the SNN snapshots help minimize the downtime and loss of data. Nevertheless, a NameNode failure requires human intervention to reconfigure the cluster to use the SNN as the primary NameNode. We'll discuss the recovery process in chapter 8 when we cover best practices for managing your cluster.

2.1.4 *JobTracker*

The JobTracker daemon is the liaison between your application and Hadoop. Once you submit your code to your cluster, the JobTracker determines the execution plan by determining which files to process, assigns nodes to different tasks, and monitors all tasks as they're running. Should a task fail, the JobTracker will automatically relaunch the task, possibly on a different node, up to a predefined limit of retries.

There is only one JobTracker daemon per Hadoop cluster. It's typically run on a server as a master node of the cluster.

2.1.5 *TaskTracker*

As with the storage daemons, the computing daemons also follow a master/slave architecture: the JobTracker is the master overseeing the overall execution of a MapReduce job and the TaskTrackers manage the execution of individual tasks on each slave node. Figure 2.2 illustrates this interaction.

Each TaskTracker is responsible for executing the individual tasks that the JobTracker assigns. Although there is a single TaskTracker per slave node, each TaskTracker can spawn multiple JVMs to handle many map or reduce tasks in parallel.

One responsibility of the TaskTracker is to constantly communicate with the JobTracker. If the JobTracker fails to receive a heartbeat from a TaskTracker within a specified amount of time, it will assume the TaskTracker has crashed and will resubmit the corresponding tasks to other nodes in the cluster.

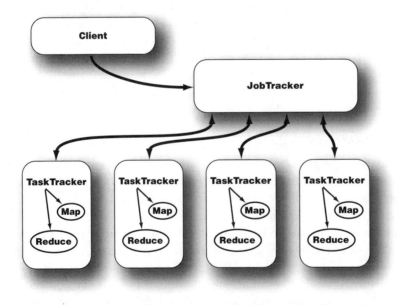

Figure 2.2   JobTracker and TaskTracker interaction. After a client calls the JobTracker to begin a data processing job, the JobTracker partitions the work and assigns different map and reduce tasks to each TaskTracker in the cluster.

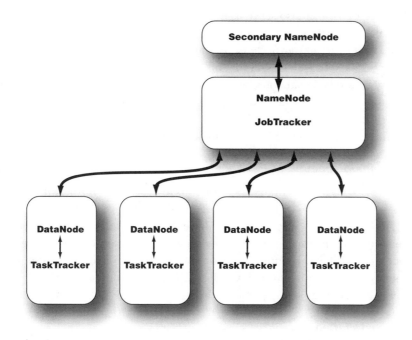

Figure 2.3   Topology of a typical Hadoop cluster. It's a master/slave architecture in which the NameNode and JobTracker are masters and the DataNodes and TaskTrackers are slaves.

Having covered each of the Hadoop daemons, we depict the topology of one typical Hadoop cluster in figure 2.3.

This topology features a master node running the NameNode and JobTracker daemons and a standalone node with the SNN in case the master node fails. For small clusters, the SNN can reside on one of the slave nodes. On the other hand, for large clusters, separate the NameNode and JobTracker on two machines. The slave machines each host a DataNode and TaskTracker, for running tasks on the same node where their data is stored.

We'll work toward setting up a complete Hadoop cluster of this form by first establishing the master node and the control channels between nodes. If a Hadoop cluster is already available to you, you can skip the next section on how to set up Secure Shell (SSH) channels between nodes. You also have a couple of options to run Hadoop using only a single machine, in what are known as standalone and pseudo-distributed modes. They're useful for development. Configuring Hadoop to run in these two modes or the standard cluster setup (fully distributed mode) is covered in section 2.3.

2.2   *Setting up SSH for a Hadoop cluster*

When setting up a Hadoop cluster, you'll need to designate one specific node as the master node. As shown in figure 2.3, this server will typically host the NameNode and

JobTracker daemons. It'll also serve as the base station contacting and activating the DataNode and TaskTracker daemons on all of the slave nodes. As such, we need to define a means for the master node to remotely access every node in your cluster.

Hadoop uses passphraseless SSH for this purpose. SSH utilizes standard public key cryptography to create a pair of keys for user verification—one public, one private. The public key is stored locally on every node in the cluster, and the master node sends the private key when attempting to access a remote machine. With both pieces of information, the target machine can validate the login attempt.

2.2.1 Define a common account

We've been speaking in general terms of one node accessing another; more precisely this access is from a user account on one node to another user account on the target machine. For Hadoop, the accounts should have the same username on all of the nodes (we use hadoop-user in this book), and for security purpose we recommend it being a user-level account. This account is only for managing your Hadoop cluster. Once the cluster daemons are up and running, you'll be able to run your actual MapReduce jobs from other accounts.

2.2.2 Verify SSH installation

The first step is to check whether SSH is installed on your nodes. We can easily do this by use of the "which" UNIX command:

```
[hadoop-user@master]$ which ssh
/usr/bin/ssh

[hadoop-user@master]$ which sshd
/usr/bin/sshd

[hadoop-user@master]$ which ssh-keygen
/usr/bin/ssh-keygen
```

If you instead receive an error message such as this,

```
/usr/bin/which: no ssh in (/usr/bin:/bin:/usr/sbin...
```

install OpenSSH (www.openssh.com) via a Linux package manager or by downloading the source directly. (Better yet, have your system administrator do it for you.)

2.2.3 Generate SSH key pair

Having verified that SSH is correctly installed on all nodes of the cluster, we use ssh-keygen on the master node to generate an RSA key pair. Be certain to avoid entering a passphrase, or you'll have to manually enter that phrase every time the master node attempts to access another node.

```
[hadoop-user@master]$ ssh-keygen -t rsa
Generating public/private rsa key pair.
Enter file in which to save the key (/home/hadoop-user/.ssh/id_rsa):
Enter passphrase (empty for no passphrase):
Enter same passphrase again:
```

```
Your identification has been saved in /home/hadoop-user/.ssh/id_rsa.
Your public key has been saved in /home/hadoop-user/.ssh/id_rsa.pub.
```

After creating your key pair, your public key will be of the form

```
[hadoop-user@master]$ more /home/hadoop-user/.ssh/id_rsa.pub
ssh-rsa AAAAB3NzaC1yc2EAAAABIwAAAQEA1WS3RG8LrZH4zL2/1oYgkV1OmVclQ2OO5vRi0Nd
K51Sy3wWpBVHx82F3x3ddoZQjBK3uvLMaDhXvncJG31JPfU7CTAfmtgINYv0kdUbDJq4TKG/fuO5q
J9CqHV71thN2M31OgcJ0Y9YCN6grmsiWb2iMcXpy2pqg8UM3ZKApyIPx99O1vREWm+4moFTg
YwIl5be23ZCyxNjgZFWk5MRlT1p1TxB68jqNbPQtU7fIafS7Sasy7h4eyIy7cbLh8x0/V4/mcQsY
5dvReitNvFVte6onl8YdmnMpAh6nwCvog3UeWWJjVZTEBFkTZuV1i9HeYHxpm1wAzcnf7az78jT
IRQ== hadoop-user@master
```

and we next need to distribute this public key across your cluster.

2.2.4 *Distribute public key and validate logins*

Albeit a bit tedious, you'll next need to copy the public key to every slave node as well as the master node:

```
[hadoop-user@master]$ scp ~/.ssh/id_rsa.pub hadoop-user@target:~/master_key
```

Manually log in to the target node and set the master key as an authorized key (or append to the list of authorized keys if you have others defined).

```
[hadoop-user@target]$ mkdir ~/.ssh
[hadoop-user@target]$ chmod 700 ~/.ssh
[hadoop-user@target]$ mv ~/master_key ~/.ssh/authorized_keys
[hadoop-user@target]$ chmod 600 ~/.ssh/authorized_keys
```

After generating the key, you can verify it's correctly defined by attempting to log in to the target node from the master:

```
[hadoop-user@master]$ ssh target
The authenticity of host 'target (xxx.xxx.xxx.xxx)' can't be established.
RSA key fingerprint is 72:31:d8:1b:11:36:43:52:56:11:77:a4:ec:82:03:1d.
Are you sure you want to continue connecting (yes/no)? yes
Warning: Permanently added 'target' (RSA) to the list of known hosts.
Last login: Sun Jan 4 15:32:22 2009 from master
```

After confirming the authenticity of a target node to the master node, you won't be prompted upon subsequent login attempts.

```
[hadoop-user@master]$ ssh target
Last login: Sun Jan 4 15:32:49 2009 from master
```

We've now set the groundwork for running Hadoop on your own cluster. Let's discuss the different Hadoop modes you might want to use for your projects.

2.3 *Running Hadoop*

We need to configure a few things before running Hadoop. Let's take a closer look at the Hadoop configuration directory:

```
[hadoop-user@master]$ cd $HADOOP_HOME
[hadoop-user@master]$ ls -l conf/
total 100
```

```
-rw-rw-r-- 1 hadoop-user hadoop  2065 Dec 1 10:07 capacity-scheduler.xml
-rw-rw-r-- 1 hadoop-user hadoop   535 Dec 1 10:07 configuration.xsl
-rw-rw-r-- 1 hadoop-user hadoop 49456 Dec 1 10:07 hadoop-default.xml
-rwxrwxr-x 1 hadoop-user hadoop  2314 Jan 8 17:01 hadoop-env.sh
-rw-rw-r-- 1 hadoop-user hadoop  2234 Jan 2 15:29 hadoop-site.xml
-rw-rw-r-- 1 hadoop-user hadoop  2815 Dec 1 10:07 log4j.properties
-rw-rw-r-- 1 hadoop-user hadoop    28 Jan 2 15:29 masters
-rw-rw-r-- 1 hadoop-user hadoop    84 Jan 2 15:29 slaves
-rw-rw-r-- 1 hadoop-user hadoop   401 Dec 1 10:07 sslinfo.xml.example
```

The first thing you need to do is to specify the location of Java on all the nodes includ-ing the master. In hadoop-env.sh define the JAVA_HOME environment variable to point to the Java installation directory. On our servers, we've it defined as

```
export JAVA_HOME=/usr/share/jdk
```

(If you followed the examples in chapter 1, you've already completed this step.)

The hadoop-env.sh file contains other variables for defining your Hadoop environment, but JAVA_HOME is the only one requiring initial modification. The default settings on the other variables will probably work fine. As you become more familiar with Hadoop you can later modify this file to suit your individual needs (logging directory location, Java class path, and so on).

The majority of Hadoop settings are contained in XML configuration files. Before version 0.20, these XML files are hadoop-default.xml and hadoop-site.xml. As the names imply, hadoop-default.xml contains the default Hadoop settings to be used unless they are explicitly overridden in hadoop-site.xml. In practice you only deal with hadoop-site.xml. In version 0.20 this file has been separated out into three XML files: core-site.xml, hdfs-site.xml, and mapred-site.xml. This refactoring better aligns the configuration settings to the subsystem of Hadoop that they control. In the rest of this chapter we'll generally point out which of the three files used to adjust a configuration setting. If you use an earlier version of Hadoop, keep in mind that all such configuration settings are modified in hadoop-site.xml.

In the following subsections we'll provide further details about the different operational modes of Hadoop and example configuration files for each.

2.3.1 *Local (standalone) mode*

The standalone mode is the default mode for Hadoop. When you first uncompress the Hadoop source package, it's ignorant of your hardware setup. Hadoop chooses to be conservative and assumes a minimal configuration. All three XML files (or hadoop-site.xml before version 0.20) are empty under this default mode:

```
<?xml version="1.0"?>
<?xml-stylesheet type="text/xsl" href="configuration.xsl"?>

<!-- Put site-specific property overrides in this file. -->

<configuration>

</configuration>
```

With empty configuration files, Hadoop will run completely on the local machine. Because there's no need to communicate with other nodes, the standalone mode doesn't use HDFS, nor will it launch any of the Hadoop daemons. Its primary use is for developing and debugging the application logic of a MapReduce program without the additional complexity of interacting with the daemons. When you ran the example MapReduce program in chapter 1, you were running it in standalone mode.

2.3.2 *Pseudo-distributed mode*

The pseudo-distributed mode is running Hadoop in a "cluster of one" with all daemons running on a single machine. This mode complements the standalone mode for debugging your code, allowing you to examine memory usage, HDFS input/output issues, and other daemon interactions. Listing 2.1 provides simple XML files to configure a single server in this mode.

Listing 2.1   Example of the three configuration files for pseudo-distributed mode

core-site.xml
```
<?xml version="1.0"?>
<?xml-stylesheet type="text/xsl" href="configuration.xsl"?>

<!-- Put site-specific property overrides in this file. -->

<configuration>

<property>
 <name>fs.default.name</name>
 <value>hdfs://localhost:9000</value>
 <description>The name of the default file system. A URI whose
 scheme and authority determine the FileSystem implementation.
 </description>
</property>

</configuration>
```

mapred-site.xml
```
<?xml version="1.0"?>
<?xml-stylesheet type="text/xsl" href="configuration.xsl"?>

<!-- Put site-specific property overrides in this file. -->

<configuration>

<property>
 <name>mapred.job.tracker</name>
 <value>localhost:9001</value>
 <description>The host and port that the MapReduce job tracker runs
 at.</description>
</property>

</configuration>
```

hdfs-site.xml
```
<?xml version="1.0"?>
<?xml-stylesheet type="text/xsl" href="configuration.xsl"?>
```

```
<!-- Put site-specific property overrides in this file. -->
<configuration>

<property>
 <name>dfs.replication</name>
 <value>1</value>
 <description>The actual number of replications can be specified when the
 file is created.</description>
</property>

</configuration>
```

In `core-site.xml` and `mapred-site.xml` we specify the hostname and port of the NameNode and the JobTracker, respectively. In `hdfs-site.xml` we specify the default replication factor for HDFS, which should only be one because we're running on only one node. We must also specify the location of the Secondary NameNode in the masters file and the slave nodes in the slaves file:

```
[hadoop-user@master]$ cat masters
localhost
[hadoop-user@master]$ cat slaves
localhost
```

While all the daemons are running on the same machine, they still communicate with each other using the same SSH protocol as if they were distributed over a cluster. Section 2.2 has a more detailed discussion of setting up the SSH channels, but for single-node operation simply check to see if your machine already allows you to `ssh` back to itself.

```
[hadoop-user@master]$ ssh localhost
```

If it does, then you're good. Otherwise setting up takes two lines.

```
[hadoop-user@master]$ ssh-keygen -t dsa -P '' -f ~/.ssh/id_dsa
[hadoop-user@master]$ cat ~/.ssh/id_dsa.pub >> ~/.ssh/authorized_keys
```

You are almost ready to start Hadoop. But first you'll need to format your HDFS by using the command

```
[hadoop-user@master]$ bin/hadoop namenode -format
```

We can now launch the daemons by use of the `start-all.sh` script. The Java `jps` command will list all daemons to verify the setup was successful.

```
[hadoop-user@master]$ bin/start-all.sh
[hadoop-user@master]$ jps
26893 Jps
26832 TaskTracker
26620 SecondaryNameNode
26333 NameNode
26484 DataNode
26703 JobTracker
```

When you've finished with Hadoop you can shut down the Hadoop daemons by the command

```
[hadoop-user@master]$ bin/stop-all.sh
```

Both standalone and pseudo-distributed modes are for development and debugging purposes. An actual Hadoop cluster runs in the third mode, the fully distributed mode.

2.3.3   *Fully distributed mode*

After continually emphasizing the benefits of distributed storage and distributed computation, it's time for us to set up a full cluster. In the discussion below we'll use the following server names:

- *master*—The master node of the cluster and host of the NameNode and Job-Tracker daemons
- *backup*—The server that hosts the Secondary NameNode daemon
- *hadoop1, hadoop2, hadoop3,* ...—The slave boxes of the cluster running both DataNode and TaskTracker daemons

Using the preceding naming convention, listing 2.2 is a modified version of the pseudo-distributed configuration files (listing 2.1) that can be used as a skeleton for your cluster's setup.

Listing 2.2   Example configuration files for fully distributed mode

core-site.xml
```
<?xml version="1.0"?>
<?xml-stylesheet type="text/xsl" href="configuration.xsl"?>

<!-- Put site-specific property overrides in this file. -->

<configuration>

<property>
 <name>fs.default.name</name>
 <value>hdfs://master:9000</value>
 <description>The name of the default file system. A URI whose
 scheme and authority determine the FileSystem implementation.
 </description>
</property>

</configuration>
```

❶ Locate NameNode for filesystem

mapred-site.xml
```
<?xml version="1.0"?>
<?xml-stylesheet type="text/xsl" href="configuration.xsl"?>

<!-- Put site-specific property overrides in this file. -->

<configuration>
```

```
<property>
 <name>mapred.job.tracker</name>
 <value>master:9001</value>
 <description>The host and port that the MapReduce job tracker runs
at.</description>
</property>

</configuration>
```

❷ Locate JobTracker master

hdfs-site.xml
```
<?xml version="1.0"?>
<?xml-stylesheet type="text/xsl" href="configuration.xsl"?>

<!-- Put site-specific property overrides in this file. -->

<configuration>

<property>
 <name>dfs.replication</name>
 <value>3</value>
 <description>The actual number of replications can be specified when the
file is created.</description>
</property>

</configuration>
```

❸ Increase HDFS replication factor

The key differences are

- We explicitly stated the hostname for location of the NameNode ❶ and JobTracker ❷ daemons.
- We increased the HDFS replication factor to take advantage of distributed storage ❸. Recall that data is replicated across HDFS to increase availability and reliability.

We also need to update the masters and slaves files to reflect the locations of the other daemons.

```
[hadoop-user@master]$ cat masters
backup
[hadoop-user@master]$ cat slaves
hadoop1
hadoop2
hadoop3
...
```

Once you have copied these files across all the nodes in your cluster, be sure to format HDFS to prepare it for storage:

```
[hadoop-user@master]$ bin/hadoop namenode-format
```

Now you can start the Hadoop daemons:

```
[hadoop-user@master]$ bin/start-all.sh
```

and verify the nodes are running their assigned jobs.

```
[hadoop-user@master]$ jps
30879 JobTracker
30717 NameNode
```

```
30965 Jps
[hadoop-user@backup]$ jps
2099 Jps
1679 SecondaryNameNode
[hadoop-user@hadoop1]$ jps
7101 TaskTracker
7617 Jps
6988 DataNode
```

You have a functioning cluster!

Switching between modes

A practice that I found useful when starting with Hadoop was to use symbolic links to switch between Hadoop modes instead of constantly editing the XML files. To do so, create a separate configuration folder for each of the modes and place the appropriate version of the XML files in the corresponding folder. Below is an example directory listing:

[hadoop@hadoop_master hadoop]$ ls -l

total 4884

drwxr-xr-x 2 hadoop-user hadoop 4096 Nov 26 17:36 bin

-rw-rw-r-- 1 hadoop-user hadoop 57430 Nov 13 19:09 build.xml

drwxr-xr-x 4 hadoop-user hadoop 4096 Nov 13 19:14 c++

-rw-rw-r-- 1 hadoop-user hadoop 287046 Nov 13 19:09 CHANGES.txt

lrwxrwxrwx 1 hadoop-user hadoop   12 Jan 5 16:06 conf -> conf.cluster

drwxr-xr-x 2 hadoop-user hadoop 4096 Jan 8 17:05 conf.cluster

drwxr-xr-x 2 hadoop-user hadoop 4096 Jan 2 15:07 conf.pseudo

drwxr-xr-x 2 hadoop-user hadoop 4096 Dec 1 10:10 conf.standalone

drwxr-xr-x 12 hadoop-user hadoop 4096 Nov 13 19:09 contrib

drwxrwxr-x 5 hadoop-user hadoop 4096 Jan 2 09:28 datastore

drwxr-xr-x 6 hadoop-user hadoop 4096 Nov 26 17:36 docs

...

You can then switch between configurations by using the Linux ln command (e.g., ln -s conf.cluster conf). This practice is also useful to temporarily pull a node out of the cluster to debug a MapReduce program in pseudo-distributed mode, but be sure that the modes have different file locations for HDFS and stop all daemons on the node before changing configurations.

Now that we've gone through all the settings to successfully get a Hadoop cluster up and running, we'll introduce the Web UI for basic monitoring of the cluster's state.

2.4   Web-based cluster UI

Having covered the operational modes of Hadoop, we can now introduce the web interfaces that Hadoop provides to monitor the health of your cluster. The browser interface allows you to access information you desire much faster than digging through logs and directories.

The NameNode hosts a general report on port 50070. It gives you an overview of the state of your cluster's HDFS. Figure 2.4 displays this report for a 2-node cluster example. From this interface, you can browse through the `filesystem`, check the status of each `DataNode` in your cluster, and peruse the Hadoop daemon logs to verify your cluster is functioning correctly.

Hadoop provides a similar status overview of ongoing MapReduce jobs. Figure 2.5 depicts one hosted at port 50030 of the JobTracker.

Again, a wealth of information is available through this reporting interface. You can access the status of ongoing MapReduce tasks as well as detailed reports about completed jobs. The latter is of particular importance—these logs describe which nodes performed which tasks and the time/resources required to complete each task. Finally, the Hadoop configuration for each job is also available, as shown in figure 2.6. With all of this information you can streamline your MapReduce programs to better utilize the resources of your cluster.

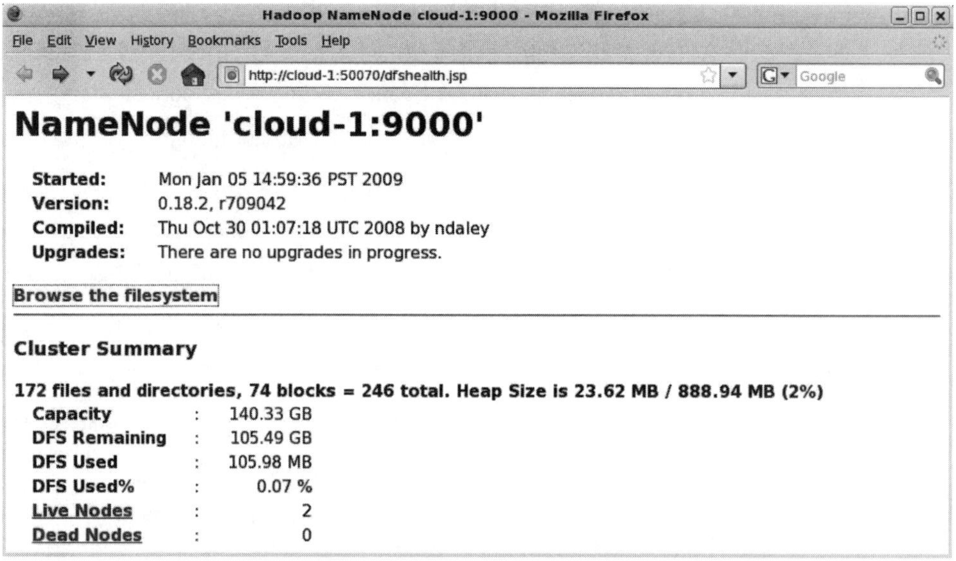

Figure 2.4   A snapshot of the HDFS web interface. From this interface you can browse through the HDFS filesystem, determine the storage available on each individual node, and monitor the overall health of your cluster.

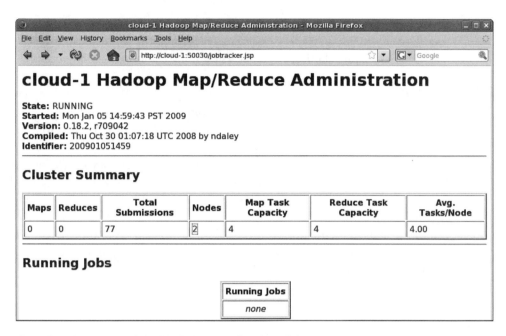

Figure 2.5 A snapshot of the MapReduce web interface. This tool allows you to monitor active MapReduce jobs and access the logs of each map and reduce task. The logs of previously submitted jobs are also available and are useful for debugging your programs.

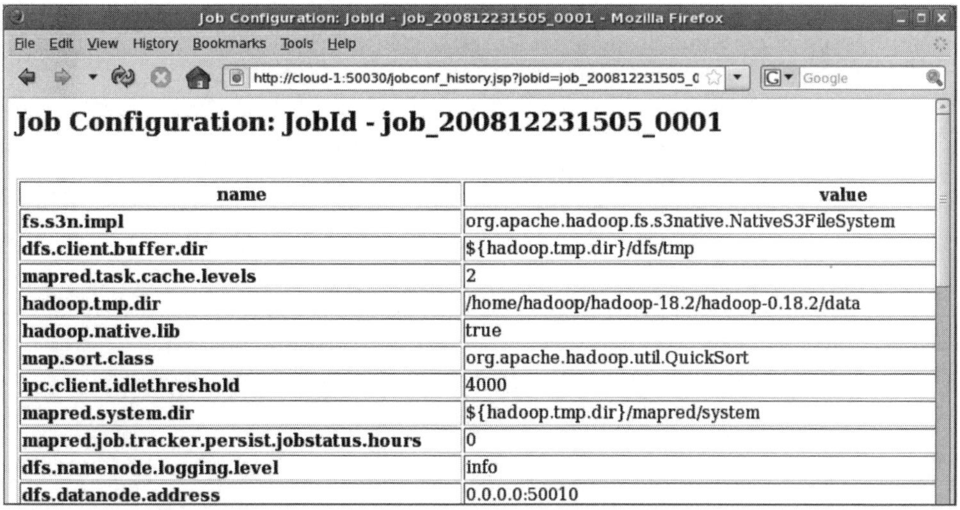

Figure 2.6 Configuration details for a specific MapReduce job. This information is potentially useful when tuning parameters to optimize the performance of your programs.

Though the usefulness of these tools may not be immediately apparent at this stage, they'll come in handy as you begin to perform more sophisticated tasks on your cluster. You'll realize their importance as we study Hadoop more in depth.

2.5   *Summary*

In this chapter we've discussed the key nodes and the roles they play within the Hadoop architecture. You've learned how to configure your cluster, as well as manage some basic tools to monitor your cluster's overall health.

Overall, this chapter focuses on one-time tasks. Once you've formatted the NameNode for your cluster, you'll (hopefully) never need to do so again. Likewise, you shouldn't keep altering the hadoop-site.xml configuration file for your cluster or assigning daemons to nodes. In the next chapter, you'll learn about the aspects of Hadoop you'll be interacting with on a daily basis, such as managing files in HDFS. With this knowledge you'll be able to begin writing your own MapReduce applications and realize the true potential that Hadoop has to offer.

Components of Hadoop

This chapter covers
- Managing files in HDFS
- Analyzing components of the MapReduce framework
- Reading and writing input and output data

In the last chapter we looked at setting up and installing Hadoop. We covered what the different nodes do and how to configure them to work with each other. Now that you have Hadoop running, let's look at the Hadoop framework from a programmer's perspective. If the previous chapter is like teaching you how to connect your turntable, your mixer, your amplifier, and your speakers together, then this chapter is about the techniques of mixing music.

We first cover HDFS, where you'll store data that your Hadoop applications will process. Next we explain the MapReduce framework in more detail. In chapter 1 we've already seen a MapReduce program, but we discussed the logic only at the conceptual level. In this chapter we get to know the Java classes and methods, as well as the underlying processing steps. We also learn how to read and write using different data formats.

3.1 *Working with files in HDFS*

HDFS is a filesystem designed for large-scale distributed data processing under frame-works such as MapReduce. You can store a big data set of (say) 100 TB as a single file in HDFS, something that would overwhelm most other filesystems. We discussed in chapter 2 how to replicate the data for availability and distribute it over multiple ma-chines to enable parallel processing. HDFS abstracts these details away and gives you the illusion that you're dealing with only a single file.

As HDFS isn't a native Unix filesystem, standard Unix file tools, such as `ls` and `cp` don't work on it,[1] and neither do standard file read/write operations, such as `fopen()` and `fread()`. On the other hand, Hadoop does provide a set of command line utilities that work similarly to the Linux file commands. In the next section we'll discuss those Hadoop file shell commands, which are your primary interface with the HDFS system. Section 3.1.2 covers Hadoop Java libraries for handling HDFS files programmatically.

> **NOTE**   A typical Hadoop workflow creates data files (such as log files) elsewhere and copies them into HDFS using one of the command line utilities discussed in the next section. Your MapReduce programs then process this data, but they usually don't read any HDFS files directly. Instead they rely on the MapReduce framework to read and parse the HDFS files into individual records (key/value pairs), which are the unit of data MapReduce programs do work on. You rarely will have to programmatically read or write HDFS files except for custom import and export of data.

3.1.1 *Basic file commands*

Hadoop file commands take the form of

```
hadoop fs -cmd <args>
```

where cmd is the specific file command and <args> is a variable number of arguments. The command cmd is usually named after the corresponding Unix equivalent. For example, the command for listing files is[2]

```
hadoop fs -ls
```

Let's look at the most common file management tasks in Hadoop, which include

- Adding files and directories
- Retrieving files
- Deleting files

---

[1] There are several ongoing projects that try to make HDFS mountable as a Unix filesystem. More details are at http://wiki.apache.org/hadoop/MountableHDFS. As of this writing these projects aren't officially part of Hadoop and they may not have the reliability needed for some production systems.

[2] Some older documentation shows file utilities in the form of `hadoop dfs -cmd <args>`. Both `dfs` and `fs` are equivalent, although `fs` is the preferred form now.

URI for specifying exact file and directory location

Hadoop file commands can interact with both the HDFS filesystem and the local filesystem. (And as we'll see in chapter 9, it can also interact with Amazon S3 as a filesystem.) A URI pinpoints the location of a specific file or directory. The full URI format is scheme://authority/path. The *scheme* is similar to a protocol. It can be `hdfs` or `file`, to specify the HDFS filesystem or the local filesystem, respectively. For HDFS, *authority* is the NameNode host and *path* is the path of the file or directory of interest. For example, for a standard pseudo-distributed configuration running HDFS on the local machine on port 9000, a URI to access the example.txt file under the directory user/chuck will look like hdfs://localhost:9000/user/chuck/example.txt. You can use the Hadoop `cat` command to show the content of that file:

```
hadoop fs -cat hdfs://localhost:9000/user/chuck/example.txt
```

As we'll see shortly, most setups don't need to specify the scheme://authority part of the URI. When dealing with the local filesystem, you'll probably prefer your standard Unix commands rather than the Hadoop file commands. For copying files between the local filesystem and HDFS, Hadoop commands, such as `put` and `get` use the local filesystem as source and destination, respectively, without you specifying the file:// scheme. For other commands, if you leave out the scheme://authority part of the URI, the default from the Hadoop configuration is used. For example, if you have changed the conf/core-site.xml file to the pseudo-distributed configuration, your fs.default.name property in the file should be

```
<property>
    <name>fs.default.name</name>
    <value>hdfs://localhost:9000</value>
</property>
```

Under this configuration, shorten the URI hdfs://localhost:9000/user/chuck/example. txt to /user/chuck/example.txt. Furthermore, HDFS defaults to a current *working directory* of /user/$USER, where $USER is your login user name. If you're logged in as chuck, then shorten the URI hdfs://localhost:9000/user/chuck/example.txt to example.txt. The Hadoop `cat` command to show the content of the file is

```
hadoop fs -cat example.txt
```

ADDING FILES AND DIRECTORIES

Before you can run Hadoop programs on data stored in HDFS, you'll need to put the data into HDFS first. Let's assume you've already formatted and started a HDFS filesystem. (For learning purposes, we recommend a pseudo-distributed configuration as a playground.) Let's create a directory and put a file in it.

HDFS has a default working directory of /user/$USER, where $USER is your login user name. This directory isn't automatically created for you, though, so let's create it with the `mkdir` command. For the purpose of illustration, we use *chuck*. You should substitute your user name in the example commands.

```
hadoop fs -mkdir /user/chuck
```

Hadoop's `mkdir` command automatically creates parent directories if they don't already exist, similar to the Unix `mkdir` command with the -p option. So the preceding command will create the /user directory too. Let's check on the directories with the `ls` command.

```
hadoop fs -ls /
```

You'll see this response showing the /user directory at the root / directory.

```
Found 1 items
drwxr-xr-x    - chuck supergroup          0 2009-01-14 10:23 /user
```

If you want to see all the subdirectories, in a way similar to Unix's `ls` with the -r option, you can use Hadoop's `lsr` command.

```
hadoop fs -lsr /
```

You'll see all the files and directories recursively.

```
drwxr-xr-x    - chuck supergroup          0 2009-01-14 10:23 /user
drwxr-xr-x    - chuck supergroup          0 2009-01-14 10:23 /user/chuck
```

Now that we have a working directory, we can put a file into it. Create some text file on your local filesystem called example.txt. The Hadoop command `put` is used to copy files from the local system into HDFS.

```
hadoop fs -put example.txt .
```

Note the period (.) as the last argument in the command above. It means that we're putting the file into the default working directory. The command above is equivalent to

```
hadoop fs -put example.txt /user/chuck
```

We can re-execute the recursive file listing command to see that the new file is added to HDFS.

```
$ hadoop fs -lsr /
drwxr-xr-x    - chuck supergroup          0 2009-01-14 10:23 /user
drwxr-xr-x    - chuck supergroup          0 2009-01-14 11:02 /user/chuck
-rw-r--r--    1 chuck supergroup        264 2009-01-14 11:02
➥/user/chuck/example.txt
```

In practice we don't need to check on all files recursively, and we may restrict ourselves to what's in our own working directory. We would use the Hadoop `ls` command in its simplest form:

```
$ hadoop fs -ls
Found 1 items
-rw-r--r--    1 chuck supergroup        264 2009-01-14 11:02
➥/user/chuck/example.txt
```

The output displays properties, such as permission, owner, group, file size, and last modification date, all of which are familiar Unix concepts. The column stating "1" reports the replication factor of the file. It should always be 1 for the pseudo-distributed configuration. For production clusters, the replication factor is typically 3 but can be any positive integer. Replication factor is not applicable to directories, so they will only show a dash (-) for that column.

After you've put data into HDFS, you can run Hadoop programs to process it. The output of the processing will be a new set of files in HDFS, and you'll want to read or retrieve the results.

RETRIEVING FILES

The Hadoop command `get` does the exact reverse of `put`. It copies files from HDFS to the local filesystem. Let's say we no longer have the example.txt file locally and we want to retrieve it from HDFS; we can run the command

```
hadoop fs -get example.txt .
```

to copy it into our local current working directory.

Another way to access the data is to display it. The Hadoop `cat` command allows us to do that.

```
hadoop fs -cat example.txt
```

We can use the Hadoop file command with Unix pipes to send its output for further processing by other Unix commands. For example, if the file is huge (as typical Hadoop files are) and you're interested in a quick check of its content, you can pipe the output of Hadoop's `cat` into a Unix `head`.

```
hadoop fs -cat example.txt | head
```

Hadoop natively supports a `tail` command for looking at the last kilobyte of a file.

```
hadoop fs -tail example.txt
```

After you finish working with files in HDFS, you may want to delete them to free up space.

DELETING FILES

You shouldn't be too surprised by now that the Hadoop command for removing files is `rm`.

```
hadoop fs -rm example.txt
```

The `rm` command can also be used to delete empty directories.

LOOKING UP HELP

A list of Hadoop file commands, together with the usage and description of each command, is given in the appendix. For the most part, the commands are modeled after their Unix equivalent. You can execute `hadoop fs` (with no parameters) to get a complete list of all commands available on your version of Hadoop. You can also use `help` to display the usage and a short description of each command. For example, to get a summary of `ls`, execute

```
hadoop fs -help ls
```

and you should see the following description:

```
-ls <path>:      List the contents that match the specified file pattern. If
                 path is not specified, the contents of /user/<currentUser>
                 will be listed. Directory entries are of the form
                       dirName (full path) <dir>
                 and file entries are of the form
                       fileName(full path) <r n> size
                 where n is the number of replicas specified for the file
                 and size is the size of the file, in bytes.
```

Although the command line utilities are sufficient for most of your interaction with the HDFS filesystem, they're not exhaustive and there'll be situations where you may want deeper access into the HDFS API. Let's see how to do so in the next section.

3.1.2 *Reading and writing to HDFS programmatically*

To motivate an examination of the HDFS Java API, we'll develop a PutMerge program for merging files while putting them into HDFS. The command line utilities don't support this operation; we'll use the API.

The motivation for this example came when we wanted to analyze Apache log files coming from many web servers. We can copy each log file into HDFS, but in general, Hadoop works more effectively with a single large file rather than a number of smaller ones. ("Smaller" is relative here as it can still be tens or hundreds of gigabytes.) Besides, for analytics purposes we think of the log data as one big file. That it's spread over multiple files is an incidental result of the physical web server architecture. One solution is to merge all the files first and then copy the combined file into HDFS. Unfortunately, the file merging will require a lot of disk space in the local machine. It would be much easier if we could merge all the files on the fly as we copy them into HDFS.

What we need is, therefore, a PutMerge-type of operation. Hadoop's command line utilities include a getmerge command for merging a number of HDFS files before copying them onto the local machine. What we're looking for is the exact opposite. This is not available in Hadoop's file utilities. We'll write our own program using the HDFS API.

The main classes for file manipulation in Hadoop are in the package org.apache.hadoop.fs. Basic Hadoop file operations include the familiar open, read, write, and close. In fact, the Hadoop file API is generic and can be used for working with filesystems other than HDFS. For our PutMerge program, we'll use the Hadoop file API to both read the local filesystem and write to HDFS.

The starting point for the Hadoop file API is the FileSystem class. This is an abstract class for interfacing with the filesystem, and there are different concrete subclasses for handling HDFS and the local filesystem. You get the desired FileSystem instance by calling the factory method FileSystem.get(Configuration conf). The Configuration class is a special class for holding key/value configuration parameters. Its default instantiation is based on the resource configuration for your HDFS system. We can get the FileSystem object to interface with HDFS by

```
Configuration conf = new Configuration();
FileSystem hdfs = FileSystem.get(conf);
```

To get a `FileSystem` object specifically for the local filesystem, there's the `FileSystem.getLocal(Configuration conf)` factory method.

```
FileSystem local = FileSystem.getLocal(conf);
```

Hadoop file API uses `Path` objects to encode file and directory names and `FileStatus` objects to store metadata for files and directories. Our PutMerge program will merge all files from a local directory. We use the `FileSystem`'s `listStatus()` method to get a list of files in a directory.

```
Path inputDir = new Path(args[0]);
FileStatus[] inputFiles = local.listStatus(inputDir);
```

The length of the `inputFiles` array is the number of files in the specified directory. Each `FileStatus` object in `inputFiles` has metadata information such as file length, permissions, modification time, and others. Of interest to our PutMerge program is each file's `Path` representation, `inputFiles[i].getPath()`. We can use this `Path` to request an `FSDataInputStream` object for reading in the file.

```
FSDataInputStream in = local.open(inputFiles[i].getPath());
byte buffer[] = new byte[256];
int bytesRead = 0;
while( (bytesRead = in.read(buffer)) > 0) {
    ...
}
in.close();
```

`FSDataInputStream` is a subclass of Java's standard java.io.DataInputStream with additional support for random access. For writing to a HDFS file, there's the analogous `FSDataOutputStream` object.

```
Path hdfsFile = new Path(args[1]);
FSDataOutputStream out = hdfs.create(hdfsFile);
out.write(buffer, 0, bytesRead);
out.close();
```

To complete the PutMerge program, we create a loop that goes through all the files in `inputFiles` as we read each one in and write it out to the destination HDFS file. You can see the complete program in listing 3.1.

Listing 3.1 A PutMerge program

```
import java.io.IOException;

import org.apache.hadoop.conf.Configuration;
import org.apache.hadoop.fs.FSDataInputStream;
import org.apache.hadoop.fs.FSDataOutputStream;
import org.apache.hadoop.fs.FileStatus;
import org.apache.hadoop.fs.FileSystem;
import org.apache.hadoop.fs.Path;

public class PutMerge {
```

```
public static void main(String[] args) throws IOException {

    Configuration conf = new Configuration();
    FileSystem hdfs  = FileSystem.get(conf);
    FileSystem local = FileSystem.getLocal(conf);

    Path inputDir = new Path(args[0]);        ❶ Specify input directory
    Path hdfsFile = new Path(args[1]);           and output file

    try {                                                   Get list of
        FileStatus[] inputFiles = local.listStatus(inputDir);  ❷ local files
        FSDataOutputStream out = hdfs.create(hdfsFile);  ❸ Create
                                                     HDFS output stream
        for (int i=0; i<inputFiles.length; i++) {
            System.out.println(inputFiles[i].getPath().getName());
            FSDataInputStream in =
    ⟹ local.open(inputFiles[i].getPath());       ❹ Open local
            byte buffer[] = new byte[256];              input stream
            int bytesRead = 0;
            while( (bytesRead = in.read(buffer)) > 0) {
                out.write(buffer, 0, bytesRead);
            }
            in.close();
        }
        out.close();
    } catch (IOException e) {
        e.printStackTrace();
    }

  }
}
```

The general flow of the program involves first setting the local directory and the HDFS destination file based on user-specified arguments ❶. In ❷ we extract information about each file in the local input directory. We create an output stream to write to the HDFS file in ❸. We loop through each file in the local directory, and ❹ opens an input stream to read that file. The rest of the code is standard Java file copy.

The FileSystem class also has methods such as delete(), exists(), mkdirs(), and rename() for other standard file operations. You can find the most recent Javadoc for the Hadoop file API at http://hadoop.apache.org/core/docs/current/api/org/apache/hadoop/fs/package-summary.html.

We have covered how to work with files in HDFS. You now know a few ways to put data into and out of HDFS. But merely having data isn't terribly interesting. You want to process it, analyze it, and do other things. Let's conclude our discussion of HDFS and move on to the other major component of Hadoop, the MapReduce framework, and how to program under it.

3.2   *Anatomy of a MapReduce program*

As we have mentioned before, a MapReduce program processes data by manipulating (key/value) pairs in the general form

map: $(K1,V1) \rightarrow list(K2,V2)$
reduce: $(K2,list(V2)) \rightarrow list(K3,V3)$

Not surprisingly, this is an overly generic representation of the data flow. In this section we learn more details about each stage in a typical MapReduce program. Figure 3.1 displays a high-level diagram of the entire process, and we further dissect each component as we step through the flow.

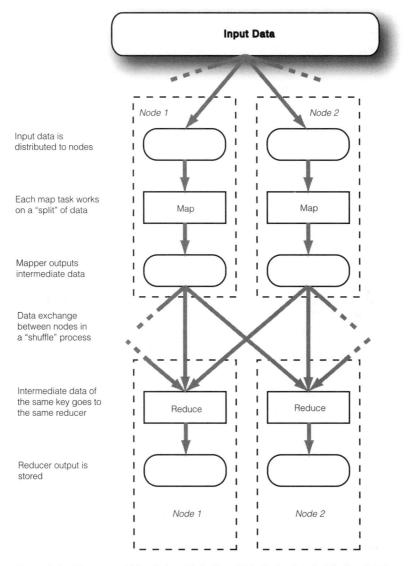

Figure 3.1 The general MapReduce data flow. Note that after distributing input data to different nodes, the only time nodes communicate with each other is at the "shuffle" step. This restriction on communication greatly helps scalability.

Before we analyze how data gets passed onto each individual stage, we should first familiarize ourselves with the data types that Hadoop supports.

3.2.1   *Hadoop data types*

Despite our many discussions regarding keys and values, we have yet to mention their types. The MapReduce framework won't allow them to be any arbitrary class. For example, although we can and often do talk about certain keys and values as integers, strings, and so on, they aren't exactly standard Java classes, such as Integer, String, and so forth. This is because the MapReduce framework has a certain defined way of serializing the key/value pairs to move them across the cluster's network, and only classes that support this kind of serialization can function as keys or values in the framework.

More specifically, classes that implement the Writable interface can be values, and classes that implement the WritableComparable<T> interface can be either keys or values. Note that the WritableComparable<T> interface is a combination of the Writable and java.lang.Comparable<T> interfaces. We need the comparability requirement for keys because they will be sorted at the reduce stage, whereas values are simply passed through.

Hadoop comes with a number of predefined classes that implement WritableComparable, including wrapper classes for all the basic data types, as seen in table 3.1.

Table 3.1 List of frequently used types for the key/value pairs. These classes all implement the WritableComparable interface.

Class	Description
BooleanWritable	Wrapper for a standard Boolean variable
ByteWritable	Wrapper for a single byte
DoubleWritable	Wrapper for a Double
FloatWritable	Wrapper for a Float
IntWritable	Wrapper for a Integer
LongWritable	Wrapper for a Long
Text	Wrapper to store text using the UTF8 format
NullWritable	Placeholder when the key or value is not needed

Keys and values can take on types beyond the basic ones which Hadoop natively supports. You can create your own custom type as long as it implements the Writable (or WritableComparable<T>) interface. For example, listing 3.2 shows a class that can represent edges in a network. This may represent a flight route between two cities.

Listing 3.2 An example class that implements the `WritableComparable` interface

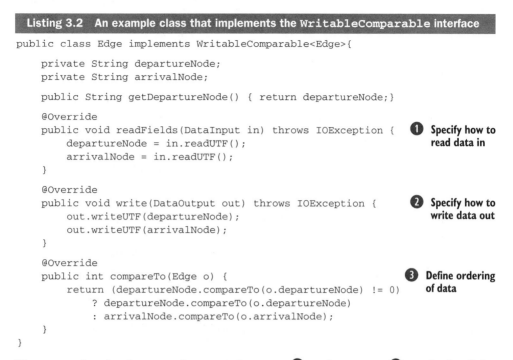

```
public class Edge implements WritableComparable<Edge>{

    private String departureNode;
    private String arrivalNode;

    public String getDepartureNode() { return departureNode;}

    @Override
    public void readFields(DataInput in) throws IOException {     ❶ Specify how to
        departureNode = in.readUTF();                               read data in
        arrivalNode = in.readUTF();
    }

    @Override
    public void write(DataOutput out) throws IOException {       ❷ Specify how to
        out.writeUTF(departureNode);                              write data out
        out.writeUTF(arrivalNode);
    }

    @Override
    public int compareTo(Edge o) {                              ❸ Define ordering
        return (departureNode.compareTo(o.departureNode) != 0)     of data
            ? departureNode.compareTo(o.departureNode)
            : arrivalNode.compareTo(o.arrivalNode);
    }
}
```

The `Edge` class implements the `readFields()` ❶ and `write()` ❷ methods of the `Writable` interface. They work with the Java `DataInput` and `DataOutput` classes to serialize the class contents. Implement the `compareTo()` method ❸ for the `Comparable` interface. It returns -1, 0, or 1 if the called `Edge` is less than, equal to, or greater than the given `Edge`.

With the data type interfaces now defined, we can proceed to the first stage of the data flow process as described in figure 3.1: the mapper.

3.2.2 Mapper

To serve as the mapper, a class implements from the Mapper interface and inherits the `MapReduceBase` class. The `MapReduceBase` class, not surprisingly, serves as the base class for both mappers and reducers. It includes two methods that effectively act as the constructor and destructor for the class:

- *void configure(JobConf job)*—In this function you can extract the parameters set either by the configuration XML files or in the main class of your application. Call this function before any data processing begins.
- *void close()*—As the last action before the map task terminates, this function should wrap up any loose ends—database connections, open files, and so on.

The `Mapper` interface is responsible for the data processing step. It utilizes Java generics of the form `Mapper<K1,V1,K2,V2>` where the key classes and value classes implement the `WritableComparable` and `Writable` interfaces, respectively. Its single method is to process an individual (key/value) pair:

```
void map(K1 key,
         V1 value,
         OutputCollector<K2,V2> output,
         Reporter reporter
         ) throws IOException
```

The function generates a (possibly empty) list of (K2, V2) pairs for a given (K1, V1) input pair. The OutputCollector receives the output of the mapping process, and the Reporter provides the option to record extra information about the mapper as the task progresses.

Hadoop provides a few useful mapper implementations. You can see some of them in the table 3.2.

Table 3.2   Some useful Mapper implementations predefined by Hadoop

Class	Description
IdentityMapper<K,V>	Implements Mapper<K,V,K,V> and maps inputs directly to outputs
InverseMapper<K,V>	Implements Mapper<K,V,V,K> and reverses the key/value pair
RegexMapper<K>	Implements Mapper<K,Text,Text,LongWritable> and generates a (match, 1) pair for every regular expression match
TokenCountMapper<K>	Implements Mapper<K,Text,Text,LongWritable> and generates a (token, 1) pair when the input value is tokenized

As the MapReduce name implies, the major data flow operation after map is the reduce phase, shown in the bottom part of figure 3.1.

3.2.3   *Reducer*

As with any mapper implementation, a reducer must first extend the MapReduce base class to allow for configuration and cleanup. In addition, it must also implement the Reducer interface which has the following single method:

```
void reduce(K2 key,
            Iterator<V2> values,
            OutputCollector<K3,V3> output,
            Reporter reporter
            ) throws IOException
```

When the reducer task receives the output from the various mappers, it sorts the incoming data on the key of the (key/value) pair and groups together all values of the same key. The reduce() function is then called, and it generates a (possibly empty) list of (K3, V3) pairs by iterating over the values associated with a given key. The OutputCollector receives the output of the reduce process and writes it to an output file. The Reporter provides the option to record extra information about the reducer as the task progresses.

Table 3.3 lists a couple of basic reducer implementations provided by Hadoop.

Table 3.3   Some useful `Reducer` implementations predefined by Hadoop

Class	Description
IdentityReducer<K,V>	Implements Reducer<K,V,K,V> and maps inputs directly to outputs
LongSumReducer<K>	Implements Reducer<K,LongWritable,K,LongWritable> and determines the sum of all values corresponding to the given key

Although we have referred to Hadoop programs as MapReduce applications, there is a vital step between the two stages: directing the result of the mappers to the different reducers. This is the responsibility of the partitioner.

3.2.4   *Partitioner—redirecting output from Mapper*

A common misconception for first-time MapReduce programmers is to use only a single reducer. After all, a single reducer sorts all of your data before processing—and who doesn't like sorted data? Our discussions regarding MapReduce expose the folly of such thinking. We would have ignored the benefits of parallel computation. With one reducer, our compute cloud has been demoted to a compute raindrop.

With multiple reducers, we need some way to determine the appropriate one to send a (key/value) pair outputted by a mapper. The default behavior is to hash the key to determine the reducer. Hadoop enforces this strategy by use of the `HashPartitioner` class. Sometimes the `HashPartitioner` will steer you awry. Let's return to the `Edge` class introduced in section 3.2.1.

Suppose you used the `Edge` class to analyze flight information data to determine the number of passengers departing from each airport. Such data may be

(San Francisco, Los Angeles)   Chuck Lam
(San Francisco, Dallas)   James Warren
...

If you used `HashPartitioner`, the two rows could be sent to different reducers. The number of departures would be processed twice and both times erroneously.

How do we customize the partitioner for your applications? In this situation, we want all edges with a common departure point to be sent to the same reducer. This is done easily enough by hashing the `departureNode` member of the `Edge`:

```
public class EdgePartitioner implements Partitioner<Edge, Writable>
{
    @Override
    public int getPartition(Edge key, Writable value, int numPartitions)
    {
        return key.getDepartureNode().hashCode() % numPartitions;
    }

    @Override
    public void configure(JobConf conf) { }
}
```

A custom partitioner only needs to implement two functions: `configure()` and `getPartition()`. The former uses the Hadoop job configuration to configure the partitioner, and the latter returns an integer between 0 and the number of reduce tasks indexing to which reducer the (key/value) pair will be sent.

The exact mechanics of the partitioner may be difficult to follow. Figure 3.2 illustrates this for better understanding.

Between the map and reduce stages, a MapReduce application must take the output from the mapper tasks and distribute the results among the reducer tasks. This process is typically called *shuffling*, because the output of a mapper on a single node may be sent to reducers across multiple nodes in the cluster.

3.2.5   *Combiner—local reduce*

In many situations with MapReduce applications, we may wish to perform a "local reduce" before we distribute the mapper results. Consider the `WordCount` example of

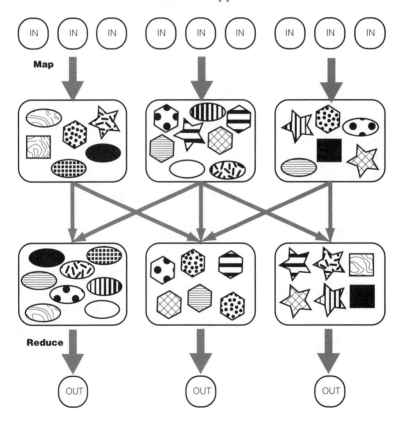

Figure 3.2   The MapReduce data flow, with an emphasis on partitioning and shuffling. Each icon is a key/value pair. The shapes represents keys, whereas the inner patterns represent values. After shuffling, all icons of the same shape (key) are in the same reducer. Different keys can go to the same reducer, as seen in the rightmost reducer. The partitioner decides which key goes where. Note that the leftmost reducer has more load due to more data under the "ellipse" key.

chapter 1 once more. If the job processes a document containing the word "the" 574 times, it's much more efficient to store and shuffle the pair ("the", 574) once instead of the pair ("the", 1) multiple times. This processing step is known as combining. We explain combiners in more depth in section 4.6.

3.2.6 Word counting with predefined mapper and reducer classes

We have concluded our preliminary coverage of all the basic components of MapReduce. Now that you've seen more classes provided by Hadoop, it'll be fun to revisit the Word-Count example (see listing 3.3), using some of the classes we've learned.

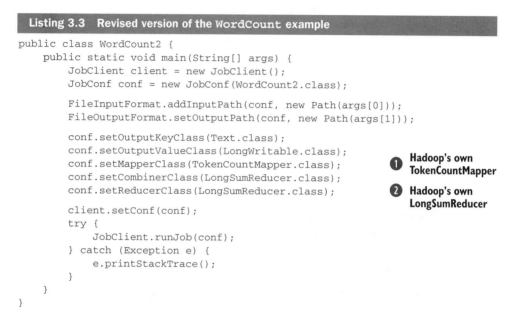

Listing 3.3 Revised version of the WordCount example

```
public class WordCount2 {
    public static void main(String[] args) {
        JobClient client = new JobClient();
        JobConf conf = new JobConf(WordCount2.class);

        FileInputFormat.addInputPath(conf, new Path(args[0]));
        FileOutputFormat.setOutputPath(conf, new Path(args[1]));

        conf.setOutputKeyClass(Text.class);
        conf.setOutputValueClass(LongWritable.class);
        conf.setMapperClass(TokenCountMapper.class);       ❶ Hadoop's own
        conf.setCombinerClass(LongSumReducer.class);           TokenCountMapper
        conf.setReducerClass(LongSumReducer.class);        ❷ Hadoop's own
                                                               LongSumReducer
        client.setConf(conf);
        try {
            JobClient.runJob(conf);
        } catch (Exception e) {
            e.printStackTrace();
        }
    }
}
```

We have to write only the driver for this MapReduce program because we have used Hadoop's predefined TokenCountMapper class ❶ and LongSumReducer class ❷. Easy, isn't it? Hadoop provides the ability to generate more sophisticated programs (this will be the focus of part 2 of the book), but we want to emphasize that Hadoop allows you to rapidly generate useful programs with a minimal amount of code.

3.3 Reading and writing

Let's see how MapReduce reads input data and writes output data and focus on the file formats it uses. To enable easy distributed processing, MapReduce makes certain assumptions about the data it's processing. It also provides flexibility in dealing with a variety of data formats.

Input data usually resides in large files, typically tens or hundreds of gigabytes or even more. One of the fundamental principles of MapReduce's processing power is the splitting of the input data into *chunks*. You can process these chunks in parallel using multiple machines. In Hadoop terminology these chunks are called *input splits*.

The size of each split should be small enough for a more granular parallelization. (If all the input data is in one split, then there is no parallelization.) On the other hand, each split shouldn't be so small that the overhead of starting and stopping the processing of a split becomes a large fraction of execution time.

The principle of dividing input data (which often can be one single massive file) into splits for parallel processing explains some of the design decisions behind Hadoop's generic `FileSystem` as well as HDFS in particular. For example, Hadoop's `FileSystem` provides the class `FSDataInputStream` for file reading rather than using Java's `java.io.DataInputStream`. `FSDataInputStream` extends `DataInputStream` with random read access, a feature that MapReduce requires because a machine may be assigned to process a split that sits right in the middle of an input file. Without random access, it would be extremely inefficient to have to read the file from the beginning until you reach the location of the split. You can also see how HDFS is designed for storing data that MapReduce will split and process in parallel. HDFS stores files in blocks spread over multiple machines. Roughly speaking, each file block is a split. As different machines will likely have different blocks, parallelization is automatic if each split/ block is processed by the machine that it's residing at. Furthermore, as HDFS replicates blocks in multiple nodes for reliability, MapReduce can choose any of the nodes that have a copy of a split/block.

Input splits and record boundaries

Note that input splits are a logical division of your records whereas HDFS blocks are a physical division of the input data. It's extremely efficient when they're the same but in practice it's never perfectly aligned. Records may cross block boundaries. Hadoop guarantees the processing of all records. A machine processing a particular split may fetch a fragment of a record from a block other than its "main" block and which may reside remotely. The communication cost for fetching a record fragment is inconsequential because it happens relatively rarely.

You'll recall that MapReduce works on key/value pairs. So far we've seen that Hadoop by default considers each line in the input file to be a record and the key/value pair is the byte offset (key) and content of the line (value), respectively. You may not have recorded all your data that way. Hadoop supports a few other data formats and allows you to define your own.

3.3.1   *InputFormat*

The way an input file is split up and read by Hadoop is defined by one of the implementations of the `InputFormat` interface. `TextInputFormat` is the default `Input-Format` implementation, and it's the data format we've been implicitly using up to now. It's often useful for input data that has no definite key value, when you want to get the content one line at a time. The key returned by `TextInputFormat` is the byte offset of each line, and we have yet to see any program that uses that key for its data processing.

POPULAR INPUTFORMAT CLASSES

Table 3.4 lists other popular implementations of `InputFormat` along with a description of the key/value pair each one passes to the mapper.

Table 3.4 Main `InputFormat` classes. `TextInputFormat` is the default unless an alternative is specified. The object type for key and value are also described.

InputFormat	Description
`TextInputFormat`	Each line in the text files is a record. Key is the byte offset of the line, and value is the content of the line. key: LongWritable value: Text
`KeyValueTextInputFormat`	Each line in the text files is a record. The first separator character divides each line. Everything before the separator is the key, and everything after is the value. The separator is set by the key.value.separator.in.input. line property, and the default is the tab (\t) character. key: Text value: Text
`SequenceFileInputFormat<K,V>`	An InputFormat for reading in *sequence files*. Key and value are user defined. Sequence file is a Hadoop-specific compressed binary file format. It's optimized for passing data between the output of one MapReduce job to the input of some other MapReduce job. key: K (user defined) value: V (user defined)
`NLineInputFormat`	Same as TextInputFormat, but each split is guaranteed to have exactly *N* lines. The mapred.line.input.format. linespermap property, which defaults to one, sets *N*. key: LongWritable value: Text

`KeyValueTextInputFormat` is used in the more structured input files where a predefined character, usually a tab (\t), separates the key and value of each line (record). For example, you may have a tab-separated data file of timestamps and URLs:

```
17:16:18    http://hadoop.apache.org/core/docs/r0.19.0/api/index.html
17:16:19    http://hadoop.apache.org/core/docs/r0.19.0/mapred_tutorial.html
17:16:20    http://wiki.apache.org/hadoop/GettingStartedWithHadoop
17:16:20    http://www.maxim.com/hotties/2008/finalist_gallery.aspx
17:16:25    http://wiki.apache.org/hadoop/
...
```

You can set your `JobConf` object to use the `KeyValueTextInputFormat` class to read this file.

```
conf.setInputFormat(KeyValueTextInputFormat.class);
```

Given the preceding example file, the first record your mapper reads will have a key of "17:16:18" and a value of "http://hadoop.apache.org/core/docs/r0.19.0/api/index.html". The second record to your mapper will have a key of "17:16:19" and a value of "http://hadoop.apache.org/core/docs/r0.19.0/mapred_tutorial.html." And so on.

Recall that our previous mappers had used `LongWritable` and `Text` as the key and value types, respectively. `LongWritable` is a reasonable type for the key under `TextInputFormat` because the key is a numerical offset. When using `KeyValueTextInputFormat`, both the key and the value will be of type `Text`, and you'll have to change your `Mapper` implementation and `map()` method to reflect the new key type.

The input data to your MapReduce job does not necessarily have to be some external data. In fact it's often the case that the input to one MapReduce job is the output of some other MapReduce job. As we'll see, you can customize your output format too. The default output format writes the output in the same format that `KeyValueTextInputFormat` can read back in (i.e., each line is a record with key and value separated by a tab character). Hadoop provides a much more efficient binary compressed file format called *sequence file*. This sequence file is optimized for Hadoop processing and should be the preferred format when chaining multiple MapReduce jobs. The `InputFormat` class to read sequence files is `SequenceFileInputFormat`. The object type for key and value in a sequence file are definable by the user. The output and the input type have to match, and your `Mapper` implementation and `map()` method have to take in the right input type.

CREATING A CUSTOM INPUTFORMAT—INPUTSPLIT AND RECORDREADER

Sometimes you may want to read input data in a way different from the standard `InputFormat` classes. In that case you'll have to write your own custom `InputFormat` class. Let's look at what it involves. `InputFormat` is an interface consisting of only two methods.

```
public interface InputFormat<K, V> {

    InputSplit[] getSplits(JobConf job, int numSplits) throws IOException;

    RecordReader<K, V> getRecordReader(InputSplit split,
                                       JobConf job,
                                       Reporter reporter) throws IOException;
}
```

The two methods sum up the functions that `InputFormat` has to perform:

- Identify all the files used as input data and divide them into input splits. Each map task is assigned one split.

- Provide an object (`RecordReader`) to iterate through records in a given split, and to parse each record into key and value of predefined types.

Who wants to worry about how files are divided into splits? In creating your own `InputFormat` class you should subclass the `FileInputFormat` class, which takes care of file splitting. In fact, all the `InputFormat` classes in table 3.4 subclass `FileInputFormat`. `FileInputFormat` implements the `getSplits()` method but leaves `getRecordReader()` abstract for the subclass to fill out. `FileInputFormat`'s `getSplits()` implementation tries to divide the input data into roughly the number of splits specified in `numSplits`, subject to the constraints that each split must have more than `mapred.min.split.size` number of bytes but also be smaller than the block size of the filesystem. In practice, a split usually ends up being the size of a block, which defaults to 64 MB in HDFS.

`FileInputFormat` has a number of protected methods a subclass can overwrite to change its behavior, one of which is the `isSplitable(FileSystem fs, Path filename)` method. It checks whether you can split a given file. The default implementation always returns true, so all files larger than a block will be split. Sometimes you may want a file to be its own split, and you'll overwrite `isSplitable()` to return false in those situations. For example, some file compression schemes don't support splits. (You can't start reading from the middle of those files.) Some data processing operations, such as file conversion, will need to treat each file as an atomic record and one should also not be able to split it.

In using `FileInputFormat` you focus on customizing `RecordReader`, which is responsible for parsing an input split into records and then parsing each record into a key/value pair. Let's look at the signature of this interface.

```
public interface RecordReader<K, V> {
  boolean next(K key, V value) throws IOException;

  K createKey();
  V createValue();

  long getPos() throws IOException;
  public void close() throws IOException;
  float getProgress() throws IOException;
}
```

Instead of writing our own `RecordReader`, we'll again leverage existing classes provided by Hadoop. For example, `LineRecordReader` implements `RecordReader <LongWritable,Text>`. It's used in `TextInputFormat` and reads one line at a time, with byte offset as key and line content as value. `KeyValueLineRecordReader` uses `KeyValueTextInputFormat`. For the most part, your custom `RecordReader` will be a wrapper around an existing implementation, and most of the action will be in the `next()` method.

One use case for writing your own custom `InputFormat` class is to read records in a specific type rather than the generic `Text` type. For example, we had previously used `KeyValueTextInputFormat` to read a tab-separated data file of timestamps and URLs. The class ends up treating both the timestamp and the URL as `Text` type. For our illustration, let's create a `TimeUrlTextInputFormat` that works exactly the same but treats the URL as a `URLWritable` type[3]. As mentioned earlier, we create our `InputFormat` class by extending `FileInputFormat` and implementing the factory method to return our `RecordReader`.

```
public class TimeUrlTextInputFormat extends
    ➥ FileInputFormat<Text, URLWritable> {

  public RecordReader<Text, URLWritable> getRecordReader(
      ➥ InputSplit input, JobConf job, Reporter reporter)
      ➥ throws IOException {

    return new TimeUrlLineRecordReader(job, (FileSplit)input);

  }
}
```

Our `URLWritable` class is quite straightforward:

```
public class URLWritable implements Writable {

  protected URL url;

  public URLWritable() { }

  public URLWritable(URL url) {
    this.url = url;
  }

  public void write(DataOutput out) throws IOException {
    out.writeUTF(url.toString());
  }

  public void readFields(DataInput in) throws IOException {
    url = new URL(in.readUTF());
  }

  public void set(String s) throws MalformedURLException {
    url = new URL(s);
  }
}
```

Our `TimeUrlLineRecordReader` will implement the six methods in the `RecordReader` interface, in addition to the class constructor. It's mostly a wrapper around `KeyValueTextInputFormat`, but converts the record value from `Text` to type `URLWritable`.

```
class TimeUrlLineRecordReader implements RecordReader<Text, URLWritable> {

  private KeyValueLineRecordReader lineReader;
  private Text lineKey, lineValue;

  public TimeUrlLineRecordReader(JobConf job, FileSplit split) throws
```

---

[3] We may also want the time key to be some type other than `Text`. For example, we can make up a type `CalendarWritableComparable` for it. We leave that as an exercise for the reader as we focus on a simpler illustration.

```
IOException {
    lineReader = new KeyValueLineRecordReader(job, split);

    lineKey = lineReader.createKey();
    lineValue = lineReader.createValue();
}
public boolean next(Text key, URLWritable value) throws IOException {
    if (!lineReader.next(lineKey, lineValue)) {
        return false;
    }
    key.set(lineKey);
    value.set(lineValue.toString());

    return true;
}
public Text createKey() {
    return new Text("");
}
public URLWritable createValue() {
    return new URLWritable();
}
public long getPos() throws IOException {
    return lineReader.getPos();
}
public float getProgress() throws IOException {
    return lineReader.getProgress();
}
public void close() throws IOException {
    lineReader.close();
}
}
```

Our `TimeUrlLineRecordReader` class creates a `KeyValueLineRecordReader` object and passes the `getPos()`, `getProgress()`, and `close()` method calls directly to it. The `next()` method casts the `lineValue` `Text` object into the `URLWritable` type.

3.3.2 *OutputFormat*

MapReduce outputs data into files using the `OutputFormat` class, which is analogous to the `InputFormat` class. The output has no splits, as each reducer writes its output only to its own file. The output files reside in a common directory and are typically named part-*nnnnn*, where *nnnnn* is the partition ID of the reducer. `RecordWriter` objects format the output and `RecordReaders` parse the format of the input.

Hadoop provides several standard implementations of `OutputFormat`, as shown in table 3.5. Not surprisingly, almost all the ones we deal with inherit from the `File OutputFormat` abstract class; `InputFormat` classes inherit from `FileInputFormat`. You specify the `OutputFormat` by calling `setOutputFormat()` of the `JobConf` object that holds the configuration of your MapReduce job.

NOTE You may wonder why there's a separation between `OutputFormat` (`InputFormat`) and `FileOutputFormat` (`FileInputFormat`) when it seems all `OutputFormat` (`InputFormat`) classes extend `FileOutputFormat` (`FileInputFormat`). Are there `OutputFormat` (`InputFormat`) classes that don't work with files? Well, the `NullOutputFormat` implements `OutputFormat` in a trivial way and doesn't need to subclass `FileOutputFormat`. More importantly, there are `OutputFormat` (`InputFormat`) classes that work with databases rather than files, and these classes are in a separate branch in the class hierarchy from `FileOutputFormat` (`FileInputFormat`). These classes have specialized applications, and the interested reader can dig further in the online Java documentation for `DBInputFormat` and `DBOutputFormat`.

Table 3.5   Main `OutputFormat` classes. `TextOutputFormat` is the default.

OutputFormat	Description
`TextOutputFormat<K,V>`	Writes each record as a line of text. Keys and values are written as strings and separated by a tab (\t) character, which can be changed in the mapred. textoutputformat.separator property.
`SequenceFileOutputFormat<K,V>`	Writes the key/value pairs in Hadoop's proprietary sequence file format. Works in conjunction with SequenceFileInputFormat.
`NullOutputFormat<K,V>`	Outputs nothing.

The default `OutputFormat` is `TextOutputFormat`, which writes each record as a line of text. Each record's key and value are converted to strings through `toString()`, and a tab (\t) character separates them. The separator character can be changed in the `mapred.textoutputformat.separator` property.

`TextOutputFormat` outputs data in a format readable by `KeyValueTextInputFormat`. It can also output in a format readable by `TextInputFormat` if you make the key type a `NullWritable`. In that case the key in the key/value pair is not written out, and neither is the separator character. If you want to suppress the output completely, then you should use the `NullOutputFormat`. Suppressing the Hadoop output is useful if your reducer writes its output in its own way and doesn't need Hadoop to write any additional files.

Finally, `SequenceFileOutputFormat` writes the output in a sequence file format that can be read back in using `SequenceFileInputFormat`. It's useful for writing intermediate data results when chaining MapReduce jobs.

3.4 *Summary*

Hadoop is a software framework that demands a different perspective on data processing. It has its own filesystem, HDFS, that stores data in a way optimized for data-intensive processing. You need specialized Hadoop tools to work with HDFS, but fortunately most of those tools follow familiar Unix or Java syntax.

The data processing part of the Hadoop framework is better known as MapReduce. Although the highlight of a MapReduce program is, not surprisingly, the Map and the Reduce operations, other operations done by the framework, such as data splitting and shuffling, are crucial to how the framework works. You can customize the other operations, such as Partitioning and Combining. Hadoop provides options for reading data and also to output data of different formats.

Now that we have a better understanding of how Hadoop works, let's go on to part 2 of this book and look at various techniques for writing practical programs using Hadoop.

Part 2

Hadoop in Action

P art 2 teaches the practical skills required to write and run data processing programs in Hadoop. We explore various examples of using Hadoop to analyze a patent data set, including advanced algorithms such as the Bloom filter. We also cover programming and administration techniques that are uniquely useful to working with Hadoop in production.

Writing basic
MapReduce programs

This chapter covers

- Patent data as an example data set to process with Hadoop
- Skeleton of a MapReduce program
- Basic MapReduce programs to count statistics
- Hadoop's Streaming API for writing MapReduce programs using scripting languages
- Combiner to improve performance

The MapReduce programming model is unlike most programming models you may have learned. It'll take some time and practice to gain familiarity. To help develop your proficiency, we go through many example programs in the next couple chapters. These examples will illustrate various MapReduce programming techniques. By applying MapReduce in multiple ways you'll start to develop an intuition and a habit of "MapReduce thinking." The examples will cover simple tasks to advanced uses. In one of the advanced applications we introduce the Bloom filter, a data structure not normally taught in the standard computer science curriculum. You'll see that processing large data sets, whether you're using Hadoop or not, often requires a rethinking of the underlying algorithms.

We assume you already have a basic grasp of Hadoop. You can set up Hadoop, and you have compiled and run an example program, such as word counting from chapter 1. Let's use examples—from a real-world data set.

4.1   Getting the patent data set

To do anything meaningful with Hadoop we need data. Many of our examples will use patent data sets, both of which are available from the National Bureau of Economic Research (NBER) at http://www.nber.org/patents/. The data sets were originally compiled for the paper "The NBER Patent Citation Data File: Lessons, Insights and Methodological Tools."[1] We use the citation data set `cite75_99.txt` and the patent description data set `apat63_99.txt`.

> **NOTE** The data sets are approximately 250 MB each, which are small enough to make our examples runnable in Hadoop's standalone or pseudo-distributed mode. You can practice writing MapReduce programs using them even when you don't have access to a live cluster. The best part of Hadoop is that you can be fairly sure your MapReduce program will run on clusters of machines processing data sets 100 or 1,000 times larger with virtually no code changes.
>
> A popular development tactic is to create a smaller, sampled subset of your large production data and call it the *development data set*. This development data set may only have several hundred megabytes. You develop your program in standalone or pseudo-distributed mode with the development data set. This gives your development process a fast turnaround time, the convenience of running on your own machine, and an isolated environment for debugging.

We have chosen these two data sets for our example programs because they're similar to most data types you'll encounter. First of all, the citation data encodes a graph in the same vein that web links and social networks are also graphs. Patents are published in chronological order; some of their properties resemble time series. Each patent is linked with a person (inventor) and a location (country of inventor). You can view them as personal or geographical data. Finally, you can look at the data as generic database relations with well-defined schemas, in a simple comma-separated format.[2]

4.1.1   The patent citation data

The patent citation data set contains citations from U.S. patents issued between 1975 and 1999. It has more than 16 million rows and the first few lines resemble the following:

---

[1] NBER Working Paper 8498, by Hall, B. H., A. B. Jaffe, and M. Tratjenberg (2001).

[2] There are more common data types than two data sets can possibly represent. An important one that's missing here is text, but you've already seen text used in the word count example. Other missing types include XML, image, and geolocation (the lat-long variety). Math matrix is not represented in general, although the citation graph can be interpreted as a sparse 0/1 matrix.

```
"CITING","CITED"
3858241,956203
3858241,1324234
3858241,3398406
3858241,3557384
3858241,3634889
3858242,1515701
3858242,3319261
3858242,3668705
3858242,3707004
...
```

The data set is in the standard comma-separated values (CSV) format, with the first line a description of the columns. Each of the other lines record one particular citation. For example, the second line shows that patent 3858241 cites patent 956203. The file is sorted by the citing patent. We can see that patent 3858241 cites five patents in total. Analyzing the data more quantitatively will give us deeper insights into it.

If you're only reading the data file, the citation data appears to be a bunch of numbers. You can "think" of this data in more interesting terms. One way is to visualize it as a graph. In figure 4.1 we've shown a portion of this citation graph. We can see that some patents are cited often whereas others aren't cited at all.[3] Patents like 5936972 and 6009552 cite a similar set of patents (4354269, 4486882, 5598422) even though they don't cite each other. We use Hadoop to derive descriptive statistics about this patent data, as well as look for interesting patterns that aren't immediately obvious.

4.1.2 *The patent description data*

The other data set we use is the patent description data. It has the patent number, the patent application year, the patent grant year, the number of claims, and other metadata about patents. Look at the first few lines of this data set. It's similar to a table in a relational database, but in CSV format. This data set has more than 2.9 million records. As in many real-world data sets, it has many missing values.

```
"PATENT","GYEAR","GDATE","APPYEAR","COUNTRY","POSTATE","ASSIGNEE",
➥ "ASSCODE","CLAIMS","NCLASS","CAT","SUBCAT","CMADE","CRECEIVE",
➥ "RATIOCIT","GENERAL","ORIGINAL","FWDAPLAG","BCKGTLAG","SELFCTUB",
➥ "SELFCTLB","SECDUPBD","SECDLWBD"
3070801,1963,1096,,"BE","",,1,,269,6,69,,1,,0,,,,,,,
3070802,1963,1096,,"US","TX",,1,,2,6,63,,0,,,,,,,,,
3070803,1963,1096,,"US","IL",,1,,2,6,63,,9,,0.3704,,,,,,,
3070804,1963,1096,,"US","OH",,1,,2,6,63,,3,,0.6667,,,,,,,
3070805,1963,1096,,"US","CA",,1,,2,6,63,,1,,0,,,,,,,
```

---

[3] As with any data analysis, we must be careful when interpreting with limited data. When a patent doesn't seem to cite any other patents, it may be an older patent for which we have no citation information. On the other hand, more recent patents are cited less often because only newer patents can be aware of their existence.

```
3070806,1963,1096,,"US","PA",,1,,2,6,63,,0,,,,,,,,,
3070807,1963,1096,,"US","OH",,1,,623,3,39,,3,,0.4444,,,,,,,
3070808,1963,1096,,"US","IA",,1,,623,3,39,,4,,0.375,,,,,,,
3070809,1963,1096,,"US","AZ",,1,,4,6,65,,0,,,,,,,,,
```

The first row contains the name of a couple dozen attributes, which are meaningful only to patent specialists. Even without understanding all the attributes, it's still useful to have some idea of a few of them. Table 4.1 describes the first ten.

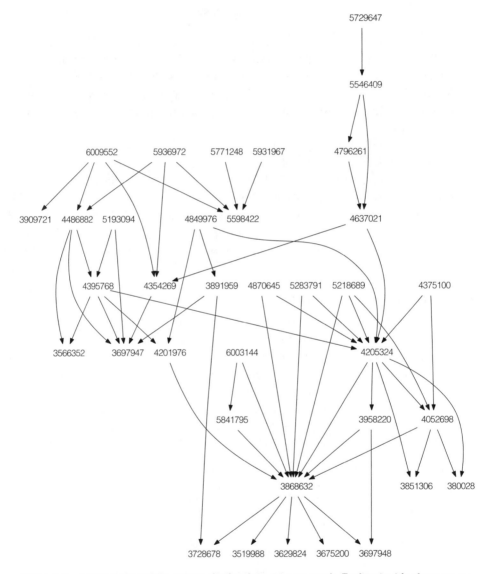

Figure 4.1   A partial view of the patent citation data set as a graph. Each patent is shown as a vertex (node), and each citation is a directed edge (arrow).

Table 4.1   Definition of the first 10 attributes in the patent description data set

Attribute name	Content
PATENT	Patent number
GYEAR	Grant year
GDATE	Grant date, given as the number of days elapsed since January 1, 1960
APPYEAR	Application year (available only for patents granted since 1967)
COUNTRY	Country of first inventor
POSTATE	State of first inventory (if country is U.S.)
ASSIGNEE	Numeric identifier for assignee (i.e., patent owner)
ASSCODE	One-digit (1-9) assignee type. (The assignee type includes U.S. individual, U.S. government, U.S. organization, non-U.S. individual, etc.)
CLAIMS	Number of claims (available only for patents granted since 1975)
NCLASS	3-digit main patent class

Now that we have two patent data sets, let's write Hadoop programs to process the data.

4.2   Constructing the basic template of a MapReduce program

We write most MapReduce programs in brief and as variations on a template. When writing a new MapReduce program, you generally take an existing MapReduce program and modify it until it does what you want. In this section, we write our first MapReduce program and explain its different parts. This program can serve as a template for future MapReduce programs.

Our first program will take the patent citation data and *invert* it. For each patent, we want to find and group the patents that cite it. Our output should be similar to the following:

```
1       3964859,4647229
10000   4539112
100000  5031388
1000006 4714284
1000007 4766693
1000011 5033339
1000017 3908629
1000026 4043055
1000033 4190903,4975983
1000043 4091523
1000044 4082383,4055371
1000045 4290571
1000046 5918892,5525001
1000049 5996916
```

```
1000051 4541310
1000054 4946631
1000065 4748968
1000067 5312208,4944640,5071294
1000070 4928425,5009029
```

We have discovered that patents 5312208, 4944640, and 5071294 cited patent 1000067. For this section we won't focus too much on the MapReduce data flow, which we've already covered in chapter 3. Instead we focus on the structure of a MapReduce program. We need only one file for the entire program as you can see in listing 4.1.

Listing 4.1 Template for a typical Hadoop program

```java
public class MyJob extends Configured implements Tool {

    public static class MapClass extends MapReduceBase
        implements Mapper<Text, Text, Text, Text> {

        public void map(Text key, Text value,
                        OutputCollector<Text, Text> output,
                        Reporter reporter) throws IOException {

            output.collect(value, key);
        }
    }

    public static class Reduce extends MapReduceBase
        implements Reducer<Text, Text, Text, Text> {

        public void reduce(Text key, Iterator<Text> values,
                        OutputCollector<Text, Text> output,
                        Reporter reporter) throws IOException {

            String csv = "";
            while (values.hasNext()) {
                if (csv.length() > 0) csv += ",";
                csv += values.next().toString();
            }
            output.collect(key, new Text(csv));
        }
    }

    public int run(String[] args) throws Exception {
        Configuration conf = getConf();

        JobConf job = new JobConf(conf, MyJob.class);

        Path in = new Path(args[0]);
        Path out = new Path(args[1]);
        FileInputFormat.setInputPaths(job, in);
        FileOutputFormat.setOutputPath(job, out);

        job.setJobName("MyJob");
        job.setMapperClass(MapClass.class);
        job.setReducerClass(Reduce.class);

        job.setInputFormat(KeyValueTextInputFormat.class);
```

```
        job.setOutputFormat(TextOutputFormat.class);
        job.setOutputKeyClass(Text.class);
        job.setOutputValueClass(Text.class);
        job.set("key.value.separator.in.input.line", ",");

        JobClient.runJob(job);

        return 0;
    }

    public static void main(String[] args) throws Exception {
        int res = ToolRunner.run(new Configuration(), new MyJob(), args);

        System.exit(res);
    }
}
```

Our convention is that a single class, called MyJob in this case, completely defines each MapReduce job. Hadoop requires the Mapper and the Reducer to be their own static classes. These classes are quite small, and our template includes them as inner classes to the MyJob class. The advantage is that everything fits in one file, simplifying code management. But keep in mind that these inner classes are independent and don't interact much with the MyJob class. Various nodes with different JVMs clone and run the Mapper and the Reducer during job execution, whereas the rest of the job class is executed *only* at the client machine.

We investigate the Mapper and the Reducer classes in a while. Without those classes, the skeleton of the MyJob class is

```
public class MyJob extends Configured implements Tool {

    public int run(String[] args) throws Exception {
        Configuration conf = getConf();

        JobConf job = new JobConf(conf, MyJob.class);

        Path in = new Path(args[0]);
        Path out = new Path(args[1]);
        FileInputFormat.setInputPaths(job, in);
        FileOutputFormat.setOutputPath(job, out);

        job.setJobName("MyJob");
        job.setMapperClass(MapClass.class);
        job.setReducerClass(Reduce.class);

        job.setInputFormat(KeyValueTextInputFormat.class);
        job.setOutputFormat(TextOutputFormat.class);
        job.setOutputKeyClass(Text.class);
        job.setOutputValueClass(Text.class);
        job.set("key.value.separator.in.input.line", ",");

        JobClient.runJob(job);

        return 0;
    }

    public static void main(String[] args) throws Exception {
```

```
    int res = ToolRunner.run(new Configuration(), new MyJob(), args);
    System.exit(res);
    }
}
```

The core of the skeleton is within the `run()` method, also known as the *driver*. The driver instantiates, configures, and passes a `JobConf` object named job to `JobClient.runJob()` to start the MapReduce job. (The `JobClient` class, in turn, will communicate with the JobTracker to start the job across the cluster.) The `JobConf` object will hold all configuration parameters necessary for the job to run. The driver needs to specify in `job` the input paths, the output paths, the `Mapper` class, and the `Reducer` class—the basic parameters for every job. In addition, each job can reset the default job properties, such as `InputFormat`, `OutputFormat`, and so on. One can also call the `set()` method on the `JobConf` object to set up any configuration parameter. Once you pass the `JobConf` object to `JobClient.runJob()`, it's treated as the master plan for the job. It becomes the blueprint for how the job will be run.

The `JobConf` object has many parameters, but we don't want to program the driver to set up all of them. The configuration files of the Hadoop installation are a good starting point. When starting a job from the command line, the user may also want to pass extra arguments to alter the job configuration. The driver can define its own set of commands and process the user arguments itself to enable the user to modify some of the configuration parameters. As this task is needed often, the Hadoop framework provides `ToolRunner`, `Tool`, and `Configured` to simplify it. When used together in the `MyJob` skeleton above, these classes enable our job to understand user-supplied options that are supported by `GenericOptionsParser`. For example, we have previously executed the `MyJob` class using this command line:

```
bin/hadoop jar playground/MyJob.jar MyJob input/cite75_99.txt output
```

Had we wanted to run the job only to see the mapper's output (which you may want to do for debugging purposes), we could set the number of reducers to zero with the option `-D mapred.reduce.tasks=0`.

```
bin/hadoop jar playground/MyJob.jar MyJob -D mapred.reduce.tasks=0
➥ input/cite75_99.txt output
```

It works even though our program doesn't explicitly understand the `-D` option. By using `ToolRunner`, `MyJob` will automatically support the options in table 4.2.

Table 4.2 Options supported by `GenericOptionsParser`

Option	Description
`-conf <configuration file>`	Specify a configuration file.
`-D <property=value>`	Set value for a `JobConf` property.
`-fs <local|namenode:port>`	Specify a `NameNode`, can be "local".

Table 4.2 Options supported by `GenericOptionsParser` (*continued*)

Option	Description
`-jt <local|jobtracker:port>`	Specify a JobTracker.
`-files <list of files>`	Specify a comma-separated list of files to be used with the MapReduce job. These files are automatically distributed to all task nodes to be locally available.
`-libjars <list of jars>`	Specify a comma-separated list of jar files to be included in the classpath of all task JVMs.
`-archives <list of archives>`	Specify a comma-separated list of archives to be unarchived on all task nodes.

The convention for our template is to call the `Mapper` class `MapClass` and the `Reducer` class `Reduce`. The naming would seem more symmetrical if we call the `Mapper` class `Map`, but Java already has a class (interface) named `Map`. Both the `Mapper` and the `Reducer` extend `MapReduceBase`, which is a small class providing no-op implementations to the `configure()` and `close()` methods required by the two interfaces. We use the `configure()` and `close()` methods to set up and clean up the map (reduce) tasks. We won't need to override them except for more advanced jobs.

The signatures for the `Mapper` class and the `Reducer` class are

```
public static class MapClass extends MapReduceBase
    implements Mapper<K1, V1, K2, V2> {

    public void map(K1 key, V1 value,
                OutputCollector<K2, V2> output,
                Reporter reporter) throws IOException { }
}
public static class Reduce extends MapReduceBase
    implements Reducer<K2, V2, K3, V3> {

    public void reduce(K2 key, Iterator<V2> values,
                OutputCollector<K3, V3> output,
                Reporter reporter) throws IOException { }
}
```

The center of action for the `Mapper` class is the `map()` method and for the `Reducer` class the `reduce()` method. Each invocation of the `map()` method is given a key/value pair of types `K1` and `V1`, respectively. The key/value pairs generated by the mapper are outputted via the `collect()` method of the `OutputCollector` object. Somewhere in your `map()` method you need to call

```
output.collect((K2) k, (V2) v);
```

Each invocation of the `reduce()` method at the reducer is given a key of type `K2` and a list of values of type `V2`. Note that it must be the same `K2` and `V2` types used in the `Mapper`. The `reduce()` method will likely have a loop to go through all the values of type `V2`.

```
while (values.hasNext()) {
    V2? v = values.next();
    ...
}
```

The reduce() method is also given an OutputCollector to gather its key/value output, which is of type K3/V3. Somewhere in the reduce() method you'll call

```
output.collect((K3) k, (V3) v);
```

In addition to having consistent K2 and V2 types across Mapper and Reducer, you'll also need to ensure that the key and value types used in Mapper and Reducer are consistent with the input format, output key class, and output value class set in the driver. The use of KeyValueTextInputFormat means that K1 and V1 must both be type Text. The driver must call setOutputKeyClass() and setOutputValueClass() with the classes of K2 and V2, respectively.

Finally, all the key and value types must be subtypes of Writable, which ensures a serialization interface for Hadoop to send the data around in a distributed cluster. In fact, the key types implement WritableComparable, a subinterface of Writable. The key types need to additionally support the compareTo() method, as keys are used for sorting in various places in the MapReduce framework.

4.3   *Counting things*

Much of what the layperson thinks of as statistics is counting, and many basic Hadoop jobs involve counting. We've already seen the word count example in chapter 1. For the patent citation data, we may want the number of citations a patent has received. This too is counting. The desired output would look like this:

```
1         2
10000     1
100000    1
1000006 1
1000007 1
1000011 1
1000017 1
1000026 1
1000033 2
1000043 1
1000044 2
1000045 1
1000046 2
1000049 1
1000051 1
1000054 1
1000065 1
1000067 3
```

In each record, a patent number is associated with the number of citations it has received. We can write a MapReduce program for this task. Like we said earlier, you hardly ever write a MapReduce program from scratch. You have an existing MapReduce program that processes the data in a similar way. You copy that and modify it until it fits what you want.

We already have a program for getting the inverted citation index. We can modify that program to output the count instead of the list of citing patents. We need the modification only at the `Reducer`. If we choose to output the count as an `IntWritable`, we need to specify `IntWritable` in three places in the `Reducer` code. We called them `V3` in our previous notation.

```
public static class Reduce extends MapReduceBase
    implements Reducer<Text, Text, Text, IntWritable> {

    public void reduce(Text key, Iterator<Text> values,
                       OutputCollector<Text, IntWritable> output,
                       Reporter reporter) throws IOException {

        int count = 0;
        while (values.hasNext()) {
            values.next();
            count++;
        }
        output.collect(key, new IntWritable(count));
    }
}
```

By changing a few lines and matching class types, we have a new MapReduce program. This program may seem a minor modification. Let's go through another example that requires more changes, but you'll see that the basic MapReduce program structure remains.

After running the previous example, we now have a data set that counts the number of citations for each patent. A neat exercise would be to count the counts. Let's build a histogram of the citation counts. We expect a large number of patents to have been only cited once, and a small number may have been cited hundreds of times. It would be interesting to see the distribution of the citation counts.

> **NOTE** As the patent citation data set only covers patents issued between 1975 and 1999, the citation count is necessarily an underestimate. (Citations from patents outside of that period aren't counted.) We also don't deal with patents that supposedly have been cited zero times. Despite these caveats, the analysis will be useful.

The first step to writing a MapReduce program is to figure out the data flow. In this case, as a mapper reads a record, it ignores the patent number and outputs an intermediate key/value pair of `<citation_count, 1>`. The reducer will sum up the number of 1s for each citation count and output the total.

After figuring out the data flow, decide on the types for the key/value pairs—`K1`, `V1`, `K2`, `V2`, `K3`, and `V3` for the input, intermediate, and output key/value pairs. Let's use the `KeyValueTextInputFormat`, which automatically breaks each input record into key/value pairs based on a separator character. The input format produces `K1` and `V1` as Text. We choose to use IntWritable for K2, V2, K3, and V3 because we know those data must be integers and it's more efficient to use IntWritable.

Based on the data flow and the data types, you'll be able to see the final program shown in listing 4.2 and understand what it's doing. You can see that it's structurally similar to the other MapReduce programs we've seen so far. We go into details about the program after the listing.

Listing 4.2 CitationHistogram.java: count patents cited once, twice, and so on

```java
public class CitationHistogram extends Configured implements Tool {

    public static class MapClass extends MapReduceBase
        implements Mapper<Text, Text, IntWritable, IntWritable> {

        private final static IntWritable uno = new IntWritable(1);
        private IntWritable citationCount = new IntWritable();

        public void map(Text key, Text value,
                        OutputCollector<IntWritable, IntWritable> output,
                        Reporter reporter) throws IOException {

            citationCount.set(Integer.parseInt(value.toString()));
            output.collect(citationCount, uno);
        }
    }

    public static class Reduce extends MapReduceBase
        implements Reducer<IntWritable,IntWritable,IntWritable,IntWritable>
    {

        public void reduce(IntWritable key, Iterator<IntWritable> values,
                        OutputCollector<IntWritable, IntWritable>output,
                        Reporter reporter) throws IOException {

            int count = 0;
            while (values.hasNext()) {
                count += values.next().get();
            }
            output.collect(key, new IntWritable(count));
        }
    }

    public int run(String[] args) throws Exception {
        Configuration conf = getConf();

        JobConf job = new JobConf(conf, CitationHistogram.class);

        Path in = new Path(args[0]);
        Path out = new Path(args[1]);
        FileInputFormat.setInputPaths(job, in);
        FileOutputFormat.setOutputPath(job, out);

        job.setJobName("CitationHistogram");
        job.setMapperClass(MapClass.class);
        job.setReducerClass(Reduce.class);

        job.setInputFormat(KeyValueTextInputFormat.class);
        job.setOutputFormat(TextOutputFormat.class);
```

```
        job.setOutputKeyClass(IntWritable.class);
        job.setOutputValueClass(IntWritable.class);

        JobClient.runJob(job);

        return 0;
    }
    public static void main(String[] args) throws Exception {
        int res = ToolRunner.run(new Configuration(),
                                 new CitationHistogram(),
                                 args);

        System.exit(res);
    }
}
```

The class name is now CitationHistogram; all references to MyJob were changed to reflect the new name. The main() method is almost always the same. The driver is mostly intact. The input format and output format are still KeyValueTextInputFormat and TextOutputFormat, respectively. The main change is that the output key class and the output value class are now IntWritable, to reflect the new type for K2 and V2. We've also removed this line:

```
job.set("key.value.separator.in.input.line", ",");
```

It sets the separator character used by KeyValueTextInputFormat to break each input line into a key/value pair. Previously it was a comma for processing the original patent citation data. By not setting this property it defaults to the tab character, which is appropriate for the citation count data.

The data flow for this mapper is similar to that of the previous mappers, only here we've chosen to define and use a couple class variables—citationCount and uno.

```
public static class MapClass extends MapReduceBase
    implements Mapper<Text, Text, IntWritable, IntWritable> {

    private final static IntWritable uno = new IntWritable(1);
    private IntWritable citationCount = new IntWritable();

    public void map(Text key, Text value,
                    OutputCollector<IntWritable, IntWritable> output,
                    Reporter reporter) throws IOException {

        citationCount.set(Integer.parseInt(value.toString()));
        output.collect(citationCount, uno);
    }
}
```

The map() method has one extra line for setting citationCount, which is for type casting. The reason for defining citationCount and uno in the class rather than inside the method is purely one of efficiency. The map() method will be called as many times as there are records (in a split, for each JVM). Reducing the number of objects created inside the map() method can increase performance and reduce garbage collection. As we pass citationCount and uno to output.collect(), we're relying on the `output.collect()` method's contract to not modify those two objects.[4]

The reducer sums up the values for each key. It seems inefficient because we know all values are 1s (uno, to be exact). Why do we need to sum the count? We've chosen this route because it will be easier for us later if we choose to add a *combiner* to enhance performance. Unlike `MapClass`, the call to `output.collect()` in `Reduce` instantiates a new `IntWritable` rather than reuse an existing one.

```
output.collect(key, new IntWritable(count));
```

We can improve performance by using an `IntWritable` class variable. But the number of times `reduce()` is called is much smaller in this particular program, probably no more than a thousand times (across all reducers). We don't have much need to optimize this particular code.

Running the MapReduce job on the citation count data will show the following result. As we suspect, a large number (900K+) of patents have only one citation, whereas some have hundreds of citations. The most popular patent has 779 citations.

```
1       921128
2       552246
3       380319
4       278438
5       210814
6       163149
7       127941
8       102155
9       82126
10      66634
...
411     1
605     1
613     1
631     1
633     1
654     1
658     1
678     1
716     1
779     1
```

As this histogram output is only several hundred lines long, we can put it into a spreadsheet and plot it. Figure 4.2 shows the number of patents at various citation frequencies. The plot is on a log-log scale. When a distribution shows as a line in a log-log plot, it's considered to be a *power law* distribution. The citation count histogram seems to fit the description, although its approximately parabolic curvature also suggests a *lognormal* distribution.

As you've seen in our examples so far, a MapReduce program is often not very big, and you can keep a certain structure across them to simplify development. Most of the work is in thinking through the data flow.

---

[4] We see in section 5.1.3 that this reliance will forbid the `ChainMapper` from using pass-by-reference.

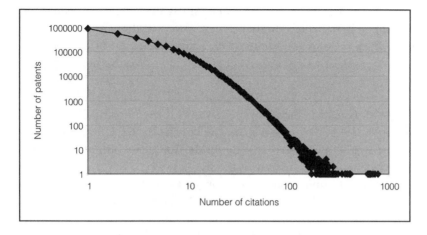

Figure 4.2 Plotting the number of patents at different citation frequencies. Many patents have one citation (or not at all, which is not shown on this graph). Some patents have hundreds of citations. On a log-log graph, this looks close enough to a straight line to be considered a power-law distribution.

4.4 *Adapting for Hadoop's API changes*

One of the main design goals driving toward Hadoop's major 1.0 release is a stable and extensible MapReduce API. As of this writing, version 0.20 is the latest release and is considered a bridge between the older API (that we use throughout this book) and this upcoming stable API. The 0.20 release supports the future API while maintaining backward-compatibility with the old one by marking it as deprecated. Future releases after 0.20 will stop supporting the older API. As of this writing, we don't recommend jumping into the new API yet for a couple reasons:

1 Many of Hadoop's own library classes in 0.20 aren't rewritten under the new API yet. You won't be able to use those classes if your MapReduce code uses the new API in 0.20.
2 Many still consider the most production-ready and stable version of Hadoop as of this writing to be 0.18.3. Some users are warming up to version 0.20, but we suggest you wait a little longer before going full production with it.[5]

By the time you read this the situation may be different. In this section we cover the changes the new API presents. Fortunately, almost all the changes affect only the basic MapReduce template. We rewrite the template under the new API to enable you to use it in the future.

---

[5] You may be wondering about version 0.19. The general consensus is that its initial release was problematic and full of bugs. Some minor releases tried fixing the problems, but the community seems to want to skip straight to 0.20 instead.

The first thing you'll notice in the new API is that many classes in `org.apache.hadoop.mapred` have been moved elsewhere. Many of them are now at `org.apache.hadoop.mapreduce`, and the library classes are under one of the packages in `org.apache.hadoop.mapreduce.lib`. After you've moved to the new API, you shouldn't have any `import` statements (or full references) to any classes under `org.apache.hadoop.mapred`, all of which are to be deprecated.

The most meaningful change in the new API is the introduction of *context* objects. Its most immediate impact is to replace the `OutputCollector` and `Reporter` objects used in the `map()` and `reduce()` methods. You now output key/value pairs by calling `Context.write()` instead of `OutputCollector.collect()`. The long-term consequences are to unify communication between your code and the MapReduce framework, and to stabilize the Mapper and Reducer API such that the basic method signatures will not change when new functionalities are added. New functionalities will only be additional methods on the context objects. Programs written before the introduction of those functionalities will be unaware of the new methods, and they will continue to compile and run against the newer releases.

The new `map()` and `reduce()` methods are contained in new *abstract classes* `Mapper` and `Reducer`, respectively. They replace the `Mapper` and `Reducer` *interfaces* in the original API (`org.apache.hadoop.mapred.Mapper` and `org.apache.hadoop.mapred.Reducer`). The new abstract classes also replace the `MapReduceBase` class, which has been deprecated.

The new `map()` and `reduce()` methods have a couple more minor changes. They can throw `InterruptedException` instead of only `IOException`. In addition, the `reduce()` method no longer accepts the list of values as an `Iterator` but as an `Iterable`, which is easier to iterate through using Java's foreach syntax. We can summarize the changes we've discussed so far in the method signatures for `MapClass` and `Reduce`. Recall the signatures under the original API:

```
public static class MapClass extends MapReduceBase
    implements Mapper<K1, V1, K2, V2> {

    public void map(K1 key, V1 value,
                    OutputCollector<K2, V2> output,
                    Reporter reporter) throws IOException { }
}
public static class Reduce extends MapReduceBase
    implements Reducer<K2, V2, K3, V3> {

    public void reduce(K2 key, Iterator<V2> values,
                    OutputCollector<K3, V3> output,
                    Reporter reporter) throws IOException { }
}
```

The new API has simplified them somewhat:

```
public static class MapClass extends Mapper<K1, V1, K2, V2> {

    public void map(K1 key, V1 value, Context context)
                    throws IOException, InterruptedException { }
```

```
}
public static class Reduce extends Reducer<K2, V2, K3, V3> {
    public void reduce(K2 key, Iterable<V2> values, Context context)
                    throws IOException, InterruptedException { }
}
```

You also need to change a few things in the driver to support the new API. `JobConf` and `JobClient` classes have been replaced. Their functionalities have been pushed to the `Configuration` class (which was originally the parent class of `JobConf`) and a new class `Job`. The `Configuration` class purely configures a job, whereas the `Job` class defines and controls the execution of a job. Methods such as `setOutputKeyClass()` and `setOutputValueClass()` have moved from `JobConf` to `Job`. A job's construction and submission for execution are now under `Job`. Originally you would construct a job using `JobConf`:

```
JobConf job = new JobConf(conf, MyJob.class);
job.setJobName("MyJob");
```

Now it's done through `Job`:

```
Job job = new Job(conf, "MyJob");
job.setJarByClass(MyJob.class);
```

Previously `JobClient` submitted a job for execution:

```
JobClient.runJob(job);
```

Now it's also done through `Job`:

```
System.exit(job.waitForCompletion(true)?0:1);
```

Listing 4.3 is the template program from listing 4.1 rewritten to use the new API in Hadoop 0.20. It incorporates all the changes we've mentioned in this section.

Listing 4.3 Template for basic Hadoop program (listing 4.1) rewritten for new API v 0.20

```
public class MyJob extends Configured implements Tool {
    public static class MapClass
                            extends Mapper<LongWritable, Text, Text, Text> {
        public void map(LongWritable key, Text value, Context context)
                    throws IOException, InterruptedException {
            String[] citation = value.toString().split(",");
            context.write(new Text(citation[1]), new Text(citation[0]));
        }
    }
    public static class Reduce extends Reducer<Text, Text, Text, Text> {
        public void reduce(Text key, Iterable<Text> values,
                    Context context)
                    throws IOException, InterruptedException {
            String csv = "";
```

```
        for (Text val:values) {                                   Iterable allows
            if (csv.length() > 0) csv += ",";                     foreach looping
            csv += val.toString();
        }

        context.write(key, new Text(csv));
    }
}
    public int run(String[] args) throws Exception {
        Configuration conf = getConf();

        Job job = new Job(conf, "MyJob");
        job.setJarByClass(MyJob.class);

        Path in = new Path(args[0]);
        Path out = new Path(args[1]);
        FileInputFormat.setInputPaths(job, in);
        FileOutputFormat.setOutputPath(job, out);

        job.setMapperClass(MapClass.class);
        job.setReducerClass(Reduce.class);

        job.setInputFormatClass(TextInputFormat.class);      ❶ Compatible
        job.setOutputFormatClass(TextOutputFormat.class);       InputFormat class
        job.setOutputKeyClass(Text.class);
        job.setOutputValueClass(Text.class);

        System.exit(job.waitForCompletion(true)?0:1);

        return 0;
    }
    public static void main(String[] args) throws Exception {
        int res = ToolRunner.run(new Configuration(), new MyJob(), args);

        System.exit(res);
    }
}
```

The code performs the same inverted indexing function as listing 4.1, but under the 0.20 API. Unfortunately, the `KeyValueTextInputFormat` class we had used in listing 4.1 hasn't been ported to the new API as of version 0.20. We have to rewrite the template using `TextInputFormat` ❶. We expect all Hadoop classes to support the new API when version 0.21 is released. To keep presentation of examples in the rest of this book unified, we continue to use the API before 0.20.

4.5   *Streaming in Hadoop*

We have been using Java to write all our Hadoop programs. Hadoop supports other languages via a generic API called Streaming. In practice, Streaming is most useful for writing simple, short MapReduce programs that are more rapidly developed in a scripting language that can take advantage of non-Java libraries.

Hadoop Streaming interacts with programs using the Unix streaming paradigm. Inputs come in through STDIN and outputs go to STDOUT. Data has to be text based and each line is considered a record. Note that this is exactly how many

Unix commands work, and Hadoop Streaming enables those commands to be used as mappers and reducers. If you're familiar with using Unix commands, such as `wc`, `cut`, or `uniq` for data processing, you can apply them to large data sets using Hadoop Streaming.

The overall data flow in Hadoop Streaming is like a pipe where data streams through the mapper, the output of which is sorted and streamed through the reducer. In pseudo-code using Unix's command line notation, it's

```
cat [input_file] | [mapper] | sort | [reducer] >[output_file]
```

The following examples will illustrate how to use Streaming with Unix commands.

4.5.1 Streaming with Unix commands

In the first example, let's get a list of cited patents in `cite75_99.txt`.

```
bin/hadoop jar contrib/streaming/hadoop-0.19.1-streaming.jar
        ➡ -input input/cite75_99.txt
        ➡ -output output
        ➡ -mapper 'cut -f 2 -d ,'
        ➡ -reducer 'uniq'
```

That's it! It's a one-line command. Let's see what each part of the command does.

The Streaming API is in a contrib package at `contrib/streaming/hadoop-*-streaming.jar`. The first part and the `-input` and the `-output` arguments specify that we're running a Streaming program with the corresponding input and output file/directory. The mapper and reducer are specified as arguments in quotes. We see that for the mapper we use the Unix `cut` command to extract the second column, where columns are separated by commas. In the citation data set this column is the patent number of a cited patent. These patent numbers are then sorted and passed to the reducer. The `uniq` command at the reducer will remove all duplicates in the sorted data. The output of this command is

```
"CITED"
1
10000
100000
1000006
...
999973
999974
999977
999978
999983
```

The first row has the column descriptor "CITED" from the original file. Note that the rows are sorted lexicographically because Streaming processes everything as text and doesn't know other data types.

After getting the list of cited patents, we may want to know how many are there. Again we can use Streaming to quickly get a count, using the Unix command `wc -l`.

```
bin/hadoop jar contrib/streaming/hadoop-0.19.1-streaming.jar
       ➥ -input output
       ➥ -output output_a
       ➥ -mapper 'wc -l'
       ➥ -D mapred.reduce.tasks=0
```

Here we use `wc -l` as the mapper to count the number of records in each split. Hadoop Streaming (since version 0.19.0) supports the `GenericOptionsParser`. The `-D` argument is used for specifying configuration properties. We want the mapper to directly output the record count without any reducer, so we set `mapred.reduce.tasks` to 0 and don't specify the `-reducer` option at all.[6] The final count is 3258984. More than 3 million patents have been cited according to our data.

4.5.2 Streaming with scripts

We can use any executable script that processes a line-oriented data stream from `STDIN` and outputs to `STDOUT` with Hadoop Streaming. For example, the Python script in listing 4.4 randomly samples data from `STDIN`. For those who don't know Python, the program has a `for` loop that reads `STDIN` one line at a time. For each line, we choose a random integer between 1 and 100 and check against the user-given argument (`sys.argv[1]`). The comparison determines whether to pass that line on to the output or ignore it. You can use the script in Unix to uniformly sample a line-oriented data file, for example:

```
cat input.txt | RandomSample.py 10 >sampled_output.txt
```

The preceding command calls the Python script with an argument of 10; `sampled_output.txt` will have (approximately) 10 percent of the records in input.txt. We can in fact specify any integer between 1 and 100 to get the corresponding percentage of data in the output.

Listing 4.4 RandomSample.py: a Python script printing random lines from STDIN

```python
#!/usr/bin/env python
import sys, random

for line in sys.stdin:
    if (random.randint(1,100) <= int(sys.argv[1])):
        print line.strip()
```

We can apply the same script in Hadoop to get a smaller sample of a data set. A sampled data set is often useful for development purposes, as you can run your Hadoop program on the sampled data in standalone or pseudo-distributed mode to quickly debug and iterate. Also, when you're looking for some "descriptive"

---

[6] You may notice that this approach counts the number of records in each split, not the entire file. With a bigger file, or multiple files, the user will have to sum up the counts herself to get the overall total. To fully automate a complete counting, the user will have to write a script at the reducer to sum up all the partial counts.

information about your data, the speed and convenience in processing a smaller data set generally outweigh any loss of precision. Finding data clusters is one example of such descriptive information. Optimized implementations of a variety of clustering algorithms are readily available in R, MATLAB, and other packages. It makes a lot more sense to sample down the data and apply some standard software package, instead of trying to process all data using some distributed clustering algorithms in Hadoop.

> **WARNING** The loss of precision from computing on a sampled data set may or may not be important. It depends on what you're trying to compute and the distribution of your data set. For example, it's usually fine to compute an average from a sampled data set, but if the data set is highly skewed and the average is dominated by a few values, sampling can be problematic. Similarly, clustering on a sampled data set is fine if it's used only to get a general understanding of the data. If you were looking for small, anomalous clusters, sampling may get rid of them. For functions such as maximum and minimum, it's not a good idea to apply them to sampled data.

Running `RandomSample.py` using Streaming is like running Unix commands using Streaming, the difference being that Unix commands are already available on all nodes in the cluster, whereas `RandomSample.py` is not. Hadoop Streaming supports a `-file` option to package your executable file as part of the job submission.[7] Our command to execute RandomSample.py is

```
bin/hadoop jar contrib/streaming/hadoop-0.19.1-streaming.jar
        ➥ -input input/cite75_99.txt
        ➥ -output output
        ➥ -mapper 'RandomSample.py 10'
        ➥ -file RandomSample.py
        ➥ -D mapred.reduce.tasks=1
```

In specifying the mapper to be `'RandomSample.py 10'` we're sampling at 10 percent. Note that we've set the number of reducers (`mapred.reduce.tasks`) to 1. As we haven't specified any particular reducer, it will use the default `IdentityReducer`. As its name implies, `IdentityReducer` passes its input straight to output. In this case we can set the number of reducers to any non-zero value to get an exact number of output files. Alternatively, we can set the number of reducers to 0, and let the number of output files be the number of mappers. This is probably not ideal for the sampling task as each mapper's output is only a small fraction of the input, and we may end up with a number of small files. We can easily correct that later using the HDFS shell command `getmerge` or other file manipulations to arrive at the right number of output files. The approach to use is more or less a personal preference.

---

[7] It's also implicitly assumed that you have installed the Python language on all the nodes in your cluster.

The random sampling script was implemented in Python, although any scripting language that works with STDIN and STDOUT would work. For illustration we've rewritten the same script in PHP[8] (listing 4.5). Execute this Stream script with

```
bin/hadoop jar contrib/streaming/hadoop-0.19.1-streaming.jar
          ➥ -input input/cite75_99.txt
          ➥ -output output
          ➥ -mapper 'php RandomSample.php 10'
          ➥ -file RandomSample.php
          ➥ -D mapred.reduce.tasks=1
```

Listing 4.5 RandomSample.php.: a PHP script printing random lines from STDIN

```php
<?php
while (!feof(STDIN)) {
    $line = fgets(STDIN);
    if (mt_rand(1,100) <= $argv[1]) {
        echo $line;
    }
}
```

The random sampling scripts don't require any custom reducer, but you can't always write a Streaming program like that. As you'll use Streaming quite often in practice, let's see another exercise. This time we create a custom reducer.

Suppose we're interested in finding the most number of claims in a single patent. In the patent description data set, the number of claims for a given patent is in the ninth column. Our task is to find the maximum value in the ninth column of the patent description data.

Under Streaming, each mapper sees the entire stream of data, and it's the mapper that takes on the responsibility of breaking the stream into (line-oriented) records. In the standard Java model, the framework itself breaks input data into records, and gives the map() method only one record at a time. The Streaming model makes it easy to keep state information across records in a split, which we take advantage of in computing the maximum. The standard Java model, too, can keep track of state across records in a split, but it's more involved. We cover that in the next chapter.

In creating a Hadoop program for computing maximum, we take advantage of the *distributive* property of maximum. Given a data set divided into many splits, the

---

[8] You may have noticed in listing 4.5 that there's no ending bracket ?> to close the opening bracket <?php. Recall that PHP was originally designed to work within static HTML content. Anything outside the PHP brackets <?php ... ?> is considered static content to be outputted. When using PHP as a pure scripting language, you need to be careful that you leave no whitespaces outside the brackets. Otherwise they will be outputted and may cause unintended behavior that is hard to debug. (It would appear whitespaces were introduced in the output data out of nowhere.)

It's easy to ensure that there's no whitespaces before the opening bracket <?php by putting the bracket at the beginning of the script file. But, it's easy to accidentally leave whitespaces after the closing bracket ?>, as ending whitespaces don't grab attention. When using a file as a PHP script, it's safer to omit the closing bracket ?>. The PHP interpreter will quietly read everything till the end-of-file as PHP commands rather than static content.

global maximum is the maximum over the maxima of the splits. That sounded like a mouthful, but a simple example will make it clear. If we have four records X1, X2, X3, and X4, and they're divided into two splits (X1, X2) and (X3, X4), we can find the maximum over all four records by looking at the maximum of each split, or

```
max(X1,X2,X3,X4) = max(max(X1,X2), max(X3,X4))
```

Our strategy is to have mapper calculate the maximum over its individual split. Each mapper will output a single value at the end. We have a single reducer that looks at all those values and outputs the global maximum. Listing 4.6 depicts the Python script for a mapper to compute the maximum over a split.

Listing 4.6   AttributeMax.py: Python script to find maximum value of an attribute

```python
#!/usr/bin/env python

import sys

index = int(sys.argv[1])
max   = 0
for line in sys.stdin:
    fields = line.strip().split(",")
    if fields[index].isdigit():
        val = int(fields[index])
        if (val > max):
            max = val
else:
    print max
```

The script is not complicated. It has a `for` loop to read one record at a time. It tokenizes the record into fields and updates the maximum if the user-specified field is bigger. Note that the mapper doesn't output any value until the end, when it sends out the maximum value of the entire split. This is different from what we've seen before, where each record sends out one or more intermediate records to be processed by the reducers.

Given the parsimonious output of the mapper, we can use the default `IdentityReducer` to record the (sorted) output of the mappers.

```
bin/hadoop jar contrib/streaming/hadoop-0.19.1-streaming.jar
        ➥ -input input/apat63_99.txt
        ➥ -output output
        ➥ -mapper 'AttributeMax.py 8'
        ➥ -file playground/AttributeMax.py
        ➥ -D mapred.reduce.tasks=1
```

The mapper is `'AttributeMax.py 8'`. It outputs the maximum of the ninth column in a split. The single reducer collects all the mapper outputs. Given seven mappers, the final output of the above command is this:

```
0
260
306
```

```
348
394
706
868
```

Each line records the maximum over a particular split. We see that one split has zero claims in all its records. This sounds suspicious until we recall that the claim count attribute is not available for patents before 1975.

We see that our mapper is doing the right thing. We can use a reducer that outputs the maximum over the values outputted by the mappers. We have an interesting situation here, due to the distributive property of maximum, where we can also use `AttributeMax.py` as the reducer. Only now the reducer is trying to find the maximum in the "first" column.

```
bin/hadoop jar contrib/streaming/hadoop-0.18.1-streaming.jar
        ➥ -input input/apat63_99.txt
        ➥ -output output
        ➥ -mapper 'AttributeMax.py 8'
        ➥ -reducer 'AttributeMax.py 0'
        ➥ -file AttributeMax.py
        ➥ -D mapred.reduce.tasks=1
```

The output of the above command should be a one-line file, and you'll find the maximum number of claims in a patent to be 868.

Classes of aggregation functions

We use aggregation functions to compute descriptive statistics. They're generally grouped into three classes: distributive, algebraic, and holistic. The maximum function is an example of a distributive function. Other distributive functions include minimum, sum, and count. As the name implies, distributive functions have distributive properties. Similar to the maximum function, you can globally compute these functions by iteratively applying them to smaller chunks of data.

Another class of aggregation functions is the algebraic functions. Examples of this class include average and variance. They don't follow the distributive property, and their derivation will require some "algebraic" computation over simpler functions. We get into examples of this in the next section.

Finally, functions such as median and *K* smallest/largest value belong to the holistic class of aggregation functions. Readers interested in a challenge should try to implement the median function in an efficient manner using Hadoop.

4.5.3 *Streaming with key/value pairs*

At this point you may wonder what happened to the key/value pair way of encoding records. Our discussion on Streaming so far talks about each record as an atomic unit rather than as composed of a key and a value. The truth is that Streaming works on key/value pairs just like the standard Java MapReduce model. By default, Streaming uses the tab character to separate the key from the value in a record. When there's no tab character, the entire record is considered the key and the value is empty text. For our data sets, which have no tab character, this provides the illusion that we're processing each individual record as a whole unit. Furthermore, even if the records do have tab characters in them, the Streaming API will only shuffle and sort the records in a different order. As long as our mapper and reducer work in a record-oriented way, we can maintain the record-oriented illusion.

Working with key/value pairs allows us to take advantage of the key-based shuffling and sorting to create interesting data analyses. To illustrate key/value pair processing using Streaming, we can write a program to find the maximum number of claims in a patent *for each country*. This would differ from `AttributeMax.py` in that this is trying to find the maximum *for each key*, rather than a maximum across all records. Let's make this exercise more interesting by computing the average rather than finding the maximum. (As we see, Hadoop already includes a package called Aggregate that contains classes that help find the maximum for each key.)

First, let's examine how key/value pairs work in the Streaming API for each step of the MapReduce data flow.

1   As we've seen, the mapper under Streaming reads a split through STDIN and extracts each line as a record. Your mapper can choose to interpret each input record as a key/value pair or a line of text.

2   The Streaming API will interpret each line of your mapper's output as a key/ value pair separated by tab. Similar to the standard MapReduce model, we apply the partitioner to the key to find the right reducer to shuffle the record to. All key/value pairs with the same key will end up at the same reducer.

3   At each reducer, key/value pairs are sorted according to the key by the Streaming API. Recall that in the Java model, all key/value pairs of the same key are grouped together into one key and a list of values. This group is then presented to the `reduce()` method. Under the Streaming API *your reducer is responsible for performing the grouping*. This is not too bad as the key/value pairs are already sorted by key. All records of the same key are in one contiguous chunk. Your reducer will read one line at a time from STDIN and will keep track of the new keys.

4   For all practical purposes, the output (STDOUT) of your reducer is written to a file directly. Technically a no-op step is taken before the file write. In this step the Streaming API breaks each line of the reducer's output by the tab character and feeds the key/value pair to the default `TextOutputFormat`, which by default re-inserts the tab character before writing the result to a file. Without tab characters in the reducer's output it will show the same

no-op behavior. You can reconfigure the default behavior to do something different, but it makes sense to leave it as a no-op and push the processing into your reducer.

To understand the data flow better, we write a Streaming program to compute the average number of claims for each country. The mapper will extract the country and the claims count for each patent and package them as a key/value pair. In accord with the default Streaming convention, the mapper outputs this key/value pair with a tab character to separate them. The Streaming API will pick up the key and the shuffling will guarantee that all claim counts of a country will end up at the same reducer. We can see the Python code in listing 4.7. For each record, the mapper extracts the country (`fields[4][1:-1]`) as key and the claims count (`fields[8]`) as value. An extra concern with our data set is that missing values do exist. We've added a conditional statement to skip over records with missing claim counts.

Listing 4.7 AverageByAttributeMapper.py: output country and claim count of patents

```python
#!/usr/bin/env python

import sys

for line in sys.stdin:
    fields = line.split(",")
    if (fields[8] and fields[8].isdigit()):
        print fields[4][1:-1] + "\t" + fields[8]
```

Before writing the reducer, let's run the mapper in two situations: without any reducer, and with the default `IdentityReducer`. It's a useful approach now for learning as we can see exactly what's being outputted by the mapper (by using no reducer) and what's being inputted into the reducer (by using `IdentityReducer`). You'll find this handy later when debugging your MapReduce program. You can at least check if the mapper is outputting the proper data and if the proper data is being sent to the reducer. First let's run the mapper without any reducer.

```
bin/hadoop jar contrib/streaming/hadoop-0.19.1-streaming.jar
        ➥ -input input/apat63_99.txt
        ➥ -output output
        ➥ -file playground/AverageByAttributeMapper.py
        ➥ -mapper 'AverageByAttributeMapper.py'
        ➥ -D mapred.reduce.tasks=0
```

The output should consist of lines where a country code is followed by a tab followed by a numeric count. The order of the output records is not sorted by (the new) key. In fact, it's in the same order as the order of the input records, although that's not obvious from looking at the output.

The more interesting case is to use the `IdentityReducer` with a non-zero number of reducers. We see how the shuffled and sorted records are presented to the reducer. To keep it simple let's try a single reducer by setting `-D mapred.reduce.tasks=1` and see the first 32 records.

AD	9		AE	23
AD	12		AE	12
AD	7		AE	16
AD	28		AE	10
AD	14		AG	18
AE	20		AG	12
AE	7		AG	8
AE	35		AG	14
AE	11		AG	24
AE	12		AG	20
AE	24		AG	7
AE	4		AG	3
AE	16		AI	10
AE	26		AM	18
AE	11		AN	5
AE	4		AN	26

Under the Streaming API, the reducer will see these text data in STDIN. We have to code our reducer to recover the key/value pairs by breaking each line at the tab character. Sorting has "grouped" together records of the same key. As you read each line from STDIN, you'll be responsible for keeping track of the boundary between records of different keys. Note that although the keys are sorted, the values don't follow any particular order. Finally, the reducer must perform its stated computation, which in this case is calculating the average value across a key. Listing 4.8 gives the complete reducer in Python.

Listing 4.8   AverageByAttributeReducer.py

```
#!/usr/bin/env python

import sys

(last_key, sum, count) = (None, 0.0, 0)

for line in sys.stdin:
    (key, val) = line.split("\t")

    if last_key and last_key != key:
        print last_key + "\t" + str(sum / count)
        (sum, count) = (0.0, 0)

    last_key = key
    sum   += float(val)
    count += 1

print last_key + "\t" + str(sum / count)
```

The program keeps a running sum and count for each key. When it detects a new key in the input stream or the end of the file, it computes the average for the previous key and sends it to STDOUT. After running the entire MapReduce job, we can easily check the correctness of the first few results.

```
AD      14.0
AE      15.4
AG      13.25
AI      10.0
AM      18.0
AN      9.625
```

NOTE   For those interested, the NBER website from where we get the patent data also has a file (`list_of_countries.txt`) that shows the full country name for each country code. Looking at the output of our job and the country codes, we see that Andorra (AD) patents have an average 14 claims. Arab Emirates (AE) patents average 15.4 claims. Antigua and Barbuda (AG) patents average 13.25 claims, and so forth.

4.5.4   *Streaming with the Aggregate package*

Hadoop includes a library package called Aggregate that simplifies obtaining aggregate statistics of a data set. This package can simplify the writing of Java statistics collectors, especially when used with Streaming, which is the focus of this section.[9]

The Aggregate package under Streaming functions as a reducer that computes aggregate statistics. You only have to provide a mapper that processes records and sends out a specially formatted output. Each line of the mapper's output looks like

```
function:key\tvalue
```

The output string starts with the name of a value aggregator function (from the set of predefined functions available in the Aggregate package). A colon and a tab-separated key/value pair follows. The Aggregate reducer applies the function to the set of values for each key. For example, if the function is `LongValueSum`, then the output is the sum of values for each key. (As the function name implies, each value is treated as a Java long type.) If the function is `LongValueMax`, then the output is the maximum value for each key. You can see the list of aggregator functions supported in the Aggregate package in table 4.3.

Table 4.3   List of value aggregator functions supported by the Aggregate package

Value aggregator	Description
DoubleValueSum	Sums up a sequence of double values.
LongValueMax	Finds the maximum of a sequence of long values.
LongValueMin	Finds the minimum of a sequence of long values.
LongValueSum	Sums up a sequence of long values.
StringValueMax	Finds the lexicographical maximum of a sequence of string values.
StringValueMin	Finds the lexicographical minimum of a sequence of string values.
UniqValueCount	Finds the number of unique values (for each key).
ValueHistogram	Finds the count, minimum, median, maximum, average, and standard deviation of each value. (See text for further explanation.)

---

[9] Using the Aggregate package in Java is explained in http://hadoop.apache.org/core/docs/current/api/org/apache/hadoop/mapred/lib/aggregate/package-summary.html.

Let's go through an exercise using the Aggregate package to see how easy it is. We want to count the number of patents granted each year. We can approach this problem in a way similar to the word counting example we saw in chapter 1. For each record, our mapper will output the grant year as the key and a "1" as the value. The reducer will sum up all the values ("1"s) to arrive at a count. Only now we're using Streaming with the Aggregate package. Our result will be the simple mapper shown in listing 4.9.

Listing 4.9   AttributeCount.py

```python
#!/usr/bin/env python

import sys

index = int(sys.argv[1])
for line in sys.stdin:
    fields = line.split(",")
    print "LongValueSum:" + fields[index] + "\t" + "1"
```

`AttributeCount.py` works for any CSV-formatted input file. The user only has to specify the column index to count the number of records for each attribute in that column. The print statement has the main "action" of this short program. It tells the Aggregate package to sum up all the values (of 1) for each key, defined as the user-specified column (`index`). To count the number of patents granted each year, we run this Streaming program with the Aggregate package, telling the mapper to use the second column (`index = 1`) of the input file as the attribute of interest.

```
bin/hadoop jar contrib/streaming/hadoop-0.19.1-streaming.jar
        ➥ -input input/apat63_99.txt
        ➥ -output output
        ➥ -file AttributeCount.py
        ➥ -mapper 'AttributeCount.py 1'
        ➥ -reducer aggregate
```

You'll find most of the options of running the Streaming program familiar. The main thing to point out is that we've specified the reducer to be `'aggregate'`. This is the signal to the Streaming API that we're using the Aggregate package. The output of the MapReduce job (after sorting) is

```
"GYEAR"  1
1963     45679
1964     47375
1965     62857
...
1996     109645
1997     111983
1998     147519
1999     153486
```

The first row is anomalous because the first row of the input data is a column description. Otherwise the MapReduce job neatly outputs the patent count for each year. As

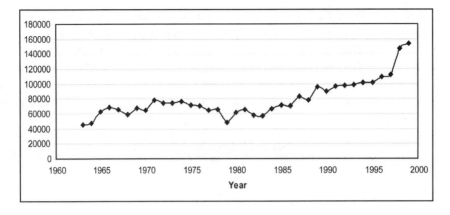

Figure 4.3   Using Hadoop to count patents published each year and Excel to plot the result. This analysis using Hadoop quickly shows the annual patent output to have almost quadrupled in 40 years.

shown in figure 4.3, we can plot the data to visualize it better. You'll see that it has a mostly steady upward trend.

Looking at the list of functions in the Aggregate package in table 4.3, you'll find that most of them are combinations of maximum, minimum, and sum for atomic data type. (For some reason `DoubleValueMax` and `DoubleValueMin` aren't supported. They would be trivial modifications of `LongValueMax` and `LongValueMin` and an added advantage.) `UniqValueCount` and `ValueHistogram` are slightly different and we look at some examples of how to use them.

`UniqValueCount` gives the number of unique values for each key. For example, we may want to know whether more countries are participating in the U.S. patent system over time. We can examine this by looking at the number of countries with patents granted each year. We use a straightforward wrapper of `UniqValueCount` in listing 4.10 and apply it to the year and country columns of `apat63_99.txt` (column index of 1 and 4, respectively).

```
bin/hadoop jar contrib/streaming/hadoop-0.19.1-streaming.jar
          ➥ -input input/apat63_99.txt
          ➥ -output output
          ➥ -file UniqueCount.py
          ➥ -mapper 'UniqueCount.py 1 4'
          ➥ -reducer aggregate
```

In the output we get one record for each year. Plotting it gives us figure 4.4. We can see that the increasing number of patents granted from 1960 to 1990 (from figure 4.3) didn't come from more countries (figure 4.4). The same number of countries had filed more.

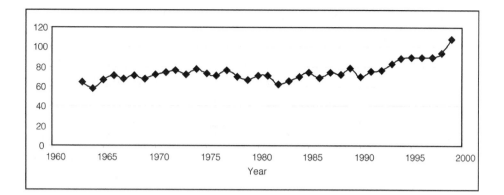

Figure 4.4 The number of countries with U.S. patents granted in each year. We performed the computation with a MapReduce job and graphed the result with Excel.

Listing 4.10 UniqueCount.py: a wrapper around the UniqValueCount function

```python
#!/usr/bin/env python

import sys

index1 = int(sys.argv[1])
index2 = int(sys.argv[2])
for line in sys.stdin:
    fields = line.split(",")
    print "UniqValueCount:" + fields[index1] + "\t" + fields[index2]
```

The aggregate function `ValueHistogram` is the most ambitious function in the Aggregate package. For each key, it outputs the following:

1 The number of unique values
2 The minimum count
3 The median count
4 The maximum count
5 The average count
6 The standard deviation

In its most general form, it expects the output of the mapper to have the form

```
ValueHistogram:key\tvalue\tcount
```

We specify the function `ValueHistogram` followed by a colon, followed by a tab-separated key, value, and count triplet. The Aggregate reducer outputs the six statistics above for each key. Note that for everything except the first statistics (number of unique values) the counts are summed over each key/value pair. Outputting two records from your mapper as

```
ValueHistogram:key_a\tvalue_a\t10
ValueHistogram:key_a\tvalue_a\t20
```

is no different than outputting a single record with the sum

```
ValueHistogram:key_a\tvalue_a\t30
```

A useful variation is for the mapper to only output the key and value, without the count and the tab character that goes with it. `ValueHistogram` automatically assumes a count of 1 in this case. Listing 4.11 shows a trivial wrapper around `ValueHistogram`.

Listing 4.11   ValueHistogram.py: wrapper around Aggregate package's `ValueHistogram`

```python
#!/usr/bin/env python

import sys

index1 = int(sys.argv[1])
index2 = int(sys.argv[2])
for line in sys.stdin:
    fields = line.split(",")
    print "ValueHistogram:" + fields[index1] + "\t" + fields[index2]
```

We run this program to find the distribution of countries with patents granted for each year.

```
bin/hadoop jar contrib/streaming/hadoop-0.19.1-streaming.jar
        ➥ -input input/apat63_99.txt
        ➥ -output output
        ➥ -file ValueHist.py
        ➥ -mapper 'ValueHist.py 1 4'
        ➥ -reducer aggregate
```

The output is a tab-separated value (TSV) file with seven columns. The first column, the year of patent granted, is the key. The other six columns are the six statistics the `ValueHistogram` is set to compute. A partial view of the output is here (we skip the first two rows for formatting reasons):

```
1964    58    1    7    38410    816.8103448275862     4997.413601595352
1965    67    1    5    50331    938.1641791044776     6104.779230296307
1966    71    1    5    54634    963.4507042253521     6443.625995189338
1967    68    1    8    51274    965.4705882352941     6177.445623039149
1968    71    1    7    45781    832.4507042253521     5401.229955880634
1969    68    1    8    50394    993.5147058823529     6080.713518728092
1970    72    1    7    47073    894.8472222222222     5527.883233761672
1971    74    1    9    55976    1058.337837837838     6492.837390992137
```

The first column after the year is the number of unique values. This is exactly the same as the output of `UniqValueCount`. The second, third, and fourth columns are the minimum, median, and maximum, respectively. For the patent data set we used, we see that (for every year) the country receiving the fewest granted patents (other than 0) received 1. Looking specifically at the output for 1964, the country receiving the most patents received 38410 patents, whereas half the countries received less than 7 patents. The average number of patents a country received in 1964 is 816.8 with a standard deviation of 4997.4. Needless to say, the number of patents granted to each country is highly skewed, given the discrepancy between the median (7) and the average (816.8).

We've seen how using the Aggregate package under Streaming is a simple way to get some popular metrics. It's a great demonstration of Hadoop's power in simplifying the analysis of large data sets.

4.6 *Improving performance with combiners*

We saw in `AverageByAttributeMapper.py` and `AverageByAttributeReducer.py` (listings 4.7 and 4.8) how to compute the average for each attribute. The mapper reads each record and outputs a key/value pair for the record's attribute and count. It shuffles the key/value pairs across the network, and the reducer computes the average for each key. In our example of computing the average number of claims for each country's patents, we see at least two efficiency bottlenecks:

1 If we have 1 billion input records, the mappers will generate 1 billion key/value pairs that will be shuffled across the network. If we were computing a function such as maximum, it's obvious that the mapper only has to output the maximum for each key it has seen. Doing so would reduce network traffic and increase performance. For a function such as average, it's a bit more complicated, but we can still redefine the algorithm such that for each mapper only one record is shuffled for each key.

2 Using country from the patent data set as key illustrates data *skew*. The data is far from uniformly distributed, as a significant majority of the records would have U.S. as the key. Not only does every key/value pair in the input map to a key/value pair in the intermediate data, most of the intermediate key/value pairs will end up at a single reducer, overwhelming it.

Hadoop solves these bottlenecks by extending the MapReduce framework with a *combiner* step in between the mapper and reducer. You can think of the combiner as a helper for the reducer. It's supposed to whittle down the output of the mapper to lessen the load on the network and on the reducer. If we specify a combiner, the MapReduce framework may apply it zero, one, or more times to the intermediate data. In order for a combiner to work, it must be an equivalent transformation of the data with respect to the reducer. If we take out the combiner, the reducer's output will remain the same. Furthermore, the equivalent transformation property must hold when the combiner is applied to arbitrary subsets of the intermediate data.

If the reducer only performs a distributive function, such as maximum, minimum, and summation (counting), then we can use the reducer itself as the combiner. But many useful functions aren't distributive. We can rewrite some of them, such as averaging to take advantage of a combiner.

The averaging approach taken by `AverageByAttributeMapper.py` is to output only each key/value pair. `AverageByAttributeReducer.py` will count the number of key/value pairs it receives and sum up their values, in order for a single final division to compute the average. The main obstacle to using a combiner is the counting operation, as the reducer assumes the number of key/value pairs it receives is the number of key/value pairs in the input data. We can refactor the MapReduce program to track the count explicitly. The combiner becomes a simple summation function with the distributive property.

Let's first refactor the mapper and reducer before writing the combiner, as the operation of the MapReduce job must be correct even without a combiner. We write the new averaging program in Java as the combiner must be a Java class.

> **NOTE** The Streaming API allows you to specify a combiner using the `-combiner` option. For versions up to at least 0.20, the combiner must still be a Java class. It's best to write your mapper and reducer in a Java language. Fortunately, the Hadoop roadmap supports native Streaming scripts as combiners. In practice, one can get the equivalent of a combiner by setting the mapper to a Unix pipe 'mapper.py | sort | combiner.py'. In addition, if you're using the Aggregate package, each value aggregator already has a built-in (Java) combiner. The Aggregate package will automatically use these combiners.

Let's write a Java mapper (listing 4.12) that's analogous to `AverageByAttributeMapper.py` of listing 4.7.

Listing 4.12   Java equivalent of AverageByAttributeMapper.py

```
public static class MapClass extends MapReduceBase
    implements Mapper<LongWritable, Text, Text, Text> {

    public void map(LongWritable key, Text value,
                    OutputCollector<Text, Text> output,
                    Reporter reporter) throws IOException {

        String fields[] = value.toString().split(",", -20);
        String country = fields[4];
        String numClaims = fields[8];
        if (numClaims.length() > 0 && !numClaims.startsWith("\"")) {
            output.collect(new Text(country),
                        new Text(numClaims + ",1"));      ❶
        }
    }
}
```

❶ Include output count of I

The crucial difference in this new Java mapper is that the output is now appended with a count of 1 ❶. We could've defined a new `Writable` data type that holds both the value and count, but things are simple enough that we're just keeping a comma-separated string in `Text`.

At the reducer, the list of values for each key are parsed. The total sum and count are then computed by summation and divided at the end to get the average.

```
public static class Reduce extends MapReduceBase
    implements Reducer<Text, Text, Text, DoubleWritable> {

    public void reduce(Text key, Iterator<Text> values,
```

```
                OutputCollector<Text, DoubleWritable> output,
                Reporter reporter) throws IOException {
    double sum = 0;
    int count = 0;
    while (values.hasNext()) {
        String fields[] = values.next().toString().split(",");
        sum += Double.parseDouble(fields[0]);
        count += Integer.parseInt(fields[1]);
    }
    output.collect(key, new DoubleWritable(sum/count));
    }
}
```

The logic of the refactored MapReduce job was not too hard to follow, was it? We added an explicit count for each key/value pair. This refactoring allows the intermediate data to be combined at each mapper before it's sent across the network.

Programmatically, the combiner must implement the `Reducer` interface. The combiner's `reduce()` method performs the combining operation. This may seem like a bad naming scheme, but recall that for the important class of distributive functions, the combiner and the reducer perform the same operations. Therefore, the combiner has adopted the reducer's signature to simplify its reuse. You don't have to rename your `Reduce` class to use it as a combiner class. In addition, because the combiner is performing an equivalent transformation, the type for the key/value pair in its output must match that of its input. In the end, we've created a `Combine` class that looks similar to the `Reduce` class, except it only outputs the (partial) sum and count at the end, whereas the reducer computes the final average.

```
public static class Combine extends MapReduceBase
    implements Reducer<Text, Text, Text, Text> {

    public void reduce(Text key, Iterator<Text> values,
                    OutputCollector<Text, Text> output,
                    Reporter reporter) throws IOException {

        double sum = 0;
        int count = 0;
        while (values.hasNext()) {
            String fields[] = values.next().toString().split(",");
            sum += Double.parseDouble(fields[0]);
            count += Integer.parseInt(fields[1]);
        }
        output.collect(key, new Text(sum + "," + count));
    }
}
```

To enable the combiner, the driver must specify the combiner's class to the `JobConf` object. You can do this through the `setCombinerClass()` method. The driver sets the mapper, combiner, and the reducer:

	Counter	Map	Reduce	Total
Job Counters	Data-local map tasks	0	0	4
	Launched reduce tasks	0	0	2
	Launched map tasks	0	0	4
Map-Reduce Framework	Reduce input records	0	151	151
	Map output records	1,984,055	0	1,984,055
	Map output bytes	18,862,764	0	18,862,764
	Combine output records	1,063	151	1,214
	Map input records	2,923,923	0	2,923,923
	Reduce input groups	0	151	151
	Combine input records	1,984,625	493	1,985,118
	Map input bytes	236,903,179	0	236,903,179
	Reduce output records	0	151	151
File Systems	HDFS bytes written	0	2.658	2,658
	Local bytes written	20,554	2,510	23,064
	HDFS bytes read	236,915,470	0	236,915,470
	Local bytes read	21,112	2,510	23,622

Figure 4.5   **Monitoring the effectiveness of the combiner in the AveragingWithCombiner job**

```
job.setMapperClass(MapClass.class);
job.setCombinerClass(Combine.class);
job.setReducerClass(Reduce.class);
```

A combiner doesn't necessarily improve performance. You should monitor the job's behavior to see if the number of records outputted by the combiner is meaningfully less than the number of records going in. The reduction must justify the extra execution time of running a combiner. You can easily check this through the JobTracker's Web UI, which we'll see in chapter 6.

Looking at figure 4.5, note that in the map phase, combine has 1,984,625 input records and only 1,063 output records. Clearly the combiner has reduced the amount of intermediate data. Note that the reduce side executes the combiner, though the benefit of this is negligible in this case.

4.7   *Exercising what you've learned*

Practice is the path to proficiency. You can try the following exercises to hone your ability to think in the MapReduce paradigm.

   1   *Top K records*—Change AttributeMax.py (or AttributeMax.php) to output the entire record rather than only the maximum value. Rewrite it such that the MapReduce job outputs the records with the top K values rather than only the maximum.

2 *Web traffic measurement*—Take a web server log file and write a Streaming program with the Aggregate package to find the hourly traffic to that site.

3 *Inner product of two sparse vectors*—A vector is a list of values. Given two vectors, $X = [x1, x2, ...]$ and $Y = [y1, y2, ...]$, their inner product is $Z = x1 * y1 + x2 * y2 + ...$. When X and Y are long but have many elements with zero value, they're usually given in a sparse representation:

1,0.46
9,0.21
17,0.92
...

where the key (first column) is the index into the vector. All elements not explicitly specified are considered to have a value of zero. Note that the keys don't need to be in a sorted order. In fact, the keys may not even be numerical. (For natural language processing, the keys can be words in a document, and the inner product is a measure of document similarity.) Write a Streaming job to compute the inner product of two sparse vectors. You can add a post-processing step after the MapReduce job to complete the computation.

4 *Time series processing*—Consider time-series data, where each record has a timestamp as key and a measurement (on that time period) as value. We want an output that is a linear function of the time series in a form: $y(t) = a0 * x(t) + a1 * x(t-1) + a2 * x(t-2) + ... + aN * x(t-N)$ where t stands for time and a0,...,aN are known constants. In signal processing, this is known as an FIR filter. A particularly popular instance is the *moving average*, where $a0 = a1 = ... = aN = 1/N$. Each point in y is the average of the previous N points in x. It's a simple way to smooth out time series.

Implement this linear filter in MapReduce. Be sure to use a combiner. If you order the time series data chronologically (as they usually are) and N is relatively small, what's the reduction in network traffic for shuffling when a combiner is used? For extra credit, write your own partitioner so the output stays ordered chronologically.

For the more advanced practitioners, this example illustrates the difference between scalability and performance. Implementing an FIR filter in Hadoop makes it *scalable* to process terabytes or more of data. Students of signal processing will recognize that a *high performance* implementation of an FIR filter often calls for a technique known as Fast Fourier Transform (FFT). A solution that is scalable *and* high performing would call for a MapReduce implementation of FFT, which is beyond the scope of this book.

5 *Commutative property*—Recall from basic math that the commutative property means the order of operation is irrelevant. For example, addition obeys the commutative property, as a+b=b+a and a+b+c=b+a+c=b+c+a=c+a+b=c+b+a. Is the

MapReduce framework fundamentally designed for implementing commutative functions? Why or why not?

6   *Multiplication (product)*—Many machine-learning and statistical-classification algorithms involve the multiplication of a large number of probability values. Usually we compare the product of one set of probabilities to the product of a different set, and choose a classification corresponding to the bigger product. We've seen that maximum is a distributive function. Is the product also distributive? Write a MapReduce program that multiplies all values in a data set. For full credit, apply the program to a reasonably large data set. Does implementing the program in MapReduce solve all scalability issues? What should you do to fix it?

(Writing your own floating-point library is a popular answer, but not a good one.)

7   *Translation into fictional dialect*—A popular assignment in introductory computer science classes is to write a program that converts English to "pirate-speak." Many variations of the exercise exist for other semi-fictional dialects, such as "Snoop Dogg" and "E-40." Usually the solution involves a dictionary look-up for exact word matches ("for" becomes "fo," "sure" becomes "sho," "the" becomes "da," etc.), simple text rules (words ending in "ing" now ends in "in'," replace the last vowel of a word and everything after it with "izzle," etc.), and random injections ("kno' wha' im sayin'?"). Write such translations and use Hadoop to apply it to a large corpus such as Wikipedia.

4.8   Summary

MapReduce programs follow a template. Often the whole program is defined within a single Java class. Within the class, a driver sets up a MapReduce job's configuration object, which is used as the blueprint for how the job is set up and run. You'll find the map and reduce functions in subclasses of `Mapper` and `Reducer`, respectively. Those classes are often no more than a couple dozen lines long, so they're usually written as inner classes for convenience.

Hadoop provides a Streaming API for writing MapReduce programs in a language other than Java. Many MapReduce programs are much easier to develop in a scripting language using the Streaming API, especially for ad hoc data analysis. The Aggregate package, when used with Streaming, enables one to rapidly write programs for counting and getting basic statistics.

MapReduce programs are largely about the map and the reduce functions, but Hadoop allows for a combiner function to improve performance by "pre-reducing" the intermediate data at the mapper before the reduce phase.

In standard programming (outside of the MapReduce paradigm), counting, summing, averaging, and so on are usually done through a simple, single pass of the data. Refactoring those programs to run in MapReduce, as we've done in this chapter, is relatively straightforward conceptually. More complex data analysis algorithms call for deeper reworking of the algorithms, which we cover in the next chapter.

4.9 *Further resources*

Although we've focused on the patent data sets in this chapter, there are other large publicly accessible data sets that you can download and play around with. Below are a few examples.

http://www.netflixprize.com/index—Netflix is an online movie rental site. A crucial part of its business is a recommendation engine that suggests new movies to a user based on the user's ratings of previous movies. As part of a competition, it released a data set of user ratings to challenge people to develop better recommendation algorithms. The uncompressed data comes at 2 GB+. It contains 100 M+ movie ratings from 480 K users on 17 K movies.

http://aws.amazon.com/publicdatasets/—Amazon has hosted for free several large public data sets for its EC2 users. As of this writing, the data sets belong to the three categories of biology, chemistry, and economics. For example, one of the biological data sets is an annotated human genome data of roughly 550 GB. Under economics you can find data sets, such as the 2000 U.S. Census (approximately 200 GB).

http://boston.lti.cs.cmu.edu/Data/clueweb09/—Carnegie Mellon University's Language Technologies Institute has released the ClueWeb09 data set to aid large-scale web research. It's a crawl of a billion web pages in 10 languages. The uncompressed data set takes up 25 TB. Given the size of the data set, the most efficient way to get it is in compressed form (which takes up 5 TB) shipped in hard disk drives. (At a certain scale, shipping hard drives through FedEx has a high "bandwidth.") As of this writing, CMU charges US$790 to ship four 1.5 TB drives with the compressed data.

Advanced MapReduce

5

This chapter covers

- Chaining multiple MapReduce jobs
- Performing joins of multiple data sets
- Creating Bloom filters

As your data processing becomes more complex you'll want to exploit different Hadoop features. This chapter will focus on some of these more advanced techniques.

When handling advanced data processing, you'll often find that you can't program the process into a single MapReduce job. Hadoop supports *chaining* MapReduce programs together to form a bigger job. You'll also find that advanced data processing often involves more than one data set. We'll explore various *joining* techniques in Hadoop for simultaneously processing multiple data sets. You can code certain data processing tasks more efficiently when processing a group of records at a time. We've seen how Streaming natively supports the ability to process a whole split at a time, and the Streaming implementation of the maximum function takes advantage of this ability. We'll see that the same is true for Java programs. We'll discover the Bloom filter and implement it with a mapper that keeps state information across records.

5.1 Chaining MapReduce jobs

You've been doing data processing tasks which a single MapReduce job can accomplish. As you get more comfortable writing MapReduce programs and take on more ambitious data processing tasks, you'll find that many complex tasks need to be broken down into simpler subtasks, each accomplished by an individual MapReduce job. For example, from the citation data set you may be interested in finding the ten most-cited patents. A sequence of two MapReduce jobs can do this. The first one creates the "inverted" citation data set and counts the number of citations for each patent, and the second job finds the top ten in that "inverted" data.

5.1.1 Chaining MapReduce jobs in a sequence

Though you can execute the two jobs manually one after the other, it's more convenient to automate the execution sequence. You can chain MapReduce jobs to run sequentially, with the output of one MapReduce job being the input to the next. Chaining MapReduce jobs is analogous to Unix pipes.

```
mapreduce-1 | mapreduce-2 | mapreduce-3 | ...
```

Chaining MapReduce jobs sequentially is quite straightforward. Recall that a driver sets up a `JobConf` object with the configuration parameters for a MapReduce job and passes the `JobConf` object to `JobClient.runJob()` to start the job. As `JobClient.runJob()` blocks until the end of a job, chaining MapReduce jobs involves calling the driver of one MapReduce job after another. The driver at each job will have to create a new `JobConf` object and set its input path to be the output path of the previous job. You can delete the intermediate data generated at each step of the chain at the end.

5.1.2 Chaining MapReduce jobs with complex dependency

Sometimes the subtasks of a complex data processing task don't run sequentially, and their MapReduce jobs are therefore not chained in a linear fashion. For example, mapreduce1 may process one data set while mapreduce2 independently processes another data set. The third job, mapreduce3, performs an inner join of the first two jobs' output. (We'll discuss data joining in the next sections.) It's dependent on the other two and can execute only after both mapreduce1 and mapreduce2 are completed. But mapreduce1 and mapreduce2 aren't dependent on each other.

Hadoop has a mechanism to simplify the management of such (nonlinear) job dependencies via the `Job` and `JobControl` classes. A `Job` object is a representation of a MapReduce job. You instantiate a `Job` object by passing a `JobConf` object to its constructor. In addition to holding job configuration information, `Job` also holds dependency information, specified through the `addDependingJob()` method. For `Job` objects x and y,

```
x.addDependingJob(y)
```

means x will not start until y has finished. Whereas `Job` objects store the configuration and dependency information, `JobControl` objects do the managing and monitoring of the job execution. You can add jobs to a `JobControl` object via the `addJob()` method. After adding all the jobs and dependencies, call `JobControl`'s `run()` method to spawn a thread to submit and monitor jobs for execution. `JobControl` has methods like `all-Finished()` and `getFailedJobs()` to track the execution of various jobs within the batch.

5.1.3 *Chaining preprocessing and postprocessing steps*

A lot of data processing tasks involve record-oriented preprocessing and postprocessing. For example, in processing documents for information retrieval, you may have one step to remove *stop words* (words like *a, the,* and *is* that occur frequently but aren't too meaningful), and another step for *stemming* (converting different forms of a word into the same form, such as *finishing* and *finished* into *finish.*) You can write a separate MapReduce job for each of these pre- and postprocessing steps and chain them together, using IdentityReducer (or no reducer at all) for these steps. This approach is inefficient as each step in the chain takes up I/O and storage to process the intermediate results. Another approach is for you to write your mapper such that it calls all the preprocessing steps beforehand and the reducer to call all the postprocessing steps afterward. This forces you to architect the pre- and postprocessing steps in a modular and composable manner. Hadoop introduced the `ChainMapper` and the `ChainReducer` classes in version 0.19.0 to simplify the composition of pre- and postprocessing.

You can think of chaining MapReduce jobs, as explained in section 5.1.1, symbolically using the pseudo-regular expression:

```
[MAP | REDUCE]+
```

where a reducer `REDUCE` comes after a mapper `MAP`, and this `[MAP | REDUCE]` sequence can repeat itself one or more times, one right after another. The analogous expression for a job using `ChainMapper` and `ChainReducer` would be

```
MAP+ | REDUCE | MAP*
```

The job runs multiple mappers in sequence to preprocess the data, and after running reduce it can optionally run multiple mappers in sequence to postprocess the data. The beauty of this mechanism is that you write the pre- and postprocessing steps as standard mappers. You can run each one of them individually if you want. (This is useful when you want to debug them individually.) You call the `addMapper()` method in `ChainMapper` and `ChainReducer` to compose the pre- and postprocessing steps, respectively. Running all the pre- and postprocessing steps in a single job leaves no intermediate file and there's a dramatic reduction in I/O.

Consider the example where there are four mappers (`Map1`, `Map2`, `Map3`, and `Map4`) and one reducer (`Reduce`), and they're chained into a single MapReduce job in this sequence:

```
Map1 | Map2 | Reduce | Map3 | Map4
```

In this setup, you should think of `Map2` and `Reduce` as the core of the MapReduce job, with the standard partitioning and shuffling applied between the mapper and reducer. You should consider `Map1` as a preprocessing step and `Map3` and `Map4` as postprocessing steps. The number of processing steps can vary. This is only an example.

You can specify the composition of this sequence of mappers and reducer with the driver. See listing 5.1. You need to make sure the key and value outputs of one task have matching types (classes) with the inputs of the next task.

Listing 5.1 Driver for chaining mappers within a MapReduce job

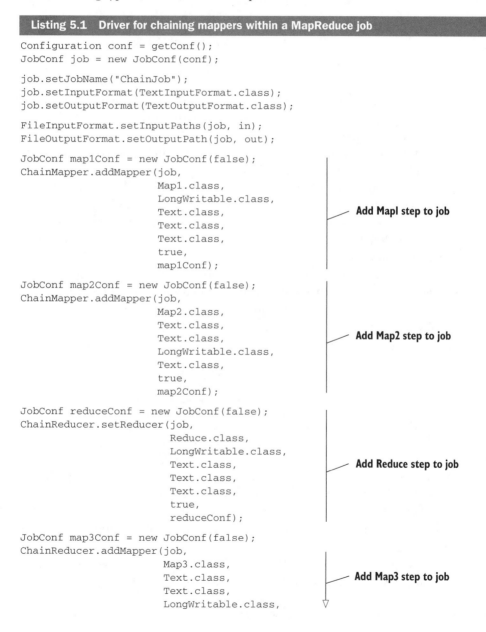

```
Configuration conf = getConf();
JobConf job = new JobConf(conf);

job.setJobName("ChainJob");
job.setInputFormat(TextInputFormat.class);
job.setOutputFormat(TextOutputFormat.class);

FileInputFormat.setInputPaths(job, in);
FileOutputFormat.setOutputPath(job, out);

JobConf map1Conf = new JobConf(false);
ChainMapper.addMapper(job,
                      Map1.class,
                      LongWritable.class,
                      Text.class,
                      Text.class,
                      Text.class,
                      true,
                      map1Conf);                    Add Map1 step to job

JobConf map2Conf = new JobConf(false);
ChainMapper.addMapper(job,
                      Map2.class,
                      Text.class,
                      Text.class,
                      LongWritable.class,
                      Text.class,
                      true,
                      map2Conf);                    Add Map2 step to job

JobConf reduceConf = new JobConf(false);
ChainReducer.setReducer(job,
                        Reduce.class,
                        LongWritable.class,
                        Text.class,
                        Text.class,
                        Text.class,
                        true,
                        reduceConf);                Add Reduce step to job

JobConf map3Conf = new JobConf(false);
ChainReducer.addMapper(job,
                       Map3.class,
                       Text.class,
                       Text.class,
                       LongWritable.class,          Add Map3 step to job
```

```
                              Text.class,
                              true,
                              map3Conf);
```
— Add Map3 step to job

```
JobConf map4Conf = new JobConf(false);
ChainReducer.addMapper(job,
                              Map4.class,
                              LongWritable.class,
                              Text.class,
                              LongWritable.class,
                              Text.class,
                              true,
                              map4Conf);
```
— Add Map4 step to job

```
JobClient.runJob(job);
```

The driver first sets up the "global" `JobConf` object with the job's name, input path, output path, and so forth. It adds the five steps of the chained job one at a time, in the sequence of the steps' execution. It adds all the steps before `Reduce` using the static `ChainMapper.addMapper()` method. It sets the reducer with the static `ChainReducer.setReducer()` method. Using the `ChainReducer.addMapper()` method, it adds the last steps. The global `JobConf` object (`job`) is passed through all five `add*` methods. In addition, each mapper and the reducer have a local `JobConf` object (`map1Conf`, `map2Conf`, `map3Conf`, `map4Conf`, and `reduceConf`) that takes precedence over the global one in configuring the individual mapper/reducer. The recommended local `JobConf` object is a new `JobConf` object initiated without defaults — `new JobConf(false)`.

Let's look at the signature of the `ChainMapper.addMapper()` method to understand in detail how to add each step to the chained job. The signature and function of `ChainReducer.setReducer()` and `ChainReducer.addMapper()` are analogous and we'll skip them.

```
public static <K1,V1,K2,V2> void
             addMapper(JobConf job,
                        Class<? extends Mapper<K1,V1,K2,V2>> klass,
                        Class<? extends K1> inputKeyClass,
                        Class<? extends V1> inputValueClass,
                        Class<? extends K2> outputKeyClass,
                        Class<? extends V2> outputValueClass,
                        boolean byValue,
                        JobConf mapperConf)
```

This method has eight arguments. The first and last are the global and local `JobConf` objects, respectively. The second argument (`klass`) is the `Mapper` class that will do the data processing. The four arguments `inputValueClass`, `inputKeyClass`, `outputKeyClass`, and `outputValueClass` are the input/output class types of the `Mapper` class.

The argument `byValue` will need a little explanation. In the standard `Mapper` model, the output key/value pairs are serialized and written to disk,[1] prepared to be shuffled

---

[1] The key and value's ability to be cloned and serialized is provided by them being implemented as `Writables`.

to a reducer that may be at a completely different node. Formally this is considered to be *passed by value*, as a copy of the key/value pair is sent over. In the current case where we can chain one `Mapper` to another, we can execute the two in the same JVM thread. Therefore, it's possible for the key/value pairs to be *passed by reference*, where the output of the initial `Mapper` stays in place in memory and the following `Mapper` refers to it directly in the same memory location. When `Map1` calls `OutputCollector.collect (K k, V v)`, the objects `k` and `v` pass directly to `Map2`'s `map()` method. This improves performance by not having to clone a potentially large volume of data between the mappers. But doing this can violate one of the more subtle "contracts" in Hadoop's MapReduce API. The call to `OutputCollector.collect(K k, V v)` is guaranteed to not alter the content of `k` and `v`. `Map1` can call `OutputCollector.collect(K k, V v)` and then use the objects `k` and `v` afterward, fully expecting their values to stay the same. But if we pass those objects by reference to `Map2`, then `Map2` may alter them and violate the API's guarantee. If you're sure that `Map1`'s `map()` method doesn't use the content of `k` and `v` after calling `OutputCollector.collect(K k, V v)`, or that `Map2` doesn't change the value of its `k` and `v` input, you can achieve some performance gains by setting `byValue` to false. If you're not sure of the `Mapper`'s internal code, it's best to play safe and let `byValue` be true, maintaining the pass-by-value model, and be certain that the `Mappers` will work as expected.

5.2   Joining data from different sources

It's inevitable that you'll come across data analyses where you need to pull in data from different sources. For example, given our patent data sets, you may want to find out if certain countries cite patents from another country. You'll have to look at citation data (`cite75_99.txt`) as well as patent data for country information (`apat63_99. txt`). In the database world it would just be a matter of joining two tables, and most databases automagically take care of the join processing for you. Unfortunately, joining data in Hadoop is more involved, and there are several possible approaches with different trade-offs.

We use a couple toy data sets to better illustrate joining in Hadoop. Let's take a comma-separated Customers file where each record has three fields: Customer ID, Name, and Phone Number. We put four records in the file for illustration:

```
1,Stephanie Leung,555-555-5555
2,Edward Kim,123-456-7890
3,Jose Madriz,281-330-8004
4,David Stork,408-555-0000
```

We store Customer orders in a separate file, called Orders. It's in CSV format, with four fields: Customer ID, Order ID, Price, and Purchase Date.

```
3,A,12.95,02-Jun-2008
1,B,88.25,20-May-2008
```

```
2,C,32.00,30-Nov-2007
3,D,25.02,22-Jan-2009
```

If we want an inner join of the two data sets above, the desired output would look a listing 5.2.

Listing 5.2   Desired output of an inner join between Customers and Orders data

```
1,Stephanie Leung,555-555-5555,B,88.25,20-May-2008
2,Edward Kim,123-456-7890,C,32.00,30-Nov-2007
3,Jose Madriz,281-330-8004,A,12.95,02-Jun-2008
3,Jose Madriz,281-330-8004,D,25.02,22-Jan-2009
```

Hadoop can also perform outer joins, although to simplify explanation we focus on inner joins.

5.2.1   *Reduce-side joining*

Hadoop has a contrib package called *datajoin* that works as a generic framework for data joining in Hadoop. Its jar file is at contrib/datajoin/hadoop-*-datajoin. jar. To distinguish it from other joining techniques, it's called the *reduce-side join*, as we do most of the processing on the reduce side. It's also known as the *repartitioned join* (or the *repartitioned sort-merge join*), as it's the same as the database technique of the same name. Although it's not the most efficient joining technique, it's the most general and forms the basis of some more advanced techniques (such as the semijoin).

Reduce-side join introduces some new terminologies and concepts, namely, data source, tag, and group key. A *data source* is analogous to a table in relational databases. We have two data sources in our toy example: Customers and Orders. A data source can be a single file or multiple files. The important point is that all the records in a data source have the same structure, analogous to a schema.

The MapReduce paradigm calls for processing each record one at a time in a stateless manner. If we want some state information to persist, we have to *tag* the record with such state. For example, given our two files, a record may look to a mapper like this:

```
3,Jose Madriz,281-330-8004
```

or:

```
3,A,12.95,02-Jun-2008
```

where the record type (Customers or Orders) is dissociated from the record itself. Tagging the record will ensure that specific metadata will always go along with the record. For the purpose of data joining, we want to tag each record with its *data source.*

The *group key* functions like a join key in a relational database. For our example, the group key is the Customer ID. As the datajoin package allows the group key to be any user-defined function, group key is more general than a join key in a relational database.

Before explaining how to use the contrib package, let's go through all the major steps in a repartitioned sort-merge join of our toy datasets. After seeing how those steps fit together, we'll see which steps are done by the datajoin package, and which ones we program. We'll have code to see the hooks for integrating our code with the datajoin package.

DATA FLOW OF A REDUCE-SIDE JOIN

Figure 5.1 illustrates the data flow of a repartitioned join on the toy data sets Customers and Orders, up to the reduce stage. We'll go into more details later to see what happens in the reduce stage.

First we see that mappers receive data from two files, Customers and Orders. Each mapper knows the filename of the data stream it's processing. The map() function is called with each record, and the main goal of map() is to package each record such that joining on the reduce side is possible.

Recall that in the MapReduce framework, map() outputs records as key/value pairs that are partitioned on the key, and all records of the same key will end up in a single reducer and be processed together. For joining, we would want the map() function to output a record package where the key is the group key for joining—the Customer ID in this case. The value in this key/value package will be the original record, tagged with the data source (i.e., filename). For example, for the record

```
3,A,12.95,02-Jun-2008
```

from the Orders file, map() will output a key/value pair where the key is "3", the Customer ID that will be used to join with records from the Customers file. The value output by map() is the entire record wrapped by a tag "Orders".

After map() packages each record of the inputs, MapReduce's standard partition, shuffle, and sort takes place. Note that as the group key is set to the join key, reduce() will process all records of the same join key together. The function reduce() will unwrap the package to get the original record and the data source of the record by its tag. We see that for group keys (Customer IDs) "1" and "2", the reduce() function gets two values. One value is tagged with "Customers" and the other value is tagged with "Orders". For the map output with (group) key "4", reduce() will only see one value, which is tagged with "Customers". This is expected as there is no record in Orders with a Customer ID of "4". On the other hand, reduce() will see three values for the (group) key "3". This is due to one record from Customers and two more from Orders.

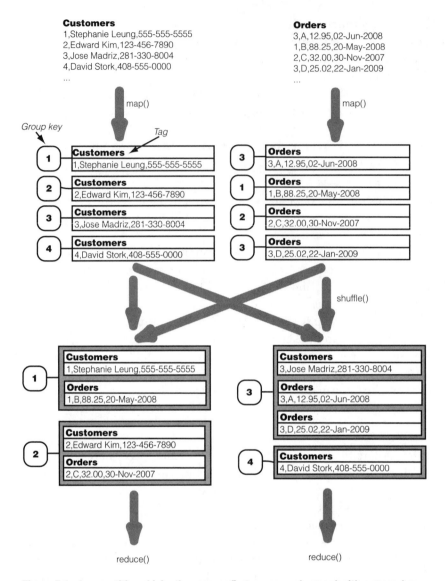

Figure 5.1   In repartitioned join, the mapper first wraps each record with a group key and a tag. The group key is the joining attribute, and the tag is the data source (*table* in SQL parlance) of the record. The partition and shuffle step will group all the records with the same group key together. The reducer is called on the set of records with the same group key.

The function `reduce()` will take its input and do a full *cross-product* on the values. `Reduce()` creates all combinations of the values with the constraint that a combination will not be tagged more than once. In cases where `reduce()` sees values of distinct tags, the cross-product is the original set of values. In our example, this is the case for group

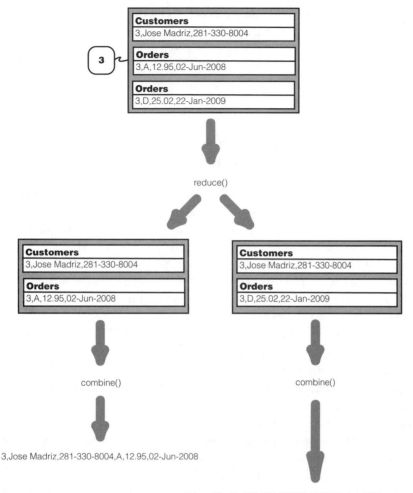

Figure 5.2   The reduce side of a repartitioned join. For a given join key, the reduce task performs a full cross-product of values from different sources. It sends each combination to `combine()` to create an output record. The `combine()` function can choose to not output any particular combination.

keys 1, 2, and 4. Figure 5.2 illustrates the cross product for group key 3. We have three values, one tagged with Customers and two tagged with Orders. The cross-product creates two combinations. Each combination consists of the Customers value and one of the Orders value.

> **NOTE**   Our toy example has an implicit schema that Customer ID identifies a unique record in Customers, making the number of combinations in a cross-product always the number of Orders records with the Customer ID (except

when it's zero, in which case the cross-product is the Customers record itself). For more complicated settings, the number of combinations generated by the cross-product is the product of the number of records under each tag. If `reduce()` sees two Customers records and three Orders records together, then the cross-product will create six (2 * 3) combinations. If there's a third data source (Accounts) with two records, then the cross-product will create twelve (2 * 2 * 3) combinations.

It feeds each combination from the cross-product into a function called `combine()`. (Don't confuse with combiners as explained in section 4.5.) Due to the nature of the cross-product, `combine()` is guaranteed to see at most one record from each of the data sources (tags), and all the records it sees have the same join key. It's the `combine()` function that determines whether the whole operation is an inner join, outer join, or another type of join. In an inner join, `combine()` drops all combinations where not all tags are present, such as our case with group key `"4"`. Otherwise `combine()` merges the records from different sources into a single output record.

Now you see why we call this joining process the repartitioned sort-merge join. The records in the original input sources can be in random order. They are *repartitioned* onto the reducers in the right grouping. The reducer can then *merge* records of the same join key together to create the desired join output. (The *sort* happens but it's not critical to understanding the operation.)

IMPLEMENTING JOIN WITH THE DATAJOIN PACKAGE

Hadoop's datajoin package implements the dataflow of a join as described previously. We have certain hooks to handle the details of our particular data structure and a special hook for us to define the exact function of `combine()`.

Hadoop's datajoin package has three abstract classes that we inherit and make concrete: `DataJoinMapperBase`, `DataJoinReducerBase`, and `TaggedMapOutput`. As the names suggest, our `MapClass` will extend `DataJoinMapperBase`, and our `Reduce` class will extend `DataJoinReducerBase`. The datajoin package has already implemented the `map()` and `reduce()` methods in these respective base classes to perform the join dataflow describe in the last section. Our subclass will only have to implement a few new methods to configure the details.

Before explaining how to use `DataJoinMapperBase` and `DataJoinReducerBase`, you need to understand a new abstract data type `TaggedMapOutput` that is used throughout the code. Recall from the dataflow description that the mapper outputs a package with a (group) key and a value that is a tagged record. The datajoin package specifies the (group) key to be of type `Text` and the value (i.e., the tagged record) to be of type `TaggedMapOutput`. `TaggedMapOutput` is a data type for wrapping our records with a `Text` tag. It trivially implements a `getTag()` and a `setTag(Text tag)` method. It specifies an abstract method `getData()`. Our subclass will implement that method to handle the type of the record. There's no explicit requirement for the subclass to have a `setData()` method but we must pass in the record data. The subclass can implement such a `setData()` method for the sake of symmetry or take in a record in the constructor. In addition, as the output of a mapper, `TaggedMapOutput` needs to be `Writable`. Therefore, our subclass has to implement the `readFields()` and `write()` methods. We created `TaggedWritable`, a simple subclass for handling any `Writable` record type.

```
public static class TaggedWritable extends TaggedMapOutput {
    private Writable data;

    public TaggedWritable(Writable data) {
        this.tag = new Text("");
        this.data = data;
    }

    public Writable getData() {
        return data;
    }

    ...
}
```

Recall from the join dataflow that the mapper's main function is to package a record such that it goes to the same reducer as other records with the same join key. `Data-JoinMapperBase` performs all the packaging, but the class specifies three abstract methods for our subclass to fill in:

```
protected abstract Text generateInputTag(String inputFile);
protected abstract TaggedMapOutput generateTaggedMapOutput(Object value);
protected abstract Text generateGroupKey(TaggedMapOutput aRecord);
```

The `generateInputTag()` is called at the start of a map task to globally specify the tag for all the records this map task will process. The tag is defined to be of type `Text`. Note that we call the `generateInputTag()` with the filename of the records. The mapper working on the Customers file will receive the string `"Customers"` as the argument to `generateInputTag()`. As we're using the tag to signify the data source, and our file-name is set up to reflect the data source, `generateInputTag()` is

```
protected Text generateInputTag(String inputFile) {
    return new Text(inputFile);
}
```

If a data source is spread out over several files (part-0000, part-0001, etc.), you would not want the tag to be the complete filename, rather some prefix of it. For example, the tag (data source) can be the filename before the dash (-) sign.

```
protected Text generateInputTag(String inputFile) {
    String datasource = inputFile.split('-')[0];
    return new Text(datasource);
}
```

We store the result of `generateInputTag()` in the `DataJoinMapperBase` object's `inputTag` variable for later use. We can also store the filename in `DataJoinMapper-Base`'s `inputFile` variable if we want to refer to it again.

After the map task's initialization, `DataJoinMapperBase`'s `map()` is called for each record. It calls the two abstract methods that we have yet to implement.

```
public void map(Object key, Object value,
            OutputCollector output, Reporter reporter) throws IOException
{
    TaggedMapOutput aRecord = generateTaggedMapOutput(value);
    Text groupKey = generateGroupKey(aRecord);
    output.collect(groupKey, aRecord);
}
```

The `generateTaggedMapOutput()` method wraps the record value into a `Tagged-MapOutput` type. Recall the concrete implementation of `TaggedMapOutput` that we're using is called `TaggedWritable`. The method `generateTaggedMapOutput()` can return a `TaggedWritable` with any `Text` tag that we want. In principle, the tag can even be different for different records in the same file. In the standard case, we want the tag to stand for the data source that our `generateInputTag()` had computed earlier and stored in `this.inputTag`.

```
protected TaggedMapOutput generateTaggedMapOutput(Object value) {
    TaggedWritable retv = new TaggedWritable((Text) value);
    retv.setTag(this.inputTag);
    return retv;
}
```

The `generateGroupKey()` method takes a tagged record (of type `TaggedMapOutput`) and returns the group key for joining. For our current purpose, we unwrap the tagged record and take the first field in the CSV-formatted value as the join key.

```
protected Text generateGroupKey(TaggedMapOutput aRecord) {
    String line = ((Text) aRecord.getData()).toString();
    String[] tokens = line.split(",");
    String groupKey = tokens[0];
    return new Text(groupKey);
}
```

In a more general implementation, the user will be able to specify which field should be the joining key and if the record separator may be some character other than a comma.

  `DataJoinMapperBase` is a simple class, and much of the mapper code is in our subclass. `DataJoinReducerBase`, on the other hand, is the workhorse of the datajoin package, and it simplifies our programming by performing a full outer join for us. Our reducer subclass only has to implement the `combine()` method to filter out unwanted combinations to get the desired join operation (inner join, left outer join, etc.). It's also in the `combine()` method that we format the combination into the appropriate output format.

  We give the `combine()` method *one combination of the cross product of the tagged records with the same join (group) key*. This may sound complicated, but recall from the dataflow diagrams in figures 5.1 and 5.2 that the cross-product is simple for the canonical case of two data sources. Each combination will have either two records (meaning there's at least one record in each data source with the join key) or one (meaning only one data source has that join key).

  Let's look at the signature of `combine()`:

```
protected abstract TaggedMapOutput
                        ➥ combine(Object[] tags, Object[] values);
```

An array of tags and an array of values represent the combination. The size of those two arrays is guaranteed to be the same and equal to the number of tagged records in the combination. The first tagged record in the combination is represented by `tags[0]` and `values[0]`, the second one is `tags[1]` and `values[1]`, and so forth. Furthermore, the tags are always in sorted order.

As tags correspond to the data sources, in the canonical case of joining two data sources, the `tags` array to `combine()` won't be longer than two. Figure 5.2 shows `combine()` being called twice. For the left side, the `tags` and `values` arrays are like this:[2]

```
tags = {"Customers", "Orders"};
values = {"3,Jose Madriz,281-330-8004", "A,12.95,02-Jun-2008"};
```

For an inner join, `combine()` will ignore combinations where not all tags are present. It does so by returning null. Given a legal combination, the role of `combine()` is to concatenate all the values into one single record for output. The order of concatenation is fully determined by `combine()`. In the case of an inner join, the length of `values[]` is always the number of data sources available (two in the canonical case), and the tags are always in sorted order. It's a sensible choice to loop through the `values[]` array to get the default alphabetical ordering based on data source names.

`DataJoinReducerBase`, like any reducer, outputs key/value pairs. For each legal combination, the key is always the join key and the value is the output of `combine()`. Note that the join key is still present in each element of the `values[]` array. The `combine()` method should strip out the join key in those elements before concatenating them. Otherwise the join key will be shown multiple times in one output record.

Finally, `DataJoinReducerBase` expects `combine()` to return a `TaggedMapOutput`. It's unclear why as `DataJoinReducerBase` ignores the tag in the `TaggedMapOutput` object.

Listing 5.3 shows the complete code, including our reduce subclass.

Listing 5.3   Inner join of data from two files using reduce-side join

```
public class DataJoin extends Configured implements Tool {

    public static class MapClass extends DataJoinMapperBase {

        protected Text generateInputTag(String inputFile) {
            String datasource = inputFile.split("-")[0];
            return new Text(datasource);
        }

        protected Text generateGroupKey(TaggedMapOutput aRecord) {
            String line = ((Text) aRecord.getData()).toString();
            String[] tokens = line.split(",");
            String groupKey = tokens[0];
            return new Text(groupKey);
```

---

[2] The `tags` array is of type `Text[]` and values is of type `TaggedWritable[]`. We ignore those details to focus on the their contents.

```
        }
        protected TaggedMapOutput generateTaggedMapOutput(Object value) {
            TaggedWritable retv = new TaggedWritable((Text) value);
            retv.setTag(this.inputTag);
            return retv;
        }
    }
    public static class Reduce extends DataJoinReducerBase {
        protected TaggedMapOutput combine(Object[] tags, Object[] values) {
            if (tags.length < 2) return null;
            String joinedStr = "";
            for (int i=0; i<values.length; i++) {
                if (i > 0) joinedStr += ",";
                TaggedWritable tw = (TaggedWritable) values[i];
                String line = ((Text) tw.getData()).toString();
                String[] tokens = line.split(",", 2);
                joinedStr += tokens[1];
            }
            TaggedWritable retv = new TaggedWritable(new Text(joinedStr));
            retv.setTag((Text) tags[0]);
            return retv;
        }
    }
    public static class TaggedWritable extends TaggedMapOutput {

        private Writable data;

        public TaggedWritable(Writable data) {
            this.tag = new Text("");
            this.data = data;
        }

        public Writable getData() {
            return data;
        }

        public void write(DataOutput out) throws IOException {
            this.tag.write(out);
            this.data.write(out);
        }

        public void readFields(DataInput in) throws IOException {
            this.tag.readFields(in);
            this.data.readFields(in);
        }
    }
    public int run(String[] args) throws Exception {
        Configuration conf = getConf();

        JobConf job = new JobConf(conf, DataJoin.class);

        Path in = new Path(args[0]);
        Path out = new Path(args[1]);
        FileInputFormat.setInputPaths(job, in);
        FileOutputFormat.setOutputPath(job, out);
```

```
            job.setJobName("DataJoin");
            job.setMapperClass(MapClass.class);
            job.setReducerClass(Reduce.class);

            job.setInputFormat(TextInputFormat.class);
            job.setOutputFormat(TextOutputFormat.class);
            job.setOutputKeyClass(Text.class);
            job.setOutputValueClass(TaggedWritable.class);
            job.set("mapred.textoutputformat.separator", ",");

            JobClient.runJob(job);
            return 0;
    }

    public static void main(String[] args) throws Exception {
        int res = ToolRunner.run(new Configuration(),
                                 new DataJoin(),
                                 args);

            System.exit(res);
    }
}
```

Next we'll look at another way of doing joins that is more efficient in some common applications.

5.2.2 *Replicated joins using DistributedCache*

The reduce-side join technique discussed in the last section is flexible, but it can also be quite inefficient. Joining doesn't take place until the reduce phase. We shuffle all data across the network first, and in many situations we drop the majority of this data during the joining process. It would be more efficient if we eliminate the unnecessary data right in the map phase. Even better would be to perform the entire joining operation in the map phase.

The main obstacle to performing joins in the map phase is that a record being processed by a mapper may be joined with a record not easily accessible (or even located) by that mapper. If we can guarantee the accessibility of all the necessary data when joining a record, joining on the map side can work. For example, if we know that the two sources of data are partitioned into the same number of partitions *and* the partitions are all sorted on the key *and* the key is the desired join key, then each mapper (with the proper `InputFormat` and `RecordReader`) can deterministically locate and retrieve all the data necessary to perform joining. In fact, Hadoop's org. apache.hadoop.mapred.join package contains helper classes to facilitate this mapside join. Unfortunately, situations where we can naturally apply this are limited, and running extra MapReduce jobs to repartition the data sources to be usable by this package seems to defeat the efficiency gain. Therefore, we'll not pursue this package further.

All hope is not lost though. There's another data pattern that occurs quite frequently that we can take advantage of. When joining big data, often only one of the sources is big; the second source may be orders of magnitude smaller. For example, a local phone company's Customers data may have only tens of millions of records (each record containing basic information for one customer), but its transaction log can have billions of records containing detailed call history. When the smaller source can fit in memory of a mapper, we can achieve a tremendous gain in efficiency by copying the smaller source to all mappers and performing joining in the map phase. This is called *replicated join* in the database literature as one of the data tables is replicated across all nodes in the cluster. (The next section will cover the case when the smaller source doesn't fit in memory.)

Hadoop has a mechanism called *distributed cache* that's designed to distribute files to all nodes in a cluster. It's normally used for distributing files containing "background" data needed by all mappers. For example, if you're using Hadoop to classify documents, you may have a list of keywords for each class. (Or better yet, a probabilistic model for each class, but we digress...) You would use distributed cache to ensure all mappers have access to the lists of keywords, the "background" data. For executing replicated joins, we consider the smaller data source as background data.

Distributed cache is handled by the appropriately named class `DistributedCache`. There are two steps to using this class. First, when configuring a job, you call the static method `DistributedCache.addCacheFile()` to specify the files to be disseminated to all nodes. These files are specified as URI objects, and they default to HDFS unless a different filesystem is specified. The JobTracker will take this list of URIs and create a local copy of the files in all the TaskTrackers when it starts the job. In the second step, your mappers on each individual TaskTracker will call the static method `DistributedCache.getLocalCacheFiles()` to get an array of local file Paths where the local copy is located. At this point the mapper can use standard Java file I/O techniques to read the local copy.

Replicated joins using `DistributedCache` are simpler than reduce-side joins. Let's begin with our standard Hadoop template.

```
public class DataJoinDC extends Configured implements Tool {

    public static class MapClass extends MapReduceBase
        implements Mapper<Text, Text, Text, Text> {

        . . .
    }

    public int run(String[] args) throws Exception {
        . . .
    }

    public static void main(String[] args) throws Exception {
        int res = ToolRunner.run(new Configuration(),
                                 new DataJoinDC(),
                                 args);

        System.exit(res);
    }
}
```

Note that we've taken out the `Reduce` class. We plan on performing the joining in the map phase and will configure this job to have no reducers. You'll find our driver method familiar too.

```
public int run(String[] args) throws Exception {
   Configuration conf = getConf();
   JobConf job = new JobConf(conf, DataJoinDC.class);

   DistributedCache.addCacheFile(new Path(args[0]).toUri(), conf);

   Path in = new Path(args[1]);
   Path out = new Path(args[2]);
   FileInputFormat.setInputPaths(job, in);
   FileOutputFormat.setOutputPath(job, out);

   job.setJobName("DataJoin with DistributedCache");
   job.setMapperClass(MapClass.class);
   job.setNumReduceTasks(0);

   job.setInputFormat(KeyValueTextInputFormat.class);
   job.setOutputFormat(TextOutputFormat.class);
   job.set("key.value.separator.in.input.line", ",");

   JobClient.runJob(job);

   return 0;
}
```

The crucial addition here is where we take the file specified by the first argument and add it to `DistributedCache`. When we run the job, each node will create a local copy of that file from HDFS. The second and third arguments denote the input and output paths of the standard Hadoop job. Note that we've limited the number of data sources to two. This is not an inherent limitation of the technique, but a simplification that makes our code easier to follow.

Up to now our `MapClass` has only had to define one method, `map()`. In fact, the `Mapper` interface (and also the `Reducer` interface) has two more abstract methods, `configure()` and `close()`. We call the method `configure()` when we first instantiate the `MapClass`, and the method `close()` when the mapper finishes processing its split. The `MapReduceBase` class provides default no-op implementations for these methods. Here we want to override `configure()` to load our join data into memory when a mapper is first initialized. This way we can have the data available each time we call `map()` to process a new record.

```
public static class MapClass extends MapReduceBase
    implements Mapper<Text, Text, Text, Text> {

   private Hashtable<String, String> joinData =
                                    new Hashtable<String, String>();

   @Override
   public void configure(JobConf conf) {
      try {
```

```
        Path [] cacheFiles = DistributedCache.getLocalCacheFiles(conf);
        if (cacheFiles != null && cacheFiles.length > 0) {
            String line;
            String[] tokens;

            BufferedReader joinReader = new BufferedReader(
                        new FileReader(cacheFiles[0].toString()));
            try {
                while ((line = joinReader.readLine()) != null) {
                    tokens = line.split(",", 2);
                    joinData.put(tokens[0], tokens[1]);
                }
            } finally {
                joinReader.close();
            }
        }
    } catch (IOException e) {
        System.err.println("Exception reading DistributedCache: " + e);
    }
}

public void map(Text key, Text value,
            OutputCollector<Text, Text> output,
            Reporter reporter) throws IOException {

    String joinValue = joinData.get(key);
    if (joinValue != null) {
        output.collect(key,
                    new Text(value.toString() + "," + joinValue));
    }
}
}
```

When we call configure(), we get an array of file paths to the local copy of files pushed by DistributedCache. As our driver method has only pushed one file (given by our first argument) into DistributedCache, this should be an array of size one. We read that file using standard Java file I/O. For our purpose, the program assumes each line is a record, the key/value pair is comma separated, and the key is unique and will be used for joining. The program reads this source file into a Java Hashtable called joinData that's available throughout the mapper's lifespan.

The joining takes place in the map() method and is straightforward now that one of the sources resides in memory in the form of joinData. If we don't find the join key in joinData, we drop the record. Otherwise, we match the (join) key to the value in joinData and concatenate the values. The result is outputted directly into HDFS as we don't have any reducer for further processing.

A not-infrequent situation in using DistributedCache is that the background data (the smaller data source in our data join case) is in the local filesystem of the client rather than stored in HDFS. One way to handle this is to add code to upload the local file on the client to HDFS before calling DistributedCache. addCacheFile(). Fortunately, this process is natively supported as one of the generic Hadoop command line arguments in GenericOptionsParser. The option is -files and it automatically copies a comma-separated list of files to all the task nodes. Our command line statement is

```
bin/hadoop jar -files small_in.txt DataJoinDC.jar big_in.txt output
```

Now that we don't need to call `DistributedCache.addCacheFile()` ourselves anymore, we no longer have to take in the filename of the smaller data source as one of the arguments. The index to the arguments has shifted.

```
Path in = new Path(args[0]);
Path out = new Path(args[1]);
```

With these minor changes our `DistributedCache` join program will take a local file on the client machine as one of the input sources.

5.2.3 *Semijoin: reduce-side join with map-side filtering*

One of the limitations in using replicated join is that one of the join tables has to be small enough to fit in memory. Even with the usual asymmetry of size in the input sources, the smaller one may still not be small enough. You can solve this problem by rearranging the processing steps to make them more efficient. For example, if you're looking for the order history of all customers in the 415 area code, it's correct but inefficient to join the Orders and the Customers tables first before filtering out records where the customer is in the 415 area code. Both the Orders and Customers tables may be too big for replicated join and you'll have to resort to the inefficient reduce-side join. A better approach is to first filter out customers living in the 415 area code. We store this in a temporary file called Customers415. We can arrive at the same end result by joining Orders with Customers415, but now Customers415 is small enough that a replicated join is feasible. There is some overhead in creating and distributing the Customers415 file, but it's often compensated by the overall gain in efficiency.

Sometimes you may have a lot of data to analyze. You can't use replicated join no matter how you rearrange your processing steps. Don't worry. We still have ways to make reduce-side joining more efficient. Recall that the main problem with reduce-side joining is that the mapper only tags the data, all of which is shuffled across the network but most of which is ignored in the reducer. The inefficiency is ameliorated if the mapper has an extra prefiltering function to eliminate most or even all the unnecessary data before it is shuffled across the network. We need to build this filtering mechanism.

Continuing our example of joining Customers415 with Orders, the join key is Customer ID and we would like our mappers to filter out any customer not from the 415 area code rather than send those records to reducers. We create a data set CustomerID415 to store all the Customer IDs of customers in the 415 area code. CustomerID415 is smaller than Customers415 because it only has one data field. Assuming CustomerID415 can now fit in memory, we can improve reduce-side join by using distributed cache to disseminate CustomerID415 across all the mappers. When processing records from Customers and Orders, the mapper will drop any record whose key is not in the set CustomerID415. This is sometimes called a *semijoin*, taking the terminology from the database world.

Last but not least, what if the file CustomerID415 is still too big to fit in memory? Or maybe CustomerID415 does fit in memory but it's size makes replicating it across all the mappers inefficient. This situation calls for a data structure called a Bloom filter. A Bloom filter is a compact representation of a set that supports only the *contain* query. ("Does this set contain this element?") Furthermore, the query answer is not completely accurate, but it's guaranteed to have no false negatives and a small probability of false positives. The slight inaccuracy is the trade-off for the data structure's compactness. By using a Bloom filter representation of CustomerID415, the mappers will pass through all customers in the 415 area code. It still guarantees the correctness of the data join algorithm. The Bloom filter will also pass a small portion of customers not in the 415 area code to the reduce phase. This is fine because those will be ignored in the reduce phase. We'll still have improved performance by reducing dramatically the amount of traffic shuffled across the network. The use of Bloom filters is in fact a standard technique for joining in distributed databases, and it's used in commercial products such as Oracle 11g. We'll describe Bloom filter and its other applications in more details in the next section.

5.3   *Creating a Bloom filter*

If you use Hadoop for batch processing of large data sets, your data-intensive computing needs probably include transaction-style processing as well. We won't cover all the techniques for running real-time distributed data processing (caching, sharding, etc.). They aren't necessarily Hadoop-related and are well beyond the scope of this book. One lesser-known tool for real-time data processing is the Bloom filter, which is a summary of a data set whose usage makes other data processing techniques more efficient. When that data set is big, Hadoop is often called in to generate the Bloom filter representation. As we mentioned earlier, a Bloom filter is also sometimes used for data joining within Hadoop itself. As a data processing expert, you'll be well rewarded to have the Bloom filter in your bag of tricks. In this section we'll explain this data structure in more detail and we'll go through an online ad network example that will build a Bloom filter using Hadoop.

5.3.1   *What does a Bloom filter do?*

At its most basic, a Bloom filter object supports two methods: add() and contains(). These two methods work in a similar way as in the Java Set interface. The method add() adds an object to the set, and the method contains() returns a Boolean true/false value denoting whether an object is in the set or not. But, for a Bloom filter, contains() doesn't always give an accurate answer. It has no *false negatives*. If contains() returns false, you can be sure that the set doesn't have the object queried. It does have a small probability of *false positives* though. contains() can return true for some objects not in the set. The probability of false positives depends on the number of elements in the set and some configuration parameters of the Bloom filter itself.

The major benefit of a Bloom filter is that its size, in number of bits, is constant and is set upon initialization. Adding more elements to a Bloom filter doesn't increase its size. It only increases the false positive rate. A Bloom filter also has another configuration parameter to denote the number of hash functions it uses. We'll discuss the reason for this parameter and how the hash functions are used later when we discuss the Bloom filter's implementation. For now, its main implication is that it affects the false positive rate. The false positive rate is approximated by the equation

$$(1 - \exp(-kn/m))k$$

where k is the number of hash functions used, m is the number of bits used to store the Bloom filter, and n is the number of elements to be added to the Bloom filter. In practice, m and n are determined by the requirement of the system, and therefore, k is chosen to minimize the false positive rate given m and n, which (after a little calculus) is

$$k = \ln(2) * (m/n) \approx 0.7 * (m/n)$$

The false positive rate with the given k is $0.6185m/n$, and k has to be an integer. The false positive rate will only be an approximation. From a design point of view, one should think in terms of (m/n), number of bits per element, rather than m alone. For example, we have to store a set containing ten million URLs (n=10,000,000). Allocating 8 bits per URL (m/n=8) will require a 10 MB Bloom filter (m = 80,000,000 bits). This Bloom filter will have a false positive rate of $(0.6185)8$, or about 2 percent. If we were to implement the Set class by storing the raw URLs, and let's say the average URL length was 100 bytes, we would have to use 1 GB. Bloom filter has shrunk the storage requirement by 2 orders of magnitude at the expense of only a 2 percent false positive rate! A slight increase in storage allocated to the Bloom filter will reduce the false positive rate further. At 10 bits per URL, the Bloom filter will take up 12.5 MB and have a false positive rate of only 0.8 percent.

In summary, the signature of our Bloom filter class will look like the following:

```
class BloomFilter<E> {
    public BloomFilter(int m, int k) { ... }
    public void add(E obj) { ... }
    public boolean contains(E obj) { ... }
}
```

More applications of the Bloom filter

The Bloom filter found its first successful applications back when memory was scarce. One of its first uses was in spellchecking. Not being able to store a whole dictionary in memory, spellcheckers used a Bloom filter representation (of the dictionary) to catch most misspellings. As memory size grew and became cheaper, such space consideration waned. Bloom filter usage is finding a resurgence in large-scale data-intensive operations as data is fast outgrowing memory and bandwidth.

We've already seen commercial products, such as Oracle 11g, using Bloom filters to join data across distributed databases. In the networking world, one successful

(continued)

product using Bloom filters is the open source distributed web proxy called Squid. Squid caches frequently accessed web content to save bandwidth and give users a faster web experience. In a cluster of Squid servers, each one can cache a different set of content. An incoming request should be routed to the Squid server holding a copy of the requested content, or in case of a cache miss, the request is passed on to the originating server. The routing mechanism needs to know what each of the Squid servers contains. As sending a list of URLs for each Squid server and storing it in memory is expensive, Bloom filters are used. A false positive means a request is forwarded to the wrong Squid server, but that server would recognize it as a cache miss and pass it on to the originating server, ensuring the correctness of the overall operation. The small performance hit from a false positive is far outweighed by the overall improvement.

Sharding systems are a similar application but more advanced. In a nutshell, database sharding is the partitioning of a database across multiple machines such that each machine only has to deal with a subset of records. Each record has some ID that determines which machine it's assigned to. In more basic designs, the ID is hashed statically to one of a fixed number of database machines. This approach is inflexible to adding more shards or rebalancing existing ones. To add flexibility, it uses a dynamic look-up for each record ID, but unfortunately that adds processing delay if the look-up is done through a database (i.e., using disk). Like Squid, more advanced shard systems use in-memory Bloom filters as a fast look-up. It needs some mechanism to handle false positives, but the occurrence is small enough to not impact the overall performance improvement.

For online display ad networks, it's important to be able to target an ad from the right category to a visitor. Given the volume of traffic a typical ad network receives and the latency requirements, one can end up spending a lot of money on hardware to have the capability of retrieving the category in real time. A design based on Bloom filters can dramatically decrease that cost. Use an offline process to tag web pages (or visitors) on a limited number of categories (sports, family-oriented, music, etc.). Build a Bloom filter for each category and store it in memory at the ad servers. When an ad request arrives, the ad servers can quickly and cheaply determine which category of ads to show. The amount of false positives is negligible.

5.3.2   *Implementing a Bloom filter*

Conceptually the implementation of a Bloom filter is quite straightforward. We describe its implementation in a single system first before implementing it using Hadoop in a distributed way. The internal representation of a Bloom filter is a bit array of size m. We have k independent hash functions, where each hash function takes an object as input and outputs an integer between 0 and m-1. We use the integer output as an index into the bit array. When we "add" an element to the Bloom filter, we use the hash functions to generate k indexes into the bit array. We set the k bits to 1. Figure 5.3 shows what happens when we add several objects (x, y, and z) over time, in a Bloom filter that uses three hash functions. Note that a bit will be set to 1 regardless of its previous state. The number of 1s in the bit array can only grow.

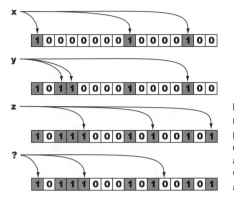

Figure 5.3 A Bloom filter is a bit array that represents a set with some probability of false positives. Objects (such as x, y, and z) are deterministically hashed into positions in the array, and those bits are set to 1. You can check whether an object is in the set or not by hashing and checking the values of those bit positions.

When an object comes in and we want to check whether it has been previously added to the Bloom filter, we use the same *k* hash functions to generate the bit array indexes as we would do in adding the object. Now we check whether *all* those *k* bits in the bit array are 1s. If all *k* bits are 1, we return true and claim that the Bloom filter contains the object. Otherwise we return false. We see that if the object has in fact been added before, then the Bloom filter will necessarily return true. There are no false negatives (returning false when the object is truly in the set). The *k* bits corresponding to the queried object can all be set to 1 even though the object has never been added to the set. It may happen that adding other objects set those bits leading to false positives.[3]

Our implementation of a Bloom filter in Java would use the Java `BitSet` class as its internal representation. We have a function `getHashIndexes(obj)` that takes an object and returns an integer array of size *k*, containing indexes into the `BitSet`. The main functions of the Bloom filter, `add()` and `contains()`, are quite straightforward:

```
class BloomFilter<E> {
    private BitSet bf;
    public void add(E obj) {
        int[] indexes = getHashIndexes(obj);
        for (int index : indexes) {
            bf.set(index);
        }
    }
    public boolean contains(E obj) {
        int[] indexes = getHashIndexes(obj);
        for (int index : indexes) {
            if (bf.get(index) == false) {
                return false;
            }
        }
```

---

[3] For an accessible introduction to Bloom Filters, see http://en.wikipedia.org/wiki/Bloom_filter.

```
        return true;
    }

    protected int[] getHashIndexes(E obj) { ... }
}
```

To implement `getHashIndexes()` such that it works truly as *k* independent hash functions is nontrivial. Instead, in our Bloom filter implementation in listing 5.4, we use a hack to generate *k* indexes that are roughly independent and uniformly distributed. The `getHashIndexes()` method seeds the Java `Random` number generator with an MD5 hash of the object and then takes *k* "random" numbers as indexes. The Bloom filter class would benefit from a more rigorous implementation of `getHashIndexes()`, but our hack suffices for illustration purposes.

An ingenious way of creating a Bloom filter for the union of two sets is by OR'ing the (bit array of the) Bloom filters of each individual set. As adding an object is setting certain bits in a bit array to 1, it's easy to see why this union rule is true:

```
public void union(BloomFilter<E> other) {
    bf.or(other.bf);
}
```

We'll be exploiting this union trick to build Bloom filters in a distributed fashion. Each mapper will build a Bloom filter based on its own data split. We'll send the Bloom filters to a single reducer, which will take a union of them and record the final output.

As the Bloom filter will be shuffled around as the mappers' output, the `BloomFilter` class will have to implement the `Writable` interface, which consists of methods `write()` and `readFields()`. For our purpose these methods transform between the internal `BitSet` representation and a byte array such that the data can be serialized to `DataInput`/`DataOutput`. The final code is in listing 5.4.

Listing 5.4   Basic Bloom filter implementation

```
class BloomFilter<E> implements Writable {

    private BitSet bf;
    private int bitArraySize = 100000000;
    private int numHashFunc = 6;

    public BloomFilter() {
        bf = new BitSet(bitArraySize);
    }

    public void add(E obj) {
        int[] indexes = getHashIndexes(obj);

        for (int index : indexes) {
            bf.set(index);
        }
    }

    public boolean contains(E obj) {
        int[] indexes = getHashIndexes(obj);

        for (int index : indexes) {
```

```
            if (bf.get(index) == false) {
                return false;
            }
        }
        return true;
    }
    public void union(BloomFilter<E> other) {
        bf.or(other.bf);
    }
    protected int[] getHashIndexes(E obj) {
        int[] indexes = new int[numHashFunc];

        long seed = 0;
        byte[] digest;
        try {
            MessageDigest md = MessageDigest.getInstance("MD5");
            md.update(obj.toString().getBytes());
            digest = md.digest();

            for (int i = 0; i < 6; i++) {
                seed = seed ^ (((long)digest[i] & 0xFF))<<(8*i);
            }
        } catch (NoSuchAlgorithmException  e) {}

        Random gen = new Random(seed);

        for (int i = 0; i < numHashFunc; i++) {
            indexes[i] = gen.nextInt(bitArraySize);
        }

        return indexes;
    }
    public void write(DataOutput out) throws IOException {
        int byteArraySize = (int)(bitArraySize / 8);

        byte[] byteArray = new byte[byteArraySize];
        for (int i = 0; i < byteArraySize; i++) {
            byte nextElement = 0;
            for (int j = 0; j < 8; j++) {
                if (bf.get(8 * i + j)) {
                    nextElement |= 1<<j;
                }
            }

            byteArray[i] = nextElement;
        }
        out.write(byteArray);
    }
    public void readFields(DataInput in) throws IOException {
        int byteArraySize = (int)(bitArraySize / 8);
        byte[] byteArray = new byte[byteArraySize];

        in.readFully(byteArray);

        for (int i = 0; i < byteArraySize; i++ ) {
            byte nextByte = byteArray[i];
```

```
            for (int j = 0; j < 8; j++) {
                if (((int)nextByte & (1<<j)) != 0) {
                    bf.set(8 * i + j);
                }
            }
        }
    }
}
```

Next we'll create the MapReduce program to make a Bloom filter using Hadoop. As we said earlier, each mapper will instantiate a `BloomFilter` object and add the key of each record in its split into its `BloomFilter` instance. (We're using the key of the record to follow our data joining example.) We'll create a union of the `BloomFilter`s by collecting them into a single reducer.

The driver for the MapReduce program is straightforward. Our mappers will output a key/value pair where the value is a `BloomFilter` instance.

```
job.setOutputValueClass(BloomFilter.class);
```

The output key will not matter in terms of partitioning because we only have a single reducer.

```
job.setNumReduceTasks(1);
```

We want our reducer to output the final `BloomFilter` as a binary file. Hadoop's `OutputFormat`s outputs either text files or assumes a key/value pair. Our reducer, therefore, won't use Hadoop's MapReduce output mechanism and instead we'll write the result out to a file ourselves.

```
job.setOutputFormat(NullOutputFormat.class);
```

> **WARNING** In general life gets a little more dangerous when you deviate from MapReduce's input/output framework and start working with your own files. Your tasks are no longer guaranteed to be idempotent and you'll need to understand how various failure scenarios can affect your tasks. For example, your files may only be partially written when some tasks are restarted. Our example here is safe(r) because all the file operations take place together only once in the `close()` method and in only one reducer. A more careful/paranoid implementation would check each individual file operation more closely.

Recall that our strategy for the mapper is to build a single Bloom filter on the entire split and output it *at the end of the split* to the reducer. Given that the `map()` method of the `Map-Class` has no state information about which record in the split it's processing, we should output the `BloomFilter` in the `close()` method to ensure that all the records in the split have been read. Although the `map()` method is passed an `OutputCollector` to collect the mapper's outputs, the `close()` method is not given one. The standard pattern in Hadoop to get around this situation is for `MapClass` itself to hold on to a reference to the `OutputCollector` when it's passed into `map()`. This `OutputCollector` is known to function even in the `close()` method. The `MapClass` looks like

```
public static class MapClass extends MapReduceBase
       implements Mapper<K1, V1, K2, V2> {

    OutputCollector<K2, V2> oc = null;

    public void map(K1 key, V1 value,
                    OutputCollector<K2,V2> output,
                    Reporter reporter) throws IOException {
        if (oc == null) oc = output;
        ...
    }

    public void close() throws IOException {
        oc.collect(k, v);
    }
}
```

The `BloomFilters` generated by all the mappers are sent to a single reducer. The `reduce()` method in the `Reduce` class will do a Bloom filter union of all of them.

```
while (values.hasNext()) {
    bf.union((BloomFilter<String>)values.next());
}
```

As we mentioned earlier, we want the final `BloomFilter` to be written out in a file of our own format rather than one of Hadoop's `OutputFormats`. We had already set the reducer's `OutputFormat` to `NullOutputFormat` in the driver to turn off that output mechanism. Now the `close()` method will have to handle the file output itself. It will have to know the output path as specified by the user, which can be found in the `mapred.output.dir` property of the `JobConf` object. But the `close()` is not given the job configuration object. We handle this oversight the same way we handled `Output-Collector` in the mapper. We keep a reference to the `JobConf` object in the `Reduce` class to be used by the `close()` method. The rest of the `close()` method will use Hadoop's file I/O to write out our `BloomFilter` in binary to a file in HDFS. The complete code is in listing 5.5.

Listing 5.5   A MapReduce program to create a Bloom filter

```
public class BloomFilterMR extends Configured implements Tool {

    public static class MapClass extends MapReduceBase
        implements Mapper<Text, Text, Text, BloomFilter<String>> {

        BloomFilter<String> bf = new BloomFilter<String>();
        OutputCollector<Text, BloomFilter<String>> oc = null;

        public void map(Text key, Text value,
                    OutputCollector<Text, BloomFilter<String>> output,
                    Reporter reporter) throws IOException {
```

```
            if (oc == null) oc = output;

            bf.add(key.toString());
        }

        public void close() throws IOException {
            oc.collect(new Text("testkey"), bf);
        }
    }

    public static class Reduce extends MapReduceBase
        implements Reducer<Text, BloomFilter<String>, Text, Text> {

        JobConf job = null;
        BloomFilter<String> bf = new BloomFilter<String>();

        public void configure(JobConf job) {
            this.job = job;
        }

        public void reduce(Text key, Iterator<BloomFilter<String>> values,
                           OutputCollector<Text, Text> output,
                           Reporter reporter) throws IOException {

            while (values.hasNext()) {
                bf.union((BloomFilter<String>)values.next());
            }
        }

        public void close() throws IOException {
            Path file = new Path(job.get("mapred.output.dir") +
                                "/bloomfilter");
            FSDataOutputStream out = file.getFileSystem(job).create(file);
            bf.write(out);
            out.close();
        }
    }

    public int run(String[] args) throws Exception {
        Configuration conf = getConf();
        JobConf job = new JobConf(conf, BloomFilterMR.class);

        Path in = new Path(args[0]);
        Path out = new Path(args[1]);
        FileInputFormat.setInputPaths(job, in);
        FileOutputFormat.setOutputPath(job, out);

        job.setJobName("Bloom Filter");
        job.setMapperClass(MapClass.class);
        job.setReducerClass(Reduce.class);
        job.setNumReduceTasks(1);

        job.setInputFormat(KeyValueTextInputFormat.class);
        job.setOutputFormat(NullOutputFormat.class);
        job.setOutputKeyClass(Text.class);
        job.setOutputValueClass(BloomFilter.class);
        job.set("key.value.separator.in.input.line", ",");

        JobClient.runJob(job);

        return 0;
    }
```

```
public static void main(String[] args) throws Exception {
    int res = ToolRunner.run(new Configuration(),
                             new BloomFilterMR(),
                             args);

    System.exit(res);
    }
}
```

5.3.3 Bloom filter in Hadoop version 0.20+

Hadoop version 0.20 has a Bloom filter class in it. It plays a support role to some of the new classes introduced in version 0.20, and it will likely stay around for future versions as well. It functions much like our `BloomFilter` class in listing 5.4, although it's much more rigorous in its implementation of the hashing functions. As a built-in class, it can be a good choice for semijoin within Hadoop. But it's not easy to separate this class from the Hadoop framework to use it as a standalone class. If you're building a Bloom filter for non-Hadoop applications, Hadoop's built-in `BloomFilter` may not be appropriate.

5.4 Exercising what you've learned

You can test your understanding of more advanced MapReduce techniques through these exercises:

1 *Anomaly detection*—Take a web server log file. Write a MapReduce program to aggregate the number of visits for each IP address. Write another MapReduce program to find the top *K* IP addresses in terms of visits. These frequent visitors may be legitimate ISP proxies (shared among many users) or they may be scrapers and fraudsters (if the server log is from an ad network). Chain these two MapReduce jobs together such that they can be easily run on a daily basis.

2 *Filter out records in input*—In both patent data sets we've used (`cite75_99.txt` and `apat63_99.txt`), the first row is metadata (column names). So far we've had to explicitly or implicitly filter out that row in our mappers, or interpret our results knowing that the metadata record has some deterministic influence. A more permanent solution is to remove the metadata row from the input data and keep track of it elsewhere. Another solution is to write a mapper as a preprocessor that filters all records that look like metadata. (For example, records that don't start with a numeric patent number.) Write such a mapper and use `ChainMapper/ChainReducer` to incorporate it into your MapReduce programs.

3 *Disjoint selection*—Using the same Customers and Orders example for the datajoin package, how will you change the code to output customers *not* in the Orders data source? Perhaps the Orders data only contains orders made within the last *N* months, and these customers haven't purchased anything in that time period.

A business may choose to re-engage these customers with discounts or other incentives.

4   *Calculating ratios*—Ratios are often a better unit of analysis than raw numbers. For example, say you have a data set of today's stock prices and another data set for stock prices from yesterday. You may be more interested in each stock's growth rate than its absolute price. Use the datajoin framework to write a program that takes two data sources and output the ratio.

5   *Product of a vector with a matrix*—Look up your favorite linear algebra text on the definition of matrix multiplication. Implement a MapReduce job to take the product of a vector and a matrix. You should use `DistributedCache` to hold the value of the vector. You may assume the matrix is in sparse representation.

6   *Spatial join*—Let's get more adventurous. Consider a two-dimensional space where both the x and y coordinates range from -1,000,000,000 to +1,000,000,000. You have one file with the location of *foos*, and another file with the location of *bars*. Each record in those files is a comma-separated (x,y) coordinate. For example, a couple lines may look like

145999.32455,888888880.001
834478899.2,5656.87660922

Write a MapReduce job to find all *foos* that are less than 1 unit distance from a *bar*. Distance is measured using the familiar Euclidean distance, $sqrt[(x1-x2)^2 + (y1-y2)^2]$. Although both *foos* and *bars* are relatively sparse in this 2D space, their respective files are too big to be stored in memory. You can't use `DistributedCache` for this spatial join.

Hint: The datajoin package as it's currently implemented doesn't work that well for this problem either, but you can solve it with your own mapper and reducer that have a similar data flow as the datajoin package.

Hint #2: In all the MapReduce programs we've discussed up till now, the keys are only extracted and passed around, whereas the values go through various computations. You should consider computing the key for the mapper's output.

7   *Spatial join, enhanced with Bloom filter*—After you've answered the last question, figure out how you can use a Bloom filter to speed up the join operation. Assume *bars* are much fewer in number than *foos*, but still too many to fit all their locations in memory.

5.5   *Summary*

We can often write the basic MapReduce programs as one job operating on one data set. We may need to write the more advanced programs as multiple jobs or we may operate them on multiple data sets. Hadoop has several different ways of coordinating multiple jobs together, including sequential chaining and executing them according to predefined dependencies. For the frequent case of chaining map-only jobs around a full MapReduce job, Hadoop has special classes to do it efficiently.

Joining is the canonical example for processing data from multiple data sources. Though Hadoop has a powerful datajoin package for doing arbitrary joins, its generality comes at the expense of efficiency. A couple other joining methods can provide faster joins by exploiting the relative asymmetry in data source sizes typical of most data joins. One of these methods leverages the Bloom filter, a data structure that's useful in many data processing tasks.

At this point, your knowledge of MapReduce programming should enable you to start writing your own programs. As all programmers know, programming is more than writing code. You have various techniques and processes—from development to deployment and testing and debugging. The nature of MapReduce programming and distributed computing adds complexity and nuance to these processes, which we'll cover in the next chapter.

5.6 *Further resources*

http://portal.acm.org/citation.cfm?doid=1247480.1247602—MapReduce's lack of simple support for joining datasets is well-known. Many of the tools to enhance Hadoop (such as Pig, Hive, and CloudBase) offer data joins as a first-class operation. For a more formal treatment, Hung-chih Yang and coauthors have published a paper "Map-reduce-merge: simplified relational data processing on large clusters" that proposes a modified form of MapReduce with an extra "merge" step that supports data joining natively.

http://umiacs.umd.edu/~jimmylin/publications/Lin_etal_TR2009.pdf—Section 5.2.2 describes the use of distributed cache to provide side data to tasks. The limitation of this technique is that the side data is replicated to every TaskTracker, and the side data must fit into memory. Jimmy Lin and colleagues explore the use of memcached, a distributed in-memory object caching system, to provide global access to side data. Their experience is summarized in the paper "Low-Latency, High-Throughput Access to Static Global Resources within the Hadoop Framework."

Programming Practices

This chapter covers

- Best practices unique to developing Hadoop programs
- Debugging programs in local, pseudo-distributed, and fully distributed modes
- Sanity checking and regression testing program outputs
- Logging and monitoring
- Performance tuning

Now that you've gone through various programming techniques in MapReduce, this chapter will step back and cover programming practices.

Programming on Hadoop differs from traditional programming mainly in two ways. First, Hadoop programs are primarily about processing data. Second, Hadoop programs are run over a distributed set of computers. These two differences will change some aspects of your development and debugging processes, which we cover in sections 6.1 and 6.2.

Performance tuning techniques tend to be specific to the programming platform, and Hadoop is no different. We cover tools and approaches to optimizing Hadoop programs in section 6.3.

Let's start with the development techniques applicable to Hadoop. Presumably you're already familiar with standard Java software engineering techniques. We focus on practices unique to data-centric programming within Hadoop.

6.1 Developing MapReduce programs

Chapter 2 discussed the three modes of Hadoop: local (standalone), pseudo-distributed, and fully distributed. They correspond roughly to development, staging, and production setups. Your development process will go through each of the three modes. You'll have to be able to switch between configurations easily. In practice you may even have more than one fully distributed cluster. Larger shops may, for example, have a "development" cluster to further harden MapReduce programs before running them on the real production cluster. You may have multiple clusters for different workloads. For example, there can be an in-house cluster for running many small- to medium-sized jobs and a cluster in the cloud that's more cost effective for running large, infrequent jobs.

Section 2.3 discussed how you can have different versions of the `hadoop-site.xml` configuration file for different setups, and you switch a symlink to point to the configuration you want to work with at the moment. You can also specify the exact configuration file you want at each Hadoop command with the `-conf` option. For example,

```
bin/hadoop fs -conf conf.cluster/hadoop-site.xml -lsr
```

will list all files in your fully distributed cluster, even though you may be currently working on a different mode or different cluster (assuming `conf.cluster/hadoop-site.xml` is where your fully distributed cluster's configuration file is).

Before you run and test your Hadoop program, you'll need to make data available for the configuration you're running. Section 3.1 describes various ways to get data into and out of HDFS. For local and pseudo-distributed modes, you'll only want a subset of your full data. Section 4.4 presents a Streaming program (`RandomSample.py`) that can randomly sample a percentage of records from a data set in HDFS. As it's a Python script, you can also use it to sample down a local file with a Unix pipe:

```
cat datafile | RandomSample.py 10
```

will give you a 10 percent sample of the file `datafile`.

Now that you have all the different configurations set up and know how to put data into each configuration, let's look at how to develop and debug in local and pseudo-distributed modes. The techniques build on top of each other as you get closer to the production environment. We defer the discussion of debugging on the fully distributed cluster 'till the next section.

6.1.1 Local mode

Hadoop in local mode runs everything within one single Java Virtual Machine (JVM) and uses the local filesystem (i.e., no HDFS). Running within one JVM allows you to use all the familiar Java development tools, such as a debugger. Using files from the local filesystem means you can quickly apply Unix commands or simple scripts on the input and output data. Examining files in HDFS, on the other hand, is limited to commands provided by the Hadoop command line. For example, to count how many records are in an output file, you can use `wc -l` if the file is in the local filesystem. If the file is in HDFS, then you'll either have to write a MapReduce program or download the file to local storage before applying the Unix commands. As you'll see, being able to access input and output files easily will be important to our development practices under local mode.

> **NOTE**   Local mode closely adheres to Hadoop's MapReduce programming model, but it doesn't support every feature. For example, it doesn't support distributed cache, and it only allows a maximum of one reducer.

A program running in local mode will output all log and error messages to the console. It will also summarize the amount of data processed at the end. For example, running our skeleton MapReduce job (`MyJob.java`) to invert the patent citation data, the output is quite verbose, and figure 6.1 is a snapshot in the middle of the job.

At the end of the job, Hadoop will print out the values of various internal counters. They're the number of records and bytes going through the different stages of MapReduce:

```
09/05/27 03:34:37 INFO mapred.TaskRunner: Task
⇒ attempt_local_0001_r_000000_0' done.
09/05/27 03:34:37 INFO mapred.TaskRunner: Saved output of task
⇒ attempt_local_0001_r_000000_0' to
⇒ file:/Users/chuck/Projects/Hadoop/hadoop-0.18.1/output/test
```

```
  ○ ○ ○                          Terminal — bash — 132x30
09/05/27 03:33:04 INFO mapred.MapTask: kvstart = 262144; kvend = 196607; length = 327680
09/05/27 03:33:05 INFO mapred.MapTask: Index: (0, 4716118, 4716118)
09/05/27 03:33:05 INFO mapred.MapTask: Finished spill 1
09/05/27 03:33:06 INFO mapred.MapTask: Spilling map output: buffer full = false and record full = true
09/05/27 03:33:06 INFO mapred.MapTask: bufstart = 8383919; bufend = 12575596; bufvoid = 99614720
09/05/27 03:33:06 INFO mapred.MapTask: kvstart = 196607; kvend = 131070; length = 327680
09/05/27 03:33:07 INFO mapred.MapTask: Index: (0, 4715965, 4715965)
09/05/27 03:33:07 INFO mapred.MapTask: Finished spill 2
09/05/27 03:33:07 INFO mapred.LocalJobRunner: file:/Users/chuck/Projects/Hadoop/hadoop-0.18.1/input/cite75_99.txt:234881024+29194407
09/05/27 03:33:07 INFO mapred.JobClient:  map 94% reduce 0%
09/05/27 03:33:07 INFO mapred.MapTask: Spilling map output: buffer full = false and record full = true
09/05/27 03:33:07 INFO mapred.MapTask: bufstart = 12575596; bufend = 16767227; bufvoid = 99614720
09/05/27 03:33:07 INFO mapred.MapTask: kvstart = 131070; kvend = 65533; length = 327680
09/05/27 03:33:09 INFO mapred.MapTask: Index: (0, 4715919, 4715919)
09/05/27 03:33:09 INFO mapred.MapTask: Finished spill 3
09/05/27 03:33:09 INFO mapred.MapTask: Spilling map output: buffer full = false and record full = true
09/05/27 03:33:09 INFO mapred.MapTask: bufstart = 16767227; bufend = 20958850; bufvoid = 99614720
09/05/27 03:33:09 INFO mapred.MapTask: kvstart = 65533; kvend = 327677; length = 327680
09/05/27 03:33:10 INFO mapred.LocalJobRunner: file:/Users/chuck/Projects/Hadoop/hadoop-0.18.1/input/cite75_99.txt:234881024+29194407
09/05/27 03:33:10 INFO mapred.JobClient:  map 96% reduce 0%
09/05/27 03:33:11 INFO mapred.MapTask: Index: (0, 4715913, 4715913)
09/05/27 03:33:11 INFO mapred.MapTask: Finished spill 4
09/05/27 03:33:11 INFO mapred.MapTask: Spilling map output: buffer full = false and record full = true
09/05/27 03:33:11 INFO mapred.MapTask: bufstart = 20958850; bufend = 25150768; bufvoid = 99614720
09/05/27 03:33:11 INFO mapred.MapTask: kvstart = 327677; kvend = 262140; length = 327680
09/05/27 03:33:13 INFO mapred.MapTask: Index: (0, 4716206, 4716206)
09/05/27 03:33:13 INFO mapred.MapTask: Finished spill 5
09/05/27 03:33:13 INFO mapred.MapTask: Starting flush of map output
09/05/27 03:33:13 INFO mapred.MapTask: bufstart = 25150768; bufend = 29194395; bufvoid = 99614720
09/05/27 03:33:13 INFO mapred.MapTask: kvstart = 262140; kvend = 187317; length = 327680
```

Figure 6.1   Running a Hadoop program in local mode outputs all the log messages to the console.

```
09/05/27 03:34:37 INFO mapred.LocalJobRunner: reduce > reduce
09/05/27 03:34:37 INFO mapred.JobClient: Job complete: job_local_0001
09/05/27 03:34:37 INFO mapred.JobClient: Counters: 11
09/05/27 03:34:37 INFO mapred.JobClient:     Map-Reduce Framework
09/05/27 03:34:37 INFO mapred.JobClient:       Map output records=16522439
09/05/27 03:34:37 INFO mapred.JobClient:       Reduce input records=33044878
09/05/27 03:34:37 INFO mapred.JobClient:       Map output bytes=264075431
09/05/27 03:34:37 INFO mapred.JobClient:       Map input records=16522439
09/05/27 03:34:37 INFO mapred.JobClient:       Combine output records=0
09/05/27 03:34:37 INFO mapred.JobClient:       Map input bytes=264075431
09/05/27 03:34:37 INFO mapred.JobClient:       Combine input records=0
09/05/27 03:34:37 INFO mapred.JobClient:       Reduce input groups=6517968
09/05/27 03:34:37 INFO mapred.JobClient:       Reduce output records=6517968
09/05/27 03:34:37 INFO mapred.JobClient:     File Systems
09/05/27 03:34:37 INFO mapred.JobClient:       Local bytes written=4246405780
09/05/27 03:34:37 INFO mapred.JobClient:       Local bytes read=4276658154
```

The input and output of the MapReduce job are both in the local filesystem. We can examine them using standard Unix commands such as `wc -l` or `head`. As we are deliberately using smaller data sets during development, we can even load them into a text editor or a spreadsheet. We can use the many features of those applications to sanity check the correctness of our program.

SANITY CHECKING

Most MapReduce programs involve at least some counting or arithmetic, and bugs (especially typos) in mathematical programming don't call attention to themselves in the form of thrown exceptions or threatening error messages. Your math can be wrong even though your program is technically "correct," and everything will run smoothly, but the end result will be useless. There's no simple way to uncover arithmetic mistakes, but some sanity checking will go a long way. At a high level you can look at the overall count, maximum, average, and so on, of various metrics and see if they match expectation. At a low level you can pick a particular output record and verify that it was produced correctly. For example, when we created the inverted citation graph, the first few lines were

```
"CITED"  "CITING"
1        3964859,4647229
10000    4539112
100000   5031388
1000006  4714284
1000007  4766693
1000011  5033339
1000017  3908629
1000026  4043055
1000033  4190903,4975983
```

Our job concludes that patent number 1 is cited twice, by 3964859 and 4647229. We can verify this claim by `grep`ping over the sampled input data to look for records where patent number 1 is cited.

```
grep ",1$" input/cite75_99.txt
```

We indeed get the two records as expected. You can verify a few more records to gain confidence in the correctness of your program's math and logic.[1]

An eyesore about the output of this inverted citation graph is that the first line is not real data.

```
"CITED" "CITING"
```

It's an artifact from the first line of the input data being used as data definition. Let's add some code to our mapper to filter out non-numeric keys and values, and in the process demonstrate regression testing.

REGRESSION TESTING

Our data-centric approach to regression testing revolves around "diff'ing" various output files from before and after code changes. For our particular change, we should only be taking out one line from the job's output. To verify that this indeed is the case, let's first save the output of our current job. In local mode, we have a maximum of only one reducer, so the job's output is only one file, which we call `job_1_output`.

For regression testing, it's also useful to save the output of the map phase. This will help us isolate bugs to either the map phase or the reduce phase. We can save the output of the map phase by running the MapReduce job with zero reducers. We can do this easily using the `-D mapred.reduce.tasks=0` option. In this mapper-only job, there will be multiple files as each map task will write its output to its own file. Let's copy all of them into a directory called `job_1_intermediate`.

Having stored away the output files, we can make the desired code changes to the `map()` method in `MapClass`. The code itself is trivial. We focus on testing it.

```
public void map(Text key, Text value,
                OutputCollector<Text, Text> output,
                Reporter reporter) throws IOException {

    try
    {
        if (Integer.parseInt(key.toString()) > 0 &&
            Integer.parseInt(value.toString()) > 0)
        {
            output.collect(value, key);
        }
    } catch (NumberFormatException e) { }
}
```

Compile and execute the new code against the same input data. Let's run it as a map-only job first and compare the intermediate data. As we've only changed the mapper, any bug should first manifest in differences in the intermediate data.

```
diff output/job_1_intermediate/ output/test/
```

---

[1] In this case, you may suspect whether patent number 1 is *really* cited by those two patents. The number 1 feels wrong, an outlier in the range of patent numbers being cited. There can be mistakes in the original input data. We have to track down the patents themselves if we want to verify this. In any case, ensuring data quality is an important topic but is beyond our discussion of Hadoop.

We get the following output from the diff utility:

```
Binary files output/job_1_intermediate/.part-00000.crc and
➥ output/test/.part-00000.crc differ
diff output/job_1_intermediate/part-00000 output/test/part-00000
1d0
< "CITED"        "CITING"
```

We found differences in the binary file `.part-00000.crc`. This is an internal file for HDFS to keep checksums for the file `part-00000`. A difference in checksum means that `part-00000` has changed, and diff prints out the exact differences later. The new intermediate file, under `output/test`, is missing the quoted field descriptors. More importantly, we find no other changes. So far so good. If we run the whole job with one reducer, we expect the final output to differ by one line too.

Well, it turns out not to be the case. If you run the whole job with one reducer and compare the final output with `job_1_output` from the original run, you'll find many differences. What do you think happened? Let's look at the first few lines of the diff to find out.

```
$ diff output/job_1_output output/test/part-00000 | head -n 15
1,2c1
< "CITED"        "CITING"
< 1      3964859,4647229
---
> 1      4647229,3964859
19c18
< 1000067        5312208,4944640,5071294
---
> 1000067        4944640,5071294,5312208
22,23c21,22
< 1000076        4867716,5845593
< 1000083        5566726,5322091
---
> 1000076        5845593,4867716
> 1000083        5322091,5566726
```

We see that the line with the field descriptors ("CITED" and "CITING") are taken out as expected. As to the rest of the differences, there's a definite pattern.

In our `reduce()` method, we have concatenated the list of values for each key in the order Hadoop has given them to us. Hadoop doesn't provide any guarantee as to the order of those values. We see that taking out one line in the intermediate data impacts the order of the values for many keys at the reducer. As we know that this job's correctness is invariant to the ordering, we can ignore the differences. Regression testing is inherently conservative and tends to set off false alarms. You should use it with that in mind.

We have advocated the use of a sampled data set for development, because it is more representative of the structure and properties of the data set we use in production. We have used the same sampled data set for regression testing, but you can also manually construct a separate input data set with edge cases that are atypical of the production data. For example, you may put in empty values or extra tab characters or other unusual records in this constructed data set. This test data set is for ensuring that your program continues to handle the edge cases even as it evolves. This test data set doesn't need to have more than several dozen records. You can visually inspect the entire output to see if your program still functions as expected.

CONSIDER USING LONG INSTEAD OF INT

Most Java programmers instinctively default to the `int` type (or `Integer` or `IntWritable`) to represent integer values. In Java the `int` type can hold any integer between 2^{31}-1 and -2^{31}, or between 2,147,483,647 and -2,147,483,648. This is adequate for most applications. Rarely do programmers put too much thought into it. When you're processing Hadoop-scale data, it's not unusual for some counter variables to need a bigger range. You won't see this requirement under your development data set, which by design is small. It may not even matter to your current production data, but as your business operation grows, your data set will get bigger. It may get to a point where some variables will outgrow the `int` range and cause arithmetic errors. Take the canonical word counting example. When processing millions of documents, you won't have any word count that goes beyond 2 billion,[2] and an `int` is adequate. But as you grow to process tens of millions or hundreds of millions of documents, counting frequent words like *the* can cross the limit of an `int` type. Rather than wait for this kind of bug to creep up on you in production, which is much harder to debug and costlier to fix, now is the time you should go through your code and carefully consider whether your numeric variables should be `long` or `LongWritable` to handle future scale.[3]

6.1.2 *Pseudo-distributed mode*

Local mode has none of the *distributed* characteristics of a production Hadoop cluster. We may not see many bugs when running in local mode. Hadoop provides a pseudo-distributed mode that has all the functionality and "nodes" of a production cluster—Name Node, SecondaryNameNode, DataNode, JobTracker, and TaskTracker, each running on a separate JVM. All the software components are distributed, and pseudo-distributed mode differs from a production cluster at only the system-and-hardware level. It uses only one physical machine—your own local computer. We should make sure our jobs can run in pseudo-distributed mode before deploying them to a full production cluster.

Chapter 2 describes the configuration and commands to start pseudo-distributed mode. You'll start all the daemons on your computer to make it function like a cluster. You interface with it as if it is a distinct Hadoop cluster. You put data into its own HDFS filesystem. You submit your jobs to it for running rather than run them in the same user space. Most importantly, you now monitor it "remotely" through log files and the web interface. You'll use the same tools later to monitor a production cluster.

---

[2] This is not absolutely true and will depend on your documents' size and content.
[3] The problem of exceeding a numeric range is not unique to Hadoop. You'll remember the famous Y2K problem where older programs only allocated two digits to represent year. More recently, almost all web operations that have experienced explosive growth (such as Facebook, Twitter, and RockYou) have had to retool their systems to handle a bigger range of user IDs or document IDs than they originally expected.

LOGGING

Let's run in the pseudo-distributed cluster the same job we had in local mode. You put the input file into HDFS using the `hadoop fs` command. Submit the job for running using the same `hadoop jar` command as in local mode.

The first thing you'll notice is that you no longer have the torrent of messages on your console. You only get a measure of progress in the map phase and reduce phase, and the same summary of counters at the end as in local mode. You can see this in figure 6.2.

```
○ ○ ○                    Terminal — bash — 124x59
09/05/29 04:47:38 INFO mapred.JobClient:  map 36% reduce 0%
09/05/29 04:47:43 INFO mapred.JobClient:  map 44% reduce 0%
09/05/29 04:47:48 INFO mapred.JobClient:  map 50% reduce 0%
09/05/29 04:48:16 INFO mapred.JobClient:  map 61% reduce 0%
09/05/29 04:48:21 INFO mapred.JobClient:  map 63% reduce 0%
09/05/29 04:48:26 INFO mapred.JobClient:  map 70% reduce 16%
09/05/29 04:48:31 INFO mapred.JobClient:  map 77% reduce 16%
09/05/29 04:48:36 INFO mapred.JobClient:  map 82% reduce 16%
09/05/29 04:48:41 INFO mapred.JobClient:  map 89% reduce 16%
09/05/29 04:48:46 INFO mapred.JobClient:  map 95% reduce 16%
09/05/29 04:48:50 INFO mapred.JobClient:  map 98% reduce 16%
09/05/29 04:48:55 INFO mapred.JobClient:  map 100% reduce 16%
09/05/29 04:49:20 INFO mapred.JobClient:  map 100% reduce 25%
09/05/29 04:49:23 INFO mapred.JobClient:  map 100% reduce 67%
09/05/29 04:49:25 INFO mapred.JobClient:  map 100% reduce 68%
09/05/29 04:49:29 INFO mapred.JobClient:  map 100% reduce 69%
09/05/29 04:49:34 INFO mapred.JobClient:  map 100% reduce 71%
09/05/29 04:49:36 INFO mapred.JobClient:  map 100% reduce 72%
09/05/29 04:49:39 INFO mapred.JobClient:  map 100% reduce 73%
09/05/29 04:49:41 INFO mapred.JobClient:  map 100% reduce 74%
09/05/29 04:49:44 INFO mapred.JobClient:  map 100% reduce 75%
09/05/29 04:49:49 INFO mapred.JobClient:  map 100% reduce 76%
09/05/29 04:49:51 INFO mapred.JobClient:  map 100% reduce 78%
09/05/29 04:49:54 INFO mapred.JobClient:  map 100% reduce 79%
09/05/29 04:49:56 INFO mapred.JobClient:  map 100% reduce 80%
09/05/29 04:49:59 INFO mapred.JobClient:  map 100% reduce 81%
09/05/29 04:50:04 INFO mapred.JobClient:  map 100% reduce 83%
09/05/29 04:50:06 INFO mapred.JobClient:  map 100% reduce 84%
09/05/29 04:50:09 INFO mapred.JobClient:  map 100% reduce 85%
09/05/29 04:50:11 INFO mapred.JobClient:  map 100% reduce 86%
09/05/29 04:50:14 INFO mapred.JobClient:  map 100% reduce 87%
09/05/29 04:50:19 INFO mapred.JobClient:  map 100% reduce 88%
09/05/29 04:50:21 INFO mapred.JobClient:  map 100% reduce 89%
09/05/29 04:50:24 INFO mapred.JobClient:  map 100% reduce 91%
09/05/29 04:50:26 INFO mapred.JobClient:  map 100% reduce 92%
09/05/29 04:50:29 INFO mapred.JobClient:  map 100% reduce 93%
09/05/29 04:50:34 INFO mapred.JobClient:  map 100% reduce 94%
09/05/29 04:50:35 INFO mapred.JobClient: Job complete: job_200905290339_0001
09/05/29 04:50:35 INFO mapred.JobClient: Counters: 16
09/05/29 04:50:35 INFO mapred.JobClient:   Job Counters
09/05/29 04:50:35 INFO mapred.JobClient:     Data-local map tasks=4
09/05/29 04:50:35 INFO mapred.JobClient:     Launched reduce tasks=1
09/05/29 04:50:35 INFO mapred.JobClient:     Launched map tasks=4
09/05/29 04:50:35 INFO mapred.JobClient:   Map-Reduce Framework
09/05/29 04:50:35 INFO mapred.JobClient:     Map output records=16522438
09/05/29 04:50:35 INFO mapred.JobClient:     Reduce input records=16522438
09/05/29 04:50:35 INFO mapred.JobClient:     Map output bytes=264075414
09/05/29 04:50:35 INFO mapred.JobClient:     Map input records=16522439
09/05/29 04:50:35 INFO mapred.JobClient:     Combine output records=0
09/05/29 04:50:35 INFO mapred.JobClient:     Map input bytes=264075431
09/05/29 04:50:35 INFO mapred.JobClient:     Combine input records=0
09/05/29 04:50:35 INFO mapred.JobClient:     Reduce input groups=3258983
09/05/29 04:50:35 INFO mapred.JobClient:     Reduce output records=3258983
09/05/29 04:50:35 INFO mapred.JobClient:   File Systems
09/05/29 04:50:35 INFO mapred.JobClient:     HDFS bytes written=158078522
09/05/29 04:50:35 INFO mapred.JobClient:     Local bytes written=1040839754
09/05/29 04:50:35 INFO mapred.JobClient:     HDFS bytes read=264087722
09/05/29 04:50:35 INFO mapred.JobClient:     Local bytes read=735943048
chuck-lams-computer:~/Projects/Hadoop/hadoop-0.18.1 chuck$ []
```

Figure 6.2 In pseudo-distributed mode, the console only outputs a job's progress and its counters at the end.

Hadoop hasn't stopped outputting debugging messages. In fact, it's outputting much more now. These messages don't go to the console screen. Instead, they're saved into log files.

You can find the log files under the /logs directory. Different services (NameNode, JobTracker, etc.) create separate log files. The filename should distinguish the service logging a file. Hadoop rotates log files daily. The most recent one ends in .log. It further appends the older ones with their date. Under the default setting, Hadoop doesn't delete old log files automatically. You should proactively archive and delete them to make sure they're not taking up too much space.

Log files for the NameNode, SecondaryNameNode, DataNode, and JobTracker are used for debugging the respective services. They're not too important in pseudo-distributed mode. In production clusters, you as a system administrator can look at them to debug problems in those corresponding nodes. As a programmer, you are always interested in the TaskTracker log though, as it records exceptions thrown.

Your MapReduce program can output to STDOUT and STDERR (System.out and System.err in Java) its own logging messages. Hadoop records those under files named stdout and stderr, respectively. There will be a distinct file for each task attempt. (A task can have more than one attempt if the first one fails.) These user log files are under the /logs/userlogs subdirectory.

Besides logging to STDOUT and STDERR, your program can also send out live status messages using the setStatus() method on the Reporter object being passed to the map() and reduce() methods. (For Streaming programs, the status information is updated by sending a string of the form reporter:status:*message* to STDERR.) This is useful for long-running jobs where you can monitor them as they run. The status message is shown on the JobTracker Web UI, to be described next.

JOBTRACKER WEB UI

By definition events occur in many different places in a distributed program. This makes monitoring more difficult. The system becomes more like a black box, and we need specialized monitoring tools to peek into the various states within it. The Job-Tracker provides a web interface for tracking the progress and various states of your jobs. Under the default configuration, you can set your browser to

```
http://localhost:50030/jobtracker.jsp
```

to view the starting page of the administration tool for your pseudo-distributed cluster.[4] It shows a summary of the Hadoop cluster, as well as lists of jobs that are running, completed, and failed. See figure 6.3.

Hadoop tracks jobs internally by their job ID. A job ID is a string prefixed with job_, followed by the cluster ID (which is a timestamp of when the cluster was started), followed by an auto-incremented job number. The web UI lists each job with the user name and job name. In pseudo-distributed mode, it's relatively easy to identify the job

---

[4] In fully distributed mode, replace "localhost" with the domain of the JobTracker master.

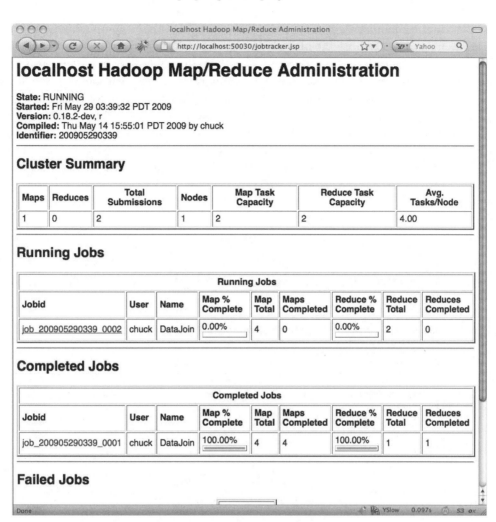

Figure 6.3 The JobTracker Web UI main page

you're currently working with, as you'll run one job at a time. When you get to a multi-user production environment, you'll have to narrow down your jobs by looking for your Hadoop user name and the name of your current job. The name of your job is set using the setJobName() method in the JobConf object. The name for a Streaming job is set through a configuration property shown in table 6.1.

Table 6.1 Configuration property for setting a job's name

Property	Description
mapred.job.name	String property denoting the name of a job

In the administration page, you can see each job with the completion percentage of its map phase. It shows the number of map tasks for the job and the number of completed ones. You can see the same metrics for the reduce side. This gives you a rough summary of your job's progress. To drill down more on a particular job, you can click on the job ID, which is a link that'll take you to the job's administration page. See figure 6.4.

The job page shows the volume of various input/output due to the running of the job. The page refreshes itself periodically but you can also refresh the page manually to get the updated numbers. You can start exploring the various aspects of your job from the many links on this page. For example, clicking on the *map* link will take you to a list of all map tasks for the job. See figure 6.5.

Hadoop job_200905290339_0002 on localhost

http://localhost:50030/jobdetails.jsp?jobid=jo   Yahoo

Hadoop job_200905290339_0002 on localhost

User: chuck
Job Name: DataJoin
Job File: hdfs://localhost:9000/tmp/hadoop-chuck/mapred/system/job_200905290339_0002/job.xml
Status: Running
Started at: Fri May 29 06:19:54 PDT 2009
Running for: 1mins, 58sec

Kind	% Complete	Num Tasks	Pending	Running	Complete	Killed	Failed/Killed Task Attempts
map	100.00%	4	0	2	2	0	0 / 0
reduce	0.00%	2	0	2	0	0	0 / 0

	Counter	Map	Reduce	Total
Job Counters	Data-local map tasks	0	0	4
	Launched reduce tasks	0	0	2
	Launched map tasks	0	0	4
Map-Reduce Framework	Map output records	8,400,584	0	8,400,584
	Map output bytes	134,217,712	0	134,217,712
	Combine output records	0	0	0
	Map input records	8,400,585	0	8,400,585
	Combine input records	0	0	0
	Map input bytes	134,217,729	0	134,217,729
File Systems	Local bytes written	380,381,217	0	380,381,217
	HDFS bytes read	134,225,921	0	134,225,921
	Local bytes read	226,849,189	0	226,849,189

Done   YSlow   0.373s   S3 ox

Figure 6.4   The JobTracker's administration page for a single job

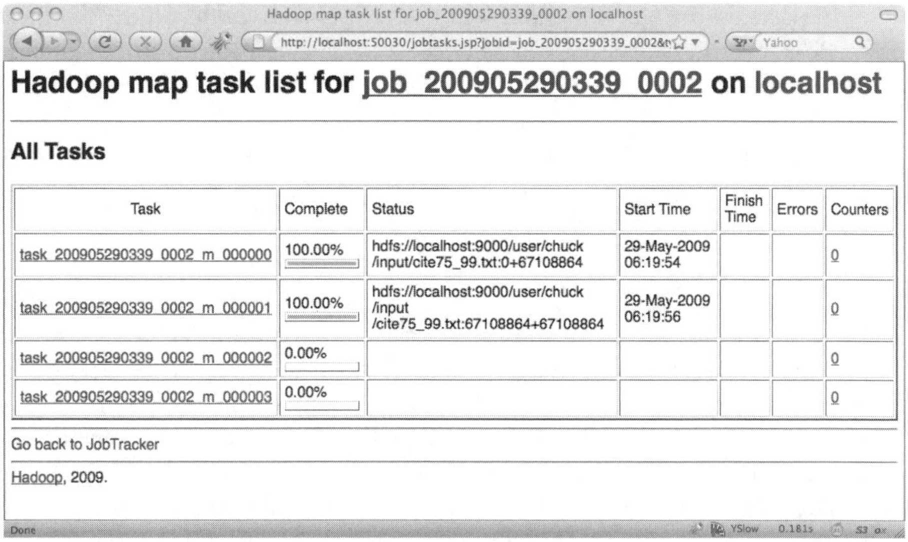

Figure 6.5   List of tasks in the TaskTracker Web UI. This figure shows all the map tasks for a single job. Each task can update its own status message.

Tasks are identified by a task ID. To construct the task ID, you start with the job ID the task runs under but replace the `job_` prefix with `task_`. You then append it with `_m` for a map task or `_r` for a reduce task. You further append it with an auto-incremented number within each group. In the TaskTracker Web UI, you'll see each task with its status, which you can programmatically set through the `setStatus()` method described earlier.

Clicking on a task ID will bring you to a page that further describes different *attempts* of a task. Hadoop makes several retry attempts at a failed task before failing the entire job.

The JobTracker and TaskTracker UIs provide many other links and metrics. Most should be self-explanatory.

KILLING JOBS

Unfortunately, sometimes a job goes awry after you've started it but it doesn't actually fail. It may take a long time to run or may even be stuck in an infinite loop. In (pseudo-) distributed mode you can manually kill a job using the command

```
bin/hadoop job -kill job_id
```

where *job_id* is the job's ID as given in JobTracker's Web UI.

6.2   *Monitoring and debugging on a production cluster*

After successfully running your job in a pseudo-distributed cluster, you're ready to run it on a production cluster using real data. We can apply all the techniques we've used for development and debugging on the production cluster, although the exact usage may be slightly different. Your cluster should still have a JobTracker Web UI, but the domain is no longer `localhost`. It's now the address of the cluster's JobTracker. The port number will still be 50030 unless it's been configured differently.

In pseudo-distributed mode, when there's only one node, all the log files are in a single `/logs` directory that you can access locally. In a fully distributed cluster, each node has its own `/logs` directory to keep its log files. You can diagnose problems on a node through the log files of that particular node.

In addition to the development and testing techniques we've mentioned so far, you also have monitoring and debugging techniques that are more useful in a production cluster on real data, which we explore in this section.

6.2.1 *Counters*

You can instrument your Hadoop job with *counters* to profile its overall operation. Your program defines various counters and increments their counts in response to specific events. Hadoop automatically sums the same counter from all tasks (of the same job) so that it reflects the profile of the overall job. It displays the value of your counters in the JobTracker's Web UI along with Hadoop's internal counters.

The canonical application of counters is for tracking different input record types, particularly for tracking "bad" records. Recall from section 4.4 our example for finding the average number of claims for patents from each country. We know the number of claims is not available for many records. Our program skips over those records, and it's useful to know the number of records we're skipping. Beyond satisfying our curiosity, such instrumentation allows us to understand the program's operation and do some "reality checks" for its correctness.

We use counters through the `Reporter.incrCounter()` method. The `Reporter` object is passed to the `map()` and `reduce()` methods. You call `incrCounter()` with the name of the counter and the amount to increment. You use uniquely named counters for each different event. When you call `incrCounter()` with a new counter name, that counter is initialized and takes on the increment value.

The `Reporter.incrCounter()` method has two signatures, depending on how you want to specify a counter's name:

```
public void incrCounter(String group, String counter, long amount)
public void incrCounter(Enum key, long amount)
```

The first form is more general in that it allows you to specify the counter name with dynamic strings at run time. The combination of two strings, `group` and `counter`, uniquely defines a counter. When counters are reported (in the Web UI or as text at the end of a job run), counters of the same group are reported together.

The second form uses a Java `enum` to specify counter names, which forces you to have them defined at compile time, but it also allows for type checking. The `enum`'s name is used as the group string, whereas the `enum`'s field is used as the counter string.

Listing 6.1 is the `MapClass` from listing 4.12 rewritten with counters to track the number of missing values and "quoted" values. (Only the first row of column description should be a "quoted" value.) An `enum` called `ClaimsCounters` is defined with values MISSING and QUOTED. Logic in the code increments the counters to reflect the record it's processing.

Listing 6.1 A `MapClass` with `Counters` to count the number of missing values

```
public static class MapClass extends MapReduceBase
    implements Mapper<LongWritable, Text, Text, Text> {

    static enum ClaimsCounters { MISSING, QUOTED };

    public void map(LongWritable key, Text value,
                    OutputCollector<Text, Text> output,
                    Reporter reporter) throws IOException {
        String fields[] = value.toString().split(",", -20);
        String country = fields[4];
        String numClaims = fields[8];

        if (numClaims.length() == 0) {
            reporter.incrCounter(ClaimsCounters.MISSING, 1);
        } else if (numClaims.startsWith("\"")) {
            reporter.incrCounter(ClaimsCounters.QUOTED, 1);
        } else {
            output.collect(new Text(country), new Text(numClaims + ",1"));
        }
    }
}
```

After running the program, we can see the defined counters along with Hadoop's internal counters in the JobTracker's Web UI. See figure 6.6.

	Counter	Map	Reduce	Total
Job Counters	Data-local map tasks	0	0	4
	Launched reduce tasks	0	0	2
	Launched map tasks	0	0	4
Map-Reduce Framework	Reduce input records	0	151	151
	Map output records	1,984,055	0	1,984,055
	Map output bytes	18,862,764	0	18,862,764
	Combine output records	1,063	151	1,214
	Map input records	2,923,923	0	2,923,923
	Reduce input groups	0	151	151
	Combine input records	1,984,625	493	1,985,118
	Map input bytes	236,903,179	0	236,903,179
	Reduce output records	0	151	151
File Systems	HDFS bytes written	0	2,658	2,658
	Local bytes written	20,554	2,510	23,064
	HDFS bytes read	236,915,470	0	236,915,470
	Local bytes read	21,112	2,510	23,622
AveragingWithCombiner$MapClass$ClaimsCounters	QUOTED	1	0	1
	MISSING	939,867	0	939,867

Figure 6.6 JobTracker's Web UI collects and shows the counter information.

We see that the enum's fully qualified Java name (with $ to separate out the inner class hierarchy) is used as the group name. The fields MISSING and QUOTED are used to define separate counters. As expected, it increments the QUOTED counter only once and the MISSING counter 939,867 times. Does the data set have that many rows with missing claim counts? The originator of the data set stated that claim counts are missing for patents granted before 1975. Merely eyeballing figure 4.3, we guess that about a third of all the patents in our data set are granted before 1975. Looking at the map input records count (from figure 6.6) we see there's a total of 2.9M+ records. The numbers seem consistent and we can feel more confident about the correctness of the processing.

A Streaming process can also use counters. It needs to send a specially formatted line to STDERR in the form of

```
reporter:counter:group,counter,amount
```

where *group*, *counter*, and *amount* are the corresponding arguments one would've passed to incrCounter() in Java. For example, in Python one can increment the ClaimsCounters. MISSING counter with

```
sys.stderr.write("reporter:counter:ClaimsCounters,MISSING,1\n")
```

Be sure to include the newline character ("\n") at the end. Hadoop Streaming will not properly interpret the string without that.

6.2.2 *Skipping bad records*

When dealing with large data sets, it is inevitable that some records will have errors. It's not unusual to focus several iterations of your development cycle on making the program robust to unexpected data.[5] Your program may never be completely foolproof, though. Your program will process new data, and new data will think of new ways to misbehave. You may even be using a parser that depends on third-party libraries you have no control over. While you should make your program as robust as possible to malformed records, you should also have a recovery mechanism to handle the cases you couldn't plan for. You don't want your whole job to fail only because it fails to handle one bad record.

Hadoop's mechanism for recovering from hardware failures doesn't work for recovering from deterministic software failures caused by bad records. Instead it provides a feature for skipping over records that it believes to be crashing a task. If this skipping feature is on, a task will enter into skipping mode after the task has been retried several times. Once in skipping mode, the TaskTracker will track and determine which record range is causing failure. The TaskTracker will then restart the task but skip over the bad record range.

---

[5] Unexpected data are not always mistakes. Someone once told me he had a program that was crashing in processing users' geographical information. Further digging revealed that one user was from a real city named Null.

CONFIGURING RECORD SKIPPING IN JAVA

The skipping feature is available starting with version 0.19, but it's disabled by default. In Java, the feature is controlled through the class `SkipBadRecords`, which consists entirely of static methods. The job driver needs to call one or both methods:

```
public static void setMapperMaxSkipRecords(Configuration conf,
        long maxSkipRecs)
public static void setReducerMaxSkipGroups(Configuration conf,
        long maxSkipGrps)
```

to turn on record skipping for map tasks and reduce tasks, respectively. The driver calls the methods with the configuration object and the maximum number of records in a skip range. If the maximum skip range size is set to 0 (default), then record skipping is disabled. Hadoop finds the skip range using a divide-and-conquer approach. It executes the task with the skip range halved each time, and determines the half with the bad record(s). The process iterates until the skip range is within the acceptable size. This is a rather expensive operation, particularly if the maximum skip range size is small. You may need to increase the maximum number of task attempts in Hadoop's normal task recovery mechanism to accommodate the extra attempts. You can do this using the methods `JobConf.setMaxMapAttempts()` and `JobConf.setMaxReduceAttempts()`, or set the equivalent properties `mapred.map.max.attempts` and `mapred.reduce.max.attempts`.

If skipping is enabled, Hadoop enters skipping mode after the task has failed twice. You can set the number of task failures needed to trigger skipping mode in `SkipBadRecords`'s `setAttemptsToStartSkipping()` method:

```
public static void setAttemptsToStartSkipping(Configuration conf,
        int attemptsToStartSkipping)
```

Hadoop will log skipped records to HDFS for later analysis. They're written as sequence files in the `_log/skip` directory. We cover sequence files in more detail in section 6.3.3. For now you can think of it as a Hadoop-specific compressed format. It can be uncompressed and read using the command:

```
bin/hadoop fs -text <filepath>
```

You can change the log directory for skipped records from `_log/skip` using the method `SkipBadRecords.setSkipOutputPath(JobConf conf, Path path)`. If `path` is set to null or to a `Path` with a string value of `"none"`, Hadoop will not record the skipped records.

CONFIGURING RECORD SKIPPING OUTSIDE OF JAVA

Although you can set the record-skipping feature in Java by calling methods in `Skip-BadRecords` in your driver, sometimes you may want to set this feature using the generic options available in `GenericOptionsParser` instead. This is because the person running the program can have a better idea about the range of bad records to expect and set the parameters more appropriately than the original developer. Furthermore, Streaming programs can't access `SkipBadRecords`; the record skipping features must

Table 6.2 Equivalent `JobConf` properties to method calls in `SkipBadRecords`

SkipBadRecords method	JobConf property
setAttemptsToStartSkipping()	mapred.skip.attempts.to.start. skipping
setMapperMaxSkipRecords()	mapred.skip.map.max.skip.records
setReducerMaxSkipGroups()	mapred.skip.reduce.max.skip.groups
setSkipOutputPath()	mapred.skip.out.dir
setAutoIncrMapperProcCount()	mapred.skip.map.auto.incr.proc.count
setAutoIncrReducerProcCount()	mapred.skip.reduce.auto.incr.proc. count

be configured using Streaming's `-D` property (`-jobconf` in version 0.18). Table 6.2 shows the `JobConf` properties being set by the `SkipBadRecords` method calls.

We haven't explained the last two properties yet. Their default values are fine for most Java programs but we need to change them for Streaming ones.

In determining the record range to skip, Hadoop needs an accurate count of the number of records a task has processed. Hadoop uses an internal counter and by default it's incremented after each call to the map (reduce) function. For Java programs this is a good approach to track the number of records processed. It can break down in some cases, such as programs that process records asynchronously (say, by spawning threads) or buffer them to process in chunks, but it usually works. In Streaming programs, this default behavior wouldn't work at all because there's no equivalent of the map (reduce) function that gets called to process each record. In those situations you have to disable the default behavior by setting the Boolean properties to false, and your task has to update the record counters itself.

In Python, the map task can update the counter with

```
sys.stderr.write(
    ➡ "reporter:counter:SkippingTaskCounters,MapProcessedRecords,1\n")
```

and the reduce task can use

```
sys.stderr.write(
    ➡ "reporter:counter:SkippingTaskCounters,ReduceProcessedGroups,1\n")
```

Java programs that cannot depend on the default record counting should use

```
reporter.incrCounter(SkipBadRecords.COUNTER_GROUP,
    SkipBadRecords.COUNTER_MAP_PROCESSED_RECORDS, 1);
```

and

```
reporter.incrCounter(SkipBadRecords.COUNTER_GROUP,
    SkipBadRecords.COUNTER_REDUCE_PROCESSED_GROUPS, 1);
```

when it has processed a key/value pair in its `Mapper` and `Reducer`, respectively.

6.2.3 *Rerunning failed tasks with IsolationRunner*

Debugging through log files is about reconstructing events using generic historical records. Sometimes there's not enough information in the logs to trace back the cause of failure. Hadoop has an IsolationRunner utility that functions like a time machine for debugging. This utility can isolate and rerun the failed task with the exact same input on the same node. You can attach a debugger to monitor the task as it runs and focus on gathering evidence specific to the failure.

To use the IsolationRunner feature, you must run your job with the configuration property keep.failed.tasks.files set to true. This tells every TaskTracker to keep all the data necessary to rerun the failed tasks.

When a job fails, you use the JobTracker Web UI to locate the node, the job ID, and the task attempt ID of the failed task. You log into the node where the task failed and go to the work directory under the directory for the task attempt. Go to

```
local_dir/taskTracker/jobcache/job_id/attempt_id/work
```

where *job_id* and *attempt_id* are the job ID and task attempt ID of the failed task. (The job ID should start with "job_" and the task attempt ID should start with "attempt_".) The root directory *local_dir* is what is set in the configuration property mapred.local.dir. Note that Hadoop allows a node to use multiple local directories (by setting mapred.local.dir to a comma-separated list of directories) to spread out disk I/O among multiple drives. If the node is configured that way, you'll have to look in all the local directories to find the one with the right *attempt_id* subdirectory.

Within the work directory you can execute IsolationRunner to rerun the failed task with the same input that it had before. In the rerun, we want the JVM to be enabled for remote debugging. As we're not running the JVM directly but through the bin/hadoop script, we specify the JVM debugging options through HADOOP_OPTS:

```
export HADOOP_OPTS="-agentlib:jdwp=transport=dt_socket,
            server=y,address=8000"
```

It tells the JVM to listen for the debugger at port 8000 and to wait for the debugger getting attached before running any code.[6] We now use IsolationRunner to rerun the task:

```
bin/hadoop org.apache.hadoop.mapred.IsolationRunner ../job.xml
```

The job.xml file contains all the configuration information IsolationRunner needs. Given our specification, the JVM will wait for a debugger's attachment before executing the task. You can attach to the JVM any Java debugger that supports the Java Debug Wire Protocol (JDWP). All the major Java IDEs do so. For example, if you're using jdb, you can attach it to the JVM via

```
jdb -attach 8000
```

---

[6] Options to configure the Sun JVM for debugging are further explained in Sun's documentation: http://java.sun.com/javase/6/docs/technotes/guides/jpda/conninv.html#Invocation.

(Of course, this is only an example. I hope you're using something better than jdb!) Consult your IDE's documentation for how to connect its debugger to a JVM.

6.3   *Tuning for performance*

After you have developed your MapReduce program and fully debugged it, you may want to start tuning it for performance. Before doing any optimization, note that one of the main attractions of Hadoop is its linear scalability. You can speed up many jobs by adding more machines. This makes economic sense when you have a small cluster. Consider the value of time it takes to optimize your program to gain a 10 percent improvement. For a 10-node cluster, you can get the same 10 percent performance gain by adding one machine (and this gain applies to *all* jobs on that cluster). The cost of your development time may well be higher than the cost of the additional computer. On the other hand, for a 1,000-node cluster, squeezing a 10 percent improvement through hardware will take 100 new machines. At that scale the brute force approach of adding hardware to boost performance may be less cost effective.

Hadoop has a number of specific levers and knobs for tuning performance, some of which boost the effectiveness of the cluster as a whole. We cover those in the next chapter when we discuss system administration issues. In this section we examine techniques that can be applied on a per-job basis.

6.3.1   *Reducing network traffic with combiner*

Combiner can reduce the amount of data shuffled between the map and reduce phases, and lower network traffic improves execution time. The details and the benefits of using combiner are thoroughly described in section 4.6. We mention it here again for the sake of completeness.

6.3.2   *Reducing the amount of input data*

When processing large data sets, sometimes a nontrivial portion of the processing time is spent scanning data from disk. Reducing the number of bytes to read can enhance overall throughput. There are several ways to do this.

The simplest way to reduce the amount of bytes processed is to reduce the amount of data processed. We can choose to process only a sampled subset of the data. This is a viable option for certain analytics applications. For those applications, sampling reduces precision but not accuracy. Their results remain useful for many decision support systems.

Often your MapReduce jobs don't use all the information in the input data set. Recall our patent description data set from chapter 4. It has almost a couple dozen fields, yet most of our jobs access only a few common ones. It's inefficient for every job on that data set to read the unused fields every time. One can "refactor" the input data into several smaller data sets. Each has only the fields necessary for a particular type of data processing. The exact refactoring will be application dependent. This technique is similar in spirit to vertical partitioning and column-oriented databases in the relational database management system (RDBMS) world.

Finally, you can reduce the amount of disk and network I/O by compressing your data. You can apply this technique to the intermediate as well as output data sets. Hadoop has many options for data compression, and we devote the next subsection to this topic.

6.3.3 *Using compression*

Even with the use of a combiner, the output of the map phase can be large. This intermediate data has to be stored on disk and shuffled across the network. Compressing this intermediate data will improve performance for most MapReduce jobs, and it's easy too.

Hadoop has built-in support for compression and decompression. Enabling compression on the mapper's output involves setting two configuration properties, as you can see in table 6.3.

Table 6.3   Configuration properties to control the compression of mapper's output

Property	Description
`mapred.compress.map.output`	Boolean property denoting whether the output of mapper should be compressed
`mapred.map.output.compression.codec`	Class property denoting which `CompressionCodec` to use for compressing mapper's output

To enable compression on the mapper's output, you set `mapred.compress.map.output` to true. In addition, you should set `mapred.map.output.compression.codec` to the appropriate codec class. All codec classes in Hadoop implement the `Compression-Codec` interface. Hadoop supports a number of compression codecs (see table 6.4). For example, to use GZIP compression, you can set the configuration object:

```
conf.setBoolean("mapred.compress.map.output", true);
conf.setClass("mapred.map.output.compression.codec",
        GzipCodec.class,
        CompressionCodec.class);
```

You can also use the convenience methods `setCompressMapOutput()` and `set-MapOutputCompressorClass()` in `JobConf` instead of setting the properties directly.

Table 6.4   List of codecs available under the org.apache.hadoop.io.compress package

Codec	Hadoop version	Description
DefaultCodec	0.18, 0.19, 0.20	Works with files in the zlib format. By Hadoop convention filenames for these files end in .deflate.
GzipCodec	0.18, 0.19, 0.20	Works with files in the gzip format. These files have a filename extension of .gz.
BZip2Codec	0.19, 0.20	Works with files in the bzip2 format. These files have a filename extension of .bz2. This compression format is unique in that it's splittable for Hadoop, even when used outside the sequence file format.

Data output from the map phase of a job is used only internally to the job, so enabling compression for this intermediate data is transparent to the developer and is a no-brainer. As many MapReduce applications involve multiple jobs, it makes sense for jobs to be able to output and input in compressed form. It's highly recommended that data that are passed between Hadoop jobs use the Hadoop-specific *sequence file* format.

Sequence file is a compressable binary file format for storing key/value pairs. It is designed to support compression while remaining *splittable*. Recall that one of the parallelisms of Hadoop is its ability to split an input file for reading and processing by multiple map tasks. If the input file is in a compressed format, Hadoop will have to be able to split the file such that each split can be decompressed by the map tasks independently. Otherwise parallelism is destroyed if Hadoop has to decompress the file as a whole first. Not all compressed file formats are designed for splitting and decompressing in chunks. Sequence files were specially developed to support this feature. The file format provides *sync markers* to Hadoop to denote splittable boundaries.[7]

In addition to its compressability and splittability, sequence files support binary keys and values. Therefore, a sequence file is often used for processing binary documents, such as images, and it works great for text documents and other large key/value objects as well. Each document is considered a record within the sequence file.

You can make a MapReduce job output a sequence file by setting its output format to `SequenceFileOutputFormat`. You'll want to change its compression type from the default RECORD to BLOCK. With record compression, each record is compressed separately. With block compression, a block of records is compressed together and achieves a higher compression ratio. Finally, you have to call the static methods `setCompressOutput()` and `setOutputCompressorClass()` in `FileOutputFormat` (or `SequenceFileOutputFormat`, which inherits those methods) to enable output compression using a specific codec. The supported codecs are the same as those given in table 6.4. You add these lines to the driver:

```
conf.setOutputFormat(SequenceFileOutputFormat.class);
SequenceFileOutputFormat.setOutputCompressionType(conf,
    ↪ CompressionType.BLOCK);
FileOutputFormat.setCompressOutput(conf, true);
FileOutputFormat.setOutputCompressorClass(conf, GzipCodec.class);
```

Table 6.5 lists the equivalent properties for configuring for sequence file output. A Streaming program can output sequence files when given the following options:

```
-outputformat org.apache.hadoop.mapred.SequenceFileOutputFormat
-D mapred.output.compression.type=BLOCK
-D mapred.output.compress=true
-D mapred.output.compression.codec=org.apache.hadoop.io.compress.GzipCode
```

---

[7] All the input files we've seen so far are uncompressed text files where each record is a line. The newline character (\n) can trivially be thought of as the sync marker pointing out to both splittable boundaries and record boundaries.

Table 6.5   Configuration properties for outputting compressed sequence file

Property	Description
`mapred.output.` `compression.type`	String property to denote the sequence file's compression type. Can be one of NONE, RECORD, or BLOCK. Default is RECORD but BLOCK almost always compresses better. **Convenience method:** `SequenceFileOutputFormat.` ➥ `setOutputCompressionType()`
`mapred.output.compress`	Boolean property on whether to compress the job's output. **Convenience method:** `FileOutputFormat.setCompressOutput()`
`mapred.output.` `compression.codec`	Class property that is used to specify which compression codec to use for compressing the job's output. **Convenience method:** `FileOutputFormat.` ➥ `setOutputCompressorClass()`

To read a sequence file as input, set the input format to `SequenceFileInputFormat`. Use

```
conf.setInputFormat(SequenceFileInputFormat.class);
```

or

```
-inputformat org.apache.hadoop.mapred.SequenceFileInputFormat
```

for Streaming. There's no need to configure the compression type or codec class, as the `SequenceFile.Reader` class (used by `SequenceFileRecordReader`) will automatically determine those settings from the file header.

6.3.4   *Reusing the JVM*

By default, the TaskTracker runs each `Mapper` and `Reducer` task in a separate JVM as a child process. This necessarily incurs the JVM start-up cost for each task. If the mapper does its own initialization, such as reading into memory a large data structure (see the example of joining using distributed cache in section 5.2.2), that initialization is part of the start-up cost as well. If each task runs only briefly, or if the mapper initialization takes a long time, then the start-up cost can be a significant portion of a task's total run time.

Starting with version 0.19.0, Hadoop allows the reuse of a JVM across multiple tasks of the same job. The start-up cost can, therefore, be amortized across many tasks. A new property, `mapred.job.reuse.jvm.num.tasks`, specifies the maximum number of tasks (of the same job) a JVM can run. The default value is 1; JVM is not reused. You can enable JVM reuse by setting the property to a higher number. You can also set it to

-1, which means there's no limit to the number of tasks a JVM can be reused for. The `JobConf` object has a convenience method, `setNumTasksToExecutePerJvm(int)`, to set the property for a job. This is summarized in table 6.6.

Table 6.6   Configuration property for enabling JVM reuse

Property	Description
`mapred.job.reuse.jvm.num.tasks`	Integer property for setting the maximum number of tasks a JVM can run. A value of -1 means no limit.

6.3.5   *Running with speculative execution*

One of the original design assumptions of MapReduce (as stated in the Google MapReduce paper) is that nodes are unreliable and the framework must handle the situation where some nodes fail in the middle of a job. Under this assumption, the original MapReduce framework specifies the map tasks and the reduce tasks to be *idempotent*. This means that when a task fails, Hadoop can restart that task and the overall job will end up with the same result. Hadoop can monitor the health of running nodes and restart tasks on failed nodes automatically. This makes fault tolerance transparent to the developer.

Often nodes don't suddenly fail but experience slowdown as I/O devices go bad. In such situations everything works but the tasks run slower. Sometimes tasks also run slow because of temporary congestion. This doesn't affect the correctness of the running job but certainly affects its performance. Even one slow-running task will delay the completion of a MapReduce job. Until *all* mappers have finished, none of the reducers will start running. Similarly, a job is not considered finished until all the reducers have finished.

Hadoop uses the idempotency property again to mitigate the slow-task problem. Instead of restarting a task only after it has failed, Hadoop will notice a slow-running task and schedule the *same* task to be run in another node *in parallel*. Idempotency guarantees the parallel task will generate the same output. Hadoop will monitor the parallel tasks. As soon as one finishes successfully, Hadoop will use its output and kill the other parallel tasks. This entire process is called *speculative execution.*

Note that speculative execution of map tasks will take place only after all map tasks have been scheduled to run, and only for map tasks that are making much less progress than is average on the other map tasks. It's the same case for speculative execution of reduce tasks. Speculative execution does not "race" multiple copies of a task to get the best completion time. It only prevents the slow tasks from dragging down the job's completion time.

By default, speculative execution is enabled. One can turn it off for map tasks and reduce tasks separately. To do this, set one or both of the properties in table 6.7 to false. They're applied on a per-job basis, but you can also change the cluster-wide default by setting them in the cluster configuration file.

Table 6.7 Configuration properties for enabling and disabling speculative execution

Property	Description
`mapred.map.tasks.speculative.execution`	Boolean property denoting whether speculative execution is enabled for map tasks
`mapred.reduce.tasks.speculative.execution`	Boolean property denoting whether speculative execution is enabled for reduce tasks

You should leave speculative execution on in general. The primary reason to turn it off is if your map tasks or reduce tasks have *side effects* and are therefore not idempotent. For example, if a task writes to external files, speculative execution can cause multiple copies of a task to collide in attempting to create the same external files. You can turn off speculative execution to ensure that only one copy of a task is being run at a time.

> **NOTE** If your tasks have side effects, you should also think through how Hadoop's recovery mechanism would interact with those side effects. For example, if a task writes to an external file, it's possible that the task dies right after writing to the external file. In that case, Hadoop will restart the task, which will try to write to that external file again. You need to make sure your tasks' operation remains correct in such situations.

6.3.6 *Refactoring code and rewriting algorithms*

If you're willing to rewrite your MapReduce programs to optimize performance, some straightforward techniques and some nontrivial, application-dependent rewritings can speed things up.

One straightforward technique for a Streaming program is to rewrite it for Hadoop Java. Streaming is great for quickly creating a MapReduce job for ad hoc data analysis, but it doesn't run as fast as Java under Hadoop. Streaming jobs that start out as one-off queries but end up being run frequently can gain from a Java re-implementation.

If you have several jobs that run on the same input data, there are probably opportunities to rewrite them into fewer jobs. For example, if you're computing the maximum as well as the minimum of a data set, you can write a single MapReduce job that computes both rather than compute them separately using two different jobs. This may sound obvious, but in practice many jobs are originally written to do one function well. This is a good design practice. A job's conciseness makes it widely applicable to different data sets for different purposes. Only after some usage should you start looking for job groupings that you can rewrite to be faster.

One of the most important things you can do to speed up a MapReduce program is to think hard about the underlying algorithm and see if a more efficient algorithm can compute the same results faster. This is true for any programming, but it is more significant for MapReduce programs. Standard text books on algorithm and data structure (sorting, lists, maps, etc.) comprehensively cover design choices for most traditional programming. Hadoop programs, on the other hand, tend to touch on "exotic" areas, such as distributed computing, functional programming, statistics, and data-intensive processing, where best practices are less known to most programmers and there is still exciting research today to explore new approaches.

One example we've already seen that leverages a new data structure to speed up MapReduce programs is the use of Bloom filters in semijoins (section 5.3). The Bloom filter is well-known in the distributed computing community but relatively unknown outside of it.

Another classic example of using a new algorithm to speed up a MapReduce program comes from statistics in the calculation of variance. Non-statisticians may compute variance using its canonical definition:

```
(1/N)  *  Sum_i[(X_i - X_avg)^2]
```

where Sum_i denotes summation over the data set. The variable X_{avg} is the average of the data set. If we don't know that average ahead of time, then a non-statistician may decide to run one MapReduce job to find the average first, and a second MapReduce job to compute the variance. Someone more familiar with computing statistics will use an equivalent definition:

```
(1/N)  *  Sum_i[(X_i)^2] - ((1/N)  *  Sum_i[X_i])^2
```

From this definition one needs the sum of X as well as the sum of X^2, but you can compute both sums together in one scan of the data, using only a single MapReduce job. (This is analogous to the example of calculating maximum and minimum in a single job.) A little statistical background has halved the processing time in computing variance.[8]

You should also pay attention to the computational complexity of your algorithms. Hadoop provides "only" linear scalability, and you can still bring it to its knees with large data sets running under computationally intensive algorithms that are quadratic or worse. You certainly should look for more efficient algorithms in those cases, and sometimes you may have to settle for faster algorithms that only give approximate results.

6.4   *Summary*

Development methodologies for Hadoop build on top of best practices for Java programming, such as unit testing and test-driven development. Hadoop's central role of processing data calls for more data-centric testing processes. Math and logic errors are more prevalent in data-intensive programs and they're often inconspicuous. The

---

[8] There's a lot of nuisance in numerical computation over large data. In this variance calculation example we note our refactored MapReduce job has lower numerical precision and is more likely to run into overflow problems.

distributed nature of Hadoop makes debugging much harder. To lessen the burden, you should test in stages, from a nondistributed (i.e., local) mode to a single-node pseudo-distributed mode, and finally to a fully distributed mode.

The famous computer scientist Donald Knuth once said that "premature optimization is the root of all evil." You should tune your Hadoop program for performance only after it's been fully debugged. Beyond thinking through general algorithmic and computational issues, performance enhancement is platform-specific, and Hadoop has a number of specific techniques to make jobs run more efficiently.

Cookbook

7

This chapter covers

- Passing custom parameters to tasks
- Retrieving task-specific information
- Creating multiple outputs
- Interfacing with relational databases
- Making output globally sorted

This book so far has covered the core techniques for making a MapReduce program. Hadoop is a big framework that supports many more functionalities than those core techniques. In this age of Bing and Google, you can look up specialized MapReduce techniques rather easily, and we don't try to be an encyclopedic reference. In our own usage and from our discussion with other Hadoop users, we've found a number of techniques generally useful, techniques such as being able to take a standard relational database as input or output to a MapReduce job. We've collected some of our favorite "recipes" in this cookbook chapter.

7.1 Passing job-specific parameters to your tasks

In writing your `Mapper` and `Reducer`, you often want to make certain aspects configurable. For example, our joining program in chapter 5 is hardcoded to take the first data column as the join key. The program can be more generally applicable if the column for the join key can be specified by the user at run time. Hadoop itself uses a configuration object to store all the configuration properties for a job. You can use the same object to pass parameters to your `Mapper` and `Reducer`.

We've seen how the MapReduce driver configures the `JobConf` object with properties, such as input format, output format, mapper class, and so forth. To introduce your own property, you give your property a unique name and set it with a value in the same configuration object. This configuration object is passed to all TaskTrackers, so the properties in the configuration object are available to all tasks in that job. Your `Mapper` and `Reducer` can read the configuration object and retrieve the property value.

The `Configuration` class (parent of `JobConf`) has a number of generic setter methods. Properties are key/value pairs, where key has to be a `String`, but value can be one of a number of common types. Signature for the common setter methods are

```
public void set(String name, String value)
public void setBoolean(String name, boolean value)
public void setInt(String name, int value)
public void setLong(String name, long value)
public void setStrings(String name, String... values)
```

Note that Hadoop stores all properties internally as strings. All the other setter methods are convenience methods for `set(String, String)`. For example, the `setStrings(String, String...)` method takes a `String` array, turns it into a single comma-separated `String`, and sets that `String` as the property value. The `get-Strings()` retrieval method similarly splits the concatenated string back into an array. With that in mind, don't keep any commas in the strings in the original array. If you want commas, you should use your own string-encoding function.

Your driver will first set the properties in the configuration object to make them available to all tasks. Your `Mapper` and `Reducer` have access to the configuration object in the `configure()` method. When a task initializes, it calls `configure()`, which you override to retrieve and store your properties . Your `map()` and `reduce()` methods will access your copy of those properties later. In the following example we call our new property `myjob.myproperty`, and it takes an integer value specified by the user.

```
public int run(String[] args) throws Exception {

    Configuration conf = getConf();
    JobConf job = new JobConf(conf, MyJob.class);

    ...

    job.setInt("myjob.myproperty", Integer.parseInt(args[2]));   ◁─┐ Set custom
                                                                   │ property
    JobClient.runJob(job);                                         ❶
    return 0;
}
```

In `MapClass`, the `configure()` method retrieves the property value and stores it in the object's scope. The getter methods of the `Configuration` class require specifying default values, which will be returned if the requested property is not set in the configuration object. For this example we use a default of 0:

```
public static class MapClass extends MapReduceBase
    implements Mapper<Text, Text, Text, Text> {

    int myproperty;

    public void configure(JobConf job) {
        myproperty = job.getInt("myjob.myproperty", 0);
    }

    ...

}
```

Get custom property ①

If you want to use the property in the `Reducer,` it will also have to retrieve the property.

```
public static class Reduce extends MapReduceBase
    implements Reducer<Text, Text, Text, Text> {

    int myproperty;

    public void configure(JobConf job) {
        myproperty = job.getInt("myjob.myproperty", 0);
    }

    ...

}
```

The `Configuration` class has a larger list of getter methods than setter methods, although they are largely self-explanatory. Almost all the getter methods require a default value as argument. The exception is `get(String)`, which returns null if the property with the specified name is not set.

```
public String get(String name)
public String get(String name, String defaultValue)
public boolean getBoolean(String name, boolean defaultValue)
public float getFloat(String name, float defaultValue)
public int getInt(String name, int defaultValue)
public long getLong(String name, long defaultValue)
public String[] getStrings(String name, String... defaultValue)
```

Given that our job class implements the `Tool` interface and uses `ToolRunner,` we can also let the user set custom properties directly using the generic options syntax, in the same way the user would set Hadoop configuration properties.

```
bin/hadoop jar MyJob.jar MyJob -D myjob.myproperty=1 input output
```

We can remove the line in the driver that requires the user to always specify the value of this property as an argument. This is more convenient for the user when the default value would work most of the time.

```
public int run(String[] args) throws Exception {

    Configuration conf = getConf();
    JobConf job = new JobConf(conf, MyJob.class);
```

```
    ...
    int myproperty = job.getInt("myjob.myproperty", 0);
    if (myproperty < 0) {
        System.err.println("Invalid myjob.myproperty: " + myproperty);
        System.exit(0);
    }
    JobClient.runJob(job);
    return 0;
}
```

When you allow the user to specify custom properties, it's good practice for the driver to validate any user input. The example above ensures that the user will not be allowed to specify a negative value for myjob.myproperty.

7.2 *Probing for task-specific information*

In addition to retrieving custom properties and global configuration, we can also use the getter methods on the configuration object to obtain certain state information about the current task and job. For example, in the Mapper you can grab the map.input.file property to get the file path to the current map task. This is exactly what the configure() method in the datajoin package's DataJoinMapperBase does to infer a tag for the data source.

```
this.inputFile = job.get("map.input.file");
this.inputTag = generateInputTag(this.inputFile);
```

Table 7.1 lists some of the other task-specific state information.

Table 7.1 Task-specific state information one can get in the configuration object

Property	Type	Description
mapred.job.id	String	The job ID
mapred.jar	String	The jar location in job directory
job.local.dir	String	The job's local scratch space
mapred.tip.id	String	The task ID
mapred.task.id	String	The task attempt ID
mapred.task.is.map	boolean	Flag denoting whether this is a map task
mapred.task.partition	int	The ID of the task within the job
map.input.file	String	The file path that the mapper is reading from
map.input.start	long	The offset into the file of the start of the current mapper's input split
map.input.length	long	The number of bytes in the current mapper's input split
mapred.work.output.dir	String	The task's working (i.e., temporary) output directory

Configuration properties are also available to Streaming programs through environment variables. Before executing a script, the Streaming API will have added all configuration properties to the running environment. The property names are reformatted such that non-alphanumeric characters are replaced with an underscore (_). For example, a Streaming script should look at the environment variable `map_input_file` for the full file path that the current mapper is reading from.

```
import os

filename = os.environ["map_input_file"]
localdir = os.environ["job_local_dir"]
```

The preceding code shows how one would access configuration properties in Python.

7.3   *Partitioning into multiple output files*

Up 'till now all the MapReduce jobs we've seen output a single set of files. However, there are often cases where it's more convenient to output multiple sets of files, or split a data set into multiple data sets. A popular example is the partitioning of a large log file into distinct sets of log files for each day.

`MultipleOutputFormat` provides a simple way of grouping similar records into separate data sets. Before writing each output record, this `OutputFormat` class calls an internal method to determine the filename to write to. More specifically, you will extend a particular subclass of `MultipleOutputFormat` and implement the `generateFileNameForKeyValue()` method. The subclass you extend will determine the output format. For example, `MultipleTextOutputFormat` will output text files whereas `MultipleSequenceFileOutputFormat` will output sequence files. In either case, you'll override the following method to return the filename for each output key/value pair:

```
protected String generateFileNameForKeyValue(K key, V value, String name)
```

The default implementation returns the argument `name`, which is the leaf filename. You can make the method return a filename that's dependent on the content of the record.

For our example here, we take the patent metadata and partition it by country. All patents from U.S. inventors will go into one set of files, all patents from Japan into another pile, and so forth. The skeleton of this example program is a map-only job that takes its input and immediately outputs it. The main change we've made is to create our own subclass of `MultipleTextOutputFormat` called `PartitionbyCountryMTOF`. (Note that *MTOF* is an acronym for `MultipleTextOutputFormat`.) Our subclass will store each record to a location based on the inventing country listed in that record. As we treat the value returned by `generateFileNameForKeyValue()` as a file path, we're able to create a subdirectory for each country by returning `country + "/" + filename`. See listing 7.1.

Listing 7.1   Partition patent metadata into multiple directories based on country

```java
public class MultiFile extends Configured implements Tool {

    public static class MapClass extends MapReduceBase
        implements Mapper<LongWritable, Text, NullWritable, Text> {

        public void map(LongWritable key, Text value,
                        OutputCollector<NullWritable, Text> output,
                        Reporter reporter) throws IOException {

            output.collect(NullWritable.get(), value);
        }
    }

    public static class PartitionByCountryMTOF
        extends MultipleTextOutputFormat<NullWritable,Text>
    {
        protected String generateFileNameForKeyValue(NullWritable key,
                                                     Text value,
                                                     String filename)
        {
            String[] arr = value.toString().split(",", -1);
            String country = arr[4].substring(1,3);
            return country + "/" + filename;
        }
    }

    public int run(String[] args) throws Exception {
        Configuration conf = getConf();

        JobConf job = new JobConf(conf, MultiFile.class);

        Path in = new Path(args[0]);
        Path out = new Path(args[1]);
        FileInputFormat.setInputPaths(job, in);
        FileOutputFormat.setOutputPath(job, out);

        job.setJobName("MultiFile");
        job.setMapperClass(MapClass.class);

        job.setInputFormat(TextInputFormat.class);
        job.setOutputFormat(PartitionByCountryMTOF.class);
        job.setOutputKeyClass(NullWritable.class);
        job.setOutputValueClass(Text.class);

        job.setNumReduceTasks(0);

        JobClient.runJob(job);

        return 0;
    }

    public static void main(String[] args) throws Exception {
        int res = ToolRunner.run(new Configuration(),
                                 new MultiFile(),
                                 args);

        System.exit(res);
    }
}
```

After executing the preceding program, we can see that the output directory now has a separate directory for each country.

ls output/

AD	BN	CS	GE	IN	LC	MT	PH	SV	VE
AE	BO	CU	GF	IQ	LI	MU	PK	SY	VG
AG	BR	CY	GH	IR	LK	MW	PL	SZ	VN
AI	BS	CZ	GL	IS	LR	MX	PT	TC	VU
AL	BY	DE	GN	IT	LT	MY	PY	TD	YE
AM	BZ	DK	GP	JM	LU	NC	RO	TH	YU
AN	CA	DO	GR	JO	LV	NF	RU	TN	ZA
AR	CC	DZ	GT	JP	LY	NG	SA	TR	ZM
AT	CD	EC	GY	KE	MA	NI	SD	TT	ZW
AU	CH	EE	HK	KG	MC	NL	SE	TW	
AW	CI	EG	HN	KN	MG	NO	SG	TZ	
AZ	CK	ES	HR	KP	MH	NZ	SI	UA	
BB	CL	ET	HT	KR	ML	OM	SK	UG	
BE	CM	FI	HU	KW	MM	PA	SM	US	
BG	CN	FO	ID	KY	MO	PE	SN	UY	
BH	CO	FR	IE	KZ	MQ	PF	SR	UZ	
BM	CR	GB	IL	LB	MR	PG	SU	VC	

And within the directory for each country are files with only records (patents) created by those countries.

ls output/AD
```
part-00003      part-00005      part-00006
```

head output/AD/part-00006
```
5765303,1998,14046,1996,"AD","",,1,12,42,5,59,11,1,0.4545,0,0,1,67.3636,,,,
5785566,1998,14088,1996,"AD","",,1,9,441,6,69,3,0,1,,0.6667,,4.3333,,,,
5894770,1999,14354,1997,"AD","",,1,,82,5,51,4,0,1,,0.625,,7.5,,,,
```

We've written this simple partitioning exercise as a map-only program. You can apply the same technique to the output of reducers as well. Be careful not to confuse this with the partitioner in the MapReduce framework. That partitioner looks at the keys of *intermediate* records and decides which reducer will process them. The partitioning we're doing here looks at the key/value pair of the *output* and decides which file to store to.

MultipleOutputFormat is simple, but it's also limited. For example, we were able to split the input data by row, but what if we want to split by column? Let's say we want to create two data sets from the patent metadata: one containing time-related information (e.g., publication date) for each patent and another one containing geographical information (e.g., country of invention). These two data sets may be of different output formats and different data types for the keys and values. We can look to MultipleOutputs, introduced in version 0.19 of Hadoop, for more powerful capabilities.

The approach taken by MultipleOutputs is different from MultipleOutputFormat. Rather than asking for the filename to output each record, MultipleOutputs creates multiple OutputCollectors. Each OutputCollector can have its own OutputFormat and types for the key/value pair. Your MapReduce program will decide what to output to each OutputCollector. Listing 7.2 shows a program that takes our patent metadata and outputs two data sets. One has chronological information, such as issued date. The other data set has geographical information associated with each patent. This, too, is a map-only program, but you can apply the multiple output collectors to reducers in a straightforward way.

Listing 7.2   Program to project different columns of input data to different files

```
public class MultiFile extends Configured implements Tool {

    public static class MapClass extends MapReduceBase
        implements Mapper<LongWritable, Text, NullWritable, Text> {

        private MultipleOutputs mos;
        private OutputCollector<NullWritable, Text> collector;

        public void configure(JobConf conf) {
            mos = new MultipleOutputs(conf);
        }

        public void map(LongWritable key, Text value,
                        OutputCollector<NullWritable, Text> output,
                        Reporter reporter) throws IOException {

            String[] arr = value.toString().split(",", -1);
            String chrono = arr[0] + "," + arr[1] + "," + arr[2];
            String geo     = arr[0] + "," + arr[4] + "," + arr[5];

            collector = mos.getCollector("chrono", reporter);
            collector.collect(NullWritable.get(), new Text(chrono));
            collector = mos.getCollector("geo", reporter);
            collector.collect(NullWritable.get(), new Text(geo));
        }

        public void close() throws IOException {
            mos.close();
        }
    }

    public int run(String[] args) throws Exception {
        Configuration conf = getConf();

        JobConf job = new JobConf(conf, MultiFile.class);

        Path in = new Path(args[0]);
        Path out = new Path(args[1]);
        FileInputFormat.setInputPaths(job, in);
        FileOutputFormat.setOutputPath(job, out);

        job.setJobName("MultiFile");
        job.setMapperClass(MapClass.class);

        job.setInputFormat(TextInputFormat.class);
        job.setOutputKeyClass(NullWritable.class);
        job.setOutputValueClass(Text.class);
        job.setNumReduceTasks(0);

        MultipleOutputs.addNamedOutput(job,
                                       "chrono",
                                       TextOutputFormat.class,
                                       NullWritable.class,
                                       Text.class);
```

```
            MultipleOutputs.addNamedOutput(job,
                                           "geo",
                                           TextOutputFormat.class,
                                           NullWritable.class,
                                           Text.class);

            JobClient.runJob(job);

            return 0;
        }

    public static void main(String[] args) throws Exception {
        int res = ToolRunner.run(new Configuration(),
                                 new MultiFile(),
                                 args);

            System.exit(res);
        }
    }
```

To use `MultipleOutputs`, the driver of the MapReduce program must set up the output collectors it expects to use. Creating the collectors involves a call to `MultipleOutputs`' static method `addNamedOutput()`. We've created one output collector called *chrono* and another one called *geo*. We've created them both to use `TextOutputFormat` and have the same key/value types, but we can choose to use different output formats or data types.

After setting up the output collectors in the driver, we need to get the `MultipleOutputs` object that tracks them when the mapper is initialized in the `configure()` method. This object must be available throughout the duration of the map task. In the `map()` function itself, we call the `getCollector()` method on the `MultipleOutputs` object to get back the chrono and the geo `OutputCollectors`. We will write out different data that's appropriate for each output collector.

We have given a name to each output collector in `MultipleOutputs`, and `MultipleOutputs` will automatically generate the output filenames. We can look at the files outputted by our script to see how `MultipleOutputs` generates the output names:

```
ls -l output/
total 101896
-rwxrwxrwx 1 Administrator None 9672703 Jul 31 06:28 chrono-m-00000
-rwxrwxrwx 1 Administrator None 7752888 Jul 31 06:29 chrono-m-00001
-rwxrwxrwx 1 Administrator None 6884496 Jul 31 06:29 chrono-m-00002
-rwxrwxrwx 1 Administrator None 6933561 Jul 31 06:29 chrono-m-00003
-rwxrwxrwx 1 Administrator None 7164558 Jul 31 06:29 chrono-m-00004
-rwxrwxrwx 1 Administrator None 7273561 Jul 31 06:29 chrono-m-00005
-rwxrwxrwx 1 Administrator None 8281663 Jul 31 06:29 chrono-m-00006
-rwxrwxrwx 1 Administrator None 9428951 Jul 31 06:28 geo-m-00000
-rwxrwxrwx 1 Administrator None 7464690 Jul 31 06:29 geo-m-00001
-rwxrwxrwx 1 Administrator None 6580482 Jul 31 06:29 geo-m-00002
-rwxrwxrwx 1 Administrator None 6448648 Jul 31 06:29 geo-m-00003
-rwxrwxrwx 1 Administrator None 6432392 Jul 31 06:29 geo-m-00004
-rwxrwxrwx 1 Administrator None 6546828 Jul 31 06:29 geo-m-00005
-rwxrwxrwx 1 Administrator None 7450768 Jul 31 06:29 geo-m-00006
```

```
-rwxrwxrwx 1 Administrator None        0 Jul 31 06:28 part-00000
-rwxrwxrwx 1 Administrator None        0 Jul 31 06:28 part-00001
-rwxrwxrwx 1 Administrator None        0 Jul 31 06:29 part-00002
-rwxrwxrwx 1 Administrator None        0 Jul 31 06:29 part-00003
-rwxrwxrwx 1 Administrator None        0 Jul 31 06:29 part-00004
-rwxrwxrwx 1 Administrator None        0 Jul 31 06:29 part-00005
-rwxrwxrwx 1 Administrator None        0 Jul 31 06:29 part-00006
```

We have a set of files prefixed with *chrono* and another set of files prefixed with *geo*. Note that the program created the default output files *part-** even though it wrote nothing explicitly. It's entirely possible to write to these files using the original `OutputCollector` passed in through the `map()` method. In fact, if this was not a map-only program, records written to the original `OutputCollector`, and only those records, would be passed to the reducers for processing.

One of the trade-offs with `MultipleOutputs` is that it has a rigid naming structure compared to `MultipleOutputFormat`. Your output collector's name cannot be *part*, because that's already in use for the default. The output filename is also strictly defined as the output collector's name followed by *m* or *r* depending on whether the output was collected at the mapper or the reducer. It's finally followed by a partition number.

```
head output/chrono-m-00000
"PATENT","GYEAR","GDATE"
3070801,1963,1096
3070802,1963,1096
3070803,1963,1096
3070804,1963,1096
3070805,1963,1096
3070806,1963,1096
3070807,1963,1096
3070808,1963,1096
3070809,1963,1096

head output/geo-m-00000
"PATENT","COUNTRY","POSTATE"
3070801,"BE",""
3070802,"US","TX"
3070803,"US","IL"
3070804,"US","OH"
3070805,"US","CA"
3070806,"US","PA"
3070807,"US","OH"
3070808,"US","IA"
3070809,"US","AZ"
```

Looking at the output files, we see that we've successfully projected out the columns on the patent data set into distinct files.

7.4 *Inputting from and outputting to a database*

Although Hadoop is useful for processing large data, relational databases remain the workhorse of many data processing applications. Oftentimes Hadoop will need to interface with databases.

Although it's possible to set up a MapReduce program to take its input by directly querying a database rather than reading a file in HDFS, the performance is less than ideal. More often you would copy a data set from a database to HDFS. You can easily do it with a standard database dump utility to get a flat file. You then upload to HDFS using its file put shell command.

But sometimes it is sensible having a MapReduce program write directly to a database. Many MapReduce programs take large data sets and process them into a manageable size for databases to handle. For example, we often use MapReduce in the ETL-like process of taking humongous log files and computing a much smaller and more manageable set of statistics for analysts to look at.

The DBOutputFormat is the crucial class for accessing databases. In your driver you set the output format to this class. You'll need to specify the configuration for connecting to your database. You can do this through the static configureDB() method in DBConfiguration:

```
public static void configureDB(JobConf job, String driverClass,
    ➥ String dbUrl, String userName, String passwd)
```

After that, you'll specify what table you're writing to and what fields are there. This is done with the static setOutput() method in DBOutputFormat.

```
public static void setOutput(JobConf job, String tableName,
    ➥ String... fieldNames)
```

Your driver should have a few lines that look like this:

```
conf.setOutputFormat(DBOutputFormat.class);
DBConfiguration.configureDB(job,
                    "com.mysql.jdbc.Driver",
                    "jdbc:mysql://db.host.com/mydb",
                    "username",
                    "password")
DBOutputFormat.setOutput(job, "Events", "event_id", "time");
```

Using DBOutputFormat forces your output key to implement the DBWritable interface. Only the key is written to the database. As usual, the keys have to implement Writable. The signatures for Writable and DBWritable are similar; only the argument types are different. The write() method in Writable takes a DataOutput, whereas write() in DBWritable takes a PreparedStatement. Similarly the read-Fields() method for Writable takes a DataInput, whereas readFields() for DBWritable takes a ResultSet. Unless you plan on fetching input data straight from the database using DBInputFormat, readFields() in DBWritable will never be called.

```
public class EventsDBWritable implements Writable, DBWritable {
    private int id;
    private long timestamp;

    public void write(DataOutput out) throws IOException {
        out.writeInt(id);
        out.writeLong(timestamp);
```

```
    }
    public void readFields(DataInput in) throws IOException {
        id = in.readInt();
        timestamp = in.readLong();
    }
    public void write(PreparedStatement statement) throws SQLException {
        statement.setInt(1, id);
        statement.setLong(2, timestamp);
    }
    public void readFields(ResultSet resultSet) throws SQLException {
        id = resultSet.getInt(1);
        timestamp = resultSet.getLong(2);
    }
}
```

We want to emphasize again that reading and writing to databases from within Hadoop is only appropriate for data sets that are relatively small by Hadoop standards. Unless your database setup is as parallel as Hadoop (which can be the case if your Hadoop cluster is relatively small while you have many shards in your database system), your DB will be the performance bottleneck, and you may not gain any scalability advantage from your Hadoop cluster. Oftentimes, it's better to bulk load data into a database rather than make direct writes from Hadoop. You'll need custom solutions for extremely large-scale databases.[1]

7.5 Keeping all output in sorted order

The MapReduce framework guarantees the input to each reducer to be in sorted order based on key. In many cases, the reducer only does a simple computation on the value part of a key/value pair. The output also stays in sorted order. Keep in mind that the MapReduce framework does not guarantee the sorted order of the reducer output. Rather, it's a byproduct of the sorted input and the typical type of operations reducers perform.

For some applications, the sorted order is unnecessary, and sometimes questions are raised about turning off the sorting operation to eliminate an unnecessary step in the reducer. The truth is that the sorting operation is not so much about enforcing the sorted order of the reducer's input. Rather, sorting is an efficient way to group all records of the same key together. If the grouping function is unnecessary, then we can directly generate an output record from a single input record. In that case, you'll be able to improve performance by eliminating the entire reduce phase. You can do this by setting the number of reducers to 0, making the application a map-only job.

---

[1] LinkedIn has an interesting blog post on challenges faced in moving massive amounts of data resulting from offline processes (i.e., Hadoop) into live systems: http://project-voldemort.com/blog/2009/06/building-a-1-tb-data-cycle-at-linkedin-with-hadoop-and-project-voldemort/.

On the other hand, for some applications it's desirable that all output is sorted *in total*. Each output file (generated by one reducer) is already in sorted order; it would be nice to also have all the records in `part-00000` be smaller than records in `part-00001`, and `part-00001` be smaller than `part-00002`, and so forth. The key to doing this is the partitioner operation in the framework.

The job of the partitioner is to deterministically assign a reducer to each key. All records of the same key are grouped and processed together in the reduce stage. An important design requirement of the partitioner is to balance load across reducers; no one reducer is given many more keys than other reducers. Without any prior information about the distribution of keys, the default partitioner uses a hashing function to uniformly assign keys to reducers. This often works well in distributing work evenly across reducers, but the assignment is intentionally arbitrary and not in any order. If we have prior knowledge that the keys are approximately uniformly distributed, we can use a partitioner that assigns key ranges to each reducer and still be certain that the reducers' loads are fairly balanced.

> **TIP** The hash partitioner can also fail to evenly distribute work if certain keys take much more time to process than others. For example, in highly skewed data sets, a significant number of records may have the same key. If possible, you should use a combiner to lessen the load at the reduce phase by doing as much preprocessing as possible at the map phase. In addition, you can also choose to write a special partitioner to distribute keys unevenly in such a way that it balances out the inherent skew of the data and its processing.

The `TotalOrderPartitioner` is a partitioner that ensures sortedness between output partitions, not only within. Sorting of large-scale data (i.e., the TeraSort benchmark) originally used a similar version of this class. This class takes a sequence file with a sorted partition keyset and proceeds to partition keys in different ranges to the reducers.

7.6   *Summary*

This chapter discussed many tools and techniques to make your Hadoop job more user-friendly or make it interface better with other components of your data processing infrastructure. The full extent of the capabilities available in a Hadoop job is documented in the Hadoop API: http://hadoop.apache.org/common/docs/current/api/index.html. You may also want to check out additional abstractions such as Pig and Hive to simplify your programming. We'll cover these tools in chapters 10 and 11.

If your role involves administrating a Hadoop cluster, you will find the tips on managing a Hadoop cluster in the next chapter useful.

Managing Hadoop

This chapter covers
- Configuring for a production system
- Maintaining the HDFS filesystem
- Setting up a job scheduler

The installation instructions in chapter 2 produced a running Hadoop cluster fairly quickly. The configuration was relatively simple, but unfortunately it's not good for a production cluster, which will be under heavy sustained use. There are various configuration parameters that you would want to tune for a production cluster, and section 8.1 will cover those parameters.

In addition, like any system, a Hadoop cluster will change over time and you (or some administrator) will have to know how to maintain it to keep it running in good shape. This is particularly true for the HDFS filesystem. In sections 8.2 through 8.5, we cover various standard filesystem maintenance tasks, such as checking its health, setting permissions, quotas, and recovering deleted files (trash). Sections 8.6 through 8.10 will cover the bigger but rarer administrative tasks more specific to HDFS. These include adding/removing nodes (capacity) and recovery from NameNode failure. We end the chapter with a section on setting up a scheduler to manage multiple running jobs.

8.1   *Setting up parameter values for practical use*

Hadoop has many different parameters. Their default values tend to target running in standalone mode. They also tend to veer toward being idiotproof. The default values are more likely to work on more systems without causing any errors. However, often-times they're far from optimal in a production cluster. Table 8.1 shows some of the system properties that you'll want to change for a production cluster.

Table 8.1   Hadoop properties that you can tune for a production cluster

Property	Description	Suggested value
dfs.name.dir	Directory in NameNode's local filesystem to store HDFS's metadata	/home/hadoop/ dfs/name
dfs.data.dir	Directory in a DataNode's local filesystem to store HDFS's file blocks	/home/hadoop/ dfs/data
mapred.system.dir	Directory in HDFS for storing shared MapReduce system files	/hadoop/ mapred/system
mapred.local.dir	Directory in a TaskNode's local filesystem to store temporary data	
mapred. tasktracker. {map|reduce} .tasks.maximum	Maximum number of map and reduce tasks that can run simultaneously in a TaskTracker	
hadoop.tmp.dir	Temporary Hadoop directories	/home/hadoop/ tmp
dfs.datanode.du .reserved	Minimum amount of free space a DataNode should have	1073741824
mapred.child. java.opts	Heap size allocated to each child task	-Xmx512m
mapred.reduce. tasks	Number of reduce tasks for a job	

The default values for dfs.name.dir and dfs.data.dir point to directories under /tmp, which is intended only for temporary storage in almost all Unix systems. You will definitely want to change those properties for a production cluster.[1] In addition, these properties can take comma-separated lists of directories. In the case of dfs.name. dir, multiple directories are good for backup purposes. If a DataNode has multiple drives, you should have a data directory in each one and list them all in dfs.data.dir.

---

[1] The rationale for using /tmp illustrates how default values are idiotproof. Every Unix system has the /tmp directory so you won't get a "directory not found" error.

The DataNode will use them all in parallel to speed up I/O.[2] You should also specify directories in multiple drives for `mapred.local.dir` to speed up processing of temporary data.

The default configuration for Hadoop's temporary directories, `hadoop.tmp.dir`, is dependent on the user name. You should avoid having any Hadoop property that depends on a user name, as there can be mismatches between the user name used to submit a job and the user name used to start a Hadoop node. You should set it to something like `/home/hadoop/tmp` to be independent of any user name. Another problem with the default value of `hadoop.tmp.dir` is that it points to the `/tmp` directory. Although that's an appropriate place for temporary storage, most default Linux configurations have a quota on `/tmp` that is too small for Hadoop. Rather than increase the quota for `/tmp`, it's better to point `hadoop.tmp.dir` to a directory that's known to have a lot of space.

By default, HDFS doesn't require DataNodes to have any reserved free space. In practice, most systems have questionable stability when the amount of free space gets too low. You should set `dfs.datanode.du.reserved` to reserve 1 GB of free space in a DataNode. A DataNode will stop accepting block writes when its amount of free space falls below the reserved amount.

Each TaskTracker is allowed to run a configurable maximum number of map and reduce tasks. Hadoop's default is four tasks (two map tasks and two reduce tasks). The right number depends on many factors, although most setups call for one to two tasks per core. You can set a quad core machine to have a maximum of six map and reduce tasks (three each), because there will already be one task each allocated for TaskTracker and DataNode, to make a total of eight. Similarly, you can set up a dual quad core machine to have a maximum of fourteen map and reduce tasks. This predicates on most MapReduce jobs being I/O heavy. You should reduce the maximum number of tasks allowed if you expect more CPU-intensive loads.

In considering the number of tasks allowed, you should also consider the amount of heap memory allocated to each task. Hadoop's default of 200 MB per task is quite underwhelming. Many setups bump up the default to 512 MB, some even at 1 GB. This is not a final property. Each job can request more (or less) heap space per task. Be sure that you have sufficient usable memory in your machines for your configuration parameters. Keep in mind that DataNode and TaskTracker each already uses 1 GB of RAM.

Although you can set the number of reduce tasks per each individual MapReduce job, it's desirable to have a default that works well most of the time. Hadoop's

---

[2] There's been some discussion in the Hadoop forums about whether one should configure multiple hard drives in a DataNode as RAID or JBOD. Hadoop doesn't need RAID's data redundancy because HDFS already replicates data across machines. Furthermore, Yahoo has stated that they were able to get noticeable performance improvement using JBOD. The stated reason is that hard drives, even of the same model, have high variance in their speed. A RAID configuration would slow down the I/O to the slowest drive. On the other hand, letting each drive function independently will allow each one to operate at its top speed, making the overall throughput of the system higher.

default of one reduce task per job is certainly suboptimal in most cases. The general recommendation is to set the default to either 0.95 or 1.75 times the maximum number of reduce TaskTrackers in the cluster. This means that the number of reduce tasks in a job should be 0.95 or 1.75 multiplied by *number of worker nodes* multiplied by mapred.tasktracker.reduce.tasks.maximum. A factor of 0.95 will have all the reduce tasks launched immediately and start copying map tasks' output as they finish. At a factor of 1.75, some reduce tasks will be able to launch immediately whereas others will wait. The faster nodes will finish the first round of reduce tasks earlier and start on the second round. The slowest nodes won't need to process any reduce tasks from the second round. This can result in better load balancing.

8.2   *Checking system's health*

Hadoop provides a filesystem checking utility called `fsck`. You call it with a file path and it'll recursively check the health of all the files under that path. Call it with the argument / and it'll check the entire filesystem. An example output looks like this:

```
bin/hadoop fsck /
Status: HEALTHY
 Total size:      143106109768 B
 Total dirs:      9726
 Total files:     41532
 Total blocks (validated):     42419 (avg. block size 3373632 B)
 Minimally replicated blocks:  42419 (100.0 %)
 Over-replicated blocks:       0 (0.0 %)
 Under-replicated blocks:      0 (0.0 %)
 Mis-replicated blocks:        0 (0.0 %)
 Default replication factor:   3
 Average block replication:    3.0
 Corrupt blocks:               0
 Missing replicas:             0 (0.0 %)
 Number of data-nodes:         8
 Number of racks:              1
```

Most of the information should be self-explanatory. By default `fsck` will ignore files still open for writing by a client. You can get a list of such files by running `fsck` with the `-openforwrite` argument.

As `fsck` checks the filesystem, it will print out a dot for each file it found healthy (not shown in the above output). It'll print out a message for each file that is less than healthy, including ones that have over-replicated blocks, under-replicated blocks, mis-replicated blocks, corrupt blocks, and missing replicas. Over-replicated blocks, under-replicated blocks, and mis-replicated blocks are not too alarming as HDFS is self-healing. But, corrupt blocks and missing replicas mean that data has been permanently lost. By default `fsck` doesn't act on those corrupt files, but you can run `fsck` with the `-delete` option to remove them. Better yet is to run `fsck` with the `-move` option, which moves corrupted files into the `/lost+found` directory for salvaging.

You can tell `fsck` to print out more information by adding `-files`, `-blocks`, `-locations`, and `-racks` options to `fsck`. Each successive option requires the preceding option be used as well. The -blocks option requires the -files option be used. The -locations option requires both -files and -blocks options be used, and so forth. The -files option tells fsck to print out, for each file it checks, a line of information containing the file's path, the file's size in bytes and blocks, and the file's status. The -blocks option tells fsck to go further and print out a line of information for each block in the file. This line will include the block's name, its length, and its number of replicas. The -locations option will include in each line the location of the block's replicas. The -racks option will add the rack name to the location information. For example, a short one-block file will have its report as

```
bin/hadoop fsck /user/hadoop/test -files -blocks -locations -racks
/user/hadoop/test/part-00000 35792 bytes, 1 block(s):  OK
0. blk_-4630072455652803568_97605 len=35792 repl=3
➡ [/default-rack/10.130.164.71:50010, /default-rack/10.130.164.177:50010,
➡ /default-rack/10.130.164.186:50010]

Status: HEALTHY
 Total size:    35792 B
 Total dirs:    0
 Total files:   1
 Total blocks (validated):      1 (avg. block size 35792 B)
 Minimally replicated blocks:   1 (100.0 %)
 Over-replicated blocks:        0 (0.0 %)
 Under-replicated blocks:       0 (0.0 %)
 Mis-replicated blocks:         0 (0.0 %)
 Default replication factor:    3
 Average block replication:     3.0
 Corrupt blocks:                0
 Missing replicas:              0 (0.0 %)
 Number of data-nodes:          8
 Number of racks:               1
```

While fsck reports on each file in HDFS, there is a dfsadmin command for reporting on each DataNode. You can get it through the -report option on the dfsadmin command:

```
bin/hadoop dfsadmin -report
Total raw bytes: 535472824320 (498.7 GB)
Remaining raw bytes: 33927731366 (31.6 GB)
Used raw bytes: 379948188541 (353.85 GB)
% used: 70.96%

Total effective bytes: 0 (0 KB)
Effective replication multiplier: Infinity
-------------------------------------------------
Datanodes available: 8

Name: 123.45.67.89:50010
State         : In Service
Total raw bytes: 76669841408 (71.4 GB)
Remaining raw bytes: 2184594843(2.03 GB)
Used raw bytes: 56598956650 (52.71 GB)
% used: 73.82%
Last contact: Sun Jun 21 16:13:32 PDT 2009
```

```
Name: 123.45.67.90:50010
State           : In Service
Total raw bytes: 76669841408 (71.4 GB)
Remaining raw bytes: 6356175381(5.92 GB)
Used raw bytes: 54220537856 (50.5 GB)
% used: 70.72%
Last contact: Sun Jun 21 16:13:33 PDT 2009

Name: 123.45.67.91:50010
State           : In Service
Total raw bytes: 76669841408 (71.4 GB)
Remaining raw bytes: 6106387206(5.69 GB)
Used raw bytes: 52412190091 (48.81 GB)
% used: 68.36%
Last contact: Sun Jun 21 16:13:33 PDT 2009

...
```

To look at the NameNode's current activity, you can use the `-metasave` option in `dfsadmin`:

bin/hadoop dfsadmin -metasave *filename*

This will save some of NameNode's metadata into its log directory under *filename*. In this metadata, you'll find lists of blocks waiting for replication, blocks being replicated, and blocks awaiting deletion. For replication each block will also have a list of DataNodes being replicated to. Finally, the metasave file will also have summary statistics on each DataNode.

8.3   *Setting permissions*

HDFS has a basic file permission system similar to the POSIX model. Each file has nine permission settings: the read (`r`), write (`w`), and execute (`x`) permissions for each of the file's associated owner, group, and other users. Not all permission settings are meaningful. Under HDFS, we can't execute files; so we can't set the `x` permission.

Permission settings for directories also closely follow the POSIX model. The `r` permission allows listing of the directory. The `w` permission allows creation or deletion of files or directories. The `x` permission allows one to access children of the directory.

Current HDFS releases don't provide much in terms of security. You should use the HDFS permission system only to prevent accidental misuse and overwriting of data among trusted users sharing a Hadoop cluster. HDFS doesn't authenticate users and believes the user identity to be whatever the host operating system says it is. Your Hadoop username is your login name, which is equivalent to what's shown by `whoami`. Your group list is equivalent to `bash -c groups`. An exception is the username that started the name node. That username has a special Hadoop username *superuser*. This superuser can perform any file operation regardless of permission settings. In addition, the administrator can specify members in a supergroup through the configuration parameter `dfs.permissions.supergroup`. All members of the supergroup are also superusers.

You can change permission settings and ownership using `bin/hadoop fs -chmod`, `-chown`, and `-chgrp`. They behave similarly to Unix commands of the same name.

8.4   Managing quotas

By default HDFS doesn't have any quota to limit how much you can put in a directory. You can enable and specify *name quotas* on specific directories, which place a hard limit on the number of file and directory names under that directory. The main use case for name quotas is to prevent users from generating too many small files and overwork the NameNode. The following commands are for setting and clearing name quotas:

```
bin/hadoop dfsadmin -setQuota <N> directory [...directory]
bin/hadoop dfsadmin -clrQuota directory [...directory]
```

Starting with version 0.19, HDFS also supports space quotas on a per directory basis. This helps manage the amount of storage a user or application can take up.

```
bin/hadoop dfsadmin -setSpaceQuota <N> directory [...directory]
bin/hadoop dfsadmin -clrSpaceQuota directory [...directory]
```

The `setSpaceQuota` command takes an argument for the number of *bytes* as each directory's quota. The argument can have a suffix to represent unit. For example, `20g` will mean 20 gigabytes, and `5t` would mean 5 terabytes. All replicas count towards the quota.

To get the quotas associated with a directory as well as a count of the number of names and bytes it uses, use the HDFS shell command `count` with the `-q` option.

```
bin/hadoop fs -count -q directory [...directory]
```

8.5   Enabling trash

In addition to file permissions, an additional safeguard against accidental deletion of files in HDFS is the trash feature. By default this feature is disabled. When this feature is enabled, the command line utilities for deleting files don't delete files immediately. Instead, they move the files temporarily to a .Trash/ folder under the user's working directory. The files are not permanently removed until after a user-configurable time delay. As long as a file is still in the .Trash/ folder, you can restore it by moving it back to its original location.

To enable the trash feature and set the time delay for the trash removal, set the `fs.trash.interval` property in core-site.xml to the delay (in minutes). For example, if you want users to have 24 hours (1,440 minutes) to restore a deleted file, you should have in core-site.xml

```
<property>
  <name>fs.trash.interval</name>
  <value>1440</value>
</property>
```

Setting the value to 0 will disable the trash feature.

8.6   Removing DataNodes

You may want to remove DataNodes from your HDFS cluster at some point. For example, you want to take a machine offline for upgrade or maintenance. Removing nodes in Hadoop can be straightforward. Although it's not recommended, you can kill the nodes or disconnect them from the cluster. HDFS is designed to be resilient. Taking one or two DataNodes offline will not affect ongoing operation. The NameNode will detect their death and will initiate replication of blocks that have fallen below the desired replication factor. For a smoother and safer operation, particularly when retiring large number of DataNodes, you should use Hadoop's decommissioning feature. Decommissioning ensures that all blocks will have the desired replication factor among the remaining active nodes. In order to use this feature, you must create an (initially empty) exclude file in the NameNode's local file- system, and the configuration parameter `dfs.hosts.exclude` must point to this file during NameNode's startup. When you want to retire DataNodes, list them in the exclude file, one node per line. You have to specify the nodes using the full hostname, IP, or IP:port format. Execute

```
bin/hadoop dfsadmin -refreshNodes
```

to force the NameNode to reread the exclude file and start the decommissioning process. Messages like "Decommission complete for node 172.16.1.55:50010" will appear in the NameNode log files when it finishes decommissioning, at which point you can remove the nodes from the cluster.

If you have started HDFS without setting `dfs.hosts.exclude` to point to an exclude file, the proper way to decommission DataNodes is this: Shut down the NameNode. Set `dfs.hosts.exclude` to point to an *empty* exclude file. Restart NameNode. After NameNode has successfully restarted, follow the procedure above. Note that if you list the retiring DataNodes in the exclude file before restarting NameNode, the NameNode will be confused and throw messages like "ProcessReport from unregistered node: node055:50010" in its logs. The NameNode thinks that it is being contacted by a DataNode outside the system rather than a node to be decommissioned.

If the decommissioned machines may rejoin the cluster at some later point, you should remove them from the exclude file and rerun `bin/hadoop dfsadmin -refreshNodes` now to update the NameNode. When the machines are ready to rejoin the cluster, you can add them using the procedure described in the next section.

8.7   Adding DataNodes

Besides bringing back a machine from offline maintenance, you may want to add DataNodes to your Hadoop cluster as you use it for more processing jobs with more data. On the new node, install Hadoop and set up the configuration files as you would any DataNode in the cluster. Start the DataNode daemon manually (`bin/hadoop datanode`). It will automatically contact the NameNode and join the cluster. You should also add the new node to the conf/slaves file in the master server. The script-based commands will recognize the new node.

When you add a new DataNode, it will initially be empty, whereas existing DataNodes will already be filled to some capacity. The filesystem is considered *unbalanced*. New files will likely go to the new node, but their replicated blocks will still go to the old nodes. One should proactively start the HDFS balancer to balance the cluster for optimal performance. Run the balancer script:

```
bin/start-balancer.sh
```

The script will run in the background until the cluster is balanced. An administrator can also terminate it earlier by running

```
bin/stop-balancer.sh
```

A cluster is considered balanced when the utilization rates of all the DataNodes are within the range of the average utilization rate plus or minus a threshold. This threshold is 10 percent by default. You can specify a different threshold when you start the balancer script. For example, to set the threshold to 5 percent for a more evenly distributed cluster, start the balancer with

```
bin/start-balancer.sh -threshold 5
```

As balancing can be network intensive, we recommend doing it overnight or over a weekend when your cluster may be less busy. Alternatively, you can set the `dfs.balance.bandwidthPerSec` configuration parameter to limit the bandwidth devoted to balancing.

8.8 *Managing NameNode and Secondary NameNode*

NameNode is one of the most important components in the HDFS architecture. It holds the filesystem's metadata and caches the cluster's blockmap in RAM for reasonable performance. When you have anything other than a tiny cluster, you should dedicate a machine to run as NameNode and don't put any DataNode, JobTracker, or TaskTracker service on it. This NameNode machine should be the most powerful machine in the cluster. Give it as much RAM as possible. Although DataNodes may have higher performance with JBOD disk drives, you should definitely use RAID drives in your NameNode for higher reliability against any single drive failure.

One approach to reducing the burden on the NameNode is to reduce the amount of filesystem metadata by increasing the block size. Doubling the block size will almost half the amount of metadata. Unfortunately, this also decreases parallelism for files that are not large. The ideal block size will depend on your specific deployment. The block size is set in the configuration parameter `dfs.block.size`. For example, to double the block size from the default 64 MB to 128 MB, set `dfs.block.size` to 134217728.

By default, the Secondary NameNode[3] and the NameNode run on the same machine. For moderate size clusters (10 or more nodes), you should separate the

---

[3] As of this writing, the Secondary NameNode is slated to be deprecated by version 0.21 of Hadoop, which should be released as this book goes to press. The Secondary NameNode will be replaced by a more robust design for warm standby. You should check the online documentation of the version of Hadoop you're using to confirm whether it's still using Secondary NameNode or not. The particular patch for this change is at https://issues.apache.org/jira/browse/HADOOP-4539.

Secondary NameNode into its own machine, the spec of which should be comparable to the NameNode. But, before going into how to set up a separate server as a Secondary NameNode, I should explain what the Secondary NameNode does and doesn't do, and in turn some of NameNode's underlying mechanics.

Due to its unfortunate naming, the Secondary NameNode (SNN) is sometimes confused with a failover backup for NameNode. It most certainly is not. The SNN only serves to periodically clean up and tighten the filesystem's state information in NameNode, helping NameNode become more efficient. NameNode manages the filesystem's state information using two files, `FsImage` and `EditLog`. The file `FsImage` is a snapshot of the filesystem at some checkpoint, and `EditLog` records each incremental change (*delta*) to the filesystem after that checkpoint. These two files can completely determine the current state of the filesystem. When you initialize NameNode, it merges these two files to create a new snapshot. At the end of NameNode's initialization, `FsImage` will contain the new snapshot and `EditLog` will be empty. Afterward any operation that changes the state of HDFS is appended to `EditLog`, whereas `FsImage` will remain unchanged. When you shut down NameNode and restart it, the consolidation will take place again and make a new snapshot. Note that the two files are only for retaining the filesystem's state information while NameNode is not running (either intentionally shut down or due to system malfunction). NameNode keeps in memory a constantly maintained copy of the filesystem's state information to quickly answer queries about the filesystem.

For a busy cluster, the `EditLog` file will grow quite large, and the next restart of NameNode will take a long time to merge `EditLog` into `FsImage`. For busy clusters, it can also be a long time in between NameNode restarts, and you may want more frequent snapshots for archival purposes. This is where SNN comes in. It consolidates `FsImage` and `EditLog` into a new snapshot and leaves the NameNode alone to serve live traffic. Therefore, it's more appropriate to think of the SNN as a checkpointing server. Merging `FsImage` and `EditLog` is memory intensive, requiring an amount of memory on the same order as normal NameNode operation. It's best for the SNN to be on a separate server that is as powerful as the primary NameNode.

To configure HDFS to use a separate server as the SNN, first list that server's host name or IP address in the `conf/masters` file. Unfortunately, this file name is also confusing. The masters in Hadoop (NameNode and JobTracker) are whichever machine you run `bin/start-dfs.sh` and `bin/start-mapred.sh` on. What's listed in `conf/masters` is the SNN, not any of the masters.

You should also modify the conf/hdfs-site.xml file on the SNN such that the `dfs.http.address` property points to port 50070 of the NameNode's host address, like

```
<property>
    <name>dfs.http.address</name>
    <value>namenode.hadoop-host.com:50070</value>
</property>
```

You should set this property because the SNN retrieves `FsImage` and `EditLog` from the NameNode by sending HTTP Get requests to the URLs:

- *FsImage*—http://*namenode.hadoop-host.com*:50070/getimage?getimage=1
- *EditLog*—http://*namenode.hadoop-host.com*:50070/getimage?getedit=1

The SNN also updates the NameNode with the merged metadata using the same address and port.

8.9 Recovering from a failed NameNode

Failures happen, and Hadoop has been designed to be quite resilient. The NameNode, unfortunately, remains a weak point. HDFS is out of commission if the NameNode is down. A common design for setting up a backup NameNode server is by reusing the SNN.[4] After all, the SNN has similar hardware specs as the NameNode, and Hadoop should've already been installed with the same directory configurations. If we do some additional work of maintaining the SNN to be a functional mirror image of the NameNode, we can quickly start this backup machine as a NameNode instance in the case of a NameNode failure. Some manual intervention and time are necessary to start the backup node as the new NameNode, but at least we wouldn't lose any data.

NameNode keeps all the filesystem's metadata, including the `FsImage` and `EditLog` files, under the `dfs.name.dir` directory. Note that the SNN server doesn't use that directory at all. It downloads the system's metadata into the `fs.checkpoint.dir` directory and proceeds to merge `FsImage` and `EditLog` there. As the `dfs.name.dir` directory on the SNN is unused, we can expose it to the NameNode via the Network File System (NFS). We instruct the NameNode to always write to this mounted directory in addition to writing to the NameNode's local metadata directory. HDFS supports this ability to write the metadata to multiple directories. You have to specify `dfs.name.dir` on the NameNode with a comma separated list, like

```
<property>
    <name>dfs.name.dir</name>
    <value>/home/hadoop/dfs/name,/mnt/hadoop-backup</value>
    <final>true</final>
</property>
```

This works, assuming the local `dfs.name.dir` directory at both the NameNode and the Secondary NameNode are at `/home/hadoop/dfs/name`, and that the directory on the SNN is mounted to the NameNode at `/mnt/hadoop-backup`. When HDFS sees a comma-separated list in `dfs.name.dir`, it writes its metadata to every directory on the list.

Given this setup, when the NameNode dies, the local `dfs.name.dir` directory at both the NameNode and the backup node (SNN) should have the same content. To have the backup node serve as the replacement NameNode, you'll have to switch its IP address to the original NameNode's IP address. (Unfortunately, changing only the hostname is not sufficient as the DataNodes cache the DNS entry.) You'll also have to run the backup node as a NameNode by executing `bin/start-dfs.sh` on it.

---

[4] Unfortunately, this common design also contributes to the misperception of the Secondary NameNode as a backup node. You can set up the backup node in a totally different machine from the NameNode and SNN, but that machine would be idle almost all the time.

To be safer, this new NameNode should *also* have a backup node set up before you start it. Otherwise you'll be in trouble if this new NameNode fails too. If you don't have a machine readily available as a backup, you should at least set up an NFS-mounted directory. This way the filesystem's state information is in more than one location.

As HDFS writes its metadata to all directories listed in `dfs.name.dir`, if your NameNode has multiple hard drives, you can specify directories from different drives to hold replicas of the metadata. This way if one drive fails, it's easier to restart the NameNode without the bad drive than to switch over to the backup node, which involves moving the IP address, setting up a new backup node, and so on.

Recall that the SNN creates a snapshot of the filesystem's metadata in the `fs.checkpoint.dir` directory. As it checkpoints only periodically (once an hour under the default setup), the metadata is too stale to rely on for failover. But it's still a good idea to archive this directory periodically over to remote storage. In catastrophic situations, recovering from stale data is better than no data at all. This can be true if both the NameNode and the backup fail simultaneously (say, a power surge affecting both machines). Another unfortunate scenario is if the filesystem's metadata has been corrupted (say, by human error or a software bug) and has poisoned all the replicas. Recovering from a checkpoint image is explained in http://issues.apache.org/jira/browse/HADOOP-2585.

HDFS's backup and recovery mechanism is undergoing active improvements as of this writing. You should check with HDFS's online documentation for the latest news. There have also been applications of specialized Linux software such as DRBD[5] to Hadoop clusters for high availability. You can find one example in http://www.cloudera.com/blog/2009/07/22/hadoop-ha-configuration/.

8.10 *Designing network layout and rack awareness*

When your Hadoop cluster gets big, the nodes will be spread out in more than one rack and the cluster's network topology starts to affect reliability and performance. You may want the cluster to survive the failure of an entire rack. You should place your backup server for NameNode, as described in the previous section, in a separate rack from the NameNode itself. This way the failure of any one rack will not destroy all copies of the filesystem's metadata.

With more than one rack, the placement of both block replicas and tasks becomes more complex. Replicas of a block should be placed in separate racks to reduce the potential of data loss. For the standard replication value of 3, the default placement policy for writing a block is this: If the client performing the write operation is part of the Hadoop cluster, place the first replica on the DataNode where the client resides. Otherwise randomly place the replica in the cluster. Place the second replica on a random rack different from the rack where the first replica resides. Write the third replica to a different node on the same rack as the second replica. For replication values higher than 3, place the subsequent replicas on random nodes. As of this

___
[5] http://www.drbd.org.

writing, this block placement policy is baked into the NameNode. A pluggable policy is targeted for version 0.21.[6]

Besides block placement, task placement is also rack aware. A task is usually placed on a node that has a copy of the block the task is assigned to process. When no such node is available to take on the new task, the task is randomly assigned to a node on a rack where a copy of the block is available somewhere on that rack. That is, when data locality can't be enforced at a node level, Hadoop tries to enforce it at the rack level. Failing that, a task would be randomly assigned to one of the remaining nodes.

At this point you may wonder how Hadoop knows which rack a node is at. It requires you to tell it. It assumes a hierarchical network topology for your Hadoop cluster, structurally similar to figure 8.1. Each node has a rack name similar to a file path. For example, the nodes H1, H2, and H3 in figure 8.1 all have a rack name of `/D1/R1`. Figure 8.1 shows a case where you have multiple datacenters (D1 and D2) each with multiple racks (R1 to R4). In most cases you'll be dealing with multiple racks co-located together. Your rack names will be in a flat namespace, such as `/R1` and `/R2`.

To help Hadoop know the location of each node, you have to provide an executable script that can map IP addresses into rack names. This *network topology script* must reside on the master node and its location is specified in the `topology.script.file.name` property in `core-site.xml`. Hadoop will call this script with a set of IP addresses as separate arguments. The script should print out (through STDOUT) the rack name corresponding to each IP address in the same order, separated by whitespace. The `topology.script.number.args` property controls the maximum number of IP addresses Hadoop will ask for at any one time. It's convenient to simplify your script by setting that value to 1. Here is an example a network topology script.

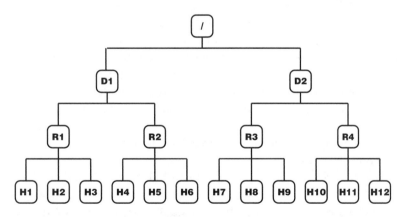

Figure 8.1 A cluster with a hierarchical network topology. This cluster spans multiples datacenters (D1 and D2). Each datacenter has multiple racks (R), and each rack has multiple machines.

---

[6] See http://issues.apache.org/jira/browse/HDFS-385 for the description of this change.

```
#!/bin/bash
ipaddr=$1
segments='echo $ipaddr | cut --delimiter=. --fields=4'
if [ "$segments" -lt 128 ]; then
    echo /rack-1
else
    echo /rack-2
fi
```

This bash script takes an IPv4 address and looks at the last of the four octets (assuming dot-decimal notation). The node is considered in rack 1 if the last octet is less than 128, and the node is considered in rack 2 otherwise. A table lookup may make more sense for more complex cluster topologies. On the other hand, if there is no network topology script, Hadoop assumes a flat topology where all nodes are assigned to `/default-rack`.

8.11 *Scheduling jobs from multiple users*

As you have more and more jobs coming from multiple users for your Hadoop cluster, you'll need some control to prevent contention. Under Hadoop's default FIFO scheduler, as soon as a job is sent to Hadoop for execution, the JobTracker will assign as many TaskTrackers as necessary to process that job. This works fairly well when things are not busy and you have a good amount of processing capacity to spare. But some big Hadoop jobs can easily tie up the cluster for a long time and force the smaller jobs to wait. Wouldn't it be great if something akin to an express checkout existed for smaller jobs in a Hadoop cluster?

8.11.1 *Multiple JobTrackers*

Back in the days before Hadoop version 0.19, you had to physically set up multiple MapReduce clusters to provide rudimentary CPU allocation among jobs. To keep storage utilization reasonably efficient though, there would still be one single HDFS cluster. Let's say, you have Z slave nodes available for your Hadoop cluster. You'll have a single NameNode that takes all Z nodes as DataNodes. All Z nodes will also be TaskTrackers. Until now, all these TaskTrackers would point to the same/only JobTracker.

The trick in making a multicluster setup is having multiple JobTrackers, and each JobTracker controls a (mutually exclusive) subset of TaskTrackers. For example, to create two MapReduce clusters, you have X TaskTrackers point to one JobTracker (via the `mapred.job.tracker` property) and Y TaskTrackers configured to use the second JobTracker. The slave nodes between the two MapReduce clusters are distinct to give X+Y=Z. To use this setup, you submit certain jobs to one JobTracker, whereas other jobs go to the other JobTracker. This limits the number of TaskTrackers available to each type of job. The job type need not necessarily determine the assignment of jobs to the MapReduce pool. More typical is to allocate each MapReduce pool to one user group. This enforces a limit to how much resource one group can take up.

Physically setting up multiple MapReduce clusters this way has many drawbacks. It's not very user-friendly as one has to remember which pool to use. It's less likely that a task is data-local. (It may be the case that all replicas are in DataNodes outside of one's pool.) The setup is not flexible to changing resource requirements. Fortunately, starting with version 0.19, Hadoop has a pluggable architecture for the scheduler, and two new schedulers have become available for resolving job contention. One is the *Fair Scheduler* developed at Facebook, and another one is the *Capacity Scheduler* developed at Yahoo.

8.11.2 Fair Scheduler

The Fair Scheduler introduced the notion of *pools*. Jobs are tagged to belong to specific pools, and each pool is configured to have a guaranteed capacity of a certain number of map slots and a certain number of reduce slots. When task slots are freed up, the Fair Scheduler will allocate them to meet these minimum guarantees first. After it meets the guarantees, slots are allocated between jobs using "fair sharing," such that each job gets roughly an equal amount of compute resource. You can set priority on jobs to give more capacity to higher priority jobs. (Some jobs are more equal than others.)

The Fair Scheduler is available as the jar file `hadoop-*-fairscheduler.jar` under the `contrib/fairscheduler` directory of the Hadoop installation. To install it, you can move the jar file directly into Hadoop's `lib/` directory. Alternatively, you can modify `HADOOP_CLASSPATH` in the script `conf/hadoop-env.sh` to include this jar.

You'll need to set a few properties in `hadoop-site.xml` to fully enable and configure the Fair Scheduler. You first instruct Hadoop to use the Fair Scheduler instead of the default one by setting `mapred.jobtracker.taskScheduler` to `org.apache.hadoop.mapred.FairScheduler`. You then configure a few Fair Scheduler properties. The most important is `mapred.fairscheduler.allocation.file`, which points to the file that defines the different pools. This file is typically named `pools.xml` and specifies each pool's name and capacity. The `mapred.fairscheduler.poolname` property defines the `jobconf` property the scheduler will use to determine which pool to use for a job. A useful configuration pattern is to set this to a new property, say `pool.name`, and assign `pool.name` to have a default value of `${user.name}`. The Fair Scheduler automatically gives each user her own individual pool. This particular `pool.name` will by default assign each job to its owner's pool. You can change the `pool.name` property in a job's `jobconf` to assign the job to a different pool.[7] Finally, the `mapred.fairscheduler.assignmultiple` property, when set to true, allows the scheduler to assign both a map task and a reduce task on each heartbeat, which improves ramp-up speed and throughput. To summarize, your `mapred-site.xml` will have the following properties set:

---

[7] Yes, you can run your job in another user's pool, but that's not very polite. The main usage is to assign special jobs to specific pools. For example, you may want all cron jobs to go to a single pool rather than have them run under each individual user's pool.

```xml
<property>
  <name>mapred.jobtracker.taskScheduler</name>
  <value>org.apache.hadoop.mapred.FairScheduler</value>
</property>
<property>
  <name>mapred.fairscheduler.allocation.file</name>
  <value>HADOOP_CONF_DIR/pools.xml</value>
</property>
<property>
  <name>mapred.fairscheduler.assignmultiple</name>
  <value>true</value>
</property>
<property>
  <name>mapred.fairscheduler.poolnameproperty</name>
  <value>pool.name</value>
</property>
<property>
  <name>pool.name</name>
  <value>${user.name}</value>
</property>
```

The allocation file `pools.xml` defines the pools for the scheduler. It gives each pool a name and capacity constraints. The constraints can include the minimum number of map slots or reduce slots. They can also include the maximum number of running jobs. In addition, you can set the maximum number of running jobs per user, and also override this maximum for specific users. An example `pools.xml` looks like this:

```xml
<?xml version="1.0"?>
<allocations>
  <pool name="ads">
    <minMaps>2</minMaps>
    <minReduces>2</minReduces>
  </pool>
  <pool name="hive">
    <minMaps>2</minMaps>
    <minReduces>2</minReduces>
    <maxRunningJobs>2</maxRunningJobs>
  </pool>
  <user name="chuck">
    <maxRunningJobs>6</maxRunningJobs>
  </user>
  <userMaxJobsDefault>3</userMaxJobsDefault>
</allocations>
```

This `pools.xml` defines two special pools, "ads" and "hive". Each is guaranteed to have at least two map slots and two reduce slots. The "hive" pool is limited to running at most two jobs at once. To use these pools, you set the `pool.name` property in a job's configuration to either "ads" or "hive". This `pools.xml` also caps the number of simultaneous running jobs a user can have to three, but the user "chuck" is given a higher cap of six.

Note that the `pools.xml` file is reread every 15 seconds. You can modify this file and dynamically reallocate capacity at run time. Any pool not defined in this file has no guaranteed capacity and no limit on number of jobs running at once.

<u>localhost</u> **Job Scheduler Administration**

Pools

Pool	Running Jobs	Min Maps	Min Reduces	Running Maps	Running Reduces
ads	0	2	2	0	0
chuck	1	0	0	1	1
hive	0	2	2	0	0
default	0	0	0	0	0

Running Jobs

Submitted	JobID	User	Name	Pool	Priority	Maps			Reduces		
						Finished	Running	Fair Share	Finished	Running	Fair Share
Aug 11, 04:08	job_200908110346_0002	chuck	streamjob6351400141424754280.jar	chuck	NORMAL	3 / 4	1	2.0	0 / 1	1	2.0

Scheduling Mode

The scheduler is currently using **Fair Sharing mode** [Switch to FIFO mode.]

Figure 8.2 The Web UI to monitor Hadoop's fair scheduler. The top table shows all the available pools and each pool's usage. The table showing "Running Jobs" has a Pool column where you can monitor or change the pool of each job.

When you have your Hadoop cluster running with the Fair Scheduler, there's a Web UI available to administer the scheduler. The page is at http://<jobtracker URL>/scheduler. Besides letting you know how the jobs are scheduled, it also allows you to change the pool a job belongs to and the job's priority. Figure 8.2 shows an example screenshot of this page.

The Capacity Scheduler shares similar goals with the Fair Scheduler. The Capacity Scheduler works on *queues* rather than *pools*. The interested reader can learn more about the Capacity Scheduler from the online documentation at http://hadoop.apache.org/common/docs/r0.20.0/capacity_scheduler.html.

8.12 *Summary*

Managing distributed clusters is complicated and Hadoop is no different. We've covered many common administrative tasks in this chapter. If you have a complex setup and have more sophisticated questions, a useful resource is the Hadoop mailing lists.[8] Many Hadoop administrators with deep expertise are active on those mailing lists, and chances are that one of them will have encountered your situation. On the other hand, if you mostly want a basic Hadoop cluster without all the hassle of administration, you may want to consider using the Cloudera distribution[9] or checking out one of the Hadoop cloud services, which we cover in the next chapter.

---

[8] http://hadoop.apache.org/common/mailing_lists.html.
[9] http://www.cloudera.com/distribution.

Part 3

Hadoop Gone Wild

P art 3 explores the larger ecosystem around Hadoop. Cloud services provide an alternative to buying and hosting your own hardware to create a Hadoop cluster. Many add-on packages provide higher-level programming abstractions over MapReduce. We show several case studies where Hadoop solves real business problems in practice.

Running Hadoop
in the cloud

This chapter covers

- Setting up a compute cloud with Amazon Web Services (AWS)
- Running Hadoop in the AWS cloud
- Transferring data into and out of an AWS Hadoop cloud

Depending on your data processing needs, your Hadoop workload can vary widely over time. You may have a few large data processing jobs that occasionally take advantage of hundreds of nodes, but those same nodes will sit idle the rest of the time. You may be new to Hadoop and want to get familiar with it first before investing in a dedicated cluster. You may own a startup that needs to conserve cash and wants to avoid the capital expense of a Hadoop cluster. In these and other situations, it makes more sense to *rent* a cluster of machines rather than buy it.

The general paradigm of provisioning compute resources as a remote service in a flexible, cost-effective manner is called *cloud computing*. The best-known infrastructure service platform for cloud computing is Amazon Web Services (AWS). You can rent computing and storage services from AWS on demand as your requirement scales. As of this writing, renting a compute unit with the equivalent power of a 1.0 GHz

32-bit Opteron with 1.7 GB RAM and 160 GB disk storage costs $0.10 per hour. Using a cluster of 100 such machines for an hour will cost a measly $10! It wasn't too long ago that only a select few had access to clusters on this scale. Thanks to AWS and other such services, large-scale compute power is available to many people today.

Because of its flexibility and cost effectiveness, running Hadoop on the AWS cloud is a popular setup, and we learn how to install and configure this configuration in this chapter.

9.1   *Introducing Amazon Web Services*

Learning all the capabilities of Amazon Web Services is worthy of a book itself. Amazon is constantly adding new services and features. We recommend you to explore the AWS website (http://aws.amazon.com) to get more details and the latest offerings. We only cover enough basics here to get a Hadoop cluster running.

Of all the services AWS offers, its Elastic Compute Cloud (EC2) and Simple Storage Service (S3) are the two core services you need to understand to run Hadoop in the cloud. The EC2 service provides compute capacity for running Hadoop nodes. You can think of EC2 as a large farm of virtual machines. An EC2 *instance* is the AWS terminology for a virtual compute unit. Each Hadoop node will take up an EC2 instance. You rent an EC2 instance for only as long as you need and pay on an hourly basis.

A car rental company throws out whatever you leave in the trunk when you return it. Similarly, all your data on an EC2 instance is deleted when you terminate the instance. If you want the data to be around for future use, you have to ensure that it's in some persistent storage. The Amazon S3 service is a cloud storage service that you may use for such purposes.

Each EC2 instance functions like a commodity Intel machine that you can access and control over the internet. You boot up an instance using an *Amazon Machine Image*, also known as an *AMI* or an *image*. More demanding users can create their own images, but most users are well served by one of the many preconfigured ones. Some images are only basic bare-bones operating systems. Supported operating systems on EC2 include more than six variants of Linux, plus Windows Server and OpenSolaris. Other images include one of the operating systems plus pre-installed software, such as database server, Apache HTTP server, Java application server, and others. AWS offers preconfigured images of Hadoop running on Linux, and Hadoop has built-in support for working with both EC2 and S3.

9.2   *Setting up AWS*

This section is a quick introduction to setting up AWS. We only cover the essentials to get a Hadoop cluster running. If you are already familiar with launching and using EC2 instances, you should skip directly to the next section on setting up Hadoop on AWS.

To start using AWS, you first have to sign up for an account. Go to http://aws.amazon.com/ and click on the button urging you to "Sign Up Now." The process is self-explanatory. It's no more complicated than buying a book from Amazon. The sign-up process sets up your Amazon account (which you may already have if you have bought stuff from Amazon before) and activates it to pay for your usage of AWS.

NOTE Amazon has introduced the Elastic MapReduce (EMR) service that vastly simplifies the use of Hadoop on AWS. The most important simplification is that you no longer have to set up and launch your own cluster of EC2 instances. The trade-off is that you lose some control over how the cluster works and you have to pay extra for this EMR service. We discuss EMR in section 9.6. But we highly encourage you to keep on reading and understand how to set up your own EC2 cluster running Hadoop, even if you don't go through the process of setting it up. At the very least, knowing more details about how Hadoop runs on an EC2 cluster will clarify what EMR is doing underneath the hood.

After you have activated your Amazon account for AWS, there are three more steps before you can start creating machine instances and using them:

1   Obtain your account IDs and your authentication keys and certificates. You'll set these up on your local machine to secure your communication with AWS. These security mechanisms ensure that only you can rent compute resources with your account.

2   Download and set up command line tools to manage your EC2 instances. These include special programs to start and stop EC2 instances in your virtual cluster.

3   Generate an SSH key pair. After you have started an EC2 instance, you'll log into it using SSH (either directly or indirectly through the use of special tools). The default SSH mechanism uses the SSH key pair to authenticate you to your EC2 instance in lieu of using a password.

We go through each step in a subsection below.

9.2.1 *Getting your AWS authentication credentials*

AWS supports two types of authentication mechanisms: the AWS Access Key Identifier and X.509 certificate. To run Hadoop on AWS you'll need both mechanisms, and they can be set up from the Access Identifiers page where you manage your AWS account (http://aws.amazon.com/account/). The AWS Access Key Identifier consists of an Access Key ID and a Secret Access Key. Figure 9.1 shows a section of the Access Identifiers page. An Access Key ID is a 20-character alphanumeric sequence whereas a Secret Access Key is a 40-character sequence. Don't share your Secret Access Key with anyone. The web page requires an extra click on Show to display it (in case anyone is looking over your shoulder). You should generate a new Secret Access Key if the one you have has been compromised. You'll need to specify your Access Key ID and Secret Access Key later when you set up the Hadoop cluster.

TIP In some situations when you want Hadoop to access S3, you'll tell Hadoop your AWS Access Key ID and Secret Access Key in a specially formatted URI. Unfortunately, AWS allows slashes (/) in its Secret Access Keys, which will cause confusion inside a URI. Although there are ways you can tell Hadoop your AWS Access Key ID without using a URI, it may be more convenient to regenerate your Secret Access Key until you get one without a slash (/) in it.

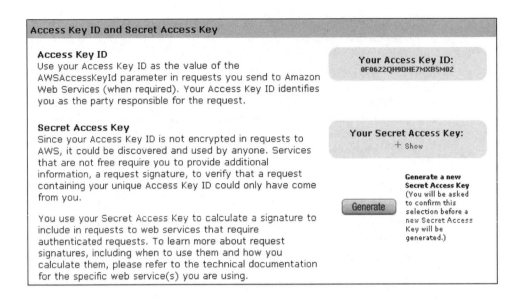

Figure 9.1   Getting AWS Access Key ID and Secret Access Key

Setting up the X.509 Certificate involves a bit more work. At the same Access Identifiers page is a section titled *X.509 Certificate*, as seen in figure 9.2. You click on Create New to generate a new X.509 certificate. A certificate has two keys: a public key and a private key. Unlike the Access Key ID and the Secret Access Key, the public and private keys in your X.509 certificate are hundreds of characters long, and they have to be stored and managed as files. After creating a new X.509 certificate, you'll arrive at a page to download both keys/files. See figure 9.3.

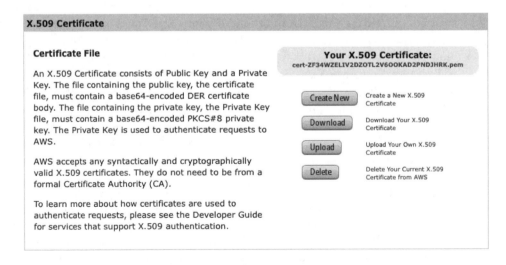

Figure 9.2   Managing your X.509 certificate. You can upload your own, or ask AWS to create one.

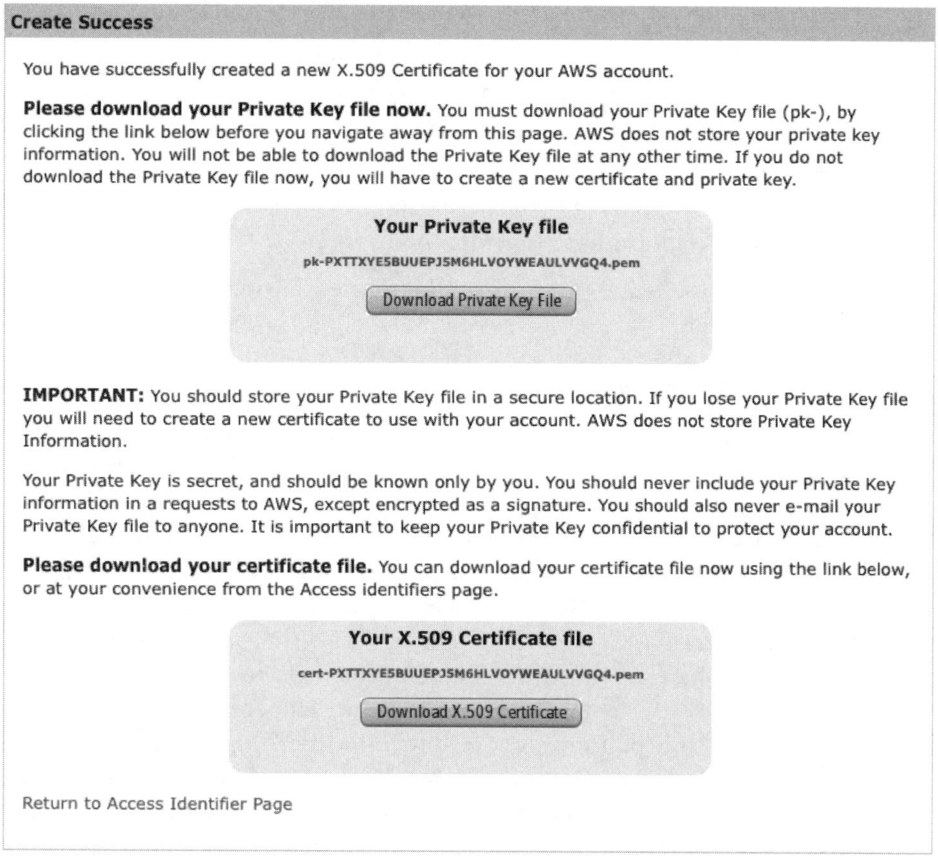

Create Success

You have successfully created a new X.509 Certificate for your AWS account.

Please download your Private Key file now. You must download your Private Key file (pk-), by clicking the link below before you navigate away from this page. AWS does not store your private key information. You will not be able to download the Private Key file at any other time. If you do not download the Private Key file now, you will have to create a new certificate and private key.

Your Private Key file

pk-PXTTXYE5BUUEPJ5M6HLVOYWEAULVVGQ4.pem

Download Private Key File

IMPORTANT: You should store your Private Key file in a secure location. If you lose your Private Key file you will need to create a new certificate to use with your account. AWS does not store Private Key Information.

Your Private Key is secret, and should be known only by you. You should never include your Private Key information in a requests to AWS, except encrypted as a signature. You should also never e-mail your Private Key file to anyone. It is important to keep your Private Key confidential to protect your account.

Please download your certificate file. You can download your certificate file now using the link below, or at your convenience from the Access identifiers page.

Your X.509 Certificate file

cert-PXTTXYE5BUUEPJ5M6HLVOYWEAULVVGQ4.pem

Download X.509 Certificate

Return to Access Identifier Page

Figure 9.3   Download the private key and certificate file of your X.509 Certificate.

The public key is also called a *certificate file.* Your private key, as the name implies, should not be shared with anyone. Even Amazon itself doesn't store a copy of it. AWS specifies filenames for the certificate and the private key, and you should keep those names when you save them. The filenames for the certificate and the private key are prefixed with cert- and pk-, respectively, and they have the .pem file extension. You should create a directory called .ec2 under your home directory on your local machine and save those two files in the new directory. On Linux you'll have saved the following files to your local machine:

```
~/.ec2/cert-HKZYKTAIG2ECMXYIBH3HXV4ZBZQ55CLO.pem
~/.ec2/pk-HKZYKTAIG2ECMXYIBH3HXV4ZBZQ55CLO.pem
```

Finally, you should also note your AWS Account Number. It's near the top right side of the Access Identifiers page, and it's a 12-digit hyphenated number that looks like "4952-1993-3132." Your Account ID is the unhyphenated version of that—something like "495219933132." Your Account ID is what you'll use in setting up Hadoop on EC2.

You may think these are a lot of values to generate and write down. To summarize, here are the five values you should have at this point:

- Your 20-character, alphanumeric Access Key ID
- Your 40-character Secret Access Key
- Your X.509 Certificate file under the .ec2 directory
- Your X.509 private key file under the .ec2 directory
- Your 12-digit (unhyphenated) AWS Account ID

You'll use these values later to authenticate yourself to AWS and control your Hadoop cluster.

9.2.2 *Getting command line tools*

After getting all the security credentials, you should download and configure the AWS command line tools to instantiate and manage your EC2 instances. These tools are written in Java, which presumably is already installed on your local machine.

The EC2 command line tools are self-contained in one downloadable ZIP file from the AWS EC2 Resource Center.[1] Unzip the file into a directory you use for your AWS work. In the unzipped files you'll see the Java tools plus shell scripts for Windows, Linux, and Mac OS X.

You don't have to configure the command line tools, but you do have to set a few environment variables before using them. The environment variable EC2_HOME should be a path pointing to the directory where the command line tools were unzipped. Unless you have renamed that directory, its name is ec2-api-tools-A.B-nnnn, where *A*, *B*, and *n* are version/release numbers. You should also set EC2_CERT and EC2_PRIVATE_KEY to point to your X.509 certificate and private key files, respectively. I've found it useful to have a script for setting up all the necessary environment variables to use the AWS command line tools. A version for Linux, Unix, and Mac OS X, called ec2-init.sh, is in listing 9.1. You run this script before using any AWS related tools by executing

```
source ec2-init.sh
```

or

```
. ec2-init.sh
```

Listing 9.1   ec2-init.sh: a Unix script setting up variables for EC2 tools

```
export JAVA_HOME = /Library/Java/Home
export EC2_HOME = ~/Projects/Hadoop/aws/ec2-api-tools-1.3-30349
export PATH = $PATH:$EC2_HOME/bin:$HADOOP_HOME/src/contrib/ec2/bin
export EC2_PRIVATE_KEY = ~/.ec2/pk-HKZYKTAIG2ECMXYIBH3HXV4ZBZQ55CLO.pem
export EC2_CERT = ~/.ec2/cert-HKZYKTAIG2ECMXYIBH3HXV4ZBZQ55CLO.pem
```

---

[1] http://developer.amazonwebservices.com/connect/entry.jspa?externalID=351&categoryID=88.

An analogous version for Windows is in listing 9.2. You can run it in a command prompt by executing ec2-init.bat.

Listing 9.2   ec2-init.bat: a Windows script setting up variables for EC2 tools

```
set JAVA_HOME = "C:\Program Files\Java\jdk1.6.0_08"
set EC2_HOME = "C:\Program Files\Hadoop\aws\ec2-api-tools-1.3-30349"
set PATH = %PATH%;%EC2_HOME%\bin;%HADOOP_HOME%\src\contrib\ec2\bin
set EC2_PRIVATE_KEY = c:\ec2\pk-HKZYKTAIG2ECMXYIBH3HXV4ZBZQ55CLO.pem
set EC2_CERT = c:\ec2\cert-HKZYKTAIG2ECMXYIBH3HXV4ZBZQ55CLO.pem
```

If you'll be working with AWS often, you may choose to not use a separate script and instead integrate it directly into your operating system's start-up script (for example, .profile and autoexec.bat).

The pathnames in the script will be different for your particular installation. The environment variable JAVA_HOME needs to be set for the AWS command line tools to work. We set it here although most likely it has already been set elsewhere. The script adds the command line tools' bin directory to your system PATH. This makes executing the tools much easier, as you don't need to specify the full path every time. The Hadoop EC2 tools' directory is also added to PATH, although we won't cover them until the next section.

AWS has machines located in different regions of the world. As of this writing, AWS supports two regions, the U.S. and the E.U. As an optional step, you can choose which region to run your EC2 instances to reduce latency. After you have run the preceding script to set up the environment variables, let's run our first AWS command line tool to ask Amazon what regions are currently available:

```
ec2-describe-regions
```

You'll get back something like this:

```
REGION          us-east-1          us-east-1.ec2.amazonaws.com
REGION          eu-west-1          eu-west-1.ec2.amazonaws.com
```

The second column is the region names (us-east-1 and eu-west-1) and the third column is the corresponding *service endpoints*. The default region is us-east-1. Set the environment variable EC2_URL to the service endpoint of a different region if you choose to. You can do this within the preceding AWS initialization shell script.

> **TIP**   Besides the official command line tools, there are also GUI tools for managing your EC2 and S3 usage. These GUI tools tend to be more user-friendly. Two of the more popular ones are both Firefox extensions: Elasticfox and S3Fox. Elasticfox (http://developer.amazonwebservices.com/connect/entry.jspa?entryID=609) provides basic EC2 management features, such as launching new EC2 instances and listing currently running ones. S3Fox (http://www.suchisoft.com/ext/s3fox.php) is a third-party tool for organizing your S3 storage. It functions much like a GUI-based FTP client in managing remote storage.

9.2.3   *Preparing an SSH key pair*

After starting an EC2 instance, you'll want to log into it to run programs and services. The default login mechanism (of public images) uses SSH with a key pair. Half of this key pair (public key) is embedded in the EC2 instance, and the other half (private key) is in your local machine. Together, the key pair secures the communication between your local machine and the EC2 instance.

> **NOTE**   Some of you may be more familiar with logging into a remote machine using SSH with a password. Using SSH with a key pair is an alternative mechanism. Instead of a password, you authenticate yourself with a private key that's stored as a file on your local machine. Like your password, your private key file should not be accessible by unauthorized people.

Each SSH key pair has a *key name* to identify it. When requesting Amazon EC2 to create an instance, you have to specify the public key to be embedded in that instance by its corresponding key name. The SSH public key has to exist and be registered with Amazon before creating any EC2 instances.

The following command generates an SSH public/private key pair and registers the public key to Amazon EC2 under the key name `gsg-keypair`.

```
ec2-add-keypair gsg-keypair
```

Interestingly, the command doesn't save the private key to a local file. Instead, it generates a standard output (stdout) similar to figure 9.4, part of which is the private key. You'll have to manually save it to a file using a text editor. Specifically, copy and paste the output between the following two lines, inclusive, to a new file named id_rsa-gsg-keypair.

```
-----BEGIN RSA PRIVATE KEY-----
-----END RSA PRIVATE KEY-----
```

For ease of management, you should save the file to the same .ec2 directory for your X.509 private key and certificate. You'll also need to lock down the file permission such that it's only readable by you. On Linux and other Unix-based systems, use the following command:

```
chmod 600 ~/.ec2/id_rsa-gsg-keypair
```

All EC2 instances in a single Hadoop cluster will have the same public key. A single private key can log into any node in the cluster, and only one SSH key pair is needed. You can also choose to use more than one SSH key pair when working with multiple Hadoop clusters, or when you use extra EC2 instances outside of your Hadoop cluster.

At this point you have finished the one-time setup of credentials and certificates to start a compute cluster in the Amazon cloud. You can manually use the AWS tools to launch EC2 instances and log into them to launch your Hadoop cluster. This approach is time consuming and error prone, though. Fortunately, Hadoop has included tools to work with AWS, which we discuss in the next section. Before we finish this section, we

```
KEYPAIR gsg-keypair  1f:51:ae:28:bf:89:e9:d8:1f:25:5d:37:2d:7d:b8:ca:9f:f5:f1:6f
-----BEGIN RSA PRIVATE KEY-----
MIIEoQIBAAKCAQBuLFg5ujHrtm1jnutSuoO8Xe56LlT+HM8v/xkaa39EstM3/aFxTHgElQiJLChp
HungXQ29VTc8rc1bWOlkdi230H5eqkMHGhvEwqa0HWASUMll4o3o/IX+0f2UcPoKCOVUR+jx71Sg
5AU52EQfanIn3ZQ8lFW7Edp5a3q4DhjGlUKToHVbicL5E+g45zfB95wIyywWZfeW/UUF3LpGZyq/
ebIUlq1qTbHkLbCC2r7RTn8vpQWp47BGVYGtGSBMpTRP5hnbzzuqj3itkiLHjU39S2sJCJ0TrJx5
i8BygR4s3mHKBj8l+ePQxG1kGbF6R4yg6sECmXn17MRQVXODNHZbAgMBAAECggEAY1tsiUsIwDl5
91CXirkYGuVfLyLflXenxfI50mDFms/mumTqloHO7tr0oriHDR5K7wMcY/YY5YkcXNo7mvUVD1pM
ZNUJs7rw9gZRTrf7LylaJ58kOcyajw8TsC4e4LPbFaHwS1d6K8rXh64o6WgW4SrsB6ICmr1kGQI7
3wcfgt5ecIu4TZf00E9IHjn+2eRlsrjBdeORi7KiUNC/pAG23I6MdDOFEQRcCSigCj+4/mciFUSA
SWS4dMbrpb9FNSIcf9dcLxVM7/6KxgJNfZc9XWzUw77Jg8x92Zd0fVhHOux5IZC+UvSKWB4dyfcI
tE8C3p9bbU9VGyY5vLCAiIb4qQKBgQDLiO24GXrIkswF32YtBBMuVgLGCwU9h9HlO9mKAc2m8Cm1
jUE5IpzRjTedc9I2qiIMUTwtgnw42auSCzbUeYMURPtDqyQ7p6AjMujp9EPemcSVOK9vXYL0Ptco
xW9MC0dtV6iPkCN7gOqiZXPRKaFbWADp16p8UAIvS/a5XXk5jwKBgQCKkpHi2EISh1uRkhxljyWC
iDCiK6JBRsMvpLbc0v5dKwP5alo1fmdR5PJaV2qvZSj5CYNpMAy1/EDNTY5OSIJU+0KFmQbyhsbm
rdLNLDL4+TcnT7c62/aH01ohYaf/VCbRhtLlBfqGoQc7+sAc8vmKkesnF7CqCEKDyF/dhrxYdQKB
gC0iZzzNAapayz1+JcVTwwEid6j9JqNXbBc+Z2YwMi+T0Fv/P/hwkX/ypeOXnIUcw0Ih/YtGBVAC
DQbsz7LcY1HqXiHKYNWNvXgww0+oiChjxvEkSdsTTIfnK4VSCvU9BxDbQHjdiNDJbL6oar92UN7V
rBYvChJZF7LvUH4YmVpHAoGAbZ2X7XvoeEO+uZ58/BGKOIGHByHBDiXtzMhdJr15HTYjxK70gTZm
gK+8zp4L9IbvLGDMJO8vft32XPEWuvI8twCzFH+CsWLQADZMZKSsBasOZ/h1FwhdMgCMcY+Qlzd4
JZKjTSu3i7vhvx6RzdSedXEMNTZWN4qlIx3kR5aHcukCgYA9T+Zrvm1F0seQPbLknn7EqhXIjBaT
P8TTvW/6bdPi23ExzxZn7KOdrfclYRph1LHMpAONv/x2xALIf91UB+v5ohy1oDoasL0gij1houRe
2ERKKdwz0ZL9SWq6VTdhr/5G994CK72fy5WhyERbDjUIdHaK3M849JJuf8cSrvSb4g==
-----END RSA PRIVATE KEY-----
```

Figure 9.4   Example output of ec2-add-keypair. The first line is a key signature and the rest is the private key.

do recommend that you spend some time reading the EC2 documentation, including the Getting Started Guide.[2] EC2 has many configuration and customization options. Understanding them will come in handy when you start to tune your AWS Hadoop cluster.

9.3   Setting up Hadoop on EC2

To run Hadoop on an EC2 cluster, you first need to install Hadoop on your local machine and be able to run it in standalone mode. Your local Hadoop installation contains scripts to help you launch and log into an EC2 Hadoop cluster. These scripts are in the directory `src/contrib/ec2/bin` under your Hadoop installation.

9.3.1   Configuring security parameters

You must configure the single initialization script at `src/contrib/ec2/bin/hadoop-ec2-env.sh`. Inside that script, set the following three variables to values you obtained in section 9.2.1:

---

[2] http://docs.amazonwebservices.com/AWSEC2/latest/GettingStartedGuide/

- *AWS_ACCOUNT_ID*—Your 12-digit AWS account ID
- *AWS_ACCESS_KEY_ID*—Your 20-character, alphanumeric Access Key ID
- *AWS_SECRET_ACCESS_KEY*—Your 40-character Secret Access Key

The tools for Hadoop on EC2 get the other security parameters from environment variables (which should be set when you source aws-init.sh) or are based on defaults that should work fine if you have followed the AWS setup in section 9.2.

9.3.2 Configuring cluster type

You'll need to specify the configuration of your Hadoop cluster in hadoop-ec2-env. sh. You need to set three main parameters: HADOOP_VERSION, INSTANCE_TYPE, and S3_BUCKET. Before telling you how to set these parameters, let's go over a little background.

Before the creation of an instance, Amazon EC2 must know the instance type and the image used to boot up the instance. Instance type is the physical configuration of the virtual machine (CPU, RAM, disk space, etc.). As of this writing, five instance types are available, grouped into two families: standard and high-CPU. High-CPU types are for compute-intensive work. Rarely are they used for Hadoop applications, which tend to be data-intensive. The standard family has three instance types, and table 9.1 lists their attributes.

The more powerful instance types cost more, and you should look up the AWS website to find the latest pricing.

Only Amazon's S3 storage service can store images for booting up EC2 instance. Many existing images are available for all kinds of setups. You can use one of the public images, or pay for special custom images, or even create your own. Similar images are stored in the same *S3 bucket*.[3] The standard public Hadoop images are either in the hadoop-ec2-images bucket or the hadoop-images bucket. In fact, we only use the hadoop-images bucket because the newer versions of Hadoop (after 0.17.1) aren't available in the hadoop-ec2-images bucket. The Hadoop team puts new EC2 images in the hadoop-images bucket when significant versions of Hadoop are released. At any point in time, execute the following EC2 command to see the available Hadoop images:

```
ec2-describe-images -x all | grep hadoop-images
```

Table 9.1 Specification for various EC2 instance types

Type	CPU	Memory	Storage	Platform	I/O	Name
Small	1 EC2 Compute Unit	1.7 GB	160 GB	32-bit	Moderate	m1.small
Large	4 EC2 Compute Unit	7.5 GB	850 GB	64-bit	High	m1.large
Extra Large	8 EC2 Compute Unit	15 GB	1690 GB	64-bit	High	m1.xlarge

---

[3] An S3 bucket is the top-level partition in S3's namespace. A bucket is owned by exactly one AWS account and must have a globally unique name.

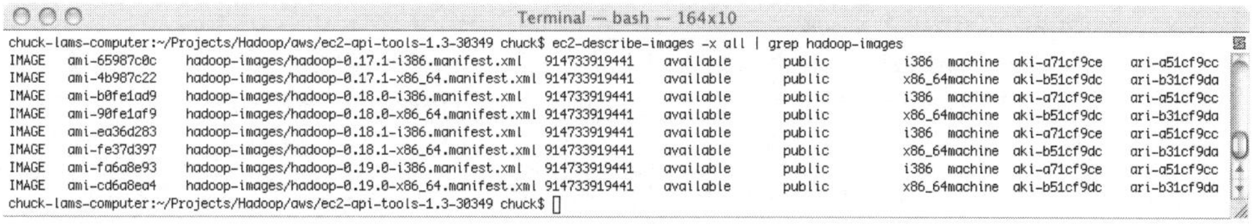

Figure 9.5 Some of the available Hadoop images in AWS.

Figure 9.5 shows an example output from the previous command. Each row describes one available EC2 image. Each image lists eleven properties, most of which are useful only for advanced AWS users. For our purpose, all the information we need can be read from the third column, also known as the *manifest location* of the image. These are expressed in a two-level hierarchy, in which the top level is the S3 bucket where the image resides. As mentioned earlier, the hadoop-images bucket is the one we focus on.

The manifest location includes the Hadoop version number. The manifest location also includes a term that's either *i386* or *x86_64*. This tells you whether the image is for a 32-bit instance or a 64-bit instance. An example image that's available as of this writing has a manifest location of hadoop-images/hadoop-0.19.0-i386.manifest.xml. That image uses Hadoop version 0.19.0 and can run on 32-bit EC2 instances.

After seeing the available Hadoop images, we're ready to set `HADOOP_VERSION`, `INSTANCE_TYPE`, and `S3_BUCKET` in `hadoop-ec2-env.sh`. Unless you're using a custom image, you should set `S3_BUCKET` to hadoop-images. `INSTANCE_TYPE` defaults to m1.small, which should work fine. The main point to remember is that the instance type directly specifies whether the CPU is 32-bit or 64-bit and must be booted from a compatible image (i386 or x86_64). Finally, `HADOOP_VERSION` should be set to the Hadoop version you want to use. The particular combination of `HADOOP_VERSION`, `INSTANCE_TYPE`, and `S3_BUCKET` has to be available as seen in the output of the `ec2-describe-images` command.

9.4   *Running MapReduce programs on EC2*

The Hadoop EC2 tools are in the directory `src/contrib/ec2/bin` under your Hadoop installation. Recall that our `ec2-init.sh` script has already added that directory to your system `PATH`. Within that directory is `hadoop-ec2`, which is a meta-command for executing other commands. To launch a Hadoop cluster on EC2, use

```
hadoop-ec2 launch-cluster <cluster-name> <number-of-slaves>
```

This first launches a master EC2 instance. After this it boots the requested number of slave nodes to point to the master node. When this command returns, it will print out the public DNS name to the master node, which we denote `<master-host>`. At this point, not all slave nodes necessarily have been fully booted. You can view the master node's JobTracker web interface at http://`<master-host>`:50030/ to monitor the cluster and the operational status of the slave nodes.

NOTE　New EC2 users can't run more than 20 concurrent instances. You can request a higher limit through the Amazon EC2 Instance Request Form at http://www.amazon.com/gp/html-forms-controller/ec2-request.

After launching a Hadoop cluster, you're ready to log into the master node and use the cluster as if you've set it up on your own machines. To log in, use this command:

```
hadoop-ec2 login <cluster-name>
```

The $HADOOP_HOME for a Hadoop EC2 instance is /usr/local/hadoop-x.y.z, where x.y.z is the Hadoop version number. We run a quick test to show that Hadoop is running in this cluster:

```
# cd /usr/local/hadoop-*
# bin/hadoop jar hadoop-*-examples.jar pi 10 10000000
```

For the rest of this chapter, a hash mark (#) character in the beginning of a command line denotes that line should be executed in the master node of your Hadoop EC2 cluster, rather than at your local machine. The commands above run an example Hadoop program to estimate the value of pi. You can monitor the job at http://<master-host>:50030/.

9.4.1　*Moving your code to the Hadoop cluster*

All Hadoop applications consist of two components: code and data. We first move our code to the Hadoop cluster. In the next subsection we discuss making our data accessible (which may or may not involve moving data to the cluster).

You'll copy your application code to the master node in your Hadoop EC2 cluster using scp. Execute the following commands from your local machine:

```
source hadoop-ec2-env.sh
scp $SSH_OPTS <local-filepath> root@$MASTER_HOST:<master-filepath>
```

where <local-filepath> points to the application code on your local machine and <master-filepath> points to the destination file path on the master node.

9.4.2　*Accessing your data from the Hadoop cluster*

As the Hadoop EC2 cluster is being rented, data stored in the cluster (including in HDFS) is not persistent. Your input data has to persist somewhere else and be brought into the EC2 cluster for processing. Many options exist for where to put your data and bring it into the Hadoop cluster, and each option has its trade-offs.

MOVING DATA DIRECTLY INTO HDFS

When the input data is small (<100 GB) and is processed only once, the simplest approach is to copy the data into the master node and then copy it from there to the cluster's HDFS. Copying data into the master node is no different than copying application code into the master node (see section 9.4.1). Once the data is in the master node, you log into the master node and copy the data into HDFS using the standard Hadoop command:

```
# bin/hadoop fs -put <master-filepath> <hdfs-filepath>
```

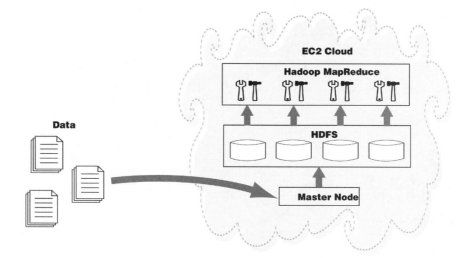

Figure 9.6   Transferring data to the Hadoop EC2 cloud directly

The data flowpath is depicted graphically in figure 9.6. Some issues are worth noting in this data flowpath. One is that AWS charges for bandwidth between AWS and the outside world (in addition to hourly charges of each EC2 instance), but bandwidth within AWS is free. In this case there's a monetary cost to copying data into the master node but not the copying of the data from the master node into HDFS. (There's also no cost to any of the communication within MapReduce processing and between MapReduce and HDFS.) Whichever way you get data into the Hadoop cluster, you'll incur this bandwidth cost at least once. The time it takes to move data into the master node will also be relatively long, as the connection between your machine and AWS is much slower than the connections within AWS. Again, this sunk time will be incurred at least once no matter how you architect the dataflow. The problem with the current dataflow architecture is that you'll incur the time and monetary costs *each time* you bring up the Hadoop cluster. If the input data will be processed in different ways over multiple sessions, this dataflow is not recommended.

Another shortcoming to the existing flowpath is the size limitation on the input data. All the data must be able to reside at the master node first, and a small EC instance only has 150 GB of disk partition. You can overcome this limitation if you can divide your input data over several chunks and move one chunk at a time. You may also choose to use bigger instances, which have multiple 420 GB disk partitions. But before trying these more complicated schemes, you should consider using S3 in your datapath.

MOVING DATA INTO HDFS THROUGH S3

S3 is a cloud storage service offered by AWS. You've already seen it in action as storage for EC2 images. Storing data in S3 is charged by bandwidth for data I/O with non-AWS machines, plus a monthly storage charge based on the size of the data. The cost

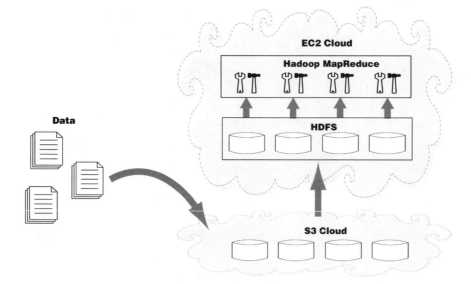

Figure 9.7 Using Hadoop on AWS with both S3 and HDFS

model makes it an attractive storage service for many applications. More particularly, it's well suited for use with Hadoop EC2 clusters.

You can see the dataflow model in figure 9.7. The main change from the dataflow of figure 9.6 is that your input data is first transferred to the S3 cloud instead of the master node. Note that, unlike the master node, the S3 cloud storage persists independently of your Hadoop EC2 cluster. You can create and terminate multiple Hadoop EC2 clusters over time, and they can all read the same input data from S3. The benefit of this setup is that you incur the monetary and time costs of copying your input data into AWS only once, when it's copied into S3, whereas in the dataflow of figure 9.6 they're incurred on every session of the Hadoop EC2 cluster. After the input data is copied into S3, copying it from the S3 cloud to the cluster's HDFS is fast and free, because both S3 and EC2 are managed within the AWS system. There's now an additional monthly storage cost for hosting your input data in S3, but it's usually minimal. If you need to have a scalable archival storage for your data, S3 can function in that role under this dataflow architecture, further justifying its cost model.

The default Hadoop installation has built-in support for using S3. There's a special Hadoop filesystem for S3, called S3 Block FileSystem, built on top of S3 to enable large file sizes. (S3 imposes a file size limit of 5 GB.) You'll need to consider the S3 Block FileSystem a separate filesystem from S3, just as HDFS is treated distinctly from the underlying Unix filesystem.

The S3 Block FileSystem requires a dedicated S3 bucket. Once you've created that S3 bucket, you can move your data from the local machine to S3:

```
bin/hadoop fs -put <local-filepath>
➥ s3://<access-key-id>:<secret-access-key>@<s3-bucket>/<s3-filepath>
```

Recall that `<access-key-id>` and `<secret-access-key>` are authentication param-eters from section 9.2.1, and `<s3-bucket>` is the name of the S3 bucket you've created for the S3 Block FileSystem.

After your data is in S3, you can copy it to any Hadoop EC2 cluster. From the master node of the cluster, run

```
# bin/hadoop distcp s3://<access-key-id>:<secret-access-key>@<s3-bucket>/
➥ <s3-filepath> <hdfs-filepath>
```

After the data is in HDFS, you can run your Hadoop program in the cluster in the usual fashion.

ACCESSING DATA DIRECTLY FROM S3

Up 'till now we've always copied data into the cluster's HDFS before running our Hadoop applications. This preserves data locality between storage and the MapReduce program. For very small jobs, you may choose to bypass HDFS and forego data locality, in return for skipping the copying of data from S3 to HDFS. You can see this datapath in figure 9.8.

To work in this architecture, specify S3 as the input filepath when executing your Hadoop application:

```
# bin/hadoop jar <app-jar-filepath> s3://<access-key-id>:
➥ <secret-access-key>@<s3-bucket>/<s3-filepath> <hdfs-filepath>
```

The preceding command will store the output file in HDFS, but you can change that to be S3 as well.

MORE OPTIONS IN USING S3 FOR HADOOP

There are a couple of variations on how you can use S3 that may be useful in some situations.

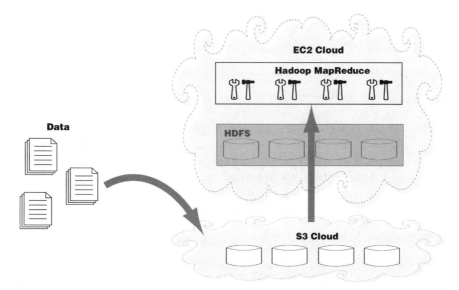

Figure 9.8 Hadoop running on EC2 can directly access data in S3.

Up 'till now we've used a special Hadoop S3 filesystem (the S3 Block FileSystem) to store data in S3. An alternative is to use S3's native filesystem. The main disadvantage with the native system is a limitation on file size of 5 GB. If the files for your input data are smaller than that limit, the native system can be an excellent option. It's compatible with all the standard S3 tools, whereas Hadoop's S3 filesystem is in a special and unique format. Standard S3 tools make the S3 native filesystem more transparent and easier to understand. To use the S3 native filesystem instead of the S3 Block FileSystem, substitute s3 with s3n when specifying file locations. For example, use

```
s3n://<access-key-id>:<secret-access-key>@<s3-bucket>/<s3-filepath>
```

in place of

```
s3://<access-key-id>:<secret-access-key>@<s3-bucket>/<s3-filepath>
```

If you're using S3 often, you'll find it cumbersome to type out the long URI for each file you want to access. One way to shorten it is to add the following to your conf/core-site.xml file:

```
<property>
  <name>fs.s3.awsAccessKeyId</name>
  <value>AWS_ACCESS_KEY_ID</value>
</property>

<property>
  <name>fs.s3.awsSecretAccessKey</name>
  <value>AWS_SECRET_ACCESS_KEY</value>
</property>
```

Note that you have to replace AWS_ACCESS_KEY_ID with your 20-character Access Key ID and AWS_SECRET_ACCESS_KEY with your 40-character Secret Access Key. After adding the two properties to core-site.xml, the URI for S3 files can be shortened to

```
s3://<s3-bucket>/<s3-filepath>
```

or

```
s3n://<s3-bucket>/<s3-filepath>
```

for the native S3 filesystem.

> **NOTE** If you're unfortunate enough to be stuck using a Secret Access Key that has a slash (/) in it, you can't embed the secret key inside a URI. The only way to use that AWS/S3 account is by embedding the secret key in core-site.xml as described before. (Some documentation has suggested escaping the secret key by replacing the slash (/) with the string *%2F* inside a URI, although that doesn't seem to work in practice.)

For an additional shortcut, it may be appropriate to make S3 your default filesystem, in place of HDFS. To do this, change the fs.default.name property in conf/core-site.xml after adding the two properties above:

```
<property>
  <name>fs.default.name</name>
```

```
   <value>s3://S3_BUCKET</value>
</property>
```

where `S3_BUCKET` is the S3 bucket you had chosen to use as your Hadoop S3 Block FileSystem (which we had denoted `<s3-bucket>` earlier).

9.5 Cleaning up and shutting down your EC2 instances

Hadoop stores the output data of your Hadoop job in the cluster's HDFS by default, and you should save it to somewhere more persistent. The options for retrieving output data are the same as the options for copying input data into the Hadoop EC2 cluster, only running in reverse. The main difference is that the output data is usually orders of magnitude smaller than the input data. Given generally small output data, copying through the master node may turn out to be your best option.

As you're renting your EC2 instances from AWS on an hourly basis, it's important that you shut down the instances when you're done and tell AWS to stop charging you. It's easy to log out of a cluster and forget that the instances are still running and you're being charged! To properly terminate a cluster, use the following command:

```
bin/hadoop-ec2 terminate-cluster <cluster-name>
```

All the EC2 instances in the cluster will shut down and data in them lost. No further cleanup is necessary.

9.6 Amazon Elastic MapReduce and other AWS services

Amazon Web Services is constantly adding new capabilities, many of which will make life easier for Hadoop developers. Two of the newest services that they've announced during the writing of this book include Amazon Elastic MapReduce (EMR) and AWS Import/Export.

9.6.1 Amazon Elastic MapReduce

For a small extra fee, the EMR service will launch a preconfigured Hadoop cluster for you to run your MapReduce programs. The major simplification this service provides is that you don't need to worry about setting up EC2 instances, and therefore you don't need to deal with all the certificates and command line tools and so forth. You interact with EMR purely through a web-based console at https://console.aws.amazon.com/elasticmapreduce/home. You can see its initial screen in figure 9.9.

The design targets the processing of single jobs. You submit a MapReduce job, either as a (Streaming, Pig, or Hive) script or a JAR file, and EMR will set up a cluster to run the job. By default the cluster will shut down at the end of the job. The input (output) of the job is read (written) directly to S3. A heavy user of Hadoop usually has many jobs running against the same data, making this setup relatively inefficient, as explained in section 9.4.2. But a light user will find EMR dramatically simplifies running MapReduce in the cloud. In addition, it's not difficult to imagine that the sophistication of EMR will only grow in the future and eventually become the primary way to run Hadoop on AWS.

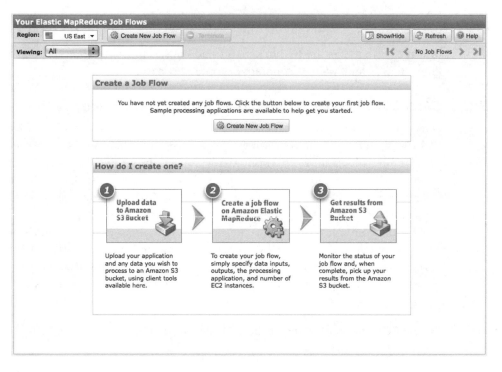

Figure 9.9   The introductory screen of the web console to Amazon Elastic MapReduce. You can follow the steps onscreen to create a job flow.

You can find more information about Amazon Elastic MapReduce at these sites:

http://aws.amazon.com/elasticmapreduce/

http://docs.amazonwebservices.com/ElasticMapReduce/latest/GettingStartedGuide/

9.6.2   AWS Import/Export

One of the main obstacles to large-scale data processing in the cloud is the difficulty of moving large data sets into the cloud. If you already have an existing process that stores your data in S3, then it's relatively straightforward to run Hadoop on EC2 to access that data. On the other hand, if you have to move data to the Amazon cloud for the sole purpose of analyzing it, then the data transfer itself can be a significant hurdle. Amazon introduced the AWS Import/Export service by which you can physically send a hard drive to them and they upload the data to S3 using their high-speed internal network. The point at which this service makes sense depends on your available internet connection speed. Table 9.2 is a rough guideline given by AWS.

Table 9.2 Size of data set at which AWS Import/Export is more practical than internet upload

Available internet connection	Theoretical min. number of days to transfer 1 TB at 80% network utilization	When to consider AWS Import/Export
T1 (1.544 Mbps)	82 days	100 GB or more
10 Mbps	13 days	600 GB or more
T3 (44.736 Mbps)	3 days	2 TB or more
100 Mbps	1 to 2 days	5 TB or more
1000 Mbps	Less than 1 day	60 TB or more

You can find more details about AWS Import/Export at http://aws.amazon.com/importexport/.

9.7   *Summary*

Cloud infrastructure is a great place for running Hadoop, as it allows you to easily scale to hundreds of nodes and gives you the financial flexibility to avoid upfront investments. Hadoop has native support for Amazon Web Services (AWS). This chapter started with the basics of setting up an account and renting compute services from AWS. Once you're ready to rent computing nodes from AWS, you'll find Hadoop tools for automating the setting up and running of a Hadoop cluster. AWS also has a cloud storage service (S3) which can be used in conjunction with or in place of HDFS. You'll find pros and cons to the different setups. Finally, it's important to remember to shut down your Hadoop cluster when you're finished. You're renting the cloud infrastructure by the hour, and fees will continue to accrue unless you explicitly shut down the machines.

Programming with Pig

10

This chapter covers

- Installing Pig and using the Grunt shell
- Understanding the Pig Latin language
- Extending the Pig Latin language with user-defined functions
- Computing similar documents efficiently, using a simple Pig Latin script

One frequent complaint about MapReduce is that it's difficult to program. When you first think through a data processing task, you may think about it in terms of data flow operations, such as loops and filters. However, as you implement the program in MapReduce, you'll have to think at the level of mapper and reducer functions and job chaining. Certain functions that are treated as first-class operations in higher-level languages become nontrivial to implement in MapReduce, as we've seen for joins in chapter 5. Pig is a Hadoop extension that simplifies Hadoop programming by giving you a high-level data processing language while keeping Hadoop's simple scalability and reliability. Yahoo, one of the heaviest user of Hadoop (and a backer of both the Hadoop Core and Pig), runs 40 percent of all its Hadoop jobs with Pig. Twitter is also another well-known user of Pig.[1]

---

[1] http://www.slideshare.net/kevinweil/hadoop-pig-and-twitter-nosql-east-2009.

Pig has two major components:

1 A high-level data processing language called Pig Latin.
2 A compiler that compiles and runs your Pig Latin script in a choice of *evaluation mechanisms.* The main evaluation mechanism is Hadoop. Pig also supports a local mode for development purposes.

Pig simplifies programming because of the ease of expressing your code in Pig Latin. The compiler helps to automatically exploit optimization opportunities in your script. This frees you from having to tune your program manually. As the Pig compiler improves, your Pig Latin program will also get an automatic speed-up.

10.1 Thinking like a Pig

Pig has a certain philosophy about its design. We expect ease of use, high performance, and massive scalability from any Hadoop subproject. More unique and crucial to understanding Pig are the design choices of its programming language (a data flow language called Pig Latin), the data types it supports, and its treatment of user-defined functions (UDFs) as first-class citizens.

10.1.1 Data flow language

You write Pig Latin programs in a sequence of steps where each step is a single high-level data transformation. The transformations support relational-style operations, such as filter, union, group, and join. An example Pig Latin program that processes a search query log may look like

```
log  = LOAD 'excite-small.log' AS (user, time, query);
grpd = GROUP log BY user;
cntd = FOREACH grpd GENERATE group, COUNT(log);
DUMP cntd;
```

Even though the operations are relational in style, Pig Latin remains a data flow language. A data flow language is friendlier to programmers who think in terms of algorithms, which are more naturally expressed by the data and control flows. On the other hand, a declarative language such as SQL is sometimes easier for analysts who prefer to just state the results one expects from a program. Hive is a different Hadoop subproject that targets users who prefer the SQL model. We'll learn about Hive in detail in chapter 11.

10.1.2 Data types

We can summarize Pig's philosophy toward data types in its slogan of "Pigs eat anything." Input data can come in any format. Popular formats, such as tab-delimited text files, are natively supported. Users can add functions to support other data file formats as well. Pig doesn't require metadata or schema on data, but it can take advantage of them if they're provided.

Pig can operate on data that is relational, nested, semistructured, or unstructured. To support this diversity of data, Pig supports complex data types, such as bags and tuples that can be nested to form fairly sophisticated data structures.

10.1.3 User-defined functions

Pig was designed with many applications in mind—processing log data, natural language processing, analyzing network graphs, and so forth. It's expected that many of the computations will require custom processing. Pig is architected from the ground up with support for user-defined functions. Knowing how to write UDFs is a big part of learning to use Pig.

10.2 Installing Pig

You can download the latest release of Pig from http://hadoop.apache.org/pig/releases.html. As of this writing, the latest versions of Pig are 0.4 and 0.5. Both of them require Java 1.6. The main difference between them is that Pig version 0.4 targets Hadoop version 0.18 whereas Pig version 0.5 targets Hadoop version 0.20. As usual, make sure to set JAVA_HOME to the root of your Java installation, and Windows users should install Cygwin. Your Hadoop cluster should already be set up. Ideally it's a real cluster in fully distributed mode, although a pseudo-distributed setup is fine for practice.

You install Pig on your local machine by unpacking the downloaded distribution. There's nothing you have to modify on your Hadoop cluster. Think of the Pig distribution as a compiler and some development and deployment tools. It enhances your MapReduce programming but is otherwise only loosely coupled with the production Hadoop cluster.

Under the directory where you unpacked Pig, you should create the subdirectories logs and conf (unless they're already there). Pig will take custom configuration from files in conf. If you are creating the conf directory just now, there's obviously no configuration file, and you'll need to put in conf a new file named pig-env.sh. This script is executed when you run Pig, and it can be used to set up environment variables for configuring Pig. Besides JAVA_HOME, the environment variables of particular interest are PIG_HADOOP_VERSION and PIG_CLASSPATH. You set these variables to instruct Pig about your Hadoop cluster. For example, the following statements in pig-env.sh will tell Pig the version of Hadoop used by the cluster is 0.18, and to add the configuration directory of your local installation of Hadoop to Pig's classpath:

```
export PIG_HADOOP_VERSION=18
export PIG_CLASSPATH=$HADOOP_HOME/conf/
```

We assume HADOOP_HOME is set to Hadoop's installation directory on your local machine. By adding Hadoop's conf directory to Pig's classpath, Pig can automatically pick up the location of your Hadoop cluster's NameNode and JobTracker.

Instead of using Pig's classpath, you can also specify the location of your Hadoop cluster by creating a pig.properties file. This properties file will be under the conf directory you created earlier. It should define fs.default.name and mapred.job.tracker, the filesystem (i.e., HDFS's NameNode) and the location of the JobTracker. An example pig. properties file pointing to a Hadoop set up in pseudo-distributed mode is

```
fs.default.name=hdfs://localhost:9000
mapred.job.tracker=localhost:9001
```

For the sake of convenience, let's add the Pig installation's `bin` directory to your path. Assume `$PIG_HOME` is pointing to your Pig's installation:

```
export PATH=$PATH:$PIG_HOME/bin
```

With Pig's `bin` directory set as part of your command line path, you can start Pig with the command `pig`. You may want to first see its usage options:

```
pig -help
```

Let's start Pig's interactive shell to see that it's reading the configurations properly.

```
pig
2009-07-11 22:33:04,797 [main] INFO
➥ org.apache.pig.backend.hadoop.executionengine.HExecutionEngine -
➥ Connecting to hadoop file system at: hdfs://localhost:9000
2009-07-11 22:33:09,533 [main] INFO
➥ org.apache.pig.backend.hadoop.executionengine.HExecutionEngine -
➥ Connecting to map-reduce job tracker at: localhost:9001
grunt>
```

The filesystem and the JobTracker Pig reports should be consistent with your configuration setup. You're now inside Pig's interactive shell, also known as Grunt.

10.3 Running Pig

We can run Pig Latin commands in three ways—via the Grunt interactive shell, through a script file, and as embedded queries inside Java programs. Each way can work in one of two modes—local mode and Hadoop mode. (Hadoop mode is sometimes called Mapreduce mode in the Pig documentation.) At the end of the previous section we've entered the Grunt shell running in Hadoop mode.

The Grunt shell allows you to enter Pig commands manually. This is typically used for ad hoc data analysis or during the interactive cycles of program development. Large Pig programs or ones that will be run repeatedly are run in script files. To enter Grunt, use the command `pig`. To run a Pig script, execute the same `pig` command with the file name as the argument, such as `pig myscript.pig`. The convention is to use the `.pig` extension for Pig scripts.

You can think of Pig programs as similar to SQL queries, and Pig provides a `PigServer` class that allows any Java program to execute Pig queries. Conceptually this is analogous to using JDBC to execute SQL queries. Embedded Pig programs is a fairly advanced topic and you can find more details at http://wiki.apache.org/pig/EmbeddedPig.

When you run Pig in local mode, you don't use Hadoop at all.[2] Pig commands are compiled to run locally in their own JVM, accessing local files. This is typically used for development purposes, where you can get fast feedback by running locally against

---

[2] There are plans to change Pig such that it uses Hadoop even in local mode, which helps to make some programming more consistent. The discussion for this topic is taking place at https://issues.apache.org/jira/browse/PIG-1053.

a small development data set. Running Pig in Hadoop mode means the compile Pig program will physically execute in a Hadoop installation. Typically the Hadoop installation is a fully distributed cluster. (The pseudo-distributed Hadoop setup we used in section 10.2 was purely for demonstration. It's rarely used except to debug configurations.) The execution mode is specified to the `pig` command via the `-x` or `-exectype` option. You can enter the Grunt shell in local mode through:

```
pig -x local
```

Entering the Grunt shell in Hadoop mode is

```
pig -x mapreduce
```

or use the `pig` command without arguments, as it chooses the Hadoop mode by default.

10.3.1 *Managing the Grunt shell*

In addition to running Pig Latin statements (which we'll look at in a later section), the Grunt shell supports some basic utility commands.[3] Typing `help` will print out a help screen of such utility commands. You exit the Grunt shell with `quit`. You can stop a Hadoop job with the `kill` command followed by the Hadoop job ID. Some Pig parameters are set with the `set` command. For example,

```
grunt> set debug on
grunt> set job.name 'my job'
```

The `debug` parameter states whether debug-level logging is turned on or off. The `job. name` parameter takes a single-quoted string and will use that as the Pig program's Hadoop job name. It's useful to set a meaningful name to easily identify your Pig job in Hadoop's Web UI.

The Grunt shell also supports file utility commands, such as `ls` and `cp`. You can see the full list of utility commands and file commands in table 10.1. The file commands are mostly a subset of the HDFS filesystem shell commands, and their usage should be self-explanatory.

Table 10.1   Utility and file commands in the Grunt shell

Utility commands	`help`
	`quit`
	`kill` ***jobid***
	`set debug [on|off]`
	`set job.name '`***jobname***`'`

File commands	`cat, cd, copyFromLocal, copyToLocal, cp, ls, mkdir,` `mv, pwd, rm, rmf, exec, run`

---

[3] Technically these are still considered Pig Latin commands, but you'll not likely use them outside of the Grunt shell.

Two new commands are `exec` and `run`. They run Pig scripts while inside the Grunt shell and can be useful in debugging Pig scripts. The `exec` command executes a Pig script in a separate space from the Grunt shell. Aliases defined in the script aren't visible to the shell and vice versa. The command `run` executes a Pig script in the same space as Grunt (also known as *interactive mode*). It has the same effect as manually typing in each line of the script into the Grunt shell.

10.4 *Learning Pig Latin through Grunt*

Before formally describing Pig's data types and data processing operators, let's run a few commands in the Grunt shell to get a feel for how to process data in Pig. For the purpose of learning, it's more convenient to run Grunt in local mode:

```
pig -x local
```

You may want to first try some of the file commands, such as `pwd` and `ls`, to orient yourself around the filesystem.

Let's look at some data. We'll later reuse the patent data we introduced in chapter 4, but for now let's dig into an interesting data set of query logs from the Excite search engine. This data set already comes with the Pig installation, and it's in the file `tutorial/data/excite-small.log` under the Pig installation directory. The data comes in a three-column, tab-separated format. The first column is an anonymized user ID. The second column is a Unix timestamp, and the third is the search query. A decidedly non-random sample from the 4,500 records of this file looks like

```
3F8AAC2372F6941C    970916093724    minors in possession
C5460576B58BB1CC    970916194352    hacking telenet
9E1707EE57C96C1E    970916073214    buffalo mob crime family
06878125BE78B42C    970916183900    how to make ecstacy
```

From within Grunt, enter the following statement to load this data into an "alias" (i.e., variable) called `log`.

```
grunt> log  = LOAD 'tutorial/data/excite-small.log' AS (user, time, query);
```

Note that nothing seems to have happened after you entered the statement. In the Grunt shell, Pig parses your statements but doesn't physically execute them until you use a DUMP or STORE command to ask for the results. The DUMP command prints out the content of an alias whereas the STORE command stores the content to a file. The fact that Pig doesn't physically execute any command until you explicitly request some end result will make sense once you remember that we're processing large data sets. There's no memory space to "load" the data, and in any case we want to verify the logic of the execution plan before spending the time and resources to physically execute it.

We use the DUMP command usually only for development. Most often you'll STORE significant results into a directory. (Like Hadoop, Pig will automatically partition the data into files named `part-nnnnn`.) When you DUMP an alias, you should be sure that its content is small enough to be reasonably printed to screen. The common way to do that is to create another alias through the LIMIT command and DUMP the new, smaller alias. The LIMIT command allows you to specify how many tuples (rows) to return back. For example, to see four tuples of log

```
grunt> lmt = LIMIT log 4;
grunt> DUMP lmt;
(2A9EABFB35F5B954,970916105432L,+md foods +proteins)
(BED75271605EBD0C,970916001949L,yahoo chat)
(BED75271605EBD0C,970916001954L,yahoo chat)
(BED75271605EBD0C,970916003523L,yahoo chat)
```

Table 10.2 summarizes the read and write operators in Pig Latin. LIMIT is technically not a read or write operator, but as it's often used alongside, we've included it in the table.

Table 10.2   Data read/write operators in Pig Latin

LOAD	alias = LOAD 'file' [USING function] [AS schema]; Load data from a file into a relation. Uses the PigStorage load function as default unless specified otherwise with the USING option. The data can be given a schema using the AS option.
LIMIT	alias = LIMIT alias n; Limit the number of tuples to *n*. When used right after alias was processed by an ORDER operator, LIMIT returns the first *n* tuples. Otherwise there's no guarantee which tuples are returned. The LIMIT operator defies categorization because it's certainly not a read/write operator but it's not a true relational operator either. We include it here for the practical reason that a reader looking up the DUMP operator, explained later, will remember to use the LIMIT operator right before it.
DUMP	DUMP alias; Display the content of a relation. Use mainly for debugging. The relation should be small enough for printing on screen. You can apply the LIMIT operation on an alias to make sure it's small enough for display.
STORE	STORE alias INTO 'directory' [USING function]; Store data from a relation into a directory. The directory must not exist when this command is executed. Pig will create the directory and store the relation in files named part-*nnnnn* in it. Uses the PigStorage store function as default unless specified otherwise with the USING option.

You may find loading and storing data not terribly exciting. Let's execute a few data processing statements and see how we can explore Pig Latin through Grunt.

```
grunt> log  = LOAD 'tutorial/data/excite-small.log'
            ➥ AS (user:chararray, time:long, query:chararray);
grunt> grpd = GROUP log BY user;
grunt> cntd = FOREACH grpd GENERATE group, COUNT(log);
grunt> STORE cntd INTO 'output';
```

The preceding statements count the number of queries each user has searched for. The content of the output files (you'll have to look at the file from outside Grunt) look like this:

```
002BB5A52580A8ED          18
005BD9CD3AC6BB38          18
00A08A54CD03EB95           3
011ACA65C2BF70B2           5
01500FAFE317B7C0          15
0158F8ACC570947D           3
018FBF6BFB213E68           1
```

Conceptually we've performed an aggregating operation similar to the SQL query:

```
SELECT user, COUNT(*) FROM excite-small.log GROUP BY user;
```

Two main differences between the Pig Latin and SQL versions are worth pointing out. As we've mentioned earlier, Pig Latin is a data processing language. You're specifying a series of data processing steps instead of a complex SQL query with clauses. The other difference is more subtle—relations in SQL always have fixed schemas. In SQL, we define a relation's schema before it's populated with data. Pig takes a much looser approach to schema. In fact, you don't need to use schemas if you don't want to, which may be the case when handling semistructured or unstructured data. Here we do specify a schema for the relation log, but it's only in the load statement and it's not enforced until we're loading in the data. Any field that doesn't obey the schema in the load operation is casted to a null. In this way the relation log is guaranteed to obey our stated schema for subsequent operations.

As much as possible, Pig tries to figure out the schema for a relation based on the operation used to create it. You can expose Pig's schema for any relation with the DESCRIBE command. This can be useful in understanding what a Pig statement is doing. For example, we'll look at the schemas for grpd and cntd. Before doing this, let's first see how the DESCRIBE command describes log.

grunt> DESCRIBE log;
```
log: {user: chararray,time: long,query: chararray}
```

As expected, the load command gives log the exact schema we've specified. The relation log consists of three fields named user, time, and query. The fields user and query are both strings (chararray in Pig) whereas time is a long integer.

A GROUP BY operation on the relation log generates the relation grpd. Based on the operation and the schema for log, Pig infers a schema for grpd:

grunt> DESCRIBE grpd;
```
grpd: {group: chararray,log: {user: chararray,time: long,query: chararray}}
```

group and log are two fields in grpd. The field log is a *bag* with subfields user, time, and query. As we haven't covered Pig's type system and the GROUP BY operation, we don't expect you to understand this schema yet. The point is that relations in Pig can have fairly complex schemas, and DESCRIBE is your friend in understanding the relations you're working with:

grunt> DESCRIBE cntd;
```
cntd: {group: chararray,long}
```

Finally, the FOREACH command operates on the relation grpd to give us cntd. Having looked at the output of cntd, we know it has two fields—the user ID and a count of the number of queries. Pig's schema for cntd, as given by DESCRIBE, also has two fields. The first one's name—group—is taken from grpd's schema. The second field has no name, but it has a type of long. This field is generated by the COUNT function, and the function doesn't automatically provide a name, although it does tell Pig that the type has to be a long.

Whereas DESCRIBE can tell you the schema of a relation, ILLUSTRATE does a sample run to show a step-by-step process on how Pig would compute the relation. Pig tries to simulate the execution of the statements to compute a relation, but it uses only a small sample of data to make the execution fast. The best way to understand ILLUSTRATE is by applying it to a relation. In this case we use cntd. (The output is reformatted to fit the width of a printed page.)

```
grunt> ILLUSTRATE cntd;
-------------------------------------------------------------------------
| log      | user: bytearray | time: bytearray | query: bytearray     |
-------------------------------------------------------------------------
|          | 0567639EB8F3751C | 970916161410   | "conan o'brien"      |
|          | 0567639EB8F3751C | 970916161413   | "conan o'brien"      |
|          | 972F13CE9A8E2FA3 | 970916063540   | finger AND download  |
-------------------------------------------------------------------------

-------------------------------------------------------------------------
| log      | user: chararray | time: long     | query: chararray     |
-------------------------------------------------------------------------
|          | 0567639EB8F3751C | 970916161410   | "conan o'brien"      |
|          | 0567639EB8F3751C | 970916161413   | "conan o'brien"      |
|          | 972F13CE9A8E2FA3 | 970916063540   | finger AND download  |
-------------------------------------------------------------------------

--------------------------------------------------------------------------------
| grpd     | group: chararray | log: bag({user: chararray,time: long,        |
|          |                  |              query: chararray})              |
--------------------------------------------------------------------------------
|          | 0567639EB8F3751C | {(0567639EB8F3751C, 970916161410,            |
|          |                  |    "conan o'brien"), .                       |
|          |                  |  (0567639EB8F3751C,970916161413,             |
|          |                  |    "conan o'brien")}                         |
|          | 972F13CE9A8E2FA3 | {(972F13CE9A8E2FA3, 970916063540,            |
|          |                  |  finger AND download)}                       |
--------------------------------------------------------------------------------

---------------------------------------------
| cntd     | group: chararray | long |
---------------------------------------------
|          | 0567639EB8F3751C | 2    |
|          | 972F13CE9A8E2FA3 | 1    |
---------------------------------------------
```

The ILLUSTRATE command shows there to be four transformations to arrive at cntd. The header row of each table describes the schema of the output relation after transformation, and the rest of the table shows example data. The log relation is shown as two transformations. The data hasn't changed from one to the next, but the schema has changed from a generic bytearray (Pig's type for binary objects) to the specified schema. The GROUP operation on log is executed on the three sample log tuples to arrive at the data for grpd. Based on this we can infer the GROUP operation to have taken the user field and made it the group field. In addition, it groups all tuples in log with the same user value into a bag in grpd. Seeing sample data in a simulated run by ILLUSTRATE can greatly aid the understanding of different operations. Finally, we see the FOREACH operation applied to grpd to arrive at cntd. Having seen the data in grpd in the previous table, one can easily infer that the COUNT() function provided the size of each bag.

Although DESCRIBE and ILLUSTRATE are your workhorses in understanding Pig Latin statements, Pig also has an EXPLAIN command to show the logical and physical execution plan in detail. We summarize the diagnostic operators in table 10.3.

Table 10.3 Diagnostic operators in Pig Latin

DESCRIBE	DESCRIBE alias; Display the schema of a relation.
EXPLAIN	EXPLAIN [-out path] [-brief] [-dot] [-param ...] [-param_file ...] alias; Display the execution plan used to compute a relation. When used with a script name, for example, EXPLAIN myscript.pig, it will show the execution plan of the script.

ILLUSTRATE	ILLUSTRATE alias;
	    Display step-by-step how data is transformed, starting with a load command, to arrive at the resulting relation. To keep the display and processing manageable, only a (not completely random) sample of the input data is used to simulate the execution.
	    In the unfortunate case where none of Pig's initial sample will survive the script to generate meaningful data, Pig will "fake" some similar initial data that will survive to generate data for alias. For example, consider these operations:
	
	`A = LOAD 'student.data' as (name, age);`
	`B = FILTER A by age > 18;`
	`ILLUSTRATE B;`
	
	If every tuple Pig samples for A happens to have age less than or equal to 18, B is empty and not much is "illustrated." Instead Pig will construct for A some tuples with age greater than 18. This way B won't be an empty relation and users can see how the script works.
	    In order for ILLUSTRATE to work, the load command in the first step must include a schema. The subsequent transformations must not include the LIMIT or SPLIT operators, or the nested FOREACH operator, or the use of the map data type (to be explained in section 10.5.1).

10.5 Speaking Pig Latin

You now know how to use Grunt to run Pig Latin statements and investigate their execution and results. We can come back and give a more formal treatment of the language. You should feel free to use Grunt to explore these language concepts as we present them.

10.5.1 *Data types and schemas*

Let's first look at Pig data types from a bottom-up view. Pig has six simple atomic types and three complex types, shown in tables 10.4 and 10.5 respectively. The atomic types include numeric scalars as well as string and binary objects. Type casting is supported and done in the usual manner. Fields default to `bytearray` unless specified otherwise.

Table 10.4   Atomic data types in Pig Latin

`int`	Signed 32-bit integer
`long`	Signed 64-bit integer
`float`	32-bit floating point
`double`	64-bit floating point
`chararray`	Character array (string) in Unicode UTF-8
`bytearray`	Byte array (binary object)

The three complex types are tuple, bag, and map.

A field in a tuple or a value in a map can be null or any atomic or complex type. This enables nesting and complex data structures. Whereas data structures can be arbitrarily complex, some are definitely more useful and occur more often than others, and nesting usually doesn't go deeper than two levels. In the Excite log example earlier, the GROUP BY operator generated a relation `grpd` where each tuple has a field that is a bag. The schema for the relation seems more natural once you think of `grpd` as the query history of each user. Each tuple represents one user and has a field that is a bag of the user's queries.

We can also look at Pig's data model from the top down. At the top, Pig Latin statements work with relations, which is a bag of tuples. If you force all the tuples in a bag

Table 10.5   Complex data types in Pig Latin

Tuple	`(12.5,hello world,-2)` A tuple is an ordered set of fields. It's most often used as a row in a relation. It's represented by fields separated by commas, all enclosed by parentheses.
Bag	`{(12.5,hello world,-2),(2.87,bye world,10)}` A bag is an unordered collection of tuples. A relation is a special kind of bag, sometimes called an outer bag. An inner bag is a bag that is a field within some complex type. A bag is represented by tuples separated by commas, all enclosed by curly brackets. Tuples in a bag aren't required to have the same schema or even have the same number of fields. It's a good idea to do this though, unless you're handling semistructured or unstructured data.
Map	`[key#value]` A map is a set of key/value pairs. Keys must be unique and be a string (`chararray`). The value can be any type.

to have a fixed number of fields and each field has a fixed atomic type, then it behaves like a relational data model—the relation is a table, tuples are rows (records), and fields are columns. But, Pig's data model has more power and flexibility by allowing *nested* data types. Fields can themselves be tuples, bags, or maps. Maps are helpful in processing semistructured data such as JSON, XML, and sparse relational data. In addition, it isn't necessary that tuples in a bag have the same number of fields. This allows tuples to represent unstructured data.

Besides declaring types for fields, schemas can also assign names to fields to make them easier to reference. Users can define schemas for relations using the AS keyword with the LOAD, STREAM, and FOREACH operators. For example, in the LOAD statement for getting the Excite query log, we defined the data types for the fields in log, as well as named the fields user, time, and query.

```
grunt> log  = LOAD 'tutorial/data/excite-small.log'
        ➥ AS (user:chararray, time:long, query:chararray);
```

In defining a schema, if you leave out the type, Pig will default to bytearray as the most generic type. You can also leave out the name, in which case a field would be unnamed and you can only reference it by position.

10.5.2 Expressions and functions

You can apply expressions and functions to data fields to compute various values. The simplest expression is a constant value. Next is to reference the value of a field. You can reference the named fields' value directly by the name. You can reference an unnamed field by n, where n is its position inside the tuple. (Position is numbered starting at 0.) For example, this LOAD command provides named fields to log through the schema.

```
log  = LOAD 'tutorial/data/excite-small.log'
        ➥ AS (user:chararray, time:long, query:chararray);
```

The three named fields are user, time, and query. For example, we can refer to the time field as either time or $1, because the time field is the second field in log (position number 1). Let's say we want to extract the time field into its own relation; we can use this statement:

```
projection = FOREACH log GENERATE time;
```

We can also achieve the same with

```
projection = FOREACH log GENERATE $1;
```

Most of the time you should give names to fields. One use of referring to fields by position is when you're working with unstructured data.

When using complex types, you use the dot notation to reference fields nested inside tuples or bags. For example, recall earlier that we'd grouped the Excite log by user ID and arrived at relation grpd with a nested schema.

```
-----------------------------------------------------------------
| grpd   | group: chararray | log: bag({user: chararray,time: long, |
|        |                  |              query: chararray})         |
-----------------------------------------------------------------
|        | 0567639EB8F3751C | {(0567639EB8F3751C, 970916161410,       |
|        |                  |    "conan o'brien"),                     |
|        |                  |  (0567639EB8F3751C,970916161413,         |
|        |                  |    "conan o'brien")}                     |
|        | 972F13CE9A8E2FA3 | {(972F13CE9A8E2FA3, 970916063540,       |
|        |                  |    finger AND download)}                 |
-----------------------------------------------------------------
```

The second field in `grpd` is named `log`, of type bag. Each bag has tuples with three named fields: user, time, and query. In this relation, `log.query` would refer to the two copies of "conan" "o'brien" when applied to the first tuple. You can get the same field with `log.$2`.

You reference fields inside maps through the pound operator instead of the dot operator. For a map named `m`, the value associated with key `k` is referenced through `m#k`.

Being able to refer to values is only a first step. Pig supports the standard arithmetic, comparison, conditional, type casting, and Boolean expressions that are common in most popular programming languages. See table 10.6.

Table 10.6 Expressions in Pig Latin

Constant	`12, 19.2, 'hello world'`	Constant values such as 19 or "hello world." Numeric values without decimal point are treated as `int` unless I or L is appended to the number to make it a `long`. Numeric values with a decimal point are treated as `double` unless f or F is appended to the number to make it a `float`.
Basic arithmetic	`+,-,*,/`	Plus, minus, multiply, and divide.
Sign	`+x, -x`	Negation (-) changes the sign of a number.
Cast	`(t)x`	Convert the value of *x* into type *t*.
Modulo	`x % y`	The remainder of x divided by *y*.
Conditional	`(x ? y : z)`	Returns *y* if x is true, z otherwise. This expression must be enclosed in parentheses.
Comparison	`==,!=,<,>, <=,>=`	Equals to, not equals to, greater than, less than, etc.
Pattern matching	`x matches regex`	Regular expression matching of string x. Uses Java's regular expression format (under the `java.util.regex.Pattern` class) to specify `regex`.
Null	`x is null, x is not null`	Check if x is null (or not).
Boolean	`x and y, x or y, not x`	Boolean and, or, not.

Furthermore, Pig also supports functions. Table 10.7 shows Pig's built-in functions, most of which are self-explanatory. We'll discuss user-defined functions (UDF) in section 10.6.

Table 10.7   Built-in functions in Pig Latin

`AVG`	Calculate the average of numeric values in a single-column bag.
`CONCAT`	Concatenate two strings (`chararray`) or two `bytearrays`.
`COUNT`	Calculate the number of tuples in a bag. See SIZE for other data types.
`DIFF`	Compare two fields in a tuple. If the two fields are bags, it will return tuples that are in one bag but not the other. If the two fields are values, it will emit tuples where the values don't match.
`MAX`	Calculate the maximum value in a single-column bag. The column must be a numeric type or a `chararray`.
`MIN`	Calculate the minimum value in a single-column bag. The column must be a numeric type or a `chararray`.
`SIZE`	Calculate the number of elements. For a bag it counts the number of tuples. For a tuple it counts the number of elements. For a `chararray` it counts the number of characters. For a `bytearray` it counts the number of bytes. For numeric scalars it always returns 1.
`SUM`	Calculate the sum of numeric values in a single-column bag.
`TOKENIZE`	Split a string (`chararray`) into a bag of words (each word is a tuple in the bag). Word separators are space, double quote ("), comma, parentheses, and asterisk (*).
`IsEmpty`	Check if a bag or map is empty.

You can't use expressions and functions alone. You must use them within relational operators to transform data.

10.5.3 *Relational operators*

The most salient characteristic about Pig Latin as a language is its relational operators. These operators define Pig Latin as a data processing language. We'll quickly go over the more straightforward operators first, to acclimate ourselves to their style and syntax. Afterward we'll go into more details on the more complex operators such as `COGROUP` and `FOREACH`.

`UNION` combines multiple relations together whereas `SPLIT` partitions a relation into multiple ones. An example will make it clear:

```
grunt> a = load 'A' using PigStorage(',') as (a1:int, a2:int, a3:int);
grunt> b = load 'B' using PigStorage(',') as (b1:int, b2:int, b3:int);
grunt> DUMP a;
(0,1,2)
(1,3,4)
grunt> DUMP b;
(0,5,2)
(1,7,8)
grunt> c = UNION a, b;
grunt> DUMP c;
```

```
(0,1,2)
(0,5,2)
(1,3,4)
(1,7,8)
grunt> SPLIT c INTO d IF $0 == 0, e IF $0 == 1;
grunt> DUMP d;
(0,1,2)
(0,5,2)
grunt> DUMP e;
(1,3,4)
(1,7,8)
```

The UNION operator allows duplicates. You can use the DISTINCT operator to remove duplicates from a relation. Our SPLIT operation on c sends a tuple to d if its first field ($0) is 0, and to e if it's 1. It's possible to write conditions such that some rows will go to both d and e or to neither. You can simulate SPLIT by multiple FILTER operators. The FILTER operator alone trims a relation down to only tuples that pass a certain test:

```
grunt> f = FILTER c BY $1 > 3;
grunt> DUMP f;
(0,5,2)
(1,7,8)
```

We've seen LIMIT being used to take a specified number of tuples from a relation. SAMPLE is an operator that randomly samples tuples in a relation according to a specified percentage.

The operations 'till now are relatively simple in the sense that they operate on each tuple as an atomic unit. More complex data processing, on the other hand, will require working on groups of tuples together. We'll next look at operators for grouping. Unlike previous operators, these grouping operators will create new schemas in their output that rely heavily on bags and nested data types. The generated schema may take a little time to get used to at first. Keep in mind that these grouping operators are almost always for generating intermediate data. Their complexity is only temporary on your way to computing the final results.

The simpler of these operators is GROUP. Continuing with the same set of relations we used earlier,

```
grunt> g = GROUP c BY $2;
grunt> DUMP g;
(2,{(0,1,2),(0,5,2)})
(4,{(1,3,4)})
(8,{(1,7,8)})

grunt> DESCRIBE c;
c: {a1: int,a2: int,a3: int}
grunt> DESCRIBE g;
g: {group: int,c: {a1: int,a2: int,a3: int}}
```

We've created a new relation, g, from grouping tuples in c having the same value on the third column ($2, also named a3). The output of GROUP always has two fields. The first field is group key, which is a3 in this case. The second field is a bag containing all the tuples with the same group key. Looking at g's dump, we see that it has three tuples, corresponding to the three unique values in c's third column. The bag in the first tuple represents all tuples in c with the third column equal to 2. The bag in the second tuple represents all tuples in c with the third column equal to 4. And so forth. After you understand how g's data came about, you'll feel more comfortable looking at its schema. The first field of GROUP's output relation is always named group, for the group key. In this case it may seem more natural to call the first field a3, but currently Pig doesn't allow you to assign a name to replace group. You'll have to adapt yourself to refer to it as group. The second field of GROUP's output relation is always named after the relation it's operating on, which is c in this case, and as we said earlier it's always a bag. As we use this bag to hold tuples from c, the schema for this bag is exactly the schema for c —three fields of integers named a1, a2, and a3.

Before moving on, we want to note that one can GROUP by any function or expression. For example, if time is a timestamp and there exists a function DayOfWeek, one can conceivably do this grouping that would create a relation with seven tuples.

```
GROUP log BY DayOfWeek(time);
```

Finally, one can put all tuples in a relation into one big bag. This is useful for aggregate analysis on relations, as functions work on bags but not relations. For example:

```
grunt> h = GROUP c ALL;
grunt> DUMP h;
(all,{(0,1,2),(0,5,2),(1,3,4),(1,7,8)})
grunt> i = FOREACH h GENERATE COUNT($1);
grunt> dump i;
(4L)
```

This is one way to count the number of tuples in c. The first field in GROUP ALL's output is always the string all.

Now that you're comfortable with GROUP, we can look at COGROUP, which groups together tuples *from multiple relations*. It functions much like a join. For example, let's cogroup a and b on the third column.

```
grunt> j = COGROUP a BY $2, b BY $2;
grunt> DUMP j;
(2,{(0,1,2)},{(0,5,2)})
(4,{(1,3,4)},{})
(8,{},{(1,7,8)})
grunt> DESCRIBE j;
j: {group: int,a: {a1: int,a2: int,a3: int},b: {b1: int,b2: int,b3: int}}
```

Whereas GROUP always generates two fields in its output, COGROUP always generates three (more if cogrouping more than two relations). The first field is the group key, whereas the second and third fields are bags. These bags hold tuples from the cogrouping relations that match the grouping key. If a grouping key matches only tuples from one relation but not the other, then the field corresponding to the nonmatching relation will have an empty bag. To ignore group keys that don't exist for a relation, one can add the INNER keyword to the operation, like

```
grunt> j = COGROUP a BY $2, b BY $2 INNER;
grunt> dump j;
(2,{(0,1,2)},{(0,5,2)})
(8,{},{(1,7,8)})
grunt> j = COGROUP a BY $2 INNER, b BY $2 INNER;
grunt> dump j;
(2,{(0,1,2)},{(0,5,2)})
```

Conceptually, you can think of the default behavior of COGROUP as an outer join, and the INNER keyword can modify it to be left outer join, right outer join, or inner join. Another way to do inner join in Pig is to use the JOIN operator. The main difference between JOIN and an inner COGROUP is that JOIN creates a flat set of output records, as indicated by looking at the schema:

```
grunt> j = JOIN a BY $2, b BY $2;
grunt> dump j;
(0,1,2,0,5,2)
grunt> DESCRIBE j;
j: {a::a1: int,a::a2: int,a::a3: int,b::b1: int,b::b2: int,b::b3: int}
```

The last relational operator we look at is FOREACH. It goes through all tuples in a relation and generates new tuples in the output. Behind this seeming simplicity lies tremendous power though, particularly when it's applied to complex data types outputted by the grouping operators. There's even a nested form of FOREACH designed for handling complex types. First let's familiarize ourselves with different FOREACH operations on simple relations.

```
grunt> k = FOREACH c GENERATE a2, a2 * a3;
grunt> DUMP k;
(1,2)
(5,10)
(3,12)
(7,56)
```

FOREACH is always followed by an alias (name given to a relation) followed by the keyword GENERATE. The expressions after GENERATE control the output. At its simplest, we use FOREACH to project specific columns of a relation into the output. We can also apply arbitrary expressions, such as multiplication in the preceding example.

For relations with nested bags (e.g., ones generated by the grouping operations), FOREACH has special projection syntax, and a richer set of functions. For example, applying nested projection to have each bag retain only the first field:

```
grunt> k = FOREACH g GENERATE group, c.a1;
grunt> DUMP k;
(2,{(0),(0)})
(4,{(1)})
(8,{(1)})
```

To get two fields in each bag:

```
grunt> k = FOREACH g GENERATE group, c.(a1,a2);
grunt> DUMP k;
(2,{(0,1),(0,5)})
```

```
(4,{(1,3)})
(8,{(1,7)})
```

Most built-in Pig functions are geared toward working on bags.

```
grunt> k = FOREACH g GENERATE group, COUNT(c);
grunt> DUMP k;
(2,2L)
(4,1L)
(8,1L)
```

Recall that g is based on grouping c on the third column. This FOREACH statement therefore generates a frequency count of the values in c's third column. As we said earlier, grouping operators are mainly for generating intermediate data that will be simplified by other operators such as FOREACH. The COUNT function is one of the aggregate functions. As we'll see, you can create many other functions via UDFs.

The FLATTEN function is designed to flatten nested data types. Syntactically it looks like a function, such as COUNT and AVG, but it's a special operator as it can change the structure of the output created by FOREACH...GENERATE. Its flattening behavior is also different depending on how it's applied and what it's applied to. For example, consider a relation with tuples of the form (a, (b, c)). The statement FOREACH... GENERATE $0, FLATTEN($1) will create one output tuple of the form (a, b, c) for each input tuple.

When applied to bags, FLATTEN modifies the FOREACH...GENERATE statement to generate new tuples. It removes one layer of nesting and behaves almost the opposite of grouping operations. If a bag contains N tuples, flattening it will remove the bag and create N tuples in its place.

```
grunt> k = FOREACH g GENERATE group, FLATTEN(c);
grunt> DUMP k;
(2,0,1,2)
(2,0,5,2)
(4,1,3,4)
(8,1,7,8)
grunt> DESCRIBE k;
k: {group: int,c::a1: int,c::a2: int,c::a3: int}
```

Another way to understand FLATTEN is to see that it produces a cross-product. This view is helpful when we use FLATTEN multiple times within a single FOREACH statement. For example, let's say we've somehow created a relation l.

```
grunt> dump l;
(1,{(1,2)},{(3)})
(4,{(4,2),(4,3)},{(6),(9)})
(8,{(8,3),(8,4)},{(9)})
grunt> describe l;
d: {group: int,a: {a1: int,a2: int},b: {b1: int}}
```

The following statement that flattens two bags outputs all combinations of those two bags for each tuple:

```
grunt> m = FOREACH l GENERATE group, FLATTEN(a), FLATTEN(b);
grunt> dump m;
```

```
(1,1,2,3)
(4,4,2,6)
(4,4,2,9)
(4,4,3,6)
(4,4,3,9)
(8,8,3,9)
(8,8,4,9)
```

We see that the tuple with group key 4 in relation 1 has a bag of size 2 in field a and also a bag size 2 in field b. The corresponding output in m therefore has four rows representing the full cross-product.

Finally, there's a nested form of FOREACH to allow for more complex processing of bags. Let's assume you have a relation (say 1) and one of its fields (say a) is a bag, a FOREACH with nested block has this form:

```
alias = FOREACH 1 {
          tmp1 = operation on a;
          [more operations...]
          GENERATE expr [, expr...]
       }
```

The GENERATE statement must always be present at the end of the nested block. It will create some output for each tuple in 1. The operations in the nested block can create new relations based on the bag a. For example, we can trim down the a bag in each element of 1's tuple.

```
grunt> m = FOREACH 1 {
         tmp1 = FILTER a BY a1 >= a2;
         GENERATE group, tmp1, b;
    }
grunt> DUMP m;
(1,{},{(3)})
(4,{(4,2),(4,3)},{(6),(9)})
(8,{(8,3),(8,4)},{(9)})
```

You can have multiple statements in the nested block. Each one can even be operating on different bags.

```
grunt> m = FOREACH 1 {
         tmp1 = FILTER a BY a1 >= a2;
         tmp2 = FILTER b by $0 < 7;
         GENERATE group, tmp1, tmp2;
    };
grunt> DUMP m;
(1,{},{(3)})
(4,{(4,2),(4,3)},{(6)})
(8,{(8,3),(8,4)},{})
```

As of this writing, only five operators are allowed in the nested block: DISTINCT, FILTER, LIMIT, ORDER, and SAMPLE. It's expected that more will be supported in the future.

NOTE Sometimes the output of FOREACH can have a completely different schema from its input. In those cases, users can specify the output schema using the `AS` option after each field. This syntax differs from the `LOAD` command where the schema is specified as a list after the `AS` option, but in both cases we use `AS` to specify a schema.

Table 10.8 summarizes the relational operators in Pig Latin. On many operators you'll see an option for `PARALLEL n`. The number n is the degree of parallelism you want for executing that operator. In practice n is the number of reduce tasks in Hadoop that Pig will use. If you don't set n it'll default to the default setting of your Hadoop cluster. Pig documentation recommends setting the value of n according to the following guideline:

```
n = (#nodes - 1) * 0.45 * RAM
```

where #nodes is the number of nodes and `RAM` is the amount of memory in GB on each node.

Table 10.8 Relational operators in Pig Latin

SPLIT	`SPLIT alias INTO alias IF expression, alias IF expression [, alias IF expression ...];` Splits a relation into two or more relations, based on the given Boolean expressions. Note that a tuple can be assigned to more than one relation, or to none at all.
UNION	`alias = UNION alias, alias, [, alias ...]` Creates the union of two or more relations. Note that • As with any relation, there's no guarantee to the order of tuples • Doesn't require the relations to have the same schema or even the same number of fields • Doesn't remove duplicate tuples
FILTER	`alias = FILTER alias BY expression;` Selects tuples based on Boolean expression. Used to select tuples that you want or remove tuples that you don't want.
DISTINCT	`alias = DISTINCT alias [PARALLEL n];` Remove duplicate tuples.

SAMPLE	`alias = SAMPLE alias factor;`
	Randomly sample a relation. The sampling factor is given in `factor`. For example, a 1% sample of data in relation `large_data` is
	`small_data = SAMPLE large_data 0.01;`
	The operation is probabilistic in such a way that the size of `small_data` will not be exactly 1% of `large_data`, and there's no guarantee the operation will return the same number of tuples each time.

FOREACH	`alias = FOREACH alias GENERATE expression [,expression ...] [AS schema];` Loop through each tuple and generate new tuple(s). Usually applied to transform columns of data, such as adding or deleting fields. One can optionally specify a schema for the output relation; for example, naming new fields.

Table 10.8 Relational operators in Pig Latin (*continued*)

| FOREACH (nested) | ```
alias = FOREACH nested_alias {
    alias = nested_op;
    [alias = nested_op; ...]
    GENERATE expression [, expression ...];
};
```<br>Loop through each tuple in nested_alias and generate new tuple(s). At least one of the fields of nested_alias should be a bag. DISTINCT, FILTER, LIMIT, ORDER, and SAMPLE are allowed operations in nested_op to operate on the inner bag(s). |
| JOIN | ```
alias = JOIN alias BY field_alias, alias BY field_alias [,
alias BY field_alias …] [USING "replicated"] [PARALLEL n];
```<br>Compute inner join of two or more relations based on common field values. When using the replicated option, Pig stores all relations after the first one in memory for faster processing. You have to ensure that all those smaller relations together are indeed small enough to fit in memory.<br>Under JOIN, when the input relations are flat, the output relation is also flat. In addition, the number of fields in the output relation is the sum of the number of fields in the input relations, and the output relation's schema is a concatenation of the input relations' schemas. |
| GROUP | ```
alias = GROUP alias { [ALL] | [BY {[field_alias [,
field_alias]] | * | [expression]] } [PARALLEL n];
```<br>Within a single relation, group together tuples with the same group key. Usually the group key is one or more fields, but it can also be the entire tuple (*) or an expression. One can also use GROUP alias ALL to group all tuples into one group.<br>The output relation has two fields with autogenerated names. The first field is always named "group" and it has the same type as the group key. The second field takes the name of the input relation and is a bag type. The schema for the bag is the same as the schema for the input relation. |
| COGROUP | ```
alias = COGROUP alias BY field_alias [INNER | OUTER] ,
alias  BY field_alias [INNER | OUTER] [PARALLEL n];
```<br>Group tuples from two or more relations, based on common group values.<br>The output relation will have a tuple for each unique group value. Each tuple will have the group value as its first field. The second field is a bag containing tuples from the first input relation with matching group value. Ditto for the third field of the output tuple.<br>In the default OUTER join semantic, all group values appearing in any input relation are represented in the output relation. If an input relation doesn't have any tuple with a particular group value, it will have an empty bag in the corresponding output tuple. If the INNER option is set for a relation, then only group values that exist in that input relation are allowed in the output relation. There can't be an empty bag for that relation in the output.<br>You can group on multiple fields. For this, you have to specify the fields in a comma-separated list enclosed by parentheses for field_alias.<br>COGROUP (with INNER) and JOIN are similar except that COGROUP generates nested output tuples. |
| CROSS | ```
alias = CROSS alias, alias [, alias …] [PARALLEL n];
```<br>Compute the (flat) cross-product of two or more relations. This is an expensive operation and you should avoid it as far as possible. |
```

Table 10.8 Relational operators in Pig Latin (*continued*)

ORDER	`alias = ORDER alias BY { * [ASC|DESC]	field_alias` `[ASC|DESC] [, field_alias [ASC|DESC] …] } [PARALLEL n];` Sort a relation based on one or more fields. If you retrieve the relation right after the ORDER operation (by DUMP or STORE), it's guaranteed to be in the desired sorted order. Further processing (FILTER, DISTINCT, etc.) may destroy the ordering.

STREAM	`alias = STREAM alias [, alias …] THROUGH {'command' |`
	`cmd_alias } [AS schema] ;`
	Process a relation with an external script.

At this point you've learned various aspects of the Pig Latin language—data types, expressions, functions, and relational operators. You can extend the language further with user-defined functions. But before discussing that we'll end this section with a note on Pig Latin compilation and optimization.

10.5.4 Execution optimization

As with many modern compilers, the Pig compiler can reorder the execution sequence to optimize performance, as long as the execution plan remains logically equivalent to the original program. For example, imagine a program that applies an expensive function (say, encryption) to a certain field (say, social security number) of every record, followed by a filtering function to select records based on a different field (say, limit only to people within a certain geography). The compiler can reverse the execution order of those two operations without affecting the final result, yet performance is much improved. Having the filtering step first can dramatically reduce the amount of data and work the encryption step will have to do.

As Pig matures, more optimization will be added to the compiler. Therefore it's important to try to always use the latest version. But there's always a limit to a compiler's ability to optimize arbitrary code. You can read Pig's web documentation for techniques to improve performance. A list of tips for enhancing performance under Pig version 0.3 is at http://hadoop.apache.org/pig/docs/r0.3.0/cookbook.html.

10.6 Working with user-defined functions

Fundamental to Pig Latin's design philosophy is its extensibility through user-defined functions (UDFs), and there's a well-defined set of APIs for writing UDFs. This doesn't mean that you'll have to write all the functions you need yourself. Part of Pig's ecosystem[4] is PiggyBank,[5] an online repository for users to share their functions. You should

---

[4] I thought about calling it a Pig pen, but PigPen is actually the name of an Eclipse plug-in for editing Pig Latin scripts. See http://wiki.apache.org/pig/PigPen.

[5] http://wiki.apache.org/pig/PiggyBank.

check PiggyBank first for any function you need. Only if you don't find an appropriate function should you consider writing your own. You should also consider contributing your UDF back to PiggyBank to benefit others in the Pig community.

10.6.1 Using UDFs

As of this writing UDFs are always written in Java and packaged in jar files. To use a particular UDF you'll need the jar file containing the UDF's class file(s). For example, when using functions from PiggyBank you'll most likely obtain a piggy-bank.jar file.

To use a UDF, you must first register the jar file with Pig using the REGISTER statement. Afterward, you invoke the UDF by its fully qualified Java class name. For example, there's an UPPER function in PiggyBank that transforms a string to uppercase:

```
REGISTER piggybank/java/piggybank.jar;
b = FOREACH a GENERATE
    ➥ org.apache.pig.piggybank.evaluation.string.UPPER($0);
```

If you need to use a function multiple times, it'll get annoying to write out the fully qualified class name every time. Pig offers the DEFINE statement to assign a name to a UDF. You can rewrite the above statements to

```
REGISTER piggybank/java/piggybank.jar;
DEFINE Upper org.apache.pig.piggybank.evaluation.string.UPPER();
b = FOREACH a GENERATE Upper($0);
```

Table 10.9 summarizes the UDF-related statements.

Table 10.9   UDF statements in Pig Latin

DEFINE	DEFINE alias { function | 'command' [...] }; Assign an alias to a function or command.
REGISTER	REGISTER alias; Register UDFs with Pig. Currently UDFs are only written in Java, and *alias* is the path of the JAR file. All UDFs must be registered before they can be used.

If you're only using UDFs written by other people, this is all you need to know. But if you can't find the UDF you need, you'll have to write your own.

10.6.2 Writing UDFs

Pig supports two main categories of UDFs: eval[6] and load/store. We use the load/store functions only in LOAD and STORE statements to help Pig read and write special formats. Most UDFs are eval functions that take one field value and return another field value.

---

[6] Some eval functions are quite common and have special considerations. They're sometimes described in their own categories. These include filter functions (eval functions that return a Boolean) and aggregate functions (eval functions that take a bag and return a scalar value).

As of this writing, you can only write a UDF using Pig's Java API.[7] To create an eval UDF you make a Java class that extends the abstract `EvalFunc<T>` class. It has only one abstract method which you need to implement:

```
abstract public T exec(Tuple input) throws IOException;
```

This method is called on each tuple in a relation, where each tuple is represented by a `Tuple` object. The `exec()` method processes the tuple and returns a type `T` corresponding to a valid Pig Latin type. `T` can be any one of the Java classes in table 10.10, some of which are native Java classes and some of which are Pig extensions.

Table 10.10 Pig Latin types and their equivalent classes in Java.

Pig Latin type	Java class
Bytearray	DataByteArray
Chararray	String
Int	Integer
Long	Long
Float	Float
Double	Double
Tuple	Tuple
Bag	DataBag
Map	Map<Object, Object>

The best way to learn about writing UDFs is to dissect one of the existing UDFs in PiggyBank. Even when writing your own, it's often useful to start with a working UDF that's functionally similar to what you want and only modify the processing logic. For our purpose, let's explore the UPPER UDF we used earlier from PiggyBank. The `exec()` method looks like this:

```java
public class UPPER extends EvalFunc<String>
{
    public String exec(Tuple input) throws IOException {
        if (input == null || input.size() == 0)
            return null;

        try {
            String str = (String)input.get(0);
            return str.toUpperCase();
        } catch(Exception e){
            System.err.println("Failed to process input; error - " +
                                  e.getMessage());
            return null;
        }
    }
}
```

---

[7] The Javadoc for the API is at http://hadoop.apache.org/pig/javadoc/docs/api/.

The object `input` belongs to the `Tuple` class, which has two methods for retrieving its content.

```
List<Object> getAll();
Object get(int fieldNum) throws ExecException;
```

The `getAll()` method return all fields in the tuple as an ordered list. `UPPER` instead uses the `get()` method to request for a specific field (at position 0). This method would throw an `ExecException` if the requested field number is greater than the number of fields in the tuple. In `UPPER` the retrieved field is casted to a Java String, which usually works but may cause a cast exception if we were casting between incompatible data types. We'll see later how to use Pig to ensure that our casting works. In any case, the try/catch block would've caught and handled any exception. If everything works, `UPPER`'s `exec()` method will return a String with characters uppercased. In addition, most UDFs should implement the default behavior that the output is null when the input tuple is null.

In addition to implementing `exec()`, `UPPER` also overrides a couple methods from `EvalFunc`, one of which is `getArgToFuncMapping`:

```
@Override
public List<FuncSpec> getArgToFuncMapping() throws FrontendException {
    List<FuncSpec> funcList = new ArrayList<FuncSpec>();
    funcList.add(new FuncSpec(this.getClass().getName(),
        ➥ new Schema(new Schema.FieldSchema(null, DataType.CHARARRAY))));

    return funcList;
}
```

The `getArgToFuncMapping()` method returns a `List` of `FuncSpec` objects representing the schema of each field in the `input` tuple. Pig will handle typecasting for you by converting the types of all fields in a tuple to conform to this schema before passing it to `exec()`. It will pass fields that can't be converted to the desired type as null.

`UPPER` only cares about the type of the first field, so it adds only one `FuncSpec` to the list, and this `FuncSpec` states that the field must be of type `chararray`, represented as `DataType.CHARARRAY`. The instantiation of `FuncSpec` is quite convoluted, which is due to Pig's ability to handle complex nested types. Fortunately, unless you work with unusually complicated types, you'll probably find a `FuncSpec` instantiation for the type you want already in one of PiggyBank's UDFs. Reuse that in your code. You can even reuse the entire `getArgToFuncMapping()` function if you have the same tuple schema as another UDF.

Besides telling Pig the input schema, you can also tell Pig the schema of your output. You may not need to do this if the output of your UDF is a simple scalar, as Pig will use Java's Reflection mechanism to infer the schema automatically. But if your UDF returns a tuple or a bag, the Reflection mechanism will fail to figure out the schema completely. In that case you should specify it so that Pig can propagate the schema correctly.

In UPPER's case it only outputs a simple String, so it's not necessary to specify the output schema. But UPPER does do this by overriding outputSchema() to tell Pig that it's returning a string (DataType.CHARARRAY).

```
@Override
public Schema outputSchema(Schema input) {
    return new Schema(
        new Schema.FieldSchema(
            getSchemaName(this.getClass().getName().toLowerCase(), input),
            DataType.CHARARRAY
        )
    );
}
```

Again, the Schema object construction looks convoluted because of Pig's ability to have complex nested types. One special case is if the schema of your UDF's output is the same as the input. We can return a copy of the input schema:

```
public Schema outputSchema(Schema input) {
    return new Schema(input);
}
```

As with the construction of FuncSpec, you'll probably find some preexisting UDFs in PiggyBank with your desired output schema.

A few types of UDFs call for special considerations. Filter functions are eval functions that return a Boolean, and we use them in Pig Latin's FILTER and SPLIT statements. They should extend FilterFunc instead of EvalFunc. Aggregate functions are eval functions that take in a bag and return a scalar. They're usually used for computing aggregate metrics, such as COUNT, and we can sometimes optimize them in Hadoop by using a combiner. We haven't covered the load/save UDFs for reading and writing data sets. These more advanced topics are covered in Pig's documentation on UDFs: http://hadoop.apache.org/pig/docs/r0.3.0/udf.html.

10.7 Working with scripts

Writing Pig Latin scripts is largely about packaging together the Pig Latin statements that you've successfully tested in Grunt. Pig scripting does have a few unique topics though. They're comments, parameter substitution, and multiquery execution.

10.7.1 Comments

As you'll reuse your Pig Latin script, it's obviously a good idea to leave comments for other people (or yourself) to understand it in the future. Pig Latin supports two forms of comments, single-line and multiline. You start the single-line comment by a double hyphen and the comment ends at the end of the line. You enclose the multiline comment by the /* and */ markers, similar to multiline comments in Java. For example, a Pig Latin script with comments can look like

```
/*
 * Myscript.pig
 * Another line of comment
```

```
*/
log = LOAD 'excite-small.log' AS (user, time, query);
lmt = LIMIT log 4; -- Only show 4 tuples
DUMP lmt;
-- End of program
```

10.7.2 *Parameter substitution*

When you write a reusable script, it's generally parameterized such that you can vary
its operation for each run. For example, the script may take the file paths of its input
and output from the user each time. Pig supports parameter substitution to allow the
user to specify such information at runtime. It denotes such parameters by the $ prefix
within the script. For example, the following script displays a user-specified number of
tuples from a user-specified log file:

```
log = LOAD '$input' AS (user, time, query);
lmt = LIMIT log $size;
DUMP lmt;
```

The parameters in this script are $input and $size. If you run this script using the
pig command, you specify the parameters using the -param name=value argument.

pig -param input=excite-small.log -param size=4 Myscript.pig

Note that you don't need the $ prefix in the arguments. You can enclose a param-
eter value in single or double quotes, if it has multiple words. A useful technique is
to use Unix commands to generate the parameter values, particularly for dates. This
is accomplished through Unix's command substitution, which executes commands
enclosed in back ticks (`).

pig -param input=web-'date +%y-%m-%d'.log -param size=4 Myscript.pig

By doing this, the input file for Myscript.pig will be based on the date the script is
run. For example, the input file will be web-09-07-29.log if the script is run on July
29, 2009.

   If you have to specify many parameters, it may be more convenient to put them in
a file and tell Pig to execute the script using parameter substitution based on that file.
For example, we can create a file Myparams.txt with the following content:

```
# Comments in a parameter file start with hash
input=excite-small.log
size=4
```

The parameter file is passed to the pig command with the -param_file filename
argument.

pig -param_file Myparams.txt Myscript.pig

You can specify multiple parameter files as well as mix parameter files with direct specification of parameters at the command line using -param. If you define a parameter multiple times, the last definition takes precedence. When in doubt about what parameter
values a script ends up using, you can run the pig command with the -debug option.

This tells Pig to run the script and also output a file named `original_script_name.substituted` that has the original script but with all the parameters fully substituted. Executing `pig` with the `-dryrun` option outputs the same file but doesn't execute the script.

The `exec` and `run` commands allow you to run Pig Latin scripts from within the Grunt shell, and they support parameter substitution using the same `-param` and `-param_file` arguments; for example:

```
grunt> exec -param input=excite-small.log -param size=4 Myscript.pig
```

However, parameter substitution in `exec` and `run` doesn't support Unix commands, and there's no `debug` or `dryrun` option.

10.7.3 Multiquery execution

In the Grunt shell, a `DUMP` or `STORE` operation processes all previous statements needed for the result. On the other hand, Pig optimizes and processes an entire Pig script as a whole. This difference would have no effect at all if your script has only one `DUMP` or `STORE` command at the end. If your script has multiple `DUMP` / `STORE`, Pig script's *multiquery execution* improves efficiency by avoiding redundant evaluations. For example, let's say you have a script that stores intermediate data:

```
a = LOAD ...
b = some transformation of a
STORE b ...
c = some further transformation of b
STORE c ...
```

If you enter the statements in Grunt, where there's no multiquery execution, it will generate a chain of jobs on the `STORE b` command to compute b. On encountering `STORE c`, Grunt will run another chain of jobs to compute c, but this time it will evaluate both a and b again! You can manually avoid this reevaluation by inserting a `b = LOAD ...` statement right after `STORE b`, to force the computation of c to use the saved value of b. This works on the assumption that the stored value of b has not been modified, because Grunt, by itself, has no way of knowing.

On the other hand, if you run all the statements as a script, multiquery execution can optimize the execution by intelligently handling intermediate data. Pig compiles all the statements together and can locate the dependency and redundancy. Multiquery execution is enabled by default and usually has no effect on the computed results. But multiquery execution can fail if there are data dependencies that Pig is not aware of. This is quite rare but can happen with, for example, UDFs. Consider this script:

```
STORE a INTO 'out1';
b = LOAD ...
c = FOREACH b GENERATE MYUDF($0,'out1');
STORE c INTO 'out2';
```

If the custom function `MYUDF` is such that it accesses a through the file `out1`, the Pig compiler would have no way of knowing that. Not seeing the dependency, the Pig compiler may erroneously think it OK to evaluate b and c before evaluating a. To disable multiquery execution, run the `pig` command with `-M` or `-no_multiquery` option.

10.8 *Seeing Pig in action—example of computing similar patents*

Given the extra power that Pig provides, we can take on more challenging data processing applications. One interesting application from the patent data set is finding similar
patents based on citation data. Patents that are often cited together must be similar
(or at least related) in some way. This application has the essence of the Amazon.com
style collaborative filtering ("Customers who have bought *this* have also bought *that*.")
and finding similar documents (by looking for documents with a similar set of words).
For our purpose here, let's suppose we want to look into patents that are cited together
more than N times, where N is a fixed number we specify.[8]

For applications that involve pair-wise computations (e.g., computing number
of cocitations for each pair of patents), it's often easy to imagine an implementation
involving a pair of nested loops enumerating all pair combinations and performing the
computation on each pair. Even though Hadoop makes it easy to scale by adding more
hardware, we should continue to remember fundamental concepts in computational
complexity. Quadratic complexity will still bring linear scalability to its knees. Even a small
data set of 3 million patents can lead to 9 trillion pairs. We need smarter algorithms.

The main insight to leverage is that the resulting data is *sparse*. Most pairs will
have zero similarity as most pairs of patents are never cited together. Our similarity
computation will become much more manageable if we redesign it to only work on
patent pairs that are known to have been cited together. Looking at our data, this
approach is quite natural. This implementation involves these steps for each patent:

1 Get the list of patents it cites
2 Generate all pair-wise combinations of the list and record each pair
3 Count how many of each pair we have

If each patent cites a fixed number of patents, say 10, this implementation would generate 45 pairs for each patent. (45 is the number of pair combinations possible from
10 items, which mathematically is derived as 10 x 9 / 2.) With 3 million patents this
creates 135 million pairs, which is orders of magnitude smaller than the brute force approach. This advantage would be even more apparent if the patent data set is larger.

Even though we've figured out the algorithm for this application, implementing it
in MapReduce can still be tedious. It'll require chaining multiple jobs together, and
each job will require its own class. Pig Latin, on the other hand, takes only a dozen
lines to implement the three-step program (listing 10.1), and further optimization can
eliminate more lines and increase efficiency still.

Listing 10.1   Pig Latin script to find patents that are often cited together

```
    cite = LOAD 'input/cite75_99.txt' USING PigStorage(',')
              ➥ AS (citing:int, cited:int);
cite_grpd = GROUP cite BY citing;
```

---

[8] Variations of this may involve more advanced scoring functions, such as normalizing for frequent items,
or computing a similarity ranking rather than a simple cutoff. The simple cutoff criterion we chose here is
easier to implement and illustrates the essence of computing similarity.

```
    cite_grpd_dbl = FOREACH cite_grpd GENERATE group, cite.cited AS cited1,
                     ⮡ cite.cited AS cited2;
            cocite = FOREACH cite_grpd_dbl
                     ⮡ GENERATE FLATTEN(cited1), FLATTEN(cited2);
      cocite_fltrd = FILTER cocite BY cited1 != cited2;
       cocite_grpd = GROUP cocite_fltrd BY *;
        cocite_cnt = FOREACH cocite_grpd
                     ⮡ GENERATE group, COUNT(cocite_fltrd) as cnt;
       cocite_flat = FOREACH cocite_cnt GENERATE FLATTEN(group), cnt;
   cocite_cnt_grpd = GROUP cocite_flat BY cited1;
        cocite_bag = FOREACH cocite_cnt_grpd
                     ⮡ GENERATE group, cocite_flat.(cited2, cnt);

cocite_final = FOREACH cocite_cnt_grpd {
    similar = FILTER cocite_flat BY cnt > 5;
    GENERATE group, similar;
}
STORE cocite_final INTO 'output';
```

Pig Latin, and probably complex data processing in general, can be hard to read. Fortunately, we can use Grunt's ILLUSTRATE command on cocite_bag to get a simulated sample run of the statements and see what each operation is generating. (We've reformatted the output to fit the width of the printed page.)

cite	citing: bytearray	cited: bytearray
	3858554	3601095
	3858554	3685034
	3859004	1730866
	3859004	3022581
	3859572	3206651

cite	citing: int	cited: int
	3858554	3601095
	3858554	3685034
	3859004	1730866
	3859004	3022581
	3859572	3206651

cite_grpd	group: int	cite: bag({citing: int,cited: int})
	3858554	{(3858554, 3601095), (3858554, 3685034)}
	3859004	{(3859004, 1730866), (3859004, 3022581)}
	3859572	{(3859572, 3206651)}

cite_grpd_dbl	group: int	cited1: bag({cited: int})	cited2: bag({cited: int})
	3858554	{(3601095), (3685034)}	{(3601095),(3685034)}
	3859004	{(1730866), (3022581)}	{(1730866),(3022581)}
	3859572	{(3206651)}	{(3206651)}

The relation `cite_grpd` contains a bag for each patent, and in this bag are the cited patents. From this relation (in this example run), we can see that patents 3601095 and 3685034 are cited together in patent 3858554. Grouping cocited patents was done by the GROUP operation in creating `cite_grpd`. The relation `cite_grpd_dbl` only removes the redundant "citing" patent and creates a duplicate column. The columns `cited1` and `cited2` have the same values. This duplication will allow the cross-product operation to generate all pair-wise combinations.

```
-----------------------------------------------------------
| cocite    | cited1::cited: int | cited2::cited: int |
-----------------------------------------------------------
|           | 3601095            | 3601095            |
|           | 3601095            | 3685034            |
|           | 3685034            | 3601095            |
|           | 3685034            | 3685034            |
|           | 1730866            | 1730866            |
|           | 1730866            | 3022581            |
|           | 3022581            | 1730866            |
|           | 3022581            | 3022581            |
|           | 3206651            | 3206651            |
-----------------------------------------------------------
```

The cross-product from flattening each row of `cite_grpd_dbl` creates `cocite`.[9] This is the record of all pairs of patents that have been cited together and is a major checkpoint for our algorithm. We know that cocite is a big relation, even under our scheme which is more efficient than brute force. There are three ways to trim down cocite further. We'll discuss them all but implement only one.

The first potential reduction is to notice that each cited patent is considered to have been cocited with itself. As we know that it's quite pointless for our application to figure out that a patent is similar to itself, we can ignore all such pairs. Note that if we keep these "identity" pairs in the calculation, the cocitation count for them will end up being exactly the citation count. These numbers can still be useful if we're looking for the percentage of times patents are cocited. As we're not computing percentages, that consideration wouldn't affect us.

As cocitation is symmetric, pairs always appear twice, in reverse order. For example, we see both (3601095,3685034) and (3685034,3601095) when they appear together once. Given our current application need to find patent pairs that are cocited more than N times together, we can put in a simple rule retaining only one of the two redundant pairs and trim cocite's size by half. This rule can be thus: retain only pairs where the first field is smaller than the second field. But keeping the redundant pairs can be useful for lookup later in some applications. For example, we can find all patents cocited with X by searching for X in the first field. In the more condensed version we'd have to look for X in both fields.

Finally, we can use heuristics to remove cocitation pairs that we don't think are important. We compromise final precision to gain efficiency. The applicability

---

[9] Note that `cocite` can be computed from `cite_grpd` directly by using a more complicated FOREACH statement, and you may choose to do it when you feel more comfortable reading Pig Latin.

and usefulness of heuristics will depend on the application semantics and the data distribution. In our case, a patent that cites many patents together will generate a quadratic number of rows in `cocite`. If we believe that such "verbose" patents don't help us understand similar patent pairs, removing them can significantly reduce the size of data to process with little impact on final results. The benefit of this heuristic is much greater if we're looking at reverse patent citation or text documents, where frequency of items are extremely skewed and quadratic expansion on a few popular items can dominate the amount of data processed. In fact, in such situations approximate heuristics are almost necessary.

An important process check is to note that we've focused on a higher level of data processing issues. We've obviated any low-level discussion about MapReduce.

cocite_fltrd	cited1::cited: int	cited2::cited: int
	3601095	3685034
	3685034	3601095
	1730866	3022581
	3022581	1730866

We've decided to only filter out "identity" patent pairs:

cocite_grpd	group: tuple({cited1::cited: int, cited2::cited: int})	cocite_fltrd: bag({cited1::cited: int, cited2::cited: int})
	(1730866, 3022581)	{(1730866, 3022581)}
	(3022581, 1730866)	{(3022581, 1730866)}
	(3601095, 3685034)	{(3601095, 3685034)}
	(3685034, 3601095)	{(3685034, 3601095)}

cocite_cnt	group: tuple({cited1::cited: int, cited2::cited: int})	cnt: long
	(1730866, 3022581)	1
	(3022581, 1730866)	1
	(3601095, 3685034)	1
	(3685034, 3601095)	1

cocite_flat	group::cited1::cited: int	group::cited2::cited: int	cnt: long
	1730866	3022581	1
	3022581	1730866	1
	3601095	3685034	1
	3685034	3601095	1

We grouped the patent pair citations together, counted them, and flattened out the relation. Unfortunately, ILLUSTRATE generates sample data that only has cocitation counts of 1. However, we see that the operations are doing basically what we wanted. If we stick to the original application requirement of only looking for patent pairs that have been cocited more than *N* times, we would apply a filter on cocite_flat and be finished. But we want to show how we can further group the tuples, which would be needed for other types of filtering. For example, you may want to find the *K* most cocited patents for each patent. Let's look at the rest of the output:

```
-------------------------------------------------------------------------
| cocite_cnt_grpd | group: int | cocite_flat: bag({group::cited1::cited: |
|                 |            | int,group::cited2::cited: int,cnt: long})|
-------------------------------------------------------------------------
|                 | 1730866    | {(1730866, 3022581, 1)}                 |
|                 | 3022581    | {(3022581, 1730866, 1)}                 |
|                 | 3601095    | {(3601095, 3685034, 1)}                 |
|                 | 3685034    | {(3685034, 3601095, 1)}                 |
-------------------------------------------------------------------------

-------------------------------------------------------------------------
| cocite_bag | group: int | cocite_flat:                                 |
|            |            |   bag({group::cited2::cited: int,cnt: long}) |
-------------------------------------------------------------------------
|            | 1730866    | {(3022581, 1)}                               |
|            | 3022581    | {(1730866, 1)}                               |
|            | 3601095    | {(3685034, 1)}                               |
|            | 3685034    | {(3601095, 1)}                               |
-------------------------------------------------------------------------
```

If we had wanted to find each patent's *K* most cocited patents, we would use a FOREACH statement to process each tuple in cocite_bag and write our own UDF to take in a bag (cocite_flat) and return a bag of at most *K* tuples (the most cocited ones). You can do this final step as an exercise. Let's see an example of a nested FOREACH statement to filter out tuples inside bags that have counts of 5 or less.

```
cocite_final = FOREACH cocite_cnt_grpd {
    similar = FILTER cocite_flat BY cnt > 5;
    GENERATE group, similar;
}
```

As you can see, Pig has simplified the implementation of this data processing application tremendously. This "similar item" feature has been known to be useful in different applications, but it's also quite challenging to implement. Using Pig and Hadoop, this turns into only an afternoon's work. Furthermore, its improved ease of development enables rapid prototyping of alternative features. For your own exercise, instead of finding patents that are often cited together, can you find patents that have similar citations?

10.9 *Summary*

Pig is a higher-level data processing layer on top of Hadoop. Its Pig Latin language provides programmers a more intuitive way to specify data flows. It supports schemas in processing structured data, yet it's flexible enough to work with unstructured text or semistructured XML data. It's extensible with the use of UDFs. It vastly simplifies data joining and job chaining—two aspects of MapReduce programming that many developers found overly complicated. To demonstrate its usefulness, our example of computing patent cocitation shows a complex MapReduce program written in a dozen lines of Pig Latin.

Hive and the Hadoop herd

This chapter covers
- What Hive is
- Setting up Hive
- Using Hive for data warehousing
- Other software packages related to Hadoop

As powerful as Hadoop is, it doesn't offer everything for everybody. Many projects have sprung up to extend Hadoop for specific purposes. The most prominent and well-supported ones have officially become subprojects under the umbrella of the Apache Hadoop project.[1] These subprojects include

- *Pig*—A high-level data flow language
- *Hive*—A SQL-like data warehouse infrastructure
- *HBase*—A distributed, column-oriented database modeled after Google's Bigtable

---

[1] What we've referred to in this book as "Hadoop" so far (HDFS and MapReduce) is technically called the "Hadoop Core" subproject of Apache Hadoop, although colloquially people tend to call it Hadoop.

- *ZooKeeper*—A reliable coordination system for managing shared state between distributed applications
- *Chukwa*—A data collection system for managing large distributed systems

We covered Pig in detail in chapter 10, and we'll learn about Hive in this chapter. Furthermore, section 11.2 will briefly describe other Hadoop-related projects. Some of these aren't associated with Apache (e.g., Cascading, CloudBase). Some are in their nascent stages (e.g., Hama, Mahout). You'll see some of these tools in action in the case studies of chapter 12.

11.1 *Hive*

Hive[2] is a data warehousing package built on top of Hadoop. It began its life at Facebook processing large amount of user and log data. It's now a Hadoop subproject with many contributors. Its target users remain data analysts who are comfortable with SQL and who need to do ad hoc queries, summarization, and data analysis on Hadoop-scale data.[3] You interact with Hive by issuing queries in a SQL-like language called HiveQL. For example, a query to get all active users from a `user` table looks like this:

```
INSERT OVERWRITE TABLE user_active
SELECT user.*
FROM user
WHERE user.active = 1;
```

Hive's design reflects its targeted use as a system for managing and querying *structured* data. By focusing on structured data, Hive can add certain optimization and usability features that MapReduce, being more general, doesn't have. Hive's SQL-inspired language separates the user from the complexity of MapReduce programming. It reuses familiar concepts from the relational database world, such as tables, rows, columns, and schema, to ease learning. In addition, whereas Hadoop naturally works on flat files, Hive can use directory structures to "partition" data to improve performance on certain queries. To support these additional features, a new and important component of Hive is a metastore for storing schema information. This metastore typically resides in a relational database.

You can interact with Hive using several methods, including a Web GUI and Java Database Connectivity (JDBC) interface. Most interactions, though, tend to take place over a command line interface (CLI), which is what we focus on. You can see a high-level architecture diagram of Hive in figure 11.1.

---

[2] http://hadoop.apache.org/hive/.
[3] Note that because Hive is built on top of Hadoop, it's still designed for a low-latency, batch-oriented type of processing. It's therefore not a direct replacement for traditional SQL data warehouses, such as ones offered by Oracle.

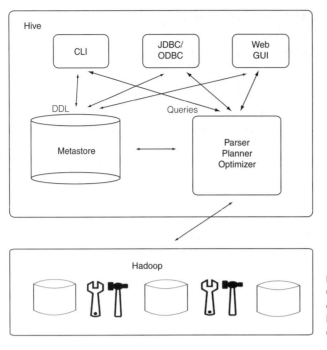

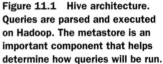

Figure 11.1   Hive architecture. Queries are parsed and executed on Hadoop. The metastore is an important component that helps determine how queries will be run.

11.1.1 Installing and configuring Hive

Hive requires Java 1.6 and Hadoop version 0.17 or above. You can find the latest release of Hive at http://hadoop.apache.org/hive/releases.html. Download and extract the tarball into a directory that we call HIVE_HOME. Hadoop needs to be up and running already. In addition, you need to set up a couple directories in HDFS for Hive to use.

```
bin/hadoop fs -mkdir /tmp
bin/hadoop fs -mkdir /user/hive/warehouse
bin/hadoop fs -chmod g+w /tmp
bin/hadoop fs -chmod g+w /user/hive/warehouse
```

If you let Hive manage your data completely for you, Hive will store your data under the /user/hive/warehouse directory. Hive can automatically add compression and special directory structures (such as partitions) to those data to improve query performance. It's good to let Hive manage your data if you plan on using Hive to query it. But if you already have your data in some other directories in HDFS and want to keep them there, Hive can work with them too. In that case, Hive will take your data as is and won't try to optimize your data storage for query processing. Some casual users don't understand this distinction, and believe that Hive requires data to be in some special Hive format. This is definitely not true.

Hive stores metadata in a standard relational database. Out-of-the-box Hive comes with an open source, lightweight, embedded SQL database called Derby,[4] which is installed and run on the client machine along with Hive. If you are the only Hive user, this default setup should be fine. But beyond the initial testing and evaluation, you'll most likely deploy Hive in a multi-user environment, where you wouldn't want each user to have their own version of the metadata. You'll need a centralized location for storing metadata. Typically, you use a shared SQL database such as MySQL, but any JDBC-compliant database will do. You'll need a database server and you'll need to create a database dedicated as a Hive metastore. This database is typically named `metastore_db`. Once you have created this, configure every Hive installation to point to it as the metastore. You configure the installations by modifying the files hive-site.xml and jpox.properties. Both are under the $HIVE_HOME/conf directory. A raw installation doesn't have a hive-site.xml file, and you'll have to create it. Properties in this file override the properties in hive-default.xml, in the same way that hadoop-site.xml overrides hadoop-default.xml. The file hive-site.xml should override three properties and look like the following:

```
<?xml version="1.0"?>
<?xml-stylesheet type="text/xsl" href="configuration.xsl"?>

<configuration>

<property>
  <name>hive.metastore.local</name>
  <value>false</value>
</property>

<property>
  <name>javax.jdo.option.ConnectionURL</name>
  <value>jdbc:mysql://<hostname>/metastore_db</value>
</property>

<property>
  <name>javax.jdo.option.ConnectionDriverName</name>
  <value>com.mysql.jdbc.Driver</value>
</property>

</configuration>
```

Table 11.1 explains these properties. Specify the `javax.jdo.option.ConnectionURL` and `javax.jdo.option.ConnectionDriverName` properties again in the file jpox. properties. In addition, the username and password to log into the database are also specified in jpox.properties. The jpox.properties file should contain the following four lines:

```
javax.jdo.option.ConnectionDriverName=com.mysql.jdbc.Driver
javax.jdo.option.ConnectionURL=jdbc:mysql://<hostname>/metastore_db
javax.jdo.option.ConnectionUserName=<username>
javax.jdo.option.ConnectionPassword=<password>
```

---

[4] http://db.apache.org/derby/.

Table 11.1   Configuration for using a MySQL database as a metadata store in multi-user mode

Property	Description
`hive.metastore.local`	Controls whether to create and use a local metastore server in the client machine. Set this to false to use a remote metastore server.
`javax.jdo.option.ConnectionURL`	JDBC connection URL specifying the database for the metastore.[5] For example, `jdbc:mysql://<hostname>/ metastore_db`.
`javax.jdo.option. ConnectionDriverName`	The class name of the JDBC driver. For example, `com.mysql.jdbc.Driver`.
`javax.jdo.option.ConnectionUserName`	Username for logging into the database.
`javax.jdo.option.ConnectionPassword`	Password for logging into the database.

Once you have the database set up, or if you're only evaluating Hive and can use its default single-user mode, you're ready to go into its CLI. Type in `bin/hive` in the `$HIVE_HOME` directory. You'll receive the Hive prompt, ready to take your Hive commands.

```
bin/hive
Hive history file=/tmp/root/hive_job_log_root_200908240830_797162695.txt
hive>
```

11.1.2 *Example queries*

Before we formally explain HiveQL, it's useful to run a few commands from the CLI. You'll get a feel of how it works and can explore on your own.

Let's assume you have the patent citation data cite75_99.txt on your local machine. Recall that this is a comma-separated data set of patent citations. In Hive, we first define a table that will store this data:

```
hive> CREATE TABLE cite (citing INT, cited INT)
    > ROW FORMAT DELIMITED
    > FIELDS TERMINATED BY ','
    > STORED AS TEXTFILE;
OK
Time taken: 0.246 seconds
```

HiveQL statements are terminated by semicolons. You can have a statement that goes over multiple lines as long as you type in a semicolon only at the end, as we've done here.

Most of the action in this four-line command is in the first line. Here we define a two-column table called *cite*. The first column is called *citing* and is of type INT, whereas the second column is called *cited* and is also of type INT. The other lines in this command

---

[5] The complete format for the MySQL JDBC driver is described in http://dev.mysql.com/doc/refman/5.0/en/connector-j-reference-configuration-properties.html.

tell Hive how the data is stored (as a text file) and how it should be parsed (fields are separated by commas).

We can see what tables are currently in Hive with the SHOW TABLES command:

```
hive> SHOW TABLES;
OK
cite
Time taken: 0.053 seconds
```

Between Hive's "OK" and "Time taken" messages, we see the cite table. We can check its schema with the DESCRIBE command:

```
hive> DESCRIBE cite;
OK
citing  int
cited   int
Time taken: 0.13 seconds
```

The table has the two columns from our definition, as expected. Managing and defining tables in HiveQL are similar to standard relational databases. Let's load the patent citation data into this table.

```
hive> LOAD DATA LOCAL INPATH 'cite75_99.txt'
    > OVERWRITE INTO TABLE cite;
Copying data from file:/root/cite75_99.txt
Loading data to table cite
OK
Time taken: 9.51 seconds
```

This tells Hive to load data from a file called cite75_99.txt in the local filesystem into our *cite* table. Underneath the hood, the local machine uploads this data into HDFS, under some directory managed by Hive. (Unless you've changed the configuration, this will be some directory under /user/hive/warehouse.)

When loading data, Hive will not let any data into a table that violates its schema. In place of those data Hive will substitute a null. We can use a simple SELECT statement to browse data in the cite table:

```
hive> SELECT * FROM cite LIMIT 10;
OK
NULL    NULL
3858241 956203
3858241 1324234
3858241 3398406
3858241 3557384
3858241 3634889
3858242 1515701
3858242 3319261
3858242 3668705
3858242 3707004
Time taken: 0.17 seconds
```

Our schema defines the two columns to be integers. We see that there's a row with nulls, indicating that a record violated the schema. This is due to the first line of cite75_99.txt, which has the column names rather than patent numbers. Overall this shouldn't be alarming.

Now that we're pretty confident that Hive has read the data and is managing it, we can run all kinds of queries on it. Let's start by counting how many rows are in the table. In SQL this is accomplished by the familiar SELECT COUNT(*). HiveQL has a slightly different syntax in this case:

```
hive> SELECT COUNT(1) FROM cite;
Total MapReduce jobs = 1
Number of reduce tasks determined at compile time: 1
In order to change the average load for a reducer (in bytes):
  set hive.exec.reducers.bytes.per.reducer=<number>
In order to limit the maximum number of reducers:
  set hive.exec.reducers.max=<number>
In order to set a constant number of reducers:
  set mapred.reduce.tasks=<number>
Starting Job = job_200908250716_0001, Tracking URL = http://ip-10-244-199-
143.ec2.internal:50030/jobdetails.jsp?jobid=job_200908250716_0001
Kill Command = /usr/lib/hadoop/bin/hadoop job  -Dmapred.job.tracker=ip-10-
244-199-143.ec2.internal:9001 -kill job_200908250716_0001
 map = 0%,  reduce =0%
 map = 12%,  reduce =0%
 map = 25%,  reduce =0%
 map = 30%,  reduce =0%
 map = 34%,  reduce =0%
 map = 43%,  reduce =0%
 map = 53%,  reduce =0%
 map = 62%,  reduce =0%
 map = 71%,  reduce =0%
 map = 75%,  reduce =0%
 map = 79%,  reduce =0%
 map = 88%,  reduce =0%
 map = 97%,  reduce =0%
 map = 99%,  reduce =0%
 map = 100%,  reduce =0%
 map = 100%,  reduce =67%
 map = 100%,  reduce =100%
Ended Job = job_200908250716_0001
OK
16522439
Time taken: 85.153 seconds
```

Reading the messages, you can see that this query had created a MapReduce job. The beauty of Hive is that the user doesn't need to know anything about MapReduce at all. As far as she's concerned, she's only querying a database using a language similar to SQL.

The result of the previous query was printed directly to the screen. In most cases the query result should be saved to disk, which usually would be some other Hive table. Our next query finds the citation frequency of each patent. We first create a table to store this result:

```
hive> CREATE TABLE cite_count (cited INT, count INT);
OK
Time taken: 0.027 seconds
```

We can execute a query to find the citation frequency. The query uses the COUNT and GROUP BY features, again in a way similar to SQL. There's an additional INSERT OVERWRITE TABLE clause to tell Hive to write the result to a table:

```
hive> INSERT OVERWRITE TABLE cite_count
    > SELECT cited, COUNT(citing)
    > FROM cite
    > GROUP BY cited;
...
 map = 100%,   reduce =89%
 map = 100%,   reduce =90%
 map = 100%,   reduce =100%
Ended Job = job_200908250716_0002
Loading data to table cite_count
3258984 Rows loaded to cite_count
OK
Time taken: 103.331 seconds
```

The query execution helpfully tells us that 3,258,984 rows were loaded into the citation frequency table. We can execute more HiveQL statements to browse this citation frequency table:

```
hive> SELECT * FROM cite_count WHERE count > 10 LIMIT 10;
Total MapReduce jobs = 1
Number of reduce tasks is set to 0 as there's no reduce operator
...
 map = 80%,   reduce =0%
 map = 100%,   reduce =100%
Ended Job = job_200908250716_0003
OK
163404   13
164184   16
217584   13
246144   14
288134   11
347644   11
366494   11
443764   11
459844   13
490484   13
```

An interesting part about this query is that Hive is intelligent enough to know that "Number of reduce tasks is set to 0 as there's no reduce operator."

When you're finished with using a table, you can delete it with the DROP TABLE command:

```
hive> DROP TABLE cite_count;
OK
Time taken: 0.024 seconds
```

Be careful when using this command. It doesn't ask you for confirmation whether you really want to delete the table or not. It's difficult to recover a table once you have dropped it.

Finally, you can exit your Hive session with the exit command.

11.1.3 HiveQL in details

Having seen Hive in action, we're ready to formally look at different aspects and usage of HiveQL.

DATA MODEL

We've already seen that Hive supports tables as a fundamental data model. Physically, Hive stores tables as directories under /user/hive/warehouse. For example, the cite table we created earlier would have its data under the /user/hive/warehouse/cite directory. The output table *cite_count* would be under /user/hive/warehouse/cite_count. In the most basic setup, the directory hierarchy under a table is only one level deep, and the table's data are spread out over many files under that one directory.

Relational databases use indexes on columns to speed up queries on those columns. Hive, instead, uses a concept of partition columns, which are columns whose values would divide the table into separate partitions. For example, a *state* column would partition a table into 50 partitions, one for each state.[6] A *date* column is a popular partition column for log data; data for each day would belong to its own partition. Hive treats partition columns differently than regular data columns, and executes queries involving partition columns much more efficiently. This is because Hive physically stores different partitions in different directories. For example, let's say you have a table named *users* that has two partition columns *date* and *state* (plus the regular data columns). Hive will have a directory structure like this for that table:

```
/user/hive/warehouse/users/date=20090901/state=CA
/user/hive/warehouse/users/date=20090901/state=NY
/user/hive/warehouse/users/date=20090901/state=TX
...
/user/hive/warehouse/users/date=20090902/state=CA
/user/hive/warehouse/users/date=20090902/state=NY
/user/hive/warehouse/users/date=20090902/state=TX
...
/user/hive/warehouse/users/date=20090903/state=CA
/user/hive/warehouse/users/date=20090903/state=NY
/user/hive/warehouse/users/date=20090903/state=TX
...
```

All user data for California (state=CA) on September 1, 2009 (date=20090901) resides in one directory, and data for other partitions is in other directories. If a query comes in asking about California users on September 1, 2009, Hive only has to process data in that one directory and ignore data in the *users* table that have been stored in other partitions. Queries over ranges in the partition columns will involve processing multiple directories, but Hive will still avoid a full scan of all data in *users*. In some sense partitioning brings similar benefits to Hive as indexing provides to a traditional relational database, although partitioning works at a much less granular level. You'll want each partition to still be big enough that a MapReduce job on it can be reasonably efficient.

---

[6] In practice you'll also have to handle District of Columbia and various territories.

In addition to partitions, the Hive data model also has a concept of *buckets*, which provide efficiency to queries that can work well on a random sample of data. (For example, in computing the average of a column, a random sample of data can provide a good approximation.) Bucketing divides data into a specified number of files based on the hash of the bucket column. If we specify 32 buckets based on user id in our *users* table, the full file structure for our table in Hive will look like

```
/user/hive/warehouse/users/date=20090901/state=CA/part-00000
...
/user/hive/warehouse/users/date=20090901/state=CA/part-00031
/user/hive/warehouse/users/date=20090901/state=NY/part-00000
...
/user/hive/warehouse/users/date=20090901/state=NY/part-00031
/user/hive/warehouse/users/date=20090901/state=TX/part-00000
...
```

Each partition will have 32 buckets. By bucketing on user id, Hive will know that each file in `part-00000 ... part-00031` has a random sample of users. The computation of many aggregate statistics remains fairly accurate on a sampled data set. Bucketing is particularly useful for speeding up those queries. For example, Hive can run a query on 1/32 of all the users in a partition by using only the data in `part-00000`, without having to even read the other files. Hive can still do sampling without buckets (or on columns other than the bucket column), but this involves scanning in all the data and randomly ignoring much of it. Much of the efficiency advantage of sampling would therefore be lost.

MANAGING TABLES

We've already seen how to create a simple table for the patent citation data set. Let's now break down the different parts of a more complicated table creation statement. This one creates a table called page_view.

```
CREATE TABLE page_view(viewTime INT, userid BIGINT,
                page_url STRING, referrer_url STRING,
                ip STRING COMMENT 'IP Address of the User')
COMMENT 'This is the page view table'
PARTITIONED BY (dt STRING, country STRING)
CLUSTERED BY (userid) INTO 32 BUCKETS
ROW FORMAT DELIMITED
        FIELDS TERMINATED BY '\t'
        LINES TERMINATED BY '\n'
STORED AS SEQUENCEFILE;
```

The first part looks much like the SQL equivalent:

```
CREATE TABLE page_view(viewTime INT, userid BIGINT,
                page_url STRING, referrer_url STRING,
                ip STRING COMMENT 'IP Address of the User')
```

It specifies the name of the table (page_view) and its schema, which includes the name of the columns as well as their type. Hive supports the following data types:

- *TINYINT*—1 byte integer
- *SMALLINT*—2 byte integer

- *INT*—4 byte integer
- *BIGINT*—8 byte integer
- *DOUBLE*—Double precision floating point
- *STRING*—Sequence of characters

Noticeably missing is the Boolean type, which is usually handled as TINYINT. Hive also has complex types, such as structs, maps, and arrays that can be nested. But they're currently not well supported in the language and are considered advanced topics.

We can attach a descriptive comment to each column, as was done here for the `ip` column. In addition, we also add a descriptive comment to the table:

```
COMMENT 'This is the page view table'
```

The next part of the CREATE TABLE statement specifies the partition columns:

```
PARTITIONED BY (dt STRING, country STRING)
```

As we've discussed previously, partition columns are optimized for querying. They're distinct from the data columns of `viewTime`, `userid`, `page_url`, `referrer_url`, and `ip`. The value of a partition column for a particular row is not explicitly stored with the row; it's implied from the directory path. But there's no syntactical difference in queries over partition columns or data columns.

```
CLUSTERED BY (userid) INTO 32 BUCKETS
```

The CLUSTERED BY (...) INTO ... BUCKETS clause specifies the bucketing information, including the column that random samples will be taken from and also how many buckets to create. The choice of the number of buckets will depend on the following:

1 The size of your data under each partition
2 The size of sample you intend to use

The first criterion is important because after you divide a partition into the specified number of buckets, you wouldn't want each bucket file to be so small that it becomes inefficient for Hadoop to handle. On the other hand, a bucket should be the same size or smaller than your intended sample size. Bucketing by user into 32 buckets is a good setting if your sample size will be about 3 percent (~1/32) of your user base.

> **NOTE** Unlike partitioning, Hive doesn't automatically enforce bucketing when data is written to a table. Specifying bucketing information merely tells Hive that you'll manually enforce the bucketing (sampling) criteria when data is written to a table and that Hive can take advantage of it in processing queries. To enforce the bucketing criteria you need to correctly set the number of reducers when populating the table. More detail can be found in http://wiki.apache.org/hadoop/Hive/LanguageManual/DDL/BucketedTables.

The ROW FORMAT clause tells Hive how the table data is stored per row. Without this clause, Hive defaults to the newline character as the row delimiter and an ASCII value of 001 (ctrl-A) as the field delimiter. Our clause tells Hive to use the tab character as the field delimiter instead. We also tell Hive to use the newline character as the line delimiter, but that's already the default and we include it here only for illustrative purposes:

```
ROW FORMAT DELIMITED
        FIELDS TERMINATED BY '\t'
        LINES TERMINATED BY '\n'
```

Finally, the last clause tells Hive the file format to store the table data:

```
STORED AS SEQUENCEFILE;
```

Currently Hive supports two formats, SEQUENCEFILE and TEXTFILE. Sequence file is a compressed format and usually provides higher performance.

We can add an EXTERNAL modifier to the CREATE TABLE statement such that the table is created to point to an existing data directory. You'll need to specify the location of this directory.

```
CREATE EXTERNAL TABLE page_view(viewTime INT, userid BIGINT,
                        page_url STRING, referrer_url STRING, ip STRING)
LOCATION '/path/to/existing/table/in/HDFS';
```

After you've created a table, you can ask Hive the table's schema with the DESCRIBE command:

```
hive> DESCRIBE page_view;
```

You can also change the table structure with the ALTER command. This includes changing the table's name:

```
hive> ALTER TABLE page_view RENAME TO pv;
```

or adding new columns:

```
hive> ALTER TABLE page_view ADD COLUMNS (newcol STRING);
```

or deleting a partition:

```
hive> ALTER TABLE page_view DROP PARTITION (dt='2009-09-01');
```

To delete the whole table, use the DROP TABLE command:

```
hive> DROP TABLE page_view;
```

To know what tables are being managed by Hive, you can show them all with

```
hive> SHOW TABLES;
```

If there are so many tables in use that it becomes unwieldy to list them all, you can narrow down the result with a Java regular expression:

```
hive> SHOW TABLES 'page_.*';
```

LOADING DATA

There are multiple ways to load data into a Hive table. The LOAD DATA command is the workhorse:

```
hive> LOAD DATA LOCAL INPATH 'page_view.txt'
   > OVERWRITE INTO TABLE page_view;
```

This takes a local file named page_view.txt and loads its content into the page_view table. If we omit the OVERWRITE modifier, the content is added to the table rather than replacing whatever already exists in it. If we omit the LOCAL modifier, the file is taken from HDFS instead of the local filesystem. The LOAD DATA command also allows you to name a specific partition in the table to load the data into:

```
hive> LOAD DATA LOCAL INPATH 'page_view.txt'
   > OVERWRITE INTO TABLE page_view
   > PARTITION (dt='2009-09-01', country='US');
```

When working with data from the local filesystem, it's useful to know that you can execute local Unix commands from within the Hive CLI. You prepend the command with the exclamation mark (!) and end it with a semicolon (;). For example, you can get a file listing

```
hive> ! ls ;
```

or examine the first few lines of a file

```
hive> ! head hive_result ;
```

Note that the spaces around ! and ; aren't necessary. We've added them for readability.

RUNNING QUERIES

For the most part, running HiveQL queries is surprisingly similar to running SQL queries. One of the general differences is that the results of HiveQL queries are relatively large. You should almost always have an INSERT clause to tell Hive to store your query result somewhere. Often it's some other table:

```
INSERT OVERWRITE TABLE query_result
```

Other times it's a directory in HDFS:

```
INSERT OVERWRITE DIRECTORY '/hdfs_dir/query_result'
```

And sometimes it's a local directory:

```
INSERT OVERWRITE LOCAL DIRECTORY '/local_dir/query_result'
```

The basic queries can look almost identical to SQL:

```
INSERT OVERWRITE TABLE query_result
SELECT *
FROM page_view
WHERE country='US';
```

Note that the query is over a partition column (country), but the query would look exactly the same if it was a data column instead. One syntax to adjust to is that HiveQL uses COUNT(1) in places where SQL typically would use COUNT(*). For example, you would use this HiveQL query to find the number of page views from the U.S.:

```
SELECT COUNT(1)
FROM page_view
WHERE country='US';
```

Like SQL, the GROUP BY clause allows one to do aggregate queries on groups. This query will list the number of page views from each country:

```
SELECT country, COUNT(1)
FROM page_view
GROUP BY country;
```

And this query will list the number of unique users from each country:

```
SELECT country, COUNT(DISTINCT userid)
FROM page_view
GROUP BY country;
```

Table 11.2 shows all the operators supported in HiveQL. These are quite standard in SQL and programming languages and we won't explain them in detail. The main exception is in regular expression matching. HiveQL provides two commands for regular expression matching—LIKE and REGEXP. (RLIKE is equivalent to REGEXP.) LIKE only performs simple SQL regular expression matching, where an underscore (_) character in B matches any single character in A and the percent (%) character matches any number of characters in A. REGEXP treats B as a full Java regular expression.[7] Tables 11.3 and 11.4 list the majority of HiveQL functions.

Table 11.2   Standard operators in HiveQL

Operator type	Operators
Comparison	A = B , A <> B , A < B , A <= B , A > B , A >= B , A IS NULL , A IS NOT NULL , A LIKE B , NOT A LIKE B , A RLIKE B , A REGEXP B
Arithmetic	A + B , A - B , A * B , A / B , A % B
Bit-wise	A & B , A | B , A ^ B, ~A
Logical	A AND B, A && B, A OR B, A || B, NOT A, !A

One of the main motivators for users to seek a higher-level language, such as Pig Latin and HiveQL, is the support of joins. Currently HiveQL only supports equijoins (joins on equality). An example join query is

```
INSERT OVERWRITE TABLE query_result
SELECT pv.*, u.gender, u.age
FROM page_view pv JOIN user u ON (pv.userid = u.id);
```

---

[7] The format of Java regular expression is fully explained in the Javadoc http://java.sun.com/j2se/1.4.2/docs/api/java/util/regex/Pattern.html.

Syntactically, in the FROM clause you add the JOIN keyword between the tables and then specify the join columns after the ON keyword. To join more than two tables, we repeat the pattern like this:

```
INSERT OVERWRITE TABLE pv_friends
SELECT pv.*, u.gender, u.age, f.friends
FROM page_view pv JOIN user u ON (pv.userid = u.id)
                  JOIN friend_list f ON (u.id = f.uid);
```

We can add sampling to any query by modifying the FROM clause. This query tries to compute the average view time, except the average is only taken from data in the first bucket out of 32 buckets:

```
SELECT avg(viewTime)
FROM page_view TABLESAMPLE(BUCKET 1 OUT OF 32);
```

The general syntax for TABLESAMPLE is

```
TABLESAMPLE(BUCKET x OUT OF y)
```

The sample size for the query is around $1/y$. In addition, y needs to be a multiple or factor of the number of buckets specified for the table at table creation time. For example, if we change y to 16, the query becomes

```
SELECT avg(viewTime)
FROM page_view TABLESAMPLE(BUCKET 1 OUT OF 16);
```

Then the sample size includes approximately 1 out of every 16 users (as the bucket column is userid). The table still has 32 buckets, but Hive tries to satisfy this query by processing buckets 1 and 17 together. On the other hand, if y is specified to be 64, Hive will execute the query on half of the data in one bucket. The value of x is only used to select which bucket to use. Under truly random sampling its value shouldn't matter.

Besides avg, Hive has many other built-in functions. You can see some of the more common ones in tables 11.3 and 11.4. Programmers can also add UDFs to Hive for custom processing. A brief introduction on how to create a UDF is given in http://wiki.apache.org/hadoop/Hive/AdminManual/Plugins.

11.1.4 Hive Sum-up

Hive is a data warehousing layer built on top of Hadoop's massively scalable architecture. By focusing on structured data, Hive has added many performance-enhancing techniques (such as partitions) and usability features (such as a SQL-like language). It makes certain frequent tasks, such as joining, easy. Hive is introducing Hadoop technology to a wider audience of analysts and other nonprogrammers. As of August 2009, Facebook counts 29 percent of its employees as Hive users, more than half of whom are outside of engineering.[8]

---

[8] This fact is cited in http://www.facebook.com/note.php?note_id=114588058858. An explanation of how Facebook decided to build out its Hadoop infrastructure is given in http://www.facebook.com/note.php?note_id=16121578919. The presentation at http://www.slideshare.net/zshao/hive-data-warehousing-analytics-on-hadoop-presentation gives a detailed description of how Facebook designed its data warehouse and analytics system around Hive.

Table 11.3   Built-in functions

Function	Description
`concat(string a, string b)`	Returns the concatenation of string *a* with string *b*.
`substr(string str, int start)` `substr(string str, int start, int length)`	Returns the substring of *str* starting at *start*. The result goes until the end of *str* unless an optional *length* argument is specified.
`round(double num)`	Returns the closest integer (BIGINT).
`floor(double num)`	Returns the largest integer (BIGINT) that's equal to or smaller than *num*.
`ceil(double num)` `ceiling(double num)`	Returns the smallest integer (BIGINT) that's equal to or bigger than *num*.
`sqrt(double num)`	Returns the square root of *num*.
`rand()` `rand(int seed)`	Returns a random number (that changes from row to row). The optional seed value can make the random number sequence deterministic.
`Ln(double num)`	Returns the natural log of *num*.
`log2(double num)`	Returns the base-2 log of *num*.
`log10(double num)`	Returns the base-10 log of *num*.
`log(double num)` `log(double base, double num)`	Returns the natural log of *num*. Or returns the base-*base* log of *num*.
`exp(double a)`	Raise *e* (the base of natural logarithm) to the power of *a*.
`power(double a, double b)` `pow(double a, double b)`	Returns *a* raised to the power of *b*.
`upper(string s)` `ucase(string s)`	Returns string *s* in uppercase.
`lower(string s)` `lcase(string s)`	Returns string *s* in lowercase.
`trim(string s)`	Returns string *s* with spaces trimmed on both ends.
`ltrim(string s)`	Returns string *s* with spaces trimmed on the left end.
`rtrim(string s)`	Returns string *s* with spaces trimmed on the right end.
`regexp(string s, string regex)`	Returns whether the string *s* matches the Java regular expression *regex*.
`regexp_replace(string s, string regex, string replacement)`	Returns a string where all parts of *s* that match the Java regular expression *regex* are replaced with *replacement*.
`day(string date)` `dayofmonth(string date)`	Returns the day part of a date or timestamp string.
`month(string date)`	Returns the month part of a date or timestamp string.
`year(string date)`	Returns the year part of a date or timestamp string.
`To_date(string timestamp)`	Returns the date part (year-month-day) of a timestamp string.
`unix_timestamp(string timestamp)`	Convert a timestamp string to UnixTime.

Table 11.3 Built-in functions (*continued*)

Function	Description
`from_unixtime(int unixtime)`	Convert integer in UnixTime to a timestamp string.
`date_add(string date, int days)`	Add a number of days to a date string.
`date_sub(string date, int days)`	Subtract a number of days from a date string.
`datediff(string date1, string date2)`	Calculate the difference in number of days. Result is negative if `date1` is earlier.

Table 11.4 Built-in aggregate functions

Function	Description
`count(1)` `count(DISTINCT col)`	Returns the number of members in the group, or the number of distinct values of the column.
`sum(col)` `sum(DISTINCT col)`	Returns the sum of the values of the column, or the sum of the distinct values of the column.
`avg(col)` `avg(DISTINCT col)`	Returns the average value of the column, or the average of the distinct values of the column.
`max(col)`	Returns the maximum value of the column.
`min(col)`	Returns the minimum value of the column.

11.2 *Other Hadoop-related stuff*

The Hadoop ecosystem is growing every day. The following are projects or vendors related to Hadoop that we find useful or that have tremendous potential. All of them except Aster Data and Greenplum are open source in some way.

11.2.1 *HBase*

http://hadoop.apache.org/hbase/—HBase is a scalable data store targeted at random read and write access of (fairly-)structured data. It's modeled after Google's Bigtable[9] and targeted to support large tables, on the order of billions of rows and millions of columns. It uses HDFS as the underlying filesystem and is designed to be fully distributed and highly available. Version 0.20 introduces significant performance improvement.

11.2.2 *ZooKeeper*

http://hadoop.apache.org/zookeeper/—ZooKeeper is a coordination service for building large distributed applications. You can use it independently from the Hadoop Core framework.

---

[9] "Bigtable: A Distributed Storage System for Structured Data" by Chang et al., OSDI '06—Seventh Symposium on Operating System Design and Implementation. http://labs.google.com/papers/bigtable.html.

It implements many of the common services used in large distributed applications, such as configuration management, naming, synchronization, and group services. Historically developers have to reinvent these services for each distributed application, which is time consuming and error prone, as these services are notoriously difficult to implement correctly. By abstracting away the underlying complexity, ZooKeeper makes it easy to implement consensus, leader election, presence protocols, and other primitives, and frees the developer to focus on the semantics of her application. ZooKeeper is often a major component in other Hadoop-related projects, such as HBase and Katta.

11.2.3 Cascading

http://www.cascading.org/—Cascading is an API for assembling and executing complex data processing workflows on Hadoop. It abstracts away the MapReduce model into a data processing model consisting of tuples, pipes, and (source and sink) taps. Pipes operate on streams of tuples, where operations include `Each`, `Every`, `GroupBy`, and `CoGroup`. Pipes can be assembled and nested to create an "assembly." We create an executable "flow" when we attach a pipe assembly to a (data) source tap and a (data) sink tap.

Cascading shares many design similarities and goals with Pig. One difference, though, is that Pig's Grunt shell makes it easier to execute ad hoc queries. Another difference is that Pig programs are written in Pig Latin, whereas Cascading works more like a Java framework in which you create a data processing flow through instantiating various Java classes (`Each`, `Every`, etc.). Using Cascading doesn't require learning a new language, and the data process flow created can be more efficient because you've written it directly yourself.

11.2.4 Cloudera

http://www.cloudera.com/—Cloudera is attempting to do for Hadoop what RedHat has done for Linux. It's supporting and packaging Hadoop to be easy and friendly to enterprise users. It provides live training sessions in major cities as well as educational videos on their web site. You can simplify your deployment of Hadoop by using their free Hadoop distribution, in either RPM or Ubuntu/Debian Packages. Their Hadoop distribution is based on the most recent stable release of Hadoop, plus useful (and tested) patches from future releases, and additional tools such as Pig and Hive. Cloudera also offers consulting and support services to help enterprises use Hadoop.

11.2.5 Katta

http://katta.sourceforge.net/—As Hadoop can trace its origin to search engines, it should not be surprising to see it being applied to distributed indexing and search. Nutch is a web search engine built on top of Hadoop.[10] But as a web search engine, Nutch has many unique requirements. It is often a mismatched solution for specific search applications.

---

[10] It may be more accurate to say that Nutch motivated the creation of Hadoop. See chapter 1 for full history.

Katta is a scalable, fault tolerant, distributed indexing system. It's more lightweight and flexible than Nutch. In some sense it's adding some extra capabilities (such as replication, redundancy, fault tolerance, and scalability) to Lucene while retaining the basic application semantics.

11.2.6 CloudBase

http://cloudbase.sourceforge.net/—CloudBase is an ANSI SQL data warehousing layer on top of Hadoop. Unlike Hive, CloudBase works directly on flat files without any meta-data store. It makes a stricter goal of ANSI SQL adherence, and interaction is primarily through a JDBC driver, which makes it easier to connect to business intelligence reporting tools. For the most part, CloudBase is a compiler that takes SQL queries and compiles them into MapReduce programs. As of this writing, CloudBase has a less active developer community than Pig or Hive, and its GPL license is more restrictive than the Apache license.

11.2.7 Aster Data and Greenplum

http://www.asterdata.com/; *http://www.greenplum.com/*—Aster Data Systems and Greenplum are both commercial vendors offering high-performance, scalable data warehousing solutions tightly combining SQL with MapReduce. Although they support the MapReduce programming model, they were both created independently from Hadoop and had made many different underlying design choices. Unlike Hadoop, their offerings are architected much more specifically toward enterprise customers looking for higher-performing SQL data warehouses. As they come at the MapReduce paradigm from a different angle than Hadoop, studying them can help understand some of Hadoop's architectural trade-offs.

11.2.8 Hama and Mahout

http://incubator.apache.org/hama/; *http://lucene.apache.org/mahout/*—Both Hama and Mahout are projects for scientific data processing using Hadoop. Hama is a matrix computation package for calculating products, inverse, eigenvalues, eigenvectors, and other matrix operations. Mahout is targeted more specifically at implementing machine learning algorithms on Hadoop (for more information, see *Mahout in Action*, Manning Publications). Mahout version 0.1 was released in April 2009 and included implementations such as Naïve Bayes classification, k-means clustering, and collaborative filtering.

At the time of this writing both projects are relatively new and under the Apache incubator. Interested readers should consider becoming contributors.

11.2.9 search-hadoop.com

As a Hadoop programmer, you'll often have the need to find some piece of documentation about Hadoop or its subprojects. Sematext, a company specializing in search and analytics, runs http://search-hadoop.com/, a site that lets you search across all

Hadoop subprojects and data sources—mailing list archives, Wikis, issue tracking systems, source code, and so on. The underlying search index is continuously updated. Search results allow filtering by project, data source, and author, and can be sorted by date, relevance, or the combination of the two.

11.3 Summary

This chapter covered many of the additional tools you can use with Hadoop. We gave special attention to Hive, a data warehousing package that allows you to process data in Hadoop using an SQL-like language. A rich ecosystem of supporting software has sprung up around Hadoop, and you'll see some of them in action in the case studies in the next chapter.

12

Case studies

This chapter covers

- The New York Times
- China Mobile
- StumbleUpon
- IBM

We've been through many exercises and sample programs by now. The next step is to integrate what you've learned about Hadoop into your own real-world applications. To help you in that transition, this chapter provides examples of how other enterprises have used Hadoop as part of the solution to their data processing problems.

The case studies serve two purposes. One is to step back and see the broader systems that utilize Hadoop as a critical part. You'll discover complementary tools, such as Cascading, HBase, and Jaql. The second purpose is to demonstrate the variety of businesses that have used Hadoop to solve their operational challenges. Our case studies span industries, including media (the New York Times), telecom (China Mobile), internet (StumbleUpon), and enterprise software (IBM).

12.1 Converting 11 million image documents from the New York Times archive

In 2007, the New York Times decided to make all their public domain articles between 1851 and 1922 freely available on their website. Doing this required a scalable image conversion system. Because the Times had stored its older articles as scanned TIFF images, they needed image processing to combine different pieces of each article together into a single file in the desired PDF format. Previously, these articles were behind a paid wall and didn't receive much traffic. The Times could use a real-time approach to scale, glue, and convert the TIFF images. Although that worked well enough for a low volume of requests, it would not scale to handle the significant traffic increase expected from the articles' free availability. The Times needed a better architecture to handle the opening of its archive.

The solution was to pregenerate all the articles as PDF files and serve them like any other static content. The New York Times already had the code to convert the TIFF images to PDF files. It looked like a simple matter of batch processing all the articles in one setting instead of dealing with each individual article as a request came in. The challenging part of this solution came when one realized that the archive had 11 million articles consisting of 4 TB of data.

Derek Gottfrid, a software programmer at the Times, thought this was a perfect opportunity to use the Amazon Web Services (AWS) and Hadoop. Storing and serving the final set of PDFs from Amazon's Simple Storage Service (S3) was already deemed a more cost-effective approach than scaling up the storage back-end of the website. Why not process the PDFs in the AWS cloud as well?

Derek copied the 4 TB of TIFF images into S3. He "started writing code to pull all the parts that make up an article out of S3, generate a PDF from them and store the PDF back in S3. This was easy enough using the JetS3t—Open Source Java toolkit for S3, iText PDF Library and installing the Java Advanced Image Extension."[1] After tweaking his code to work within the Hadoop framework, Derek deployed it to Hadoop running on 100 nodes in Amazon's Elastic Compute Cloud (EC2). The job ran for 24 hours and generated another 1.5 TB of data to be stored in S3.

At 10 cents per instance per hour, the whole job ended up costing only $240 (100 instances x 24 hours x $0.10) in computation. The storage cost for S3 was extra, but as the Times had decided to archive its files in S3 anyway, that cost was already amortized. Data transfer between S3 and EC2 being free, the Hadoop job didn't incur any bandwidth cost at all.

The whole effort took only a single employee. Thanks to Derek's work, it has become much easier for people to look up the New York Times' account of historic events.

12.2 Mining data at China Mobile

Contributed by ZHIGUO LUO, MENG XU, *and* SHAOLING SUN—*Research Institute of China Mobile Communication Corporation.*

---

[1] http://open.blogs.nytimes.com/2007/11/01/self-service-prorated-super-computing-fun/.

China Mobile Communication Corporation (CMCC) is the largest mobile phone operator in the world. Traded on NYSE under the symbol CHL, China Mobile is seventh in BrandZ's global brand equity ranking for 2009, behind McDonald's and Apple but ahead of General Electric. With more than two-thirds of China's mobile phone market, CMCC serves the communication needs of 500 million subscribers. Even at its size, China Mobile has experienced rapid growth. For example, in 2006 when its subscriber base was only 300 million, its subscriber growth rate was at 22 percent, its voice usage was growing at 30 percent, and its SMS usage was growing at 41 percent annually.

As with any telecom operator, China Mobile generates a lot of data in the normal course of running its communication network. For example, each call generates a call data record (CDR), which includes information such as the caller's phone number, the callee's phone number, the start time of the call, the call's duration, information about the call's routing, and so forth. In addition to CDR, a phone network also generates signaling data between various switches, nodes, and terminals within the network. At a minimum, we need this data for completing calls and accurately billing customers. We also need it to analyze for marketing, network tuning, and other purposes.

At China Mobile, the size of its network naturally leads to large amounts of data created. Every day the network generates 5 TB to 8 TB of CDR data. A branch company of China Mobile can have more than 20 million subscribers, leading to more than 100 GB of CDR data for voice calls and between 100 GB to 200 GB of CDR data for SMS every day. In addition, a typical branch company generates around 48 GB of data per day for General Packet Radio Service (GPRS) signaling and 300 GB of data per day for 3G signaling.

China Mobile looks to data warehousing and mining of this data to extract insights for improving marketing operations, network optimization, and service optimization. Some typical applications include

- Analyzing user behavior
- Predicting customer churn
- Analyzing service association
- Analyzing network quality of service (QOS)
- Analyzing signaling data
- Filtering spam messages

China Mobile has experiences with commercial data mining tools from some well-known vendors. These tools' architectural design limits China Mobile's current data mining system because it requires all data to be processed within a single server. Hardware capacity thus becomes a performance bottleneck. The current system at one of the branch companies is based on commercial solutions and consists of a Unix server with eight CPU cores, 32 GB memory, and a storage array. It can only perform user behavior analysis for up to 1.4 million customers, or only about 10 percent of customer data of that particular branch company. Even within the limitation on the amount of data that can be processed, the current system takes too much time for many applications.

In addition, the high-end Unix servers and storage arrays are expensive, and the commercial package software don't support custom algorithms well.

Because of the limitations of the current system, China Mobile initiated an experimental project to develop a parallel data mining tool set on Hadoop and evaluated it against its current system. They named the project Big Cloud–based Parallel Data Mining (BC-PDM) and it was architected to achieve four objectives:

- *Massive scalability*—Using Hadoop for a scale-out architecture
- *Low cost*—Built around cheap commodity hardware and free software
- *Customizable*—Applications built around specific business requirements
- *Ease of use*—Graphical user interface similar to ones in commercial tools

BC-PDM implemented many of the standard ETL operations and data mining algorithms in MapReduce. The ETL operations include computing aggregate statistics, attribute processing, data sampling, redundancy removal, and others. It implemented nine data mining algorithms from three categories. The categories include clustering (e.g., K-means), classification (e.g., C4.5), and association analysis (e.g., Apriori). The MapReduce programs were executed and evaluated within a Hadoop cluster consisting of 256 nodes connected to a single 264-port Gbps switch. The hardware for the nodes are

- *Datanode/TaskTracker*—1-way 4-core Xeon 2.5 GHz CPU, 8 GB RAM, 4 x 250 GB SATA II disks
- *Namenode/JobTracker*—2-way 2-core AMD Opteron 2.6 GHz CPU, 16 GB RAM, 4 x 146 GB SAS disks

China Mobile compared BC-PDM against their existing data mining solution using real data from China Mobile's Business Analysis Support System (BASS). There were three different data sets. They were all fairly large, and for certain evaluation tasks smaller, sampled subsets were needed. You'll see the original size (*Large scale*) as well as the size of the sampled subsets (*Middle scale* and *Small scale*) in table 12.1.

Table 12.1 Size of data sets used for evaluation

Data	Large scale	Middle scale	Small scale
Users' behavior	12 TB	120 GB	12 GB
Users' accessing	16 TB	160 GB	16 GB
New service association	120 GB	12 GB	1.2 GB

China Mobile evaluated BC-PDM on four dimensions: correctness, performance, cost, and scalability. Correctness was, of course, necessary for the new system to be useful. They verified BC-PDM's parallel ETL operations by ensuring the same results were generated as the existing serial ETL implementation. The data mining algorithms, on the other hand, were not expected to generate the *exact same* results as the existing system. This is because minor implementation and execution details, such as initial conditions and ordering of the input data, can affect the exact output. They examined the results and checked for general consistency. In addition, the UCI data sets were also employed to verify BC-PDM's parallel data mining algorithms. The UCI data sets are popular among researchers in the machine-learning community and are well understood. China Mobile can verify BC-PDM's output with known expected models.

After establishing the correctness of the MapReduce implementations, the performance of BC-PDM was compared to the current system. The comparison used only a 16-node Hadoop cluster. As we'll see, this small cluster is cheaper than the monolithic big-iron server of the current system. Figure 12.1 shows the timing between the two setups for ETL operations (left graph) and data mining tasks (right graph).

Note that BC-PDM was tasked to process *10 times* the amount of data as the current system. BC-PDM was faster for all ETL operations, resulting in general performance improvement of 12 to 16 times. For data mining tasks BC-PDM was further stress-tested with 100 times the amount of data as the current system. Even with data size two orders of magnitude larger, BC-PDM was faster than the current system at the Apriori (association) and C4.5 (classification) algorithms. The K-means clustering algorithm took slightly longer to complete than the current system at 10 times the data size. Full end-to-end testing of three applications from the Shanghai Branch Company showed performance improvement of 3 to 7 times. These real-world applications include channel preference modeling, new service association modeling, and subscriber subdivision modeling. Recall that BC-PDM in this evaluation is based on a relatively small 16-node Hadoop cluster. As we'll see later, BC-PDM and Hadoop scale well with additional nodes. At the full size of our cluster of 256 nodes, we expect BC-PDM to be able to store, process, and mine data at the 100-TB scale.

Not only is the 16-node BC-PDM cluster outperforming the current system, it's also significantly cheaper. Table 12.2 shows a cost breakdown of the two systems. (As of this writing, one USD converts to a little less than seven RMB.) The 16-node Hadoop/BC-PDM cluster is roughly one fifth the cost of the current commercial solution. The biggest saving comes from the use of low-cost commodity servers. In fact, the hardware

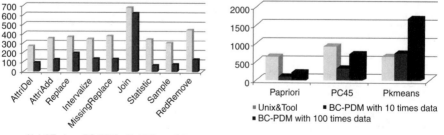

Figure 12.1   Performance comparison of the Hadoop cluster versus existing commercial Unix server. The left graph tests ETL operations whereas the right graph is for data mining algorithms.

Table 12.2 Comparison of cost and configuration between existing solution and a 16-node Hadoop cluster. (As of this writing, one USD converts to a little less than seven RMB.)

		BC-PDM (16 nodes)	Existing commercial Unix server
Hardware cost	Computing ability	CPU: 64 cores memory: 128 GB	CPU: 8 cores memory: 32 GB
	Storage ability	16 TB (4 x 256 GB SATA II each node)	storage array
Software cost	Cost	240,000 RMB	4,000,000 RMB
	Database	500,000 RMB	1,000,000 RMB
	Application software	300,000 RMB	500,000 RMB
	Maintenance cost	200,000 RMB	500,000 RMB
Total		1,240,000 RMB	6,000,000 RMB

cost of the 16-node cluster is less than one sixteenth the hardware cost of the current scale-up solution.

'Till now, we've investigated the correctness, performance, and cost of the new BC-PDM system. Let's examine the scalability of the system as we add more nodes to the cluster. We ran the ETL operations and data mining algorithms on three cluster sizes: 32 nodes, 64 nodes, and 128 nodes. We measured the speed-up in execution on larger clusters, taking the execution time in the 32-node cluster as baseline. You'll see the results in figure 12.2, with the left graph showing the speed-up for ETL operations and the right graph showing data mining operations. Note that the horizontal axis (representing cluster size) is exponential, with marks doubling from 32 to 64 to 128. As exact linear scalability of the operations is the best that we can hope for, the ideal graph would have the speed-up go from 1 to 2 to 4. We see that many ETL operations are close to this linear scalability ideal. In fact, when the cluster size quadrupled, from

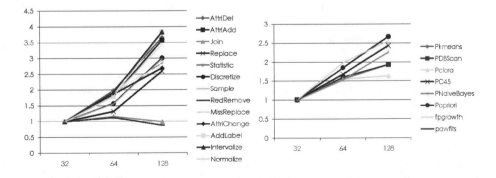

Figure 12.2 Scalability of ETL (left) and data mining (right) algorithms on Hadoop cluster as extra nodes are added. The horizontal axis represents the number of nodes in the BC-PDM cluster. The vertical axis represents the speed-up, relative to the execution time on the 32-node cluster.

32 nodes to 128 nodes, all but two had a speed-up greater than 2.5.[2] The data mining algorithms are more complex, yet they achieve respectable scalability as well. Our performance testing earlier (figure 12.1) used only a small 16-node cluster, which we don't even consider in the current scalability benchmark. Yet the 16-node cluster could handle an order of magnitude more data faster than the existing commercial solution. Together these evaluations demonstrate our BC-PDM cluster's ability to handle data at the 100-TB level going forward.

After the thorough evaluation of the BC-PDM system, we worked with the Shanghai Branch to apply our system to some of their business needs. One application was to characterize their user base to enable precision marketing. More specifically, they wanted to know how their users are segmented, the characteristics and differences of each segment, and to classify each user for targeted marketing. We used the parallel K-means algorithm from our data mining toolset to cluster their user base and created the market segmentation graph in figure 12.3. Further analysis helped to characterize each segment according to the average bill and types of service used. BC-PDM performed this analysis 3 times faster than their existing Unix solution.

In conclusion, China Mobile is a large mobile communication provider, and there's tremendous and growing need to analyze large data sets. Current commercial offerings are expensive and inadequate for analyzing our user data. We investigated the use of Hadoop. We built a data mining system called BC-PDM on top of MapReduce and HDFS and found this system to be accurate, fast, cheap, and scalable. Going forward, we'll improve BC-PDM's efficiency as well as expand its scope by implementing more ETL operations and data mining algorithms. More importantly, we intend to establish BC-PDM as a service platform for data analysis across China Mobile's branch companies.

12.3 *Recommending the best websites at StumbleUpon*

Contributed by KEN MACINNIS and RYAN RAWSON

Using a combination of human opinions and machine learning to immediately deliver relevant content, StumbleUpon presents only websites that have been suggested by other like-minded Stumblers. Each time you click the Stumble button, you are presented with a high-quality website based on the collective opinions of other like-minded web surfers.

StumbleUpon uses ratings of "like" and "dislike" to form collaborative opinions on website quality. When you "stumble," you'll only see pages that friends and like-minded

---

[2] The two exceptions were the Join and the Duplicate Removal operations. They ran in roughly constant time irrespective of the cluster size. We are currently investigating the underlying reason for it. One possible explanation for Hadoop running a job in constant time (independent of cluster size) is that the job is not evenly distributed and one task is the bottleneck to the job's completion.

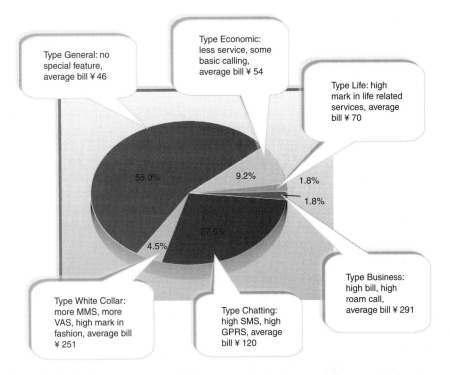

Figure 12.3   Cluster analysis of user base for China Mobile's Shanghai Branch using the K-means algorithm. The result can be used for the company's marketing campaigns.

Stumblers have recommended. This will help you discover great content that is hard to find using a traditional search engine.

12.3.1 Distributed beginnings at StumbleUpon

To collect and analyze this stumbling data, StumbleUpon requires its highly available back-end platform to collect, analyze, and transform millions of ratings per day. With nearly 10 million users at present, StumbleUpon fairly quickly surpassed the abilities a traditional LAMP (Linux, Apache, MySQL, PHP) stack afforded us, and we began to build a distributed platform for the following reasons:

- *Scalability*—Commodity hardware scales easily in many cases. Twenty Hadoop nodes may cost only as much as a single redundant database slave pair.
- *Freedom of development*—Developers have fewer restrictions when compared to designing around a carefully architected, somewhat fragile RDBMS.
- *Operational concerns*—Removing as many single-point-of-failure cases as possible is crucial to smooth operation of a world-class service.
- *Data processing speed*—Many system-wide calculations were simply not possible to perform with a monolithic system.

12.3.2 *HBase and StumbleUpon*

HBase plays a critical part in StumbleUpon's distributed platform. HBase is a distributed, column-oriented database that harnesses the power of the Hadoop and HDFS platform underneath it. But, as with any complex system, there are trade-offs: HBase shelves traditional relational database concepts, such as joins, foreign key relations, and triggers in the pursuit of a system that hosts immensely large, sparsely populated data on commodity hardware in a scalable manner.

AN INTRODUCTION TO HBASE

HBase is modeled after Google's Bigtable,[3] a distributed storage system. Let's recap the basics of Bigtable and Bigtable-like systems:

- Shares concepts of both column- and row-oriented databases. As described by the authors, Bigtable is a "a sparse, distributed multidimensional sorted map." The basic unit of storage, a table, is split into multiple *tablets* (*regions* in HBase parlance).
- Writes are buffered in memory, then flushed into read-only files after a while.
- To keep the number of files low, they are merged in a *compaction* process that rewrites *N* files into 1.
- Special tablets or regions are used to track the locations of the data.
- Due to the column-oriented nature of the datastore, *sparse* tables—those with a majority of null cell values—are virtually free as null values aren't stored explicitly.
- Column families are used to group row columns. All columns in a family are stored together (for locality) and share storage and configuration parameters.
- Table cells are stored with multiple versions instead of overwriting existing data.
- Capacity (both storage size and processing speed) can be increased by simply adding machines to the cluster, with no special configuration needed.

HBase provides many additional features:

- REST and Thrift[4] gateways allowing for easy access from non-Java development environments
- Easy integration with Hadoop MapReduce for data processing
- Harnesses the proven reliability and scalability of Hadoop and HDFS
- Web-based UIs for management of both the master and region servers
- Strong open source community

---

[3] Bigtable: A Distributed Storage System for Structured Data. Chang, et al. http://labs.google.com/papers/bigtable.html.

[4] Thrift is a remote procedure call library originally developed at Facebook. It's now an Apache incubator project at http://incubator.apache.org/thrift/.

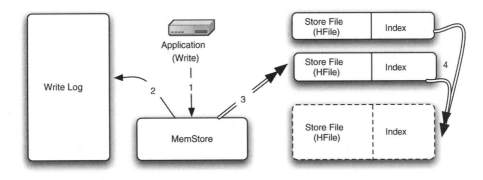

Figure 12.4   HBase write operations

Figure 12.4 describes a simplistic version of the data write path in an HBase *region server*. The write is appended to the server's write-ahead log:

1   Data is then inserted in to the MemStore.
2   As the MemStore grows beyond a threshold, it's flushed to a new file on disk.
3   When there are too many files on disk, data store files are compacted into fewer files (minor compaction).

Please visit the project site for further information on obtaining, running, and enhancing HBase.[5]

USING HBASE AT STUMBLEUPON

StumbleUpon carefully selected HBase from a host of candidate database and database-like storage and retrieval systems. We value full consistency, where any query subsequent to a write operation is guaranteed to reflect that write. In addition, StumbleUpon is committed to the open source model where we are free to contribute back to the community, and HBase's strong development community both reflected that commitment and offered a valuable resource with which to drive improvements to the product.

Our first large test of HBase was in importing existing, legacy data from our MySQL-based systems. In the past, we undertook this process only when absolutely necessary (such as migrating tables or hosts) and could take days or weeks to complete.

COLUMN VERSUS ROW STORE

You can see one example of the column-store design pattern in the storage of arbitrary attributes for a user across multiple logical attribute groupings. In this example, we assume a user has

---

[5] http://hadoop.apache.org/hbase/.

- *Contact data*—Email and web addresses, instant messaging names, profile photo URLs
- *Statistics*—"Signup date," "last login time," "last client version seen"
- *Attributes*—For remote login credentials, to authenticate to a third-party service
- *Permissions*—For access to site features and data

In the traditional RDBMS world, we may arbitrarily assign each group to a table. User attributes may be retrieved and associated simultaneously with joins and foreign keys. With careful design[6] and a relatively moderate amount of data, such a system is flexible and maintainable. However, as access patterns change—for instance, we desire to store multiple credentials per user where we assumed only one to begin—the design is difficult to change.

Furthermore, this design suffers its most fatal flaws when the data volume scales past a moderate amount and the schema needs to be refactored. The idea of doing an ALTER TABLE on a production database table containing millions or billions of rows as well as the headache of vetting systemic schema changes for both correctness and completeness is a daunting prospect. Even with a perfect, static, concrete table, data analysis becomes bottlenecked by the selection, input, and output of records.

Let's take a look at listing 12.1. It's a simple example where our typical user only has an ID and a record per Stumble:

Listing 12.1 Determining Stumbles per user, per URL

```
public class CountUserUrlStumbles {
  public static class Map extends MapReduceBase
      implements Mapper<ImmutableBytesWritable, RowResult,
      Text, Text> {
    @Override
    public void map(ImmutableBytesWritable key,
                    RowResult value,
                    OutputCollector<Text, Text> output,
                    Reporter reporter) throws IOException {
      byte [] row = value.getRow();
      int userid = StumbleUtils.UserIndex.getUserId(row);
      int urlid = StumbleUtils.UserIndex.getUrlId(row);

      Text one = new Text("1");
      output.collect(new Text("U:" + Integer.toString(userid)), one);
      output.collect(new Text("Url:" + Integer.toString(urlid)), one);
    }
  }

  public static class Reduce extends MapReduceBase
      implements Reducer<Text,Text,Text,Text> {
    @Override
    public void reduce(Text key,
                       Iterator<Text> values,
                       OutputCollector<Text, Text> output,
                       Reporter reporter) throws IOException {
```

---

[6] Rarely achieved on the first attempt, since final schemas are rarely known fully a priori!

```
      int count = 0;
      while (values.hasNext()) {
        values.next();
        count++;
      }
      output.collect(key, new Text(Integer.toString(count)));
    }
  }

  public static void main(String []args) throws IOException {
    if (args.length < 2) {
      System.out.println("Give the name of the by-userid stumble table");
      return;
    }
    JobConf job = new JobConf(CountUserUrlStumbles.class);
    job.setInputFormat(TableInputFormat.class);
    FileInputFormat.setInputPaths(job, args[0]);
    job.setMapperClass(Map.class);
    job.setReducerClass(Reduce.class);
    job.setOutputFormat(TextOutputFormat.class);
    TextOutputFormat.setOutputPath(job, new Path(args[1]));
    job.setNumMapTasks(5000);
    JobClient jc = new JobClient(job);
    jc.submitJob(job);
  }
}
```

In this example, we look at a routine StumbleUpon task: counting stumbles per user as well as stumbles per URL. Although this task is not particularly complex or insightful, we provide it here as a concrete example to the reader of a type of analytic task we perform on a daily basis. The most interesting bit is that this trivial example completes in about 1 hour (using twenty commodity nodes) when processing a key count in the tens of billions. The MySQL-based counterpart doesn't complete in a reasonable amount of time—at least not without special handling and support to dump the data from MySQL, split the lines to a reasonable chunk size, and then combine the results.

You may find this series of operations familiar: mapping, then reducing! By using the generalized facilities of both HBase and Hadoop, we are able to conduct similar statistical surveys as needed, without special preparation and runtime handling. To apply this straightforward example to the real world, we are now able to complete all analysis tasks in the same day they're requested. We can provide the ability to run ad hoc queries at a rate not thought possible before Hadoop and HBase were powering our platform. As a business thrives and dies on the data it can analyze, this decreased turnaround time makes an incredible impact from the front office number crunching to the research engineers doing instant spam analysis on content submissions.

One can only imagine the difficulty of refactoring the custom-processing pipeline when the data schema is more complex than this trivial example, if we didn't have our distributed processing platform to power the extraction, transformation, and analysis.

TRANSCENDING A SINGLE MACHINE

As we've outlined, one of the most important scalability features of HBase is the ability to (finally) transcend the write limits of a single machine.

Typically, scaling a database involves adding read slaves and caching to the system. Read slaves can only help if your application is reading more than writing. Caching only helps if your data set doesn't change too often. Even so, these architectural features frequently add vast application-side complexity.

HBase hosts each region on any one of the machines in the cluster (each is a *region server*). Writes touch the region server hosting that region, and the HBase region server writes to three (by default) HDFS data nodes.[7] With a large table and a similarly large cluster, writes are spread out to many different machines, inherently avoiding the single machine write problem that master-slave data stores have.

This feature can help you scale beyond traditional relational systems at a fraction of the cost. As larger hardware tends to become expensive faster than the actual performance delivered, this is a fairly profound and important ability. For the large work loads at StumbleUpon, the savings could literally be millions of dollars. Some problems simply aren't approachable on a single machine setup!

For highly dynamic data sets, where we frequently read things that were just written, caching in a system, such as memcached, may not help much. HBase holds recently written data in a write buffer. Reads for that data come directly out of memory. This action could completely obviate the need for a caching layer.

One example of a highly dynamic data set is event counters. This is a difficult problem because most high-speed solutions tend to be RAM-only for performance (e.g., memcached), while requiring high durability as well. Enter HBase and its `incrementColumnValue()` call. These mutates are internally treated as any other change, by both logging to disk and buffering up in the write buffer. Reads can come directly from the write buffer, accelerating both and achieving high performance and durability. StumbleUpon harnesses the natural ability of HBase to support event counters in just about every niche of the site—clicks, hits, ads served, and so on.

Furthermore, HBase offers a superior choice to typical sharding solutions. Most traditional sharding approaches require a priori assumptions of the key space. This can have surprising performance implications when the hashing function isn't evenly distributed or when the keys are distributed outside the assumptions of your sharding scheme.

HBase takes a data-sized approach to splitting tables into regions; as the data in a region grows and reaches a configured size (currently defaulted to 256 MB), a mid-key is picked from the middle of the data, splitting the region into two roughly equal chunks. Each chunk becomes its own region and now has room to grow. Repeating this procedure thousands of times gives a net result of a table with 2000 roughly equal-sized regions. Figure 12.5 shows the operation of a simplified HBase cluster with three writes and one read concurrently operating on a key space of 256 keys (0x00-0xFF).

---

[7] HDFS writes to multiple data nodes to achieve durability of data, as well as locality-based performance.

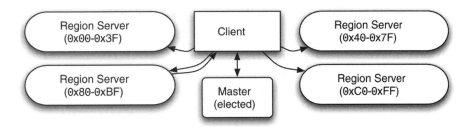

Figure 12.5 HBase easily and automatically "shards."

- The client bootstraps the ROOT table location from ZooKeeper.
- The ROOT table contains pointers to other META tables that hold user table locations.
- The client finds the region for the selected operation. The location is cached in the client.
- The request is sent to the region for execution.

As StumbleUpon's data continues to grow in an uneven manner, we don't end up with unbalanced shards or regions requiring manual intervention later, a problem frequently encountered by most manual sharding solutions involving RDBMS.

LUDICROUS-SPEED HBASE

For all the talk about HBase's advantages, initially we found that the performance of the system was not up to online data servicing. To fix that, Ryan contributed back a large number of internal performance and reliability enhancements to the HBase project.

The first major contribution was the HFile format. The previous format had inefficiencies in the index strategy, read paths, and internal APIs. Several issues were identified:

- Stream-oriented format made caching difficult.
- Index efficiency was sensitive to the size of the data.
- Lots of byte array copies were made.
- Object creation rates were too high.

HFile is an immutable file format. Once written, no value in it can change. The reader and writer are separated in code and there are no mutate or update methods available. As most HFiles are hosted on HDFS, it would be impossible anyway because HDFS files are immutable as well.

The HFile writer has a straightforward write path, with four elements:

- Open file, provide compression, block size, and comparator arguments.
- These never change for the lifetime of the file.
- Append keys, in comparator sorted order.
- Any attempt to add keys in nonsorted order results in exceptions.
- Optionally append metadata blocks.

- Useful for additional data, or features, such as Bloom filters.
- Close the file, finalize the index and write the trailers.

As keys and values are appended to the HFile, the code keeps track of how large the current block is. Once it exceeds the block size specified, it's flushed and the compression system is reset for the next block. As HFile writer appends a block, an in-memory index of the first key of each block is formed, along with its in-file offset. When the close method is called, the block index is written immediately behind the last block. Optional metadata blocks are appended next, followed by the metadata block index. Finally, a trailer with pointers to the indexes is appended and the file is closed.

When a file is opened for reading, the data block index and the meta block index are loaded. They stay in resident for the duration, until the reader object is reclaimed. The index allows for fast seek and reads of blocks of data. To find a key in the file, first the reader does a binary search of the index. Finding a block number, it reads in and decompresses the data block and stores it in the block cache. Code then iterates through the block in memory finding the key, or the closest match. Pointers are then returned, allowing clients a view into the single copy of data.

HFile gains its strengths from simplicity in both concept and implementation. The implementation is one file (tests excepted) and is about 1,600 lines for both reader and writer.

HFile provided a new internal platform to rewrite the rest of the region server. The internal algorithms for read-merging multiple files into a single-scan result had grown organically over time and needed a fresh look. Jon Gray and Erik Holstad at Streamy.com designed and implemented a brand-new read implementation by adding new delete semantics and restructuring the internal key formats. By using more efficient algorithms and redoing the implementation on the 0-copy HFile, more speed enhancements were gained from the code.

Overall speed increases were extremely impressive, ranging from 30 times to 100 times, depending on the particular API call involved. On the low end, scanning a series of rows got a 30 times speed-up. On the high end, single row gets can be up to 100 times faster. With these performance improvements, HBase can truly be labeled as "web ready."

HBASE AND PARALLELISM

HBase demonstrates excellent parallel speed-up on read and write workloads. As StumbleUpon has stored so much data in MySQL, insert performance is important. To copy data into HBase, Hadoop jobs with only mappers that read from MySQL and subsequently write into HBase were written. Running on a 20-node cluster with about 80 times parallelism, aggregate insert performance ranged from 100,000 operations a second up to as much as 300,000 operations a second. The rows involved were about 100 bytes.

As impressive as the write performance is, the read performance is exceptional. Using an 80-times-parallel MapReduce read aggregation job, it achieves a total read speed of 4.5 million rows a second. At this rate, reading our largest tables takes less than an hour. The ability to write entire table analytics is a powerful ability that previously didn't exist.

All the machines involved were dual quad core Intels, with 16 GB of RAM. Each node had two SATA disks, each 1 TB in size. These relatively modest and standard nodes provide an excellent level of performance, and the cluster only performs better with more.

12.3.3 More Hadoop at StumbleUpon

At StumbleUpon, we subscribe to the mantra of "Log early, log often, log everything." No piece of data is too small or too noisy to be useful down the road. Hadoop excels in this traditionally strong area for distributed processing: log-and-click collection combined with analysis. StumbleUpon harnesses this natural aptitude of Hadoop for a variety of analysis tasks, including Apache log file collection and user-session analysis.

As an example, a basic need for any web product in the days of search engine optimization experts and "black hat" attackers is to look back at a combination of web browser user agent strings combined with the (apparent) originating IP address and action context. Now imagine needing to do this across a fleet of web server frontends, millions of users, and billions of clicks.

Scribe,[8] a Facebook project made public, is a platform for aggregating real-time streamed log data in such a context. The service is failure tolerant at both the machine and network level and easily integrates into just about any infrastructure.

StumbleUpon uses Scribe to collect data directly into HDFS where it's reviewed and processed by a number of systems. A combination of Cascading and plain MapReduce-based analysis jobs extract data from the logs for vanilla statistics (such as click counts), while more sophisticated consumers feed data into real-time feedback systems based around BerkeleyDB and TokyoCabinet. A second set of systems use this streamed data for search index updates and thumbnail generation. Figure 12.6 illustrates several data processing modules around Hadoop.

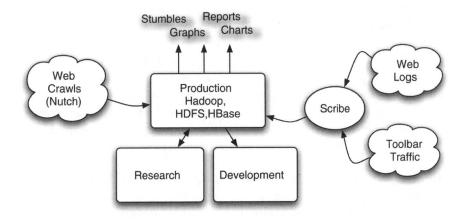

Figure 12.6　StumbleUpon data collection, analysis, and storage using Hadoop

---

[8] http://github.com/facebook/scribe.

We obtained an illustrative result by processing 10 GB of standard Apache log files with the Cascading log analysis example.[9] Using Hadoop 0.19.1, Cascading 1.0.9, and the previously mentioned node configuration, we obtained the number of Apache hits per minute with this example by bucketing the hits in MapReduce jobs. We wrote a naive single-node Perl hash-based program as an example of a typical quick solution a sysadmin may create. The results shown in table 12.3 confirm that our results easily achieve linear (or better) speed-up with the simple addition of more nodes to the cluster. Times are the average of 10 mixed executions, to allow for variances.

Table 12.3   Apache log processing with Cascading

System	Performance measure	Result
1 Node	Runtime	21m46s
	Sec/MB	0.127
	Sec/MB/Node	0.127
3 Nodes	Runtime	8m3s
	Sec/MB	0.0471
	Sec/MB/Node	0.0157
15 Nodes	Runtime	1m30s
	Sec/MB	0.00878
	Sec/MB/Node	0.000585
Naive Perl	Runtime	42m49s
	Sec/MB	0.251
	Sec/MB/Node	0.251

We see that even the single-node Cascading solution achieves double the throughput of the naive Perl application due to the intelligent segmentation and bucketing built in to the MapReduce framework versus the effect of keeping all data mapped to a single Perl hash. Given familiarity with Cascading, you may also consider the Perl code more complex to optimize (and maintain) to boot!

To wit, StumbleUpon uses the native map and reduce functionality in Hadoop and related products, including Nutch and custom-written content surveyors, to perform this data retrieval, analysis, and storage. Keeping the resultant data close to the processing pipeline maximizes our data locality benefits.

Putting it all together, StumbleUpon has taken the maximum advantage of the vast power the MapReduce paradigm unlocks by adopting and extending Hadoop, HDFS, and HBase. We're excited to help lead the future of distributed processing.

12.4   *Building analytics for enterprise search—IBM's Project ES2*

Contributed by VUK ERCEGOVAC, RAJASEKAR KRISHNAMURTHY, SRIRAM RAGHAVAN, FREDERICK REISS, EUGENE SHEKITA, SANDEEP TATA, SHIVAKUMAR VAITHYANATHAN, and HUAIYU ZHU

In contrast with the radical advances in web search over the last several years, search over enterprise intranets has remained a difficult and largely unsolved problem. Based

---

[9] http://code.google.com/p/cascading/wiki/ApacheLogCascade.

on a study of the IBM intranet, Fagin et. al. [1] highlighted some critical differences between the search problem on the intranet and that on the web. They observed that an overwhelming majority of the queries in the intranet are "navigational." They have a small set of correct answers [2,3]. For instance, a manual examination of the top 6,500 queries (as of July 2008) on the IBM intranet revealed that more than 90 percent of those queries were navigational.

Several enterprise-specific factors complicate the task of finding the "correct" answers for these queries:

- Absence of an economic incentive for content creators to make their pages easily discoverable (in contrast with the presence of such incentives on the web)
- The use of enterprise-specific vocabulary, abbreviations, and acronyms, in the search queries and in the intranet pages
- The fact that the same query can have a different "correct" answer depending on the location and organizational role of the person issuing the query (of particular importance for corporations like IBM with employees and locations in over 80 countries)

From earlier efforts at IBM [4], we learned that these problems are difficult to overcome using traditional information retrieval techniques. Subsequently, in [5], we proposed an approach consisting of detailed offline analyses to pre-identify navigational pages and the use of a special-purpose navigational index. We demonstrated the viability of this approach through experiments over a 5.5-million-page corpus from the IBM intranet. The system in [5], uses a mix of proprietary platforms and relational databases. We have, since, crawled a much larger portion of the IBM intranet, having discovered over 100 million URLs and indexed over 16 million documents. In order to tackle these sizes and beyond, and having learned from previous efforts [4,5], we have developed ES2—a scalable, high-quality search engine for the IBM intranet. ES2 is based on the analytics described in [5], but it leverages a number of open source platforms and tools, such as Hadoop, Nutch, Lucene, and Jaql.[10]

In principle, the Nutch crawler, the Hadoop MapReduce framework, and the Lucene indexing engine provide a full suite of software components for building a complete search engine. But, to truly address the challenges described earlier, it's not sufficient to merely stitch these systems together. We describe how to use sophisticated analysis and mining of the crawled pages, and special-purpose navigational indexes in conjunction with intelligent query processing to ensure effective search quality. To understand how these elements come together, we now examine some illustrative search queries and their corresponding results on ES2. See figure 12.7.

Figure 12.7 shows the result of running the query *idp* on ES2. The IDP is an acronym for *Individual Development Plan*, a web-based HR application in IBM to assist in tracking employee career development. The first two results returned by ES2 represent two different URLs that both allow the user to launch the IDP web application. The third

---

[10] http://code.google.com/p/jaql/.

result entry is, in fact, a set of pages describing the IDP process, one per country, that have been grouped together (indicated visually through indentation and the presence of a globe icon). We make the following observations:

1   The first result in figure 12.7 doesn't have the word idp in the title and indeed not even in the content of the page. ES2 was able to associate this page with the word idp by extracting the term from the URL http://w3.ibm.com/hr/idp/. For the second result in figure 12.7, besides idp in the URL, we also extract idp from the title by applying a regular expression pattern that explicitly looks for titles ending in phrases such as "Launch Page," "Portal," "Main Page," and so on. In ES2, we use several hundred such carefully crafted patterns applied to the URL, title, META headers, and various other features of a web page to detect and associate index terms with navigational pages. Section 12.4.3 describes how we execute such analysis, known as *Local Analysis*, in parallel on a Hadoop cluster.

2   Our current crawl of the IBM intranet has close to 500 pages that have a URL containing *idp* and over a 1,000 pages that have either *idp* or *individual development plan* in the title. To narrow down the result to the two specific URLs shown in figure 12.7, we use a complex set of analysis algorithms as part of a

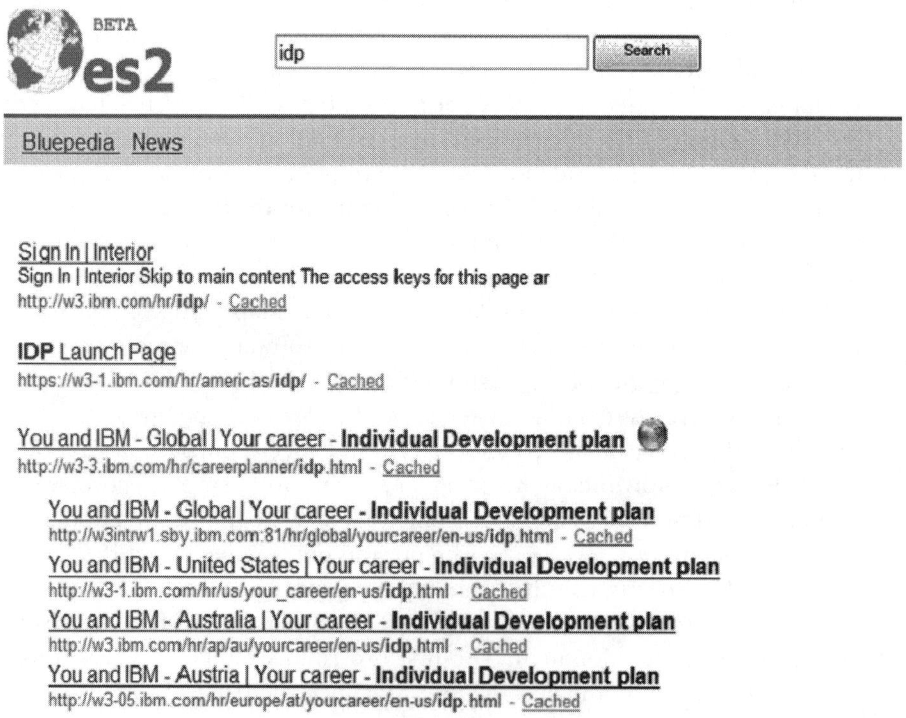

BETA

es2

idp | Search |

Bluepedia News

Sign In | Interior
Sign In | Interior Skip to main content The access keys for this page ar
http://w3.ibm.com/hr/**idp**/ - Cached

IDP Launch Page
https://w3-1.ibm.com/hr/americ as/**idp**/ - Cached

You and IBM - Global | Your career - **Individual Development plan**
http://w3-3.ibm.com/hr/careerplanner/**idp**.html - Cached

   You and IBM - Global | Your career - **Individual Development plan**
   http://w3intrw1.sby.ibm.com:81/hr/global/yourcareer/en-us/**idp**.html - Cached
   You and IBM - United States | Your career - **Individual Development plan**
   http://w3-1.ibm.com/hr/us/your_career/en-us/**idp**.html - Cached
   You and IBM - Australia | Your career - **Individual Development plan**
   http://w3.ibm.com/hr/ap/au/yourcareer/en-us/**idp**.html - Cached
   You and IBM - Austria | Your career - **Individual Development plan**
   http://w3-05.ibm.com/hr/europe/at/yourcareer/en-us/**idp**.html - Cached

Figure 12.7   Illustrative search results in ES2

process known as *Global Analysis.* Section 12.4.3 describes how to implement such analysis in ES2 using the Hadoop framework.

3 Notice that in all the result pages grouped as part of the third result in figure 12.7, the text *Individual Development Plan* in the title has been highlighted to indicate a match against the query term *idp.* To accomplish this match, the following two steps took place during offline analysis: (1) the phrase *Individual Development Plan* was extracted as part of local analysis using patterns applied to the title and (2) during indexing, the extracted phrase was recognized to be the expansion of the acronym *idp* and resulted in the term *idp* being added to the index as well. In general, we employ a process known as *variant generation* whereby multiple variants of the terms extracted through local analysis are generated and added to the index. ES2 employs a suite of variant generation strategies—from simple n-grams over the extracted phrase to more sophisticated ones. In the interest of space we don't describe these algorithms in detail.

4 Finally, to enable results to be customized based on the search users' geography and to support the type of result grouping shown in figure 12.7, we label each page in the intranet with a specific geography (country, region, and/or IBM location). In ES2, this labeling is accomplished using a rule-driven classifier that uses a number of page features extracted during local analysis.

The examples in figure 12.7 motivate the vital role of offline analysis and variant generation in ES2. Each page in the ES2 collection is pushed through multiple logical workflows, each consisting of a local analysis phase, a global analysis phase, and an appropriate variant generation strategy. The output of a workflow is some subset of the input pages along with a set of index terms. Depending on the particular extraction patterns and variant generation rules, the output of two different workflows will have correspondingly different "precision" characteristics. For example, a workflow consisting of careful extraction of a person's name from the title followed by name-specific variant generation is likely to yield much higher-quality answers than a workflow that only generates all possible n-grams of the title of a page.

The creation of an index structure consisting of the output of multiple workflows with different precision characteristics is only half the story. To fully leverage such an index, ES2 employs a sophisticated runtime query processing strategy. A discussion of the runtime component of ES2 is beyond the scope of this case study. We restrict our attention to the offline analysis workflows and their implementation on Hadoop.

12.4.1 *ES2 architecture*

We assume that readers are broadly familiar with Hadoop and Nutch.[11] Nutch is an open source crawler implemented on the Hadoop MapReduce platform for web crawling.

---

[11] http://nutch.apache.org/.

ES2 also uses Jaql,[12] a data flow language designed for JSON (a popular semi-structured data model). Jaql provides a Unix pipes-like syntax to connect multiple stages of processing over semistructured JSON data. The ES2 workflow involves invoking multiple algorithms for local analysis, global analysis, and variant generation before inserting data into indexes. Without adequate data management support, this complex multistage workflow quickly becomes overwhelming. To address this problem, ES2 uses JSON to represent its data and Jaql to specify the workflow (see figure 12.8).

Figure 12.8 shows the architecture of ES2. There are six components in ES2: the crawler, local analysis, global analysis, variant generation and indexing, background mining, and search runtime. ES2 uses an enhanced version of Nutch (version 0.9)—a scalable open source crawler based on the Hadoop platform. In addition, ES2 also gathers information from IBM's social bookmarking service (called Dogear). Much like delicious.com, Dogear contains various URLs that have been bookmarked by the IBM community along with a collection of tags associated with each URL. The tags associated with the URLs contain valuable clues about the page, and ES2 uses this information in building its indexes. All the stages use a common distributed filesystem, HDFS, for both input and output. Local analysis processes each page to extract features about the pages and stores the results as JSON objects in HDFS. ES2 uses Jaql to push each page through the rest of the pipeline, transforming the data as needed at each

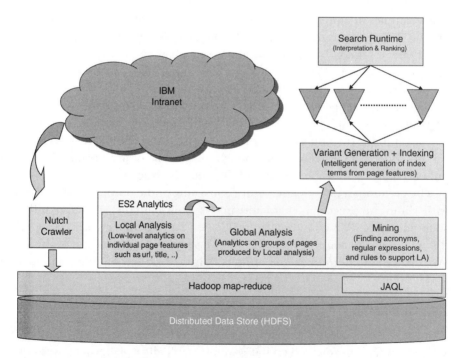

Figure 12.8   ES2 Architecture

---

[12] http://code.google.com/p/jaql/.

stage. Jaql queries are used to bring together the results of different local analyses and invoke global analysis. Jaql is also used to invoke the variant generation and indexing workflow using the outputs of local and global analyses. The indexes are periodically copied to a different set of machines that serve user queries.

Although not part of the main workflow, ES2 periodically executes several mining and classification tasks. Examples of this include algorithms to automatically produce acronym libraries, regular expression libraries [6], and geo-classification rules.

12.4.2 ES2 crawler

ES2 uses Nutch version 0.9. A primary data structure in Nutch is the CrawlDB: a key-value set where the keys are the URLs known to Nutch and the value is the status of the URL. The status contains metadata about the URL, such as the time of discovery, whether it has been fetched, and so on. Nutch is architected as a sequence of three MapReduce jobs:

- *Generate*—In this phase, a fetch list is generated by scanning the input key/value pairs (from CrawlDB) for URLs that have been discovered, but not fetched. A common choice in generating this list is to select the top k unfetched URLs using an appropriate scoring mechanism (k is a configuration parameter in Nutch).
- *Fetch*—In this phase, the pages associated with the URLs in the input fetch list are fetched and parsed. The output consists of the URL and the parsed representation of the page.
- *Update*—The update phase collects all the URLs that have been discovered by parsing the contents of the pages in the fetch phase and merges them with the CrawlDB.

The pages fetched in each cycle of generate-fetch-update are referred to as a *segment*.

Out of the box, the first problem we encountered was crawl speed. Nutch's crawl rate was under three pages per second—far less than the network bandwidth available to the cluster. A deeper problem we encountered after a sample crawl of 80 million pages was that the quality of discovered pages was surprisingly low. In this section, we identify the underlying reasons for both these problems and describe the enhancements made to Nutch to adapt it to the IBM intranet.

MODIFICATIONS FOR PERFORMANCE

Nutch's design was aimed at web crawling. When using it to crawl the IBM intranet, we observed multiple performance bottlenecks. We discovered that the reason for the bottlenecks was that the enterprise intranet contains far fewer hosts than the web, and some of the design choices made in Nutch assume a large number of distinct hosts. We describe two ways in which this problem manifests itself, and the approach used in ES2 to adapt Nutch's design for the enterprise.

A major performance bottleneck in the fetch phase, called *long tail problem*, exhibits the following behavior. The crawl rate in the early part of the fetch phase is relatively high (typically dozens of pages a second). But this deteriorates relatively quickly to less than a page per second, where it remains until completion of the segment. A quick examination revealed that this behavior is heavily influenced by the host with the largest number of URLs in the fetch list. You can understand this by observing that the fetch rate in Nutch is controlled by two parameters: the number of distinct hosts in the fetch list that Nutch can concurrently crawl from, and the duration for which Nutch waits before making consecutive requests to the same host. A straightforward solution to the long tail problem is to restrict the number of URLs for a particular host in the fetch list. Unfortunately, this is not sufficient because not all host servers are identical, and the time required to fetch the same number of pages from different hosts can be dramatically different. We added a time-shutoff parameter that terminates the fetcher after a fixed amount of time as an engineering fix to this problem. While this terminates the fetch phase early (and fewer pages are retrieved in total in the segment), by avoiding the slow tail phase, we sustain a higher average crawl rate. In practice, we observed that by appropriately setting this shutoff parameter, the average crawl rate could be improved to nearly three times the original crawl rate. Ideally, the current fetch rate should determine such a shutoff; this unfortunately requires pooling information across map tasks and can't easily be performed in Hadoop today.

A main-memory data structure in the fetcher causes a different performance bottleneck. The fetcher works by first creating a set of queues where each queue stores URLs for a particular host—we call this data structure *FetchQueues*. A fixed amount of memory is allocated to FetchQueues to be shared across the individual queues. The fetcher reads the URLs to be fetched from its input and inserts them into FetchQueues until it exhausts the allocated memory. Worker threads assigned to each queue in FetchQueues concurrently fetch pages from different hosts as long as their queues are non-empty. The bottleneck arises because URLs in the input are ordered by host (this is an artifact of the generate phase) and the fetcher exhausts the memory allocated to FetchQueues with URLs from very few hosts. Such a design is appropriate for crawling a large number of hosts on the web as each host in the fetch list would then have only a few URLs. In the enterprise, host diversity is limited to a few thousand at best. As a result, few worker threads are actively fetching from FetchQueues, leading to severe under-utilization of resources. We address this problem by replacing FetchQueues with a disk-based data structure without any limits on the total size. This allows the fetcher to populate FetchQueues with all the URLs in the input, thereby keeping the maximum possible number of worker threads active. This simple change improved the fetch rate several fold.

12.4.3 *ES2 analytics*

Much of the complexity and power in ES2 lies in its analytics. In this section, we briefly describe the different algorithms, paying special attention to the design choices made in mapping these algorithms onto Hadoop.

LOCAL ANALYSIS

In local analysis, each page is individually analyzed to extract clues that help decide whether that page is a *candidate navigational page*. In ES2, five different local analysis algorithms, namely *TitleHomePage*, *PersonalHomePage*, *URLHomePage*, *AnchorHome*, and *NavLink* are used. These algorithms use rules based on regular expression patterns, dictionaries, and information extraction tools [7] to identify candidate navigational pages. For instance, using a regular expression like "\ A\ W*(.+)\s<Home>" (Java regular expression syntax), the *PersonalHomePage* algorithm can detect that a page with a title "G. J. Chaitin's Home" indicates that this is the home page of G. J. Chaitin. The algorithm outputs the name of a feature ("Personal Home Page") and associates a value with this feature ("G. J. Chaitin"). The next section describes the impact of redirections on local analysis and discusses a solution.

REDIRECTION RESOLUTION

Many sites in IBM's intranet employ redirection for updating, load balancing, upgrading, and handling internal reorganizations. Unfortunately, redirections can cause complications in the local analysis algorithms. For instance, URLHomePage uses the text of the URL to detect a candidate navigational page. After redirection, the target URL may not contain the same features as the original URL. As an illustrative example, consider the URL http://w3.can.ibm.com/hr/erbp. Local analysis algorithms can correctly identify this URL as the home page for the Employee Referral Bonus Program (ERBP) using clues from the URL. But this URL gets redirected to a Lotus Domino server at http://w3-03.ibm.com/hr/hrc.nsf/3f31db8c0ff0ac90852568f7006d 51ea/ac3f2f04ba60a6d585256d05004cef97?OpenDocument, where a Lotus Domino database serves information about the Employee Referral Bonus Program. The clues in the source URL are no longer available in the target, and the local analysis algorithm can no longer identify this page as navigational. To prevent this, ES2 resolves all redirections, collects the set of URLs that lead to the target page through redirections, and provides local analysis with the appropriate URLs.

To track redirections, we modified Nutch to tag every page that was a target of redirection with the source URL. Consider figure 12.9. The crawler follows redirections from a page A to page B, and from page B to arrive at page C. We track these redirections by tagging pages B and C with the source URL, A. This tag is stored as a metadata field in the *segment* file. A segment file is a key/value set

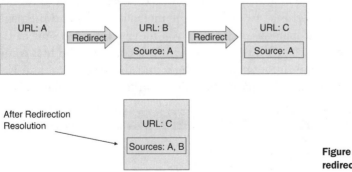

Figure 12.9   Resolving redirections

where the key is the URL of a page and the value is contents of the page (along with additional metadata fields).

Listing 12.2 (called *ResolveSimple*) outlines the map and reduce functions that are used to resolve redirections on a segment and invoke local analysis. The map phase outputs the source URL and the page contents. The reduce phase brings all the pages with the same source URL into a single group. In the preceding example of figure 12.9, the common source URL for pages A, B, and C is A. The target page in this group (C) is then passed to local analysis along with the other URLs in the group—A and B.

Listing 12.2   ResolveSimple

```
Map (Key: URL, Value: PageData)
if PageData.SourceURL exists then
    Ouput [PageData.SourceURL, PageData]
else
    Output [URL, Pagedata]
end if
End

Reduce (Key: URL, Values: Pageset)
Let URLset = Set of all URLs in Pageset
Let page = Target of redirection in Pageset
result = LocalAnalysis(page, URLset)
output [page.URL, result]
End
```

HADOOP IMPLEMENTATION

In ResolveSimple, local analysis is invoked in the reducer. This requires Hadoop to pass along the contents of each page from the map phase to the reduce phase. This involves sorting and moving a large amount of data across the network. To avoid this, we modify ResolveSimple (listing 12.2) and separate the task of redirection resolution and the local analysis so that the algorithms in local analysis are run in the map phase. This allows the local analysis computation to be colocated with the data, and therefore results in significant performance improvement.

We have outlined the modified algorithm, called *Resolve2Step*, in listing 12.3. In the map phase of this algorithm, we only pass the metadata along and the page content (which accounts for a majority of the data volume) is projected out. In the reduce phase of ResolveSimple, we output a table with two columns: the first column is the URL of the target page in the group of pages, and the second column is the set of URLs to be associated with the page when it's submitted to local analysis.

Listing 12.3   Resolve2Step

```
1: Resolve Redirections
Map (Key: URL, Value: Page)
if PageData.SourceURL exists then
    Ouput [PageData.SourceURL, PageData.metadata]
else
```

```
        Output [URL, Pagedata.metadata]
end if
End
Reduce (Key: URL, Values: Pageset)
Let URLset = Set of all URLs in Pageset
Let page = Target of redirections in Pageset
output [page.URL, URLset]
End

2: Run Local Analysis
Map (Key: URL, Value: Page)
Load resolveTable from output of previous step if needed
Let URLSet = resolveTable[URL]
result = LocalAnalysis(page, URLset)
output [page.URL, result]
End
```

If a URL results in a redirection, we don't add an entry for it in this table. Table 12.4 shows an example of such a table. The chain of redirections shown in the preceding figure 12.9 results in the first row in table 12.4. In a subsequent map-only job for local analysis, the map tasks read the redirection table into memory. This table is fairly small for typical segments and easily fits in memory. For each URL in the input segment, the mapper looks up the table if it finds a non-empty entry. It passes these URLs on to local analysis. By invoking local analysis in the map phase, Resolve2Step avoids the transfer of the page contents over the network to the reducers as in ResolveSimple. We executed both algorithms for local analysis on a segment of around 400,000 pages on the cluster using eight nodes. Whereas ResolveSimple completed in about 22 minutes, Resolve2Step took only 7 minutes.

In order to understand how Resolve2Step scales, we ran this algorithm on the same segment (400,000 pages) and varied the cluster size from one to eight servers. The times are shown in figure 12.10. The speed-up graph shows that for the early part of the curve, we get linear scaling; the benefits of adding more nodes decreases after this point. This is because the input consists of only a single segment of 400,000 pages. Hadoop is unable to efficiently divide this task at a finer granularity. We'll see in the next section that with larger input data sets, Hadoop can efficiently divide the task and provide linear scaling.

Table 12.4 Resolution table in Resolve2Step

URL	Sources
C	{A,B}
...	...
X	{Y}
...	...

GLOBAL ANALYSIS

The local analysis tasks described in the previous section identify candidate navigational pages by extracting relevant features from each page. But as described in section 12.4.1, the same navigational feature can be associated with multiple pages. Consider the case where homepage authors use the same title for many of their web pages. For example, "G. J. Chaitin home page" is the title for many pages on G. J. Chaitin's website. Local analysis for personal home pages considers all such pages to be candidates. ES2 uses global analysis to determine an appropriate subset of pages

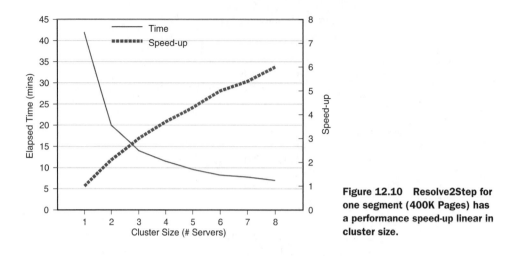

Figure 12.10   Resolve2Step for one segment (400K Pages) has a performance speed-up linear in cluster size.

as navigational. [5] describes two algorithms: *site root analysis* and *anchor text analysis*. We briefly review these algorithms and describe how Jaql is used to implement these algorithms on large data sets.

GLOBAL ANALYSIS ALGORITHMS

Each global analysis task takes as input a set of pages and the associated features discovered during local analysis. Listing 12.4 shows an example JSON record corresponding to the page titled "G. J. Chaitin home page." The fields produced by local analysis are in the record titled "LA" and those produced by global analysis are in "GA."

Listing 12.4   Example JSON output from global analysis and Jaql query

```
[...,
{docid: 1879495641814943578,
  url: "http://w3.watson.ibm.com/~chaitin/index.html",
  title: "G J Chaitin Home Page",
  ...
  LA: {
      personalHomepage: {name: G J Chaitin, begin: 0, end: 11},
      geography: {countries: "USA", ...}
      ...},
  GA: {
      personalHomepageSiteRootAnalysis: {marked: true, ...},
      ...}
}, ...]

$alldocs  = file "laDocs.json";
$results  = file "phpGADocs.json";

$alldocs
-> filter not isnull($.LA.personalHomepage.name)
-> partition by $t = $.LA.personalHomepage.name
   |- SiteRootAnalysis($t, $) -|
-> write $results;
```

The two algorithms of global analysis are

- *Site root analysis*—Both algorithms are used to group candidate pages and identify a set of representative pages. Given a collection of candidate pages, it's first partitioned by the feature of interest, for example, PersonalHomePage. For each group, a forest of pages is constructed where each URL is a node in the forest, relating the two URLS *A* and *B* as parent and child if *A* is the longest prefix of *B*. (Shorter prefixes are higher ancestors.) The forest is pruned using some complex logic that may involve inputs from other local analysis algorithms, the details of which are beyond the scope of this case study. We use site root analysis not only for the output from PersonalHomePage, but also for TitleHomePage (e.g., pages titled "Working at Almaden Research Center" or "IT Help Central").
- *Anchor text analysis*—This algorithm collects all the anchor text for each page by examining all the pages that point to it. The aggregated anchor text is processed to pick a set of representative terms for that URL. For further details on this algorithm, see [5].

HADOOP IMPLEMENTATION

In global analysis, first, a merge step joins together the results of local analysis on the main crawl and the tags for the URLs collected from Dogear. This is followed by a deduplication step where duplicate pages are eliminated. Each global analysis task then involves some standard data manipulation (e.g., partitioning, filtering, joining) in conjunction with some task-specific user-defined function, such as URL forest generation and pruning. Jaql is used to specify these tasks at a high level, and execute them in parallel using Hadoop.

Consider the Jaql query in listing 12.4 used for the global analysis on PersonalHomePage data. The first two lines specify the input and output files. The input is assumed to be a JSON array—in this case, an array of records—each record representing a page and the associated results from local analysis. The third line is the start of a Jaql pipe: pages flow from the input file, referred to by *$allDocs*, to subsequent operators. The connection between pipe operators is denoted by ->. Following the input, the "filter" operator produces a value when its predicate evaluates to true. In the example, only pages that have a local analysis (LA) field, a PersonalHomePage field, and a non-null name are output to the next operator. The *$* is a variable that refers to the current value in the pipe. The filtered pages are partitioned according to name. For each partition, the user-defined function *SiteRootAnalysis* is evaluated. The function takes as input the partitioning field *$t* (a variable for *name*), and all pages in the partition (*$*). Finally, the annotated pages are written to *$results* output file.

Jaql evaluates the query shown in the preceding listing 12.4 by translating to a MapReduce job and submitting the job to Hadoop for evaluation. In this example, the map stage filters pages and extracts the partitioning key. The reduce stage evaluates the SiteRootAnalysis function per partition and writes the output to a file. In general,

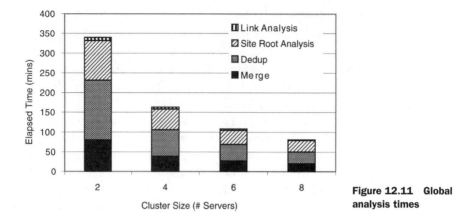

Figure 12.11   Global analysis times

Jaql automatically translates a collection of pipe definitions into a directed acyclic graph of MapReduce jobs.

In figures 12.11 and 12.12, we present how the global analysis task scaled on a collection of 16 million documents using Jaql and Hadoop as the cluster size was increased from two to eight servers. Figure 12.11 shows detailed elapsed times for each stage involved after local analysis through the end of global analysis. Figure 12.12 shows that as servers were added to the cluster, the total time to evaluate merge, dedup, and global analysis improved proportionally.

MINING TASKS

ES2 builds acronym libraries, regular expression patterns, and geo-classification rules automatically using the crawled data in background mining tasks. Recall that

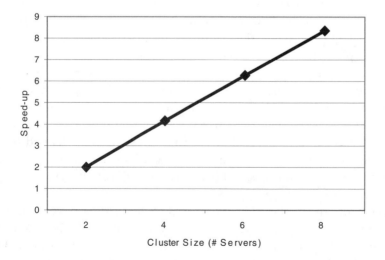

Figure 12.12   Global analysis speed-up

local analysis algorithms use these resources. Periodically, the local analysis is rerun on all the pages after updating these resources. As an example, we provide a brief description of the acronym mining algorithm and the geo-classification algorithm used in ES2 below.

Acronym mining is a computationally intensive task that benefits from a parallel implementation on Hadoop. The algorithm used in ES2 is adapted from [8]. It works by examining the text of each page to first identify patterns of the form "*longForm* (*shortForm*)" or "*shortForm* (*longForm*)". After identifying acronyms and their candidate longForms, the map function outputs [shortForm, longForm] as a key/value pair. The reduce function gathers all the possible longForms together for a given shortForm and ranks them by frequency before producing the output. The reduce function merges together longForms that are nearly identical, such as "Individual Development Plan" and "Individual Development Plans" as longForms for "idp." You can see the map and reduce functions for the mining task in listing 12.5. This task is easily parallelized on a cluster.

Listing 12.5 Mining for acronyms

```
Map (Key: URL, Value: PageText)
Identify all (shortForm, longForm) pairs in the text
For each instance, output [shortForm, longForm]
End

Reduce (Key: shortForm, Values: longForms)
Canonicalize longForms that differ slightly
Compute frequency of each longForm
Output longForms in sorted order
End
```

Figure 12.13 shows the running time of this algorithm on a sample of 10 million documents as the number of nodes is increased from two to eight. As can be seen, the overall task completes in less than 25 minutes even with two nodes. But we see that this task doesn't scale linearly with the size of the cluster. We suspect that this is because the input data is fragmented over several segments, and Hadoop chooses to split this job into a large number of tasks in the map phase which imposes a large, fixed overhead independent of the cluster size. We're investigating methods to overcome these performance issues.

The goal of the geo-classification task is to label each page on the intranet with the country, region, and/or IBM location for which the page is most relevant. Numerous factors make this task particularly nontrivial. For instance, many new business processes and web applications within IBM are first deployed in the U.S. before being extended to other countries and regions across the world. Site administrators responsible for developing the content for the subsequent rounds of deployment often use the U.S. page as a starting point and make appropriate edits to tailor the pages to their respective countries. But when performing this customization, quite often the administrators don't edit the corresponding HTML meta headers that

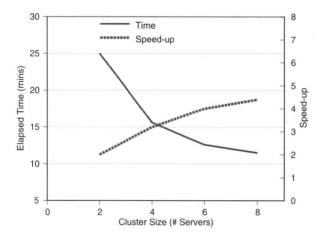

Figure 12.13   Acronym mining has a speed-up linear in cluster size.

convey the locale, language, and other geo-specific information.[13] A simple-minded classifier that directly exploits information from the meta headers is therefore prone to errors. In ES2, we're currently employing a complex rule-driven classifier consisting of a robust set of manually created rules over a small set of page features (e.g., presence of a country name in the title, a country code in the URL, etc.). While the rules have been hand-tuned for high precision, the recall—the number of pages for which the classifier is able to assign non-empty geo labels—is limited. Improvement in recall requires the use of significantly more features from a page than is used by our current classifier. But manually developing accurate rule sets over these larger feature sets is extremely laborious. We're now in the process of developing a scalable mining algorithm to automatically "induce" additional classification rules over these new features, given the high-quality rule set already available today. The use of a platform like Hadoop is critical to scale our mining algorithms to millions of pages, each with several hundred features.

12.4.4 Conclusions

We described the architecture of ES2—a scalable enterprise search system developed at IBM using open source components, such as Nutch, Hadoop, Lucene, and Jaql. We also outlined the changes we needed to make to Nutch for the purposes of crawling the enterprise. We mapped the local and global analysis algorithms from [5] on to Hadoop. In implementing a complex workflow involving crawling, local analysis, global analysis, and indexing, we found JSON to be a convenient data format and Jaql to be an extremely powerful tool. In summary, we believe that Hadoop, Nutch, Lucene, and Jaql constitute a powerful set of tools with which sophisticated, scalable systems like ES2 can be built.

---

[13] Note that the meta headers are intended for consumption by browsers and crawlers and not visible when the page is rendered.

12.4.5 References

Fagin, R., R. Kumar, K. S. McCurley, J. Novak, D. Sivakumar, J. A. Tomlin, and D. P. Williamson. "Searching the workplace web." In *WWW*, pages 366–375, 2003.

Broder, A. "A taxonomy of web search." *SIGIR Forum*, 36(2):3–10, 2002.

Hawking, D. "Challenges in enterprise search." In *ADC*, pages 15–24, 2004.

Fontura, M., E. J. Shekita, J. Y. Zien, S. Rajagopalan, and A. Neumann. "High performance index build algorithms for intranet search engines." In *VLDB*, pages 1158–1169, 2004.

Zhu, H., S. Raghavan, S. Vaithyanathan, and A. Löser. "Navigating the intranet with high precision." In *WWW*, pages 491–500, 2007.

Li, Y., R. Krishnamurthy, S. Raghavan, S. Vaithyanathan, and H. V. Jagadish. "Regular expression learning for information extraction." In *EMNLP*, 2008.

Reiss, F., S. Raghavan, R. Krishnamurthy, H. Zhu, and S. Vaithyanathan. "An algebraic approach to rule-based information extraction." In *ICDE*, pages 933–942, 2008.

Schwartz, A. S., and M. A. Hearst. "A simple algorithm for identifying abbreviation definitions in biomedical text." In *Pacific Symposium on Biocomputing*, pages 451–462, 2003.

Appendix
HDFS file commands

This appendix lists the HDFS commands for managing files. They're in the form of

```
hadoop fs -cmd <args>
```

where cmd is the specific file command and <args> is a variable number of arguments.

You can see the command usage in the following convention. Parameters inside brackets ([]) are optional and ellipsis (...) means the optional parameter can be repeated. FILE is for filenames whereas PATH can be either filenames or directory names. SRC and DST are path names but they function specifically as source and destination, respectively. LOCALSRC and LOCALDST are further required to be on the local filesystem.

Command	Usage and description
cat	`hadoop fs -cat FILE [FILE ...]` Displays the files' content. For reading compressed files, you should use the text command instead.
chgrp	`hadoop fs -chgrp [-R] GROUP PATH [PATH ...]` Changes the group association for files and directories. The -R option applies the change recursively. The user must be the files' owner or a superuser. See section 8.3 for more background information on the HDFS file permission system.

Command	Usage and description
chmod	`hadoop fs -chmod [-R] MODE[,MODE ...] PATH [PATH ...]` Changes the permissions of files and directories. Similar to its Unix equivalent, MODE can be a 3-digit octal mode, or `{augo}+/-{rwxX}`. The `-R` option applies the change recursively. The user must be the files' owner or a superuser. See section 8.3 for more background information on the HDFS file permission system.
chown	`hadoop fs -chown [-R] [OWNER][:[GROUP]] PATH [PATH ...]` Changes the ownership of files and directories. The `-R` option applies the change recursively. The user must be a superuser. See section 8.3 for more background information on the HDFS file permission system.
copyFromLocal	`hadoop fs -copyFromLocal LOCALSRC [LOCALSRC ...] DST` Identical to `put` (copy files from the local file system).
copyToLocal	`hadoop fs -copyToLocal [-ignorecrc] [-crc] SRC [SRC ...] LOCALDST` Identical to `get` (copy files to the local file system).
count	`hadoop fs -count [-q] PATH [PATH ...]` Displays the number of subdirectories, number of files, number of bytes used, and name for all files/directories identified by PATH. The `-q` option displays quota information.
cp	`hadoop fs -cp SRC [SRC ...] DST` Copies files from source to destination. If multiple source files are specified, destination has to be a directory.
du	`hadoop fs -du PATH [PATH ...]` Displays file sizes. If PATH is a directory, the size of each file in the directory is reported. Filenames are stated with the full URI protocol prefix. Note that although `du` stands for *disk usage*, it should not be taken literally, as disk usage depends on block size and replica factors.
dus	`hadoop fs -dus PATH [PATH ...]` Similar to `du`, but for a directory, `dus` reports the sum of file sizes in aggregate rather than individually.
expunge	`hadoop fs -expunge` Empties the trash. If the trash feature is enabled, when a file is deleted, it is first moved into the temporary .Trash/ folder. The file will be permanently deleted from the .Trash/ folder only after a user-configurable delay. The `expunge` command forcefully deletes all files from the .Trash/ folder. Note that as long as a file is in the .Trash/ folder, it can be restored by moving it back to its original location.
get	`hadoop fs -get [-ignorecrc] [-crc] SRC [SRC ...] LOCALDST` Copies files to the local filesystem. If multiple source files are specified, local destination has to be a directory. If LOCALDST is -, the files are copied to stdout. HDFS computes a checksum for each block of each file. The checksums for a file are stored separately in a hidden file. When a file is read from HDFS, the checksums in that hidden file are used to verify the file's integrity. For the `get` command, the `-crc` option will copy that hidden checksum file. The `-ignorecrc` option will skip the checksum checking when copying.

Command	Usage and description
getmerge	`hadoop fs -getmerge SRC [SRC ...] LOCALDST [addnl]` Retrieves all files identified by SRC, merges them, and writes the single merged file to LOCALDST in the local filesystem. The option `addnl` will add a newline character to the end of each file.
help	`hadoop fs -help [CMD]` Displays usage information for the command CMD. If CMD is omitted, it displays usage information for all commands.
ls	`hadoop fs -ls PATH [PATH ...]` Lists files and directories. Each entry shows name, permissions, owner, group, size, and modification date. File entries also show their replication factor.
lsr	`hadoop fs -lsr PATH [PATH ...]` Recursive version of `ls`.
mkdir	`hadoop fs -mkdir PATH [PATH ...]` Creates directories. Any missing parent directories are also created (like Unix `mkdir -p`).
moveFromLocal	`hadoop fs -moveFromLocal LOCALSRC [LOCALSRC ...] DST` Similar to `put`, except the local source is deleted after it's been successfully copied to HDFS.
moveToLocal	`hadoop fs -moveToLocal [-crc] SRC [SRC ...] LOCALDST` Displays a "not implemented yet" message.
mv	`hadoop fs -mv SRC [SRC ...] DST` Moves files from source(s) to destination. If multiple source files are specified, destination has to be a directory. Moving across filesystems is not permitted.
put	`hadoop fs -put LOCALSRC [LOCALSRC ...] DST` Copies files or directories from local system to destination filesystem. If LOCALSRC is set to -, input is set to `stdin` and DST must be a file.
rm	`hadoop fs -rm PATH [PATH ...]` Deletes files and empty directories.
rmr	`hadoop fs -rmr PATH [PATH ...]` Recursive version of `rm`.
setrep	`hadoop fs -setrep [-R] [-w] REP PATH [PATH ...]` Sets the target replication factor to REP for given files. The -R option will recursively apply the target replication factor to files in directories identified by PATH. The replication factor will take some time to get to the target. The -w option will wait for the replication factor to match the target.
stat	`hadoop fs -stat [FORMAT] PATH [PATH ...]` Displays "statistical" information on files. The FORMAT string is printed exactly but with the following format specifiers replaced. %b Size of file in blocks %F The string "directory" or "regular file" depending on file type %n Filename %o Block size %r Replication %y UTC date in yyyy-MM-dd HH:mm:ss format %Y Milliseconds since January 1, 1970 UTC

Command	Usage and description
tail	`hadoop fs -tail [-f] FILE` Displays the last one kilobyte of FILE.
test	`hadoop fs -test -[ezd] PATH` Performs one of the following type checks on PATH: `-e` PATH existence. Returns 0 if PATH exists. `-z` Empty file. Returns 0 if file length is 0. `-d` Returns 0 if PATH is a directory.
text	`hadoop fs -text FILE [FILE ...]` Displays the textual content of files. Identical to `cat` if files are text files. Files in known compressed format (gzip and Hadoop's binary sequence file format) are uncompressed first.
touchz	`hadoop fs -touchz FILE [FILE ...]` Creates files of length 0. Fails if files already exist and have nonzero length.

index

A

Access Key Id   195–196, 198
acronym libraries   295
acronyms, mining for   295
ad hoc queries   247
ad networks   124
aggregated   13
Aggregate package   90–94, 99
aggregating operation   219
algebraic property   86
algorithms
  computational
      complexity   158
  data mining   272
  ES2   296
  global analysis   293
allDocs   293
ALTER   257
ALTER TABLE,
     limitations   276
Amazon AWS   101
Amazon Machine Image   194
Amazon Web Services. See AWS
AMI. See Amazon
     Machine Image
anchor text analysis   291, 293
anomaly detection   131
Apache
  log file collection   281
  log files   42
  log processing with
     Cascading   282
  Lucene   19
  Top Level Project   20
Apriori   269
  vs. BC-PDM   270
arrays   256
association analysis   269
Aster Data Systems   264
authentication   195
authority   39
average, computing   86–87,
    93–98

AVG   225
AWS   194
  account ID   195
  command line tools   198
  Import/Export   210
    service recommendations
     211
  New York Times   267
  regional support   199
  setting up   194–201
AWS Account
    Number   197–198

B

Bag   222
bags
  grouping operators   226
  Pig and   213
basic arithmetic   224
BASS. See Business Analysis
    Support System
BC-PDM   269
  cost breakdown   270
  four-dimensional
    evaluation   269
  Hadoop cluster   270
  vs. Apriori   270
BerkeleyDB   281
Big Cloud–based Parallel Data
    Mining. See BC-PDM
BIGINT   256
bigram   11
Bigtable   262
  basic details   274
BitSet, Bloom filter   125
blocks   52
  replica placement   184
Bloom filter   122–131, 158, 279
  applications of   123–124
  end-of-split output   128
  implementing   124
  overview   122
  using Hadoop   128

BloomFilter   126, 129
  Hadoop v 0.20   131
Boolean expressions   224
bottleneck   10
buckets   202
  Hive   255
  specified number   256
Business Analysis Support
    System   269
bytearray   220, 222

C

caching   278–279
call data record   268
candidate navigational
    page   288
Capacity Scheduler   189
Carnegie Mellon
    University   101
Cascading   263
  Apache log processing   282
  MapReduce   281
case studies
  China Mobile   267, 269,
    271–272
  ES2   282–296
  New York Times   267
  StumbleUpon   272–273, 275,
    277, 279, 281–282
cast   224
casting   236
cat command   39
cat, command   298
CDR. See call data record
certificate file   197
chaining   102
  driver   105
  jobs in sequence   103
  MapReduce jobs   131
  pre- and postprocessing
    steps   104
chaining MapReduce
    jobs   103–107

ChainMapper 104–107, 131
ChainReducer 104, 131
chararray 222
checksums, in HDFS files 139
chgrp, command 298
China Mobile 4, 267–272
chmod, command 299
chown, command 299
chunks 51
citation graph 65
  cite_count 254
cite_grpd 242
cite table 251
classification 269
CLI 247
  Hive 250
close 57
cloud 5
CloudBase 264
cloud computing 194
  EC2 194
  multiple reducers 49
  S3 194
  S3 data storage 205
Cloudera 263
ClueWeb09 101
cluster ID 142
clustering 269
clusters
  accessing data from 204
  busy 182
  launching 200
  metadata handling 181
  moving code to 204
  multicluster setup 186
  of one 29
  private key, public key 26
  production, monitoring 140
  SSH setup for Hadoop
    25–27
  topology 25
  type configuration 202
CMU 4, 101
cocitation, symmetric 242
cocite 242
cocite_bag 241
cocite_flat 244
codecs 153
COGROUP 227
collaborative filtering 240
columns 254, 256
column store 275
combiner 76, 95–98, 152
command line interface.
  See CLI

command line tools 198
comments 237
commutative property 99
comparison 224
compiler, Pig 233
complex statistical model 8
compression 153–155
  Hive 248
CONCAT 225
conditional 224
-conf 70
Configuration 42, 161–162
configuration object, state
  information 163
configuration properties
  dfs.permissions.supergroup
    178
  Hadoop 28
configure 50, 161
Configured 70
constant 224
copyFromLocal, command
  299
copyToLocal, command 299
core-site.xml 28
COUNT 220, 225, 253
COUNT(*) 258
count, command 299
counters 98, 136, 146–148
  missing values 147
  names 146
  summary 141
  tracking records 146
counting 72–80, 86, 91–92
cp, command 299
CrawlDB 287
crawling 287
cross-product 110
  flattening 242
  record combinations 112
Cutting, Doug 4, 19
cygwin 14

D

daemons
  DataNode 22
  Hadoop 22
  JobTracker 24
  logs 34
  NameNode 22
  Secondary NameNode 23
  shut down 31
  TaskTracker 24
data, semistructured 223

databases
  accessing 170
  bulk loading into 171
  input and output 169
data block index 280
data flow language 213
DataInput 47
DataInputStream 52
data joining 103
  cross-product 114
  from different sources 107
DataJoinMapperBase 112, 163
datajoin package 131
DataJoinReducerBase 112
DataJoinReducerBase.
    combine() 114
DataNode 140, 142
  adding 180
  daemon 180
  dfsadmin 177
  multiple drives 174
  NameNode interaction 23
  offline 180
  overview 22
  RAM 175
  removing 180
DataOutput 47
data processing model 8
data sets 64–67, 101
  Amazon AWS Public Data
    Sets 101
  analysis, China Mobile 272
  collaborative filtering 101
  development 140
  human genome 101
  maximum and minimum
    computation 157
  multiple 164
  Netflix 101
  patent citation 64
  patent country codes 90
  reducing 152
  sparse 240
  test 140
  UCI 270
  US Census 101
data skew 83, 94–95
data source, reduce-side
  join 108
data types 213
  nested 223
data warehousing 268
DayOfWeek 227
DBConfiguration 170
DBOutputFormat 170

DBWritable   170
Debian   263
debugger   136, 151
debugging   70, 145–152
   arithmetic mistakes   137
   local mode   135
   modes   31
   pre- and postprocessing   104
decommissioning   180
deflate   154
departureNode   49
Derby   249
DESCRIBE   219, 251, 257
development data set   64
DIFF   225
diff'ing data   138
directories, adding   39
distributed applications   4
distributed cache   118, 136
   reduce-side join   121
DistributedCache   118
   replicated joins   117
distributed system   6
   HDFS   22
distributive functions   97
distributive property   84, 86,
      95, 100
document similarity   99
Dogear   286
dot notation   223
dot operator   224
double   222
DOUBLE   256
DoubleValueSum   90
DRBD   184
driver   103, 161
   MapReduce program   128
DROP TABLE   253, 257
du, command   299
DUMP   217
dus, command   299

E

EC2   4, 101
   command line tools   195,
      198
   concurrent instances   204
   GUI tools   199
   images   203
   instance handling   209
   MapReduce programs
      and   203, 205–209
   New York Times   267
   SSH key pair   195
   supported OSs   194

Edge   47, 49
EditLog   182
Elastic Compute Cloud.
      See EC2
Elastic MapReduce. *See* EMR
emit() function   14
Employee Referral Bonus
      Program   289
EMR   209
equijoins   259
Ercegovac, Vuk   282
ES2   282–297
   analytics   288
   architecture   285
   crawler   287
   global analysis algorithms   292
   Hadoop implementation
      293
   IBM   283
   idp query   283
   JSON   286
   local analysis   288
   mining tasks   295
   offline analysis   285
   redirection resolution   289
   variant generation   285
ETL operations   269, 270
   speed-up   271
evaluation mechanisms   213
Excite query log   217
exercises
   advanced MapReduce
      techniques   131–132
   MapReduce paradigm
      98–100
expressions, constant
      value   223
expunge, command   299
EXTERNAL   257

F

Facebook   4
   Hadoop and   247
   Hive and   260
   Scribe   281
failed tasks
   recovering   183
   rerunning   151
Fair Scheduler   187, 189
false negatives, Bloom
      filter   122
false positives, Bloom
      filter   122
Fast Fourier Transform   99
fetch list   287–288

FetchQueues   288
FFT   99
field, referencing   223
field delimiter   257
FIFO scheduler   186
file commands   38, 298–301
file management tasks   38
FileOutputFormat   57
-files   83, 120
files
   adding   39
   deleting   41
   I/O   128, 129
   merging   42
   multiple   42
   retrieving   41
   storing multiple   267
file splits   154
FileStatus   43
filesystem
   block replication   176
   checking   176–178
   corrupt block   176
   fsck   176
   metadata, handling   181
   S3, default   208
   unbalanced   181
FileSystem   42
   operations   44
FILTER   237
filter and transform   12
FIR filter   99
FLATTEN   229
flattening   229
   cross-product   242
float   222
FOREACH   219, 228
   output/input schema   230
fsck   176
FSDataInputStream   43, 52
FSDataOutputStream   43
FsImage   182
fully distributed mode   31, 135,
      145–152
FuncSpec   236
functions in Aggregate
      package   90

G

garbage collection, Java   75
General Packet Radio
      Service   268
GenericOptions   70
GenericOptionsParser   70, 82,
      120, 149

geo-classification 295
geographical data 64
get 39
get() 236
getAll() 236
getCollector 168
get, command 300
getmerge 42
getmerge, command 300
getPartition 50
getPos 57
getProgress 57
getRecordReader 55
getSplits 55
get(String) 162
getter methods 163
GFS. *See* Google File System
global analysis
  algorithms 293
  ES2 291
  Jaql and Hadoop 294
Global Analysis 284
Google File System 19
Gottfrid, Derek 267
GPRS. *See* General Packet Radio
    Service
graph data 64
Gray, Jon 280
Greenplum 264
GROUP 242
GROUP BY 219, 253, 259
group key
  join key 109
  reduce-side join 108
Grunt
  managing shell 216
  Pig Latin and 217
  shell 215
GUI tools 199

H

Hadoop 4–5
  building blocks 21–25
  cluster performance 270
  clusters, key pairs 200
  command line utilities 38
  configuration 173
  configuration directory 27
  datajoin package 112
  data processing modules
    281
  data types 46
  default settings 28
  distributed systems 6
  EC2 setup 201–203

EMR 209
ES2 293
file API 42
file commands 38
file operations 40–41
fully distributed cluster 216
history 19, 20
kill command 216
modes 135, 140
linear scalability 152
production cluster
    properties 174
related projects and
    vendors 262–265
ResolveSimple 290
running 27–33
SQL databases 7–8
subprojects list 246
HADOOP_CLASSPATH 187
Hadoop cluster 5, 25
Hadoop Core 212
hadoop-default.xml 28
hadoop-env.sh 28
Hadoop-related projects
  Aster Data 264
  Cascading 263
  CloudBase 264
  Cloudera 263
  Greenplum 264
  Hama 264
  HBase 262
  Katta 263
  Mahout 264
  ZooKeeper 262
Hadoop site properties
  dfs.balance.bandwidth
      PerSec 181
  dfs.block.size 181
  dfs.hosts.exclude 180
  dfs.http.address 182
  dfs.name.dir 183
  fs.checkpoint.dir 183
  fs.trash.interval 179
  mapred.job.tracker 186
  mapred.jobtracker.
      taskScheduler 187
  topology.script.file.
      name 185
  topology.script.number.
      args 185
hadoop-site.xml 28, 135
Hama 264
hash partitioner 172
HashPartitioner 49
hash table 10
HBase 262

added features 274
HFile 279
introduction 274
parallelism 280
region server 275, 278
SATA disks 280
StumbleUpon 274–275
table splitting 278
transcending single
    machine 277
ZooKeeper 263
HDFS 6, 129, 170, 248
  balancer 181
  blocks 52
  data nodes 278
  dataset storage 38
  directory creation 39
  file permission 178
  filesystem 216
  free space 175
  HBase 262
  metadata snapshots 23
  moving data into 204
  NameNode 22, 214
  quota 179
  reading and writing to 42
  replication factor 32
  security 178
  shell commands 83
  web interface 34
  working directory 39
  working with files 38–44
hdfs-site.xml 28
heap memory 175
help, looking up 41
help, command 300
heuristics 242
HFile 279
  internal platform 280
  keys and values 280
  write path 279
histogram 73, 93
Hive 247–250
  buckets 255
  complex types 256
  database 249
  directory structure
      example 254
  installing and configuring
      248–250
  loading data 257
  MapReduce 247, 252
  metadata 249
  metastore 247
  queries 250–253
  relational database 247

running queries   258
structured data   247
tables, managing   255
table storage   254
tarball   248
HiveQL   247
  built-in aggregate functions
    262
  built-in functions   260–262
  data model   254
  joins   259
  queries   258
  SELECT COUNT   252
  standard operators, list   259
  statements   250
  usage   254–260
hive-site.xml   249
holistic property   86
Holstad, Erik   280

I

IBM   4
IBM intranet   282–283
idempotent   156
identity   243
IdentityReducer   83, 85, 88,
    104
idp query   285, 295
  ES2   283
ILLUSTRATE   220, 241
indexes   254
Individual Development Plan.
    See IDP
information retrieval   104
INNER   227
inner join   108, 112, 115
inner product of vectors   99
InputFormat   52
  classes   53
  custom class   54
  joining   117
  KeyValueTextInput
    Format   75
  SequenceFileInput-
    Format   155
InputSplit   54
input splits   51
INSERT   258
INSERT OVERWRITE
    TABLE   253
int   222
INT   250, 256
interactive mode   217
intermediate data   11
intermediate records   166

in total   172
intranet vs. web issues   283
int type   140
IntWritable   17
inverted index   67, 73,
    103, 136
IsEmpty   225
IsolationRunner   151
isSplitable   55

J

Jaql   285
  ES2   283
  global analysis   292
jar files   15
Java   14
  generics   47
  regular expression   257
Java Advanced Image
    Extension   267
JAVA_HOME   28
java.io.DataInputStream   52
java.lang.Comparable<T>   46
JBOD   181
jdb   151
JDBC, interface   247
JetS3t   267
joining data   107–122
Job   103
JobClient   70
JobClient.runJob()   103
JobConf   54, 70, 103, 161
  chaining   106
  object   129
  set()   70
  setCombinerClass()   97
  setCompressMapOutput()
    153
  setInputFormat()   72, 155
  setJobName()   70, 143
  setMapOutputCompressor-
    Class()   153
  setMaxMapAttempts()   149
  setMaxReduceAttempts()
    149
  setNumTasksToExecute
    PerJvm()   156
  setOutputKeyClass()   72
  setOutputValueClass()   72
JobConf object   106
JobConf properties
  keep.failed.tasks.files   151
  key.value.separator.in.input.
    line   75
  mapred.job.name   143

mapred.job.reuse.jvm.num.
    tasks   155
mapred.local.dir   151
mapred.map.max.attempts
    149
mapred.output.dir   129
mapred.reduce.max.
    attempts   149
mapred.reduce.tasks   70, 138
  table   150
JobConf.setOutputFormat   128
JobControl   103
job ID   142, 151
  killing jobs   145
jobs
  chaining in sequence   103
  EMR   209
  ID   142
  kill   145, 216
  maximum per user   188
  name   142
  pools   187
  scheduling   186–189
  tracking   142
JobTracker   70, 140, 142, 269
  administration page   144
  counter information   147
  multiple   186
  overview   24
  TaskTracker interaction   24
  Web UI   143
join
  datajoin package   112
  HiveQL   259
  inner   112
  outer   112
  reduce-side   109, 121
  repartitioned   110, 111
join, reduce-side   102, 108
join key, group key   109
join process   107
jpox.properties   249
JSON, ES2   286
JVM
  mapred.job.reuse.jvm.num.
    tasks   156
  reusing   155
  TaskTracker   24
JVM usage   69

K

Katta   264
  ZooKeeper   263
key pair, RSA   26
key pairs   200

KeyValueLineRecordReader
    55, 57
key/value pairs   7, 12, 38
    Configuration   42
    data flow   44
    list   46
    splits and   55
KeyValueTextInputFormat
    53, 55, 72–73
key/value types   72
    in data flow   71
klass   106
K-means   269
    Shanghai Branch   272
Krishnamurthy, Rajasekar   282

L

LAMP   273
LIKE   259
LIMIT   218
linear scalability   152, 158
LineRecordReader   55
LinkedIn   4
Linux   14
lists   12
listStatus   43
LOAD DATA   257
Local Analysis   284
local mode   135–140
local reduce   50
log files   141–142
logging   141
    messages   142
login, validating   27
log-normal distribution   76
long   222
LongSumReducer   51
long tail problem   287
long type   140
LongValueMax   90
LongValueMin   90
LongValueSum   90
LongWritable   17, 54
ls, command   300
lsr   40
lsr, command   300
Lucene   264
    ES2   283
Lucene engine   19
Luo, Zhiguo   267

M

machine learning   100
MacInnis, Ken   272

Mac OS X   14
Mahout   264
map   54
Map   222
MapClass   71, 161
map_input_file   164
-mapper   81
Mapper   47, 69, 160
    class list   48
    close()   71
    configure()   71
    map()   71
    model   106
Mapper.configure()   119
Mapper.map()   107
mappers   8, 47
    configuration properties
        description   153
    mapred.compress.map.
        output   153
    mapred.map.output.
        compression.
        codec   153
    with Bloom   102
mapping   12
mapred.join package   117
mapred.min.split.size   55
mapred-site.xml   28
MapReduce   8–14
    algorithms, efficient   157
    chaining jobs   103
    configuration details   35
    data flow   45
    EC2 and   203, 205
    framework   19
    key/value pairs   38
    partitioning and shuffling
        50
    program anatomy   44–51
    reading and writing
        51–58
    tasks   156
    tuning for performance   152
    web interface   35
    writing to database   170
MapReduceBase   47, 71, 119
maps   256
map-side join   117
master files   32
master/slave architecture   22
    copying public key   27
    Hadoop cluster   25
MAX   225
maximum   84, 86, 90,
    93–95, 98
median   86, 93–94

memcached   133
MemStore   275
messaging queues   8
meta block index   280
metadata
    block size   181
    partitioning   167
metastore   247
MIN   225
minimum   86, 93–94
missing values   65, 88
mkdir   40
mkdir, command   300
Modulo   224
Moore's law   6
move   6
moveFromLocal, command
    300
moveToLocal, command   300
moving average   99
multiple machines   11
MultipleOutputFormat
    164, 166
MultipleOutputs   166
    filename generation   168
    naming structure   169
multiple parameter files   238
multiple relations   227
MultipleTextOutputFormat
    164
multiquery   239
multiset   10
mutates   278
mv, command   300
MySQL database
    at StumbleUpon   277
    legacy data   275
    metadata store
        configuration   250

N

NameNode   140, 142
    backup node   184
    DataNode interaction   23
    dfsadmin   178
    failure, recovering   183–184
    multiple hard drives   184
    name quotas   179
    overview   22
    RAID   181
name quotas   179
National Bureau of Economic
    Research   64
natural language processing
    11, 99, 118

navigational 283
NBER 64, 90
nested data types 223
nested schema 223
nesting 222
Netflix 101
network topology 184–185
New York Times 4, 267
next 55, 57
nodes 50
null 224
NullOutputFormat 58
nulls 251
NullWritable 58
numSplits 55
Nutch 19, 263
   ES2 283
   generate, fetch, update 287
   StumbleUpon 282
   web crawling 287

O

offline analysis 285
offline processing 8
open source framework 4
operators, grouping 226
org.apache.hadoop.fs 42
org.apache.hadoop.
   io.compress 153
outer join 112
   datajoin package 114
output
   files 57
   in total sorting 172
   sorting 171
OutputCollector 48, 71, 107,
   128–129, 166
OutputCollector.collect
   (K k, V v) 107
OutputFormat 57
   classes 58
   FileOutputFormat 154
   NullOutputFormat 129
   SequenceFileOutput
      Format 154
   TextOutputFormat 75, 87
OutputFormat class 164
outputs, multiple 164

P

page_view 255
pair-wise combinations 242
   patents example 240

pair-wise computations 240
parallelization, granular 52
PARALLEL n 231
parameters
   for practical use 174–176
   multiple files 238
   passing custom 160
   security 201
   substitution 238
partitioner 87, 166, 172
   hash 172
   Mapper output redirecting
      49
   TotalOrderPartitioner 172
partitioning 11
   data 254
   Hive 248
   into multiple output
      files 164
   LOAD DATA 258
   metadata 165
pass by reference, in output
   collector 107
pass by value, in output
   collector 107
patent citation data 64–65,
   107, 131
patent description data
   64–65, 107
patents
   cocitation 240
   cocitation counts 244
path 39
Path 43
pattern matching 224
performance improvement
   107
Perl 282
permissions, setting 178
petabytes 3
Pig
   and Cascading 263
   Cygwin 214
   data types 213
   Hadoop cluster 214
   installing 214–215
   interactive shell 215
   Java API 235
   JAVA_HOME 214
   JobTracker 214
   JVM 215
   like SQL queries 215
   multiquery execution 239
   NameNode 214
   parameters, setting 216

philisophy 213, 215
   running 215–217
   similar patents 240–244
   UDFs and 214
PIG_CLASSPATH 214
PiggyBank 233
   UDF 236
piggybank.jar 234
PIG_HADOOP_VERSION 214
Pig Latin 213, 217–233
   APIs 233
   atomic data types 222
   built-in expressions 225
   comments 237
   complex data types 222
   data flow language 213
   data read/write operators
      218
   data types and schemas
      221–223
   diagnostic operators 221
   execution optimization 233
   expressions 224
   expressions and functions
      223–225
   Hadoop mode 215
   Java equivalent classes 235
   like SQL query 219
   local mode 215
   relational operators 225–233
   schema 219
   script 213
   scripts 237–239
   type 235
   UDF statements 234
   user-defined functions 233,
      235–237
pig.properties file 214
PigServer 215
pipelines 8
pipes, Cascading 263
pirate-speak 100
pools 187
POSIX 178
pound operator 224
power law distribution 76
prefix 238
primitives 8
private key 197, 198
   SSH 26, 200
production cluster 174
pseudo-code 9
pseudo-distributed
   mode 29, 39, 41, 64,
      135, 140

public key   197
  cryptography   26
  distribution   27
  EC2   200
  SSH   200
put   39
put, command   300
PutMerge   42, 43

Q

QOS   268
quadratic complexity   240
quality of service. *See* QOS
queries, column   254
query processing
  Hive   248
  Hive examples   250
quotas, managing   179

R

rack awareness   184–185
Raghavan, Sriram   282
RAID   181
RAM storage   10
Rawson, Ryan   272
RDBMS   276
readFields   47
read-many-times   8
read-slaves   278
RecordReader   54–55
  joining   117
RecordReader<LongWritable,
    Text>   55
records
  processing guaranteed   52
  skipping bad   148
RedHat, Cloudera   263
reduce   48, 139
Reduce, class   71
reducer   8, 48, 139
  multiple   49
  partitioner and   172
  ResolveSimple   290
Reducer   48, 69, 97, 160
  class list   49
  reduce()   71, 97
reduce-side join   108–115
reducing   12
Reflection   236
REGEXP   259
region server   275
  HBase   278
REGISTER   234

regression testing   138–140
regular expression patterns
    295
Reiss, Frederick   282
relational data   64–65, 108
  aggregate analysis   227
  model   223
  nonmatching   227
relational database   7, 152
  interfacing with   169
remote storage   184
repartitioned join   108
replicated join   118–121
replication factor   40
Reporter   48, 142, 146
  incrCounter   146
  setStatus   142, 145
Resolve2Step   290
  resolution table   291
ResolveSimple   290
results   293
rm   41
rm, command   300
rmr, command   300
ROW FORMAT   256
row store   275
RPM   263

S

S3   194
  accessing data directly   207
  dataflow model   206
  datapath   207
  GUI tools   199
  Hadoop options   207
  moving data through   205
  New York Times   267
  storage service   202
S3 Block FileSystem   206
S3 bucket   202, 206
s3n   208
sampling data   64, 82, 84,
    135, 152
sanity checking   137–138
scheduler   189
schema   7
  data source records   108
  fixed   219
  nested   223
scheme   39
Scribe   281
search engine optimization
    281
search-hadoop.com   264

Secondary NameNode
    23, 181–183
  confusing name   182
  location specification   30
  server   183
  snapshots   23, 182
SecondaryNameNode   140,
    142
Secret Access Key   198
  slashes and   195
  slash problem   208
Secure Shell. *See* SSH
security, parameters   201
segment   287
segment file   289
SELECT   251
Sematext   264
semijoin   108, 121–122, 131
semistructured data   223
SequenceFileInputFormat   54
SequenceFileOutputFormat
    58
sequence file   54, 154–155
  configuration properties
      155
  SequenceFileOutput-
      Format   154
set command   216
SETI@home   6
setOutputFormat   57
setrep, command   301
setSpaceQuota command   179
Shanghai Branch   270
  K-means   272
Shekita, Eugene   282
SHOW TABLES   251, 257
shuffle   45
shuffle, MapReduce   87
shuffling   11, 50
sign   224
signal processing   99
Simple Storage Service. *See* S3
site root analysis   291, 293
SIZE   225
SkipBadRecords   149, 150
skipping bad records   148–150
slave machines   25
slave nodes   186
  location specification   30
slaves files   32
SMALLINT   255
SNN. *See* Secondary NameNode
Snoop Dogg   100
social networks   64
Solaris   14

sorted order 171
spam filter 10
sparse data 240
sparse vector representation 99, 132
spatial join 132
speculative execution 156
  configuration properties 157
SPLIT 225, 237
splits
  Bloom filters and 128
  input 52
  InputFormat class 55
splittable file formats 154
SQL 7
  and Hive 213
  engine 8
  vs. Pig Latin 213
Squid, Web proxy server 124
SSH
  channels 30
  installation 26
SSH login 200
SSN. See Secondary NameNode
standalone mode 28, 64, 135
standalone node 25
standard deviation 93
Stanford 4
stat, command 301
status messages 142, 145
STDERR 142, 148
STDOUT 142
stemming 104
stop words 104
STORE 217
Streaming 80–94
  configuration properties 164
  outputting logs 142
  PHP scripting 84
  Python scripting 82, 89
  rewriting for Hadoop Java 157
  setting job name 143
  skipping bad records 150
  split processing 102
  Unix commands 81–82
  updating status 142
  use of combiner 96
  use of compressed files 155
  use of counters 148, 150
Streamy.com 280
String 161
STRING 256
StringValueMax 90

StringValueMin 90
structs 256
structured query language. See SQL
Stumblers 272
Stumbles, per user 276
StumbleUpon 272–273, 275, 277, 279, 281–282
  architecture 273
  data handling 281
  HBase 274–275
  ratings 272
SUM 225
summarization 247
summing 86, 90
Sun, Shaoling 267
supergroup 178
superuser 178
symbolic links 33
sync markers in files 154
system malfunction 182

T
tab character 58
tables, splitting, HBase 278
tag, reduce-side join 108
TaggedMapOutput 112, 115
TaggedWritable datajoin 113
tail 41
tail, command 301
taps 263
tarball, Hive 248
task attempt ID 151
task ID 145
task initialization 155
tasks
  CPU-intensive loads 175
  failed, rerunning 156
  parallel running 156
  passing parameters 160
  placement 185
  reduce, side effects 157
  retrieving information 163
TaskTracker 140, 269
  bad record tracking 148
  configuration object 161
  default tasks 175
  JobTracker interaction 24
  overview 24
  RAM 175
  Web UI 145
Tata, Sandeep 282
template, for MapReduce program 67, 118

terabytes 3
test, command 301
Text 17, 54, 72
  datajoin 112
text, command 301
TEXTFILE 257
TextInputFormat 52
TIFF, image processing 267
time series 64, 99
TimeUrlLineRecordReader 56
TINYINT 255
TokenCountMapper 51
tokenization 16
TOKENIZE 225
TokyoCabinet 281
Tool 70, 162
Tool.run() 70
ToolRunner 70, 162
toString 58
touchz, command 301
trash 179
trigram 11
Tuple 222
tuples
  Cascading 263
  Pig and 213
Twitter 4
type casting 224

U
Ubuntu 263
UCI data sets 270
UDFs 213
  eval 234
  filter functions 237
  jar file 234
  load/store 234
  Pig Latin and 233
  simple scalar 236
unique values, computing 92–93
UniqValueCount 90
Unix
  commands, parameter values 238
  cost breakdown 270
  Hive CLI 258
  pipes 8, 41, 103
  server 268
  server performance 270
  wc -l 136
Unix command 137
UPPER UDF 235
URI, format 39

user-defined functions. *See* UDFs
username 178

V

Vaithyanathan, Shivakumar 282
ValueHistogram 90, 93
variance, computing 86, 158
  variant generation 285
visualization 65, 77, 92
void close 47
void configure(JobConf job) 47

W

web
  interfaces 34
  search engine 19
Web GUI 247

web server, log analysis 99, 131
Web UI 98, 142, 147, 189
  cluster 34–36
  Hadoop 216
whitespace characters 16
Windows 14
word count 9, 72
  predefined classes 51
  with Hadoop 14–19
Writable 72, 170
  Bloom filter 126
  datajoin 113
  IntWritable 73, 140
  LongWritable 140
  Text 73
WritableComparable 72
  example 47
WritableComparable<T> 46
write-once 8

X

X.509 Certificate 195, 198
Xu, Meng 267

Y

Yahoo 4, 212

Z

Zhu, Huaiyu 282
ZooKeeper 262, 278

Lucene in Action, Second Edition
by Michael McCandless, Erik Hatcher, and
   Otis Gospodnetić

   ISBN: 978-1-933988-17-7
   532 pages, $49.99
   July 2010

Mahout in Action
by Sean Owen, Robin Anil, Ted Dunning,
   and Ellen Friedman

   ISBN: 978-1-935182-68-9
   375 pages, $44.99
   February 2011

Algorithms of the Intelligent Web
by Haralambos Marmanis
   and Dmitry Babenko

   ISBN: 978-1-933988-66-5
   368 pages, $44.99
   MaY 2009

Collective Intelligence in Action
by Satnam Alag

   ISBN: 978-1-933988-31-3
   424 pages, $44.99
   October 2008

For ordering information go to www.manning.com

RELATED MANNING TITLES

MongoDB in Action
by Kyle Banker

> ISBN: 978-1-935182-87-0
> 375 pages, $44.99
> March 2011

The Quick Python Book, Second Edition
Revised edition of The Quick Python Book
by Vernon L. Ceder

> ISBN: 978-1-935182-20-7
> 360 pages, $39.99
> January 2010

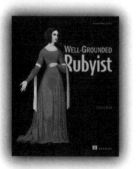

The Well-Grounded Rubyist
Covering Ruby 1.9
by David A. Black

> ISBN: 978-1-933988-65-8
> 520 pages, $44.99
> May 2009

DSLs in Action
by Debasish Ghosh

> ISBN: 978-1-935182-45-0
> 375 pages, $44.99
> December 2010

For ordering information go to www.manning.com